MARVEL ATLAS

Head Writer/Coordinator
Michael Hoskin

Writers
Anthony Flamini, Stuart Vandal & Eric J. Moreels

Cartographer
Eliot R. Brown

Art Coordinator
Mike Fichera

Cover Art
Staz Johnson & Chris Sotomayor

Cover Design & Select Layout
Brian O'Dell

Editors
Jeff Youngquist & John Denning

Editors, Special Projects
Jennifer Grünwald & Mark D. Beazley

Assistant Editor
Cory Levine

Senior Vice President of Sales
David Gabriel

Copy Editor
Brian Overton

Production
Jerron Quality Color

Editor in Chief
Joe Quesada

Publisher
Dan Buckley

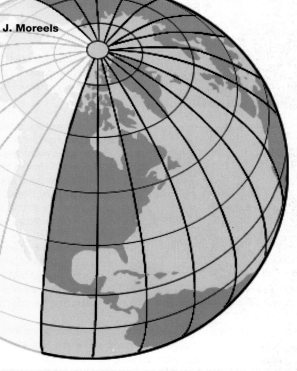

The Official Handbook of the Marvel Universe Frequently Asked Questions page — including data corrections and explanations, complete bibliographies, and Power Grid legends:
http://www.marvel.com/universe/OHOTMU

Special thanks to the guys at the Appendix (www.marvunapp.com), Bob Almond, Ronald Byrd, Tom Brevoort, Jeff Christiansen, Roy Thomas, Avril Cullen, Luis Olavo Dantas, Peter David, Craig Dylke, Christos N. Gage, Kevin Garcia, Kim Henckel, Jody LeHeup, Nick Lowe, Beatrix Nanai, Mark O'English, Mark Paniccia, Joe Quesada, Brian Reed, Alex Roth, Dan Slott, Frank Tieri, Sal Velluto, Zeb Wells & David Wiltfong

INTRODUCTION

It has been said that part of the allure of the Marvel Universe, which Stan Lee and Jack Kirby ushered into existence back in 1961, was that it painted a more realistic view of people and the world they existed in than other super hero comics of the time (as well as those Marvel itself had previously published). Most stories told in the Marvel Universe are set in the USA, and with the exception of a few minor towns and some major buildings, it isn't that far from the USA of the real world. However, as far back as Fantastic Four #1 itself the Marvel Universe had diverged from the real world with the existence of hidden civilizations. This wasn't exactly new to Marvel — Namor's kingdom of Atlantis stretched back to the first Marvel title, Marvel Comics #1 — but at first, the Marvel Universe seemed closely tied to the real world, avoiding the means where 1940s books would avoid invoking real places by substituting obviously made-up names (memorable stand-ins for Germany in the '40s included Prussland and Swastikia).

Art by Jack Kirby

The first truly great addition to the landscape of Marvel's nations was Latveria in Fantastic Four Annual #2. Although it may seem strange to consider it now, that familiar tiny European nation where the Fantastic Four's greatest nemesis rules with an iron fist was not originally part of his back story. However, the addition of Latveria was perhaps the final piece in establishing Doom as the Marvel Universe's premier villain because it granted him a power no other villain of the time enjoyed — diplomatic immunity.

Over the years many other memorable nations have been added to the Marvel Universe's Earth, from the Black Panther's advanced nation of Wakanda to mutant-dominated Genosha to Latveria's friendly neighbor Symkaria, home of Silver Sable. As in the 1940s, many of these nations exist to parallel developments in the real world, but others exist entirely to play off famous Marvel nations (such as Wakanda's relationship with Rudyarda or Azania).

Marvel's interpretation of real nations such as Germany and Russia have sought to keep abreast of changes in those countries, to the extent that some Russian characters originally conceived of as villains have become heroes in their own right. Perhaps the most significant development in Marvel's treatment of international heroes was the 1975 "All-New, All-Different" X-Men team, which made headliners out of heroes from countries including Canada, Germany, Ireland, Japan, Kenya and Russia! Many of Marvel's international fan base have had the thrill of seeing their own native land depicted in the Marvel Universe, and perhaps even granted its own hero.

Although the occasional map of Marvel's Earth has been glimpsed in the pages of the Official Handbook of the Marvel Universe titles, there has never before been a single reference tome to cover the expanse of Marvel's Earth, one that sorts out the exact geographical location of each and every Marvel country. The staff of the Official Atlas of the Marvel Universe are pleased to bring this subject matter before its audience for the first time.

New Yorker Eliot R. Brown is a familiar name to longtime Marvel fans with an interest in maps and technical schematics. In the original incarnations of the Official Handbook of the Marvel Universe, Eliot provided illustrations of everything from the lands of Asgard to the Unicorn's power horn. He also wrote and designed related works such as the Punisher Armory and Iron Manual. Eliot was the obvious choice to become cartographer of Marvel's first official foray into mapping the Earth.

The Atlas writers have each been a part of the Official Handbook of the Marvel Universe *since its 2004 revival, and together bring a true international flavor to the project — each hails from a different country!*

 From the USA is New Jersey's Anthony Flamini. Anthony is possibly the most widely read of the handbook team, having headed up Civil War Files, Civil War: Battle Damage Report, Dark Tower: Gunslinger's Guidebook *and the* Planet Hulk: Gladiator Guidebook.

 Eric J. Moreels of Adelaide, Australia has gone solo with the Astonishing X-Men Saga *and headed up the X-Men handbooks and* 198 Files. *Eric was instrumental in the push for approval of an official* Marvel Atlas.

 Scot Stuart Vandal is an expert not only on his place of origin, but also the many Marvel UK books that have been published over the decades. Stuart has headed up works such as the Ultimate Universe *handbooks and the* Anita Blake: Guilty Pleasures *handbook, as well as writing for Image's* Invincible *handbooks.*

 Hailing from Calgary, Canadian Michael Hoskin took the responsibility of heading up the Marvel Atlas. *He previously spearheaded* Marvel Monsters: From the Files of Ulysses Bloodstone, Marvel Westerns: Outlaw Files, Annihilation: Nova Corps Files *and* Annihilation Saga.

MARVEL ATLAS CONTENTS

NOTE: Only Marvel Universe-specific nations are labeled.

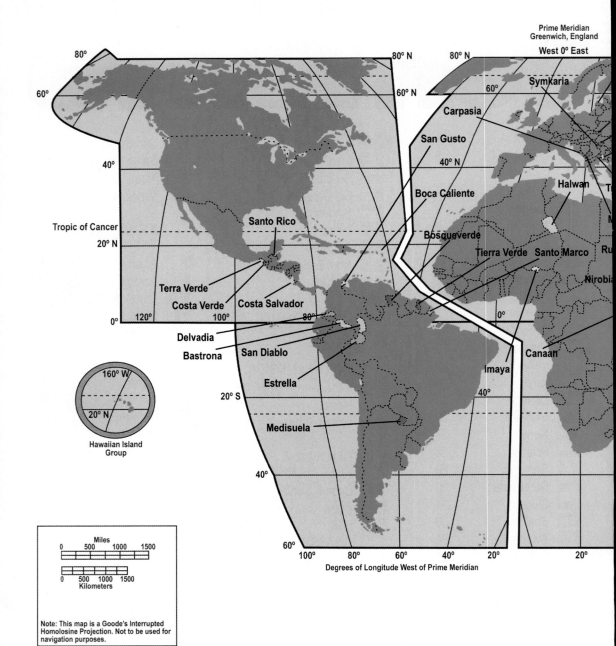

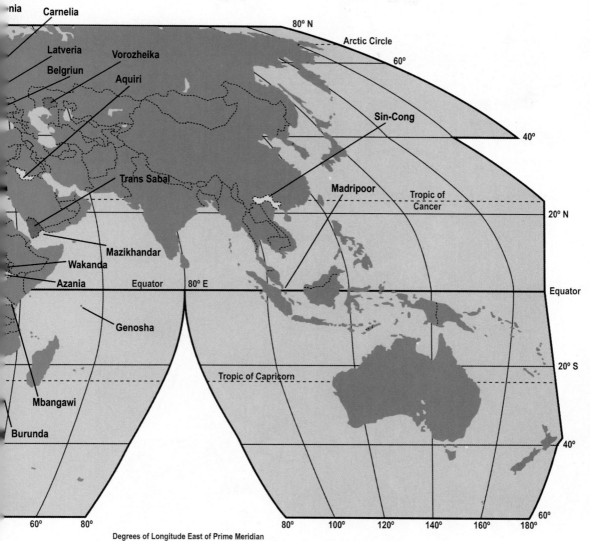

nia

Carnelia

Latveria

Belgriun

Vorozheika

Aquiri

80° N

Arctic Circle

60°

Sin-Cong

40°

Trans Sabal

Madripoor

Tropic of
Cancer

20° N

Mazikhandar

Wakanda

Azania

Equator

80° E

Equator

Genosha

20° S

Tropic of Capricorn

Mbangawi

40°

Burunda

60°

60°   80°

80°   100°   120°   140°   160°   180°

Degrees of Longitude East of Prime Meridian

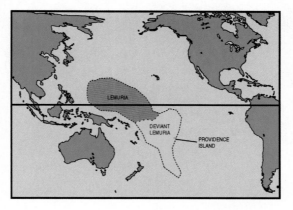

LEMURIA

DEVIANT
LEMURIA

PROVIDENCE
ISLAND

MARVEL
ATLAS
BOOK I

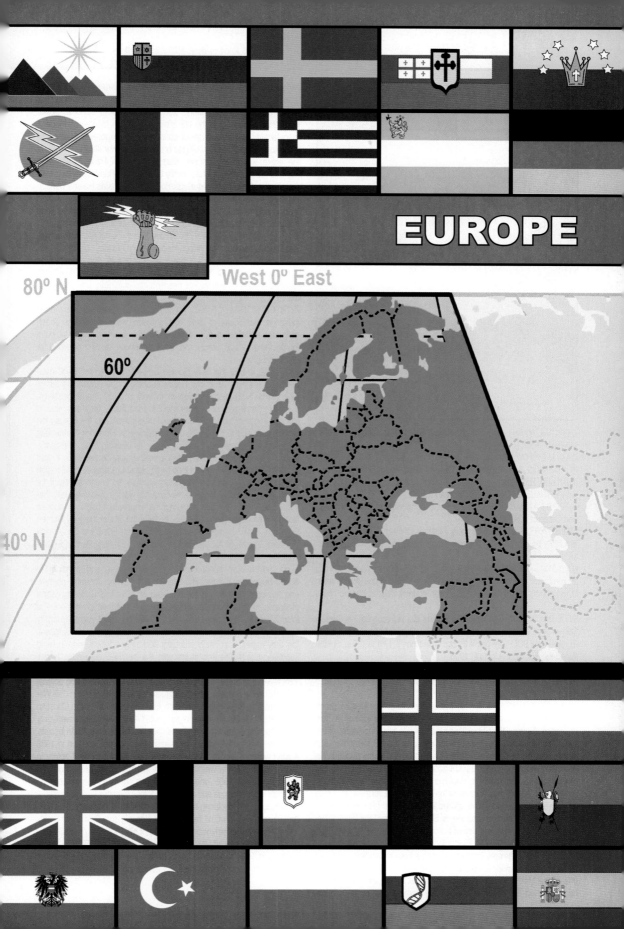

EUROPE

West 0º East

80º N

60º

40º N

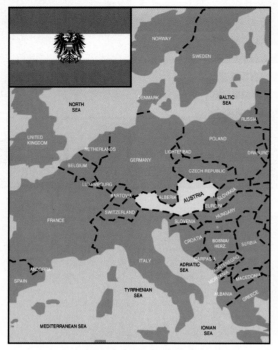

OFFICIAL NAME: Republic of Austria (Republik Österreich)
POPULATION: 8,199,000
CAPITAL CITY: Vienna
PLACES OF INTEREST: Alps, Castle Frankenstein, Dermafree Labs (Salzburg), Salzburg
GOVERNMENT: Democratic Federal republic
MAJOR LANGUAGES: German; sizeable minorities of Turkish, Sebrian and Croatian speakers
MONETARY UNIT: Euro; formerly Austrian schilling
MAJOR RESOURCES: Tourism, machinery, metallurgical products, textiles
NATIONAL DEFENSE: Bundesheer, split mainly into Land Forces (Kommando Landstreitkräfte; KdoLaSK) and Air Forces (Kommando Luftstreitkräfte; KdoLuSK). A landlocked country, Austria has no Naval Forces.
INTERNATIONAL RELATIONS: Austria is a signatory to the Geneva Convention, as well as a member of the United Nations, Council of Europe, UNESCO, Interpol, IMF, and World Health Organization. Austria joined the European Union in 1995.
EXTRATERRESTRIAL RELATIONS: The Golden Angel was active in Austria during its centuries-long torment of Dracula.
NONHUMAN POPULATION: None known.
DOMESTIC SUPERHUMANS: Mutant terrorist couple Destiny (Irene Adler) and Mystique hail from Salzburg, though the former is now deceased. Austrian Fritz Tiboldt was the founder and Ringmaster of the wartime "Circus of Crime," sent by the Nazis to the US to murder high ranking government officials, before being deported home a failure; his son, Maynard, emigrated to the US and became a naturalized American citizen, but has continued the Tiboldt criminal legacy as the new Circus' Ringmaster. Austria has a small vampire population, formerly including the "Pure Blood" Legride, who resided for centuries in his native Vienna, before his recent demise, and Henry Sage, turned by Dracula in 1794, who became a "sunwalker" before his destruction.
PROMINENT CITIZENS: Psychologist Sigmund Freud, pioneer of psychoanalysis, remains probably Austria's best-known son, and has been commemorated alongside mankind's other greatest minds as one of the Mad Thinker's "Intellectual Robots." Sadly Johann Fennhoff has perverted his illustrious countryman's profession, as the criminal psychiatrist Dr. Faustus. Reports suggest that there was an Austrian branch of the extensive Frankenstein family, complete with their own castle and illicit experiments. Concentration camp survivor Itzhak Berditchev emigrated to the US after becoming a billionaire weapons manufacturer, but the paranoia caused by his experiences saw him steal Austrian plutonium, hoping to prevent World War III by blackmailing the entire world. Inline speed skating champion Hilda Altman was headhunted by America's roller derby team Racine Ramjets, helping take them to the World Championships. Former Miss Austria Helena Carlson is now the CEO of Dermafree, based in Salzburg, one of the world's leading cosmetics firms, although their stock has been in decline since Interpol investigated them for using unwilling mutant test subjects.
SUPERHUMAN RESIDENTS: Throughout the centuries the vampire lord Dracula has been an infrequent resident of Austria.
DOMESTIC CRIME: Austria has a low crime rate, and violent crime is rare. The Tiboldt Circus, colorfully called "the Circus of Crime," was founded in Austria, but did not descend into criminality until moving to the USA.
INTERNATIONAL CRIME: An Interpol investigation of Dermafree indicated that many of their test subjects were kidnapped Czech nationals, trafficked in from Prague. Austria is a transshipment point for Southwest Asian heroin and South American cocaine destined for Western Europe
HISTORY: In 976 AD, Holy Roman Emperor Otto II, "the Red," gave the Margraviate of Ostarrîchi (Eastern Lands) to the Babenberg family, who gradually grew the region in power. In 1150 the Babenberg's transferred their residence from the Bavarian duchy they also held to Vienna (originally founded during the 1st century AD as the Roman fort Vindobona), and in 1156 Holy Roman Emperor Frederick Barbarossa detached the Margraviate from Bavaria, establishing it as a separate Duchy. During the Crusades, Austria was an ally of the Black Knight (Eobar Garrington). In 1278 Rudolf von Habsburg acquired the region through conquest, and the Habsburg dynasty continued to rule it for centuries to come. During the Napoleonic wars it became clear that the Holy Roman Empire had become impotent, unable to oppose Napoleon's occupations of Vienna; in 1804 the last of the Holy Roman Emperors, Franz II, proclaimed himself Emperor Franz I of Oesterreich (Eastern Empire, or Austria), before dissolving the Holy Roman Empire in 1806. In 1876 Franz Joseph of Austria signed the Ausgleich, becoming the dual monarch of Austria and Hungry, and founding the Austro-Hungarian Empire. However in 1914, Franz Joseph's nephew and heir presumptive was assassinated while visiting Sarajevo, capital of Bosnia (then a province of the Empire), a spark which lit the fire of World War I. By 1918, with defeat by the Allies imminent, Austro-Hungary sundered, with various territories, including Czechoslovakia, Carpasia, the Slav states, and finally Hungary declaring independence in rapid succession. With the end of the war, the last Habsburg ruler, Karl I, renounced participation in affairs of state and fled to Switzerland, and on 12th November 1918, Austria became a republic. Financial and political instability in the post-war years eventually led to a brief Austrian Civil War in February 1934, which ended with Engelbert Dollfuß of the Christian Social Party in control, who sought to avoid Austria losing its sovereignty to neighboring Germany by allying himself with Mussolini's Italian fascists. However later that year Austrian Nazis assassinated him, and in 1938 Austria was annexed by Nazi Germany. Following the Allies' victory in World War II, Austria was occupied by French, British, American and Soviet forces until 1955, when all four powers signed a treaty recognizing Austria's independence and pulled their forces out after Austria passed a constitutional law declaring the country's "perpetual neutrality," satisfying the Soviets that it would remain nonaligned in the Cold War. Swiftly rebuilding her economy with Marshall Plan aid, Austria's neutrality saw her become an official UN seat during the 1970s. The Soviet Union's collapse in 1991 allowed some more flexibility in interpreting Austria's neutral stance, and it joined the European Union in 1995.

OFFICIAL NAME: Kingdom of Belgium (Koninkrijk België [Dutch], Royaume de Belgique [French], Königreich Belgien [German])
POPULATION: 10,392,000
CAPITAL CITY: Brussels
PLACES OF INTEREST: Antwerp, Manneken Pis, Waterloo
GOVERNMENT: Democratic constitutional monarchy
MAJOR LANGUAGES: Dutch, French; German is also an official language, although only spoken by a small percentage of the population. English, though not an official language, is widely spoken.
MONETARY UNIT: Euro, formerly Belgium Franc
MAJOR RESOURCES: Chocolate and beer. Belgium produces over 172,000 tons of chocolate each year and over 450 different varieties of beer.
NATIONAL DEFENSE: Belgian Armed Forces, split into Land, Naval, and Air Operations Commands
INTERNATIONAL RELATIONS: Brussels is the seat of both the European Union and NATO, thanks in part to its relatively central location within Western Europe. The Northern port city of Antwerp is a world center for the diamond industry. Belgium is a Geneva Convention signatory, and member of Benelux (an economic union with neighbors the Netherlands and Luxembourg), Interpol, UNESCO, the United Nations, the Council of Europe, IMF, and World Health Organization. Belgium has cooperated with the Avengers. Brussels also hosted the recent International Symposium on Mutant Research.
EXTRATERRESTRIAL RELATIONS: None known.
NONHUMAN POPULATION: Created from human corpses by scientist Dr. Jennifer Nyles, using techno-organic technology developed by Dr. Meyer Herzog, the bestial Were-borgs were originally under the command of Commander Courage, but are now believed to be in Belgian government custody.
DOMESTIC SUPERHUMANS: The superintelligent but disembodied Marcel Deflandre, unofficially dubbed "the Belgian Brain" by foreign press organizations, is Belgium's representative on the Super Heroes of Europe (SHE). Rem-Ram (Marcus Andrews), one of the mutant Acolytes hails from Antwerp. Leading scientist Dr. Meyer Herzog tested his own techno-organic process on himself, briefly turning himself into the first Were-borg, but died shortly thereafter when his unstable implants exploded. After American scientist Jennifer Nyles perfected the technology for him, Lieutenant-Commander Guillaume Courage, formerly of the Belgian Ministry of Defense, transformed himself into a Were-borg, and planned to use the implant technology to secretly take control of various influential international figures, including Russia's Red Guardian, the USA's Henry Peter Gyrich and Tony Stark, Canada's Madison Jeffries, and Latveria's Victor von Doom. However his plans were thwarted by the combined efforts of the Beast (Hank McCoy), Constrictor (Frank Payne) and Red Ghost (Ivan Kragoff), the last of whom destroyed Courage.
PROMINENT CITIZENS: Before his transformation and demise, Dr. Herzog was one of Belgium's greatest scientists. The appearance of a crime-fighting Spider-Man imitator in the neighboring Netherlands briefly inspired a craze of non-powered costumed wannabes in Belgium, including Ma Yonaise, Pa Tat, Frietzak, Atomiumman, and Manneke Pis; luckily all apparently swiftly retired before any of them were seriously injured. Possibly the most famous of Belgium's citizens overseas was the actress Edda van Heemstra Hepburn-Ruston, better known as Audrey Hepburn.
SUPERHUMAN RESIDENTS: None known.
DOMESTIC CRIME: Though Belgium as a whole has a relatively low crime rate, Brussels has one of the highest recorded crime rates amongst European capitals. However there is minimal recorded super-powered criminal activity.
INTERNATIONAL CRIME: The international mercenaries Constrictor (Frank Payne) and Paladin as well as rogue Russian agent Red Ghost (Ivan Kragoff) have operated out of Belgium in the past.
HISTORY: Around 57 BC the Roman armies under Gaius Julius Caesar conquered the northern part of Gaul, an area that was home to a mixture of Germanic and Celtic tribes, whom Caesar described as the bravest of

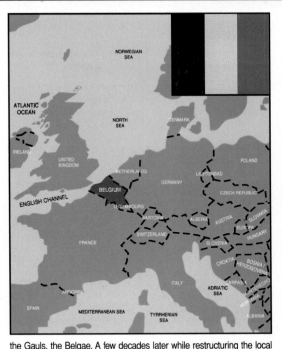

the Gauls, the Belgae. A few decades later while restructuring the local government, the Romans named the province in recognition of them, Gallia Belgica; in the modern day, this area encompasses the southern Netherlands, western Germany, northeastern France, Luxembourg, and Belgium. During the 4th century AD Frankish mercenaries employed by the Romans took control of the region, establishing first the Merovingian kingdom (named after their leader, Merovech), and then a few centuries later the Carolingian (after Charlemagne, whose empire came to encompass almost all of Europe). With Charlemagne's death, the Empire was split between three of his grandsons in 843 AD; most of what would become Belgium fell into Middle Francia, ruled by Lothair, but the northwest was part of his half-brother Charles the Bald's kingdom West Francia (forming the foundation of France), and within a few decades came under the influence of the increasingly autonomous Counts of Flanders. All the kingdoms the Treaty established fragmented over the following centuries, and over intervening centuries what would later become Belgium was the site of innumerable territorial wars, eventually becoming part of the Holy Roman Empire. In 1789, inspired by the French Revolution, the Austrian Netherlands revolted and declared independence as the United States of Belgium, only to be conquered a few years later by Napoleon's France. After Napoleon fell, Belgium was given to William of Orange as part of the Kingdom of the Netherlands, but in 1830 the Belgians revolted again, finally becoming an independent nation, a constitutional monarchy under Leopold Saxe-Coburg. Despite claiming neutrality, Belgium's strategic location between France and Germany saw them invaded during World War I; the Canadian soldier later known as Night Raven would lose his childhood innocence fighting for its liberation at the Third Battle of Ypres. Two decades later neutrality again failed to stop the German army from occupying the country; during the Second World War, Allied soldiers such as the Howling Commandos, Deadly Dozen and Maulers all saw action in occupied Belgium. Since the war Belgium's central location has seen it chosen as the ideal headquarters for the European Community (later the European Union) and NATO; ironically, as Europe has moved closer to union in the post-war years, regional differences within the country have seen its provinces gain greater autonomy.

BELGRIUN

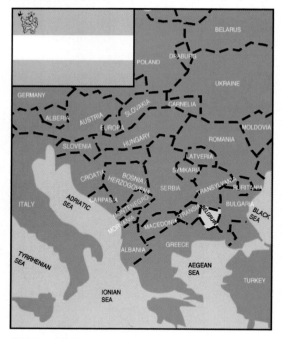

OFFICIAL NAME: Kingdom of Belgriun (Kraljewina Belgryun)
POPULATION: 968,000
CAPITAL CITY: Radisgrad
PLACES OF INTEREST: Royal Palace, Radisgrad
GOVERNMENT: Constitutional Monarchy
MAJOR LANGUAGES: Belgriunese, Russian, Romanian, Symkarian
MONETARY UNIT: Belgriunese leu
MAJOR RESOURCES: Coal, iron ore, machinery and transport equipment
NATIONAL DEFENSE: Land Forces (Army), Air Force, Air Defense Force, National Guard
INTERNATIONAL RELATIONS: Belgriun holds membership in the United Nations, UNESCO, and Interpol, and has cooperated with MI-6 and SHIELD. Although allegations of human rights abuses committed against political dissidents has made the monarchy unpopular with western nations, it nonetheless maintains strong diplomatic and economic relations with its neighboring countries, such as Symkaria and Montenegro.
EXTRATERRESTRIAL RELATIONS: None known.
NONHUMAN POPULATION: None known.
DOMESTIC SUPERHUMANS: None known.
PROMINENT CITIZENS: King Bogdan Radischev (head of government), Princess Bogdana (heir to the Belgriunese throne), Gergori Grebenko (former rebel leader, deceased)
SUPERHUMAN RESIDENTS: None documented.
DOMESTIC CRIME: Belgriun was once notorious for its high crime rate. Armed robbery and theft occurrences soared as the taxes levied by the monarchy became increasingly oppressive. However, following the temporary coup in which King Radischev was held captive by the Sinister Syndicate, wealth accumulated in the Royal Treasury was redistributed among the population, resulting in a sharp decline in violent crime. Today, most arrests in Belgriun are of a political nature, as those critical of the royal family's policies are often branded traitors and incarcerated.
INTERNATIONAL CRIME: Rumors abound that the Chaeyi, a secretive international organization dedicated to destabilizing national governments for profit, has built a power base in the easternmost regions of Belgriun.

The Belgriunese royal family has been rebuked by the UN Committee Against Torture on several occasions for alleged violations of Convention Against Torture.
FIRST APPEARANCE: Webspinners: Tales of Spider-Man #17 (2000)
HISTORY: Ruled by the same royal family for hundreds of years, the Kingdom of Belgriun has been a longtime ally and trading partner of Symkaria, its larger neighbor. However, in recent generations, the Belgriunese monarchy fell out of favor with its subjects as the royal family became more interested in lining the Royal Treasury with money and artifacts stolen from the populace rather than tending to the needs of Belgriun's increasingly impoverished lower class. As the rebel movement grew more powerful, the royal family began imprisoning and hanging political dissidents, which only proved to strengthen the opposition to the throne. The rebel movement came to a head during the reign of the tyrannical King Bogdan Radischev, when Gregori Grebenko, the rebel leader, hired Doctor Octopus (Otto Octavius), the Beetle (Abner Jenkins), Boomerang (Fred Myers), Hydro-Man (Morris Bench), the Rhino (Aleksei Mikhailovich Sytsevich), and Speed Demon (James Sanders) — a team of super-powered mercenaries collectively known as the Sinister Syndicate — to overthrow the royal family. With the Sinister Syndicate aiding the rebellion, the royal family was soon dethroned and imprisoned by the Syndicate within the Royal Palace. Belgriun was immediately placed under martial law with a compulsory curfew as the masses flocked into the streets celebrating the end of the corrupt monarchy. The Sinister Syndicate were hailed as national heroes, but the people of Belgriun were unaware that the Syndicate's true motive for aiding the rebellion was to loot the nation's Royal Treasury during the temporary chaos caused by the change in political regimes.

Parties sympathetic to the Belgriun royal family hired Silver Sable Inc., a mercenary team operating out of neighboring Symkaria, to obtain their release from captivity by any means necessary. Silver Sable (Silver Sablinova), the proprietor of Silver Sable Inc., agreed to accept the mission because she did not want any harm to befall the 11-year-old Princess Bogdana, who was imprisoned by the Syndicate alongside her father. In turn, Silver Sable recruited Spider-Man (Peter Parker), who had previously defeated the Syndicate in the USA, into her undercover strike force. As Spider-Man, Silver Sable, and her associate Sandman (William Baker) infiltrated the capital city of Radisgrad, Grebenko offered the king his freedom if he agreed to publicly embrace and legitimize the new government. However, Grebenko soon discovered the Sinister Syndicate in the act of looting the Royal Treasury and was killed by Dr. Octopus, much to the chagrin of the Beetle, who had come to admire Grebenko's dedication to his people. As Spider-Man and Sandman defeated several Sinister Syndicate members and Silver Sable rescued the king and his daughter, the Beetle attempted to escape with a helicopter filled with the Royal Treasury's riches. However, a well-placed bazooka rocket fired by Silver Sable downed the helicopter, causing its contents to rain down among the people of Belgriun (who believed the downpour of riches was a parting gift from the Beetle). The ungrateful King was reinstalled upon the throne, only without the contents of the Royal Treasury and without his Royal Palace (which had been detonated by Dr. Octopus in his failed escape attempt).

Art by Ron Frenz

Art by Barry Kitson

OFFICIAL NAME: Republic of Carnelia (Respublika Carneliya)
POPULATION: 3,000,000
CAPITAL CITY: Pershyy Misto
PLACES OF INTEREST: Castle Bagsyk, House of Parliament
GOVERNMENT: Parliamentary democracy
MAJOR LANGUAGES: Russian, Ukrainian, English
MONETARY UNIT: Euro
MAJOR RESOURCES: Machinery, electronics, oil, gas, coal, iron ore, copper, lead, zinc, nickel, gold, silver
NATIONAL DEFENSE: Carnelian Armed Forces, includes Army and Air Force, totaling over 100,000 members.
INTERNATIONAL RELATIONS: Member of the European Union, Interpol, UNESCO and United Nations. On friendly terms with Trebekistan and USA, former satellite state in the USSR.
EXTRATERRESTRIAL RELATIONS: None known.
NONHUMAN POPULATION: None known.
DOMESTIC SUPERHUMANS: None known.
PROMINENT CITIZENS: Sergei Kotznin, the country's ambassador to the UN who was killed by Iron Man (Tony Stark) when his armor's systems were hijacked by Justin Hammer. Former Prime Minister Maurus Vasilyev held a distinguished office, which included signing Carnelia's treaty with Trebekistan. However, the term of succeeding Prime Minister Nicolas Kitsenko was marred by his attempted development of a secret fusion reactor facility.
SUPERHUMAN RESIDENTS: None known.
DOMESTIC CRIME: Recurring drug smuggling and money laundering problems.
INTERNATIONAL CRIME: Carnelia attained worldwide notoriety for secretly devising a fusion reactor facility, only to have their plans exposed by the Thunderbolts and the plant rendered useless. The country has also faced terrorist actions from ULTIMATUM over their alliance with Trebekistan.
FIRST APPEARANCE: (Embassy depicted) Iron Man #117 (1978); (country depicted) Thunderbolts #11 (1998)
HISTORY: Nestled in the Carpathian Mountains, Carnelia was founded as a state in the 1920s. As a satellite in the USSR since its foundation, it is only in recent years that Carnelia has begun to interact with the greater western world. As a significant first gesture, Carnelia sought bids for a major industrial plant. Although Justin Hammer was determined to obtain the contract, the country favored Anthony Stark and his Stark International firm. Carnelian ambassador Sergei Kotznin was sent to attend a formal meeting with Stark's bodyguard Iron Man (actually Stark himself), with Bethany Cabe serving as Kotznin's security. However, Hammer obtained remote access to the systems of Iron Man's armor through his specialist Philip Barnett, and he had Barnett activate the armor's repulsor rays to kill Kotznin. The resulting scandal cost Stark International the Carnelian contract, which was given to Hammer instead. Iron Man eventually cleared his name by obtaining a confession from Barnett.

When the Thunderbolts led by Helmut Zemo began to conquer the Earth using the bio-modem, a device that brainwashes individuals through computer screens, Carnelia was among the countries affected, and their own armed forces found themselves at war with each other. They attempted to retaliate against Zemo and assault his satellite base,

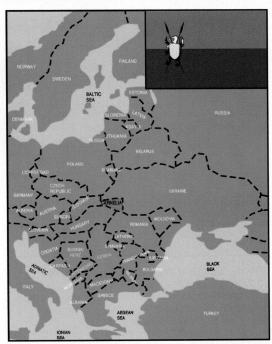

but Zemo had already infiltrated their defense grid and destroyed their missiles from remote. Carnelia and all other invaded nations were finally released when the Avengers were aided by rebellious members of the Thunderbolts in overthrowing Zemo. Later, Carnelia began to prepare a treaty with their neighbor Trebekistan, which earned them the ire of the ULTIMATUM terrorist faction, who believed that peace between their nations would stall ULTIMATUM's goal of a one world government. An ULTIMATUM agent called the Ultimator took Prime Minister Maurus Vasilyev hostage while he was in New York, but the Avengers came to the man's rescue. Carnelia later encountered the Thunderbolts again when Zemo — now reformed — sought to dismantle their secret fusion reactor facility, turning over the evidence to Russia and damaging Carnelia's international reputation. Prime Minister Nicolas Kitsenko attempted to retaliate against the Thunderbolts with the country's air force, but Zemo reacted by releasing images of Kitsenko in compromising situations with the wives of his top military advisers, causing Kitsenko to lose all support amongst his men.

CASTLE BAGSYK

Art by Mark Bagley

CARPASIA

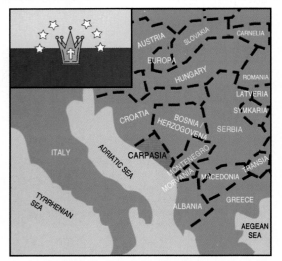

OFFICIAL NAME: Republic of Carpasia (Republika Crpasija)
POPULATION: 254,000
CAPITAL CITY: Crnilobara
PLACES OF INTEREST: Krakow
GOVERNMENT: Democratic republic
MAJOR LANGUAGES: Carpasian, Serbian
MONETARY UNIT: Euro, formerly Yugoslavian dinar
MAJOR RESOURCES: Textiles, wine
NATIONAL DEFENSE: In the wake of Carpasia's independence from Montenegro, it has no standing army, lacking the finances to maintain any large force. During the Hydra-induced civil war, the Carpasian Defense Force hastily formed to oppose the insurgents; in the post-war era, it has been recognized by the government as an official volunteer militia, currently some 1500 members strong. Despite their small size, the CDF is relatively well equipped at the moment, as they have inherited abandoned Hydra tanks and ordinance left behind after the conflict. Carpasia has signed a mutual defense pact with Montenegro, so that their larger neighbor's navy/coast guard also patrols Carpasia's relatively small coastline.
INTERNATIONAL RELATIONS: Carpasia is a member of the United Nations, UNESCO, Interpol and World Health Organization, and recently joined both the European Union and Council of Europe. Formerly tense relations with neighboring Montenegro and Croatia are gradually easing since independence was achieved.
EXTRATERRESTRIAL RELATIONS: None known.
NONHUMAN POPULATION: None.
DOMESTIC SUPERHUMANS: Though born overseas while his family was in exile during the communist regime, Scorpio (Mikel Fury) considers himself Carpasian, descendant of the former Petar Carpasian Royal Family; armed with the Scorpio Key, Mikel fought against the Hydra incursion during the Civil War, and briefly served as acting president, before resigning upon realizing that he did not have the skills to rebuild Carpasia's economy in the wake of rampant ministerial corruption.
PROMINENT CITIZENS: King Djuradj Pavel was the last Carpasian monarch; during communist rule Djuradj was officially an average citizen and factory worker, and after the birth of his son, he brokered a deal with Tito's regime to be allowed to take his family into the west in return for officially abdicating the throne. Baltazar, his son, attempted to reclaim the throne with Hydra backing shortly after Carpasia became independent, willing to turn his country into a puppet state in return for the crown. During the last years of the communist regime, the subsequent breakup of Yugoslavia and the wars which followed, Jasnia Schweik, Milovan Tankosic, Dmitri Cabrinovic, Sofia Rudavsk (a former Miss Carpasia and Miss Yugoslavia) and Josip Potiorek distinguished themselves fighting for democracy and independence; popular opinion saw them form the new

Carpasian cabinet, with Dmitri as minister of the interior, Sofia foreign affairs minister, Josip industry and Schweik defense, under President Tankosic, but all were assassinated by Hydra within a day of entering office. Under President Mikel Fury, businessmen Vasilje Burzan, Goce Petrovic and Svetozar Gvenkovski were appointed ministers of state, trade and defense respectively, but were soon exposed as using their offices to run a lucrative chocolate smuggling ring; Fury destroyed their stock before angrily resigning.
SUPERHUMAN RESIDENTS: None known.
DOMESTIC CRIME: Carpasia has a thriving black market, smuggling in luxury commodities such as chocolate and jeans, and exporting knock-off brand name items produced in illegal sweatshops. Governmental corruption is rife, with many ministers either accepting bribes or even being behind much of the country's illegal activities.
INTERNATIONAL CRIME: Shortly after independence was declared from Montenegro, Hydra engineered a civil war, intending to place a puppet ruler, Baltazar Pavel on the throne; having assassinated the newly elected President Tankosic and his cabinet, Hydra supplied the rebels with weaponry and Life Model Decoy soldiers, but the plot was ended when Nick Fury, Scorpio and Wolverine (James Howlett) exposed it and blew up the LMD plant.
FIRST APPEARANCE: Wolverine/Nick Fury: Scorpio Rising (1994)
HISTORY: The earliest known inhabitants in what is now Carpasia are believed to be the Illyrians and Thracians circa 1500 BC; the name Caerpacia first shows in Greek writings around 500 BC, when they established first trade routes and then colonies in the region. During the 2nd century BC the area was annexed by the expanding Roman Empire, and Carpasia became part of the Eastern Roman Empire (later called the Byzantine Empire) in 395 AD. The region gradually gained greater autonomy, especially following the Slavic migrations in the 5th and 6th centuries, and later fell under the rule of the Republic of Venice in the 13th century. In 1628 Carpasia gained independence under King Petar, whose dynasty lasted into the 20th century. Carpasia was devastated economically by World War I, and after the war was merged into the new Kingdom of Serbs, Croats and Slovenes (later Yugoslavia). The Axis invasion of 1941 saw the brief creation of the Independent State of Carpasia, a puppet country under Italian control, which placed the Pavels on the throne. In 1945 Carpasia fell under Soviet control, and was merged back into Yugoslavia soon after. With the collapse of communism, Yugoslavia violently sundered; Carpasia initially remained tied to its larger neighbor, Montenegro, but a couple of years ago an independence referendum saw it become an independent republic. Despite an attempted Hydra coup, brief civil war, and ongoing financial crisis, Carpasia is striving valiantly to find its place in the 21st century international community.

OFFICIAL NAME: French Republic (Republique française)

POPULATION: 63,714,000

CAPITAL CITY: Paris

PLACES OF INTEREST: Palace of Versailles, Pont du Gard, la Citadel, Cathedral of Notre Dame, Eiffel Tower

GOVERNMENT: Democratic republic

MAJOR LANGUAGES: French, several regional languages including Alsatian, Corsican, Catalan, Basque, Flemish

MONETARY UNIT: Euro; formerly French franc

MAJOR RESOURCES: Wine, cosmetics, perfume, pharmaceutical products, aircraft, textiles, iron.

NATIONAL DEFENSE: Armée de Terre, Marine Nationale, Armée de l'Air, Gendarmerie Nationale

INTERNATIONAL RELATIONS: France is a one of the UN Security Council's five permanent members, and also belongs to UNESCO, NATO, Interpol, the European Union, the G-8 and World Health Organization. SHIELD and X-Corporation both maintained French branches.

EXTRATERRESTRIAL RELATIONS: Hoping to help humans achieve enlightenment the Ludberdites of Zaar and Ul'lula'n Nebulon spread their Celestial Mind Control Movement to Paris, where they battled both the Headmen and Defenders. The Brethren launched an assault on Paris, and battled the Avengers.

NONHUMAN POPULATION: Trapped in another dimension for centuries, the Ruined (Armure, B'arr, Casque, C'hin, Exalt, Feuille, Griffe, Katar, Martyr, M'stapha, S'pyke, Stem, Touffe, T'urnaround) escaped into Paris by possessing human hosts, but were repelled by the Fantastic Four. The demon Ningal was trapped for several years by mystical energies in a cave in southern France. Niamh, the Lady of the Lake, is believed to reside beneath Lake Benoye. Crux (Cristal Lemiuex) was a nanotech life form; believing herself a human mutant, she was recruited into Cerebro's X-Men.

DOMESTIC SUPERHUMANS: During World War I, the Crimson Cavalier battled the Germans as one of Freedom's Five; during World War II the ghost of an unidentified swordsman, the Fourth Musketeer, rose to fight his country's enemies. Paulette Brazee was the resistance fighter She-Wolf (and later Citizen V). French mutants include former 12th century Crusader and modern-day Acolyte Exodus; his fellow Acolyte Gargouille (Lavinia LeBlanc); Bevatron (Fabian Marechal-Julbin) and Tarot (Marie-Ange Colbert) of the Hellfire Club's Hellions; Elsa Ames, born with gills; Flambé of the mercenary Hell's Belles; the kyphotic Half-Mad, who died fighting the werewolf Jack Russell; and X-Force's la Nuit (Pierre Truffaut). Batroc the Leaper (Georges Batroc) is a famous mercenary; his daughter Marie has followed him into the family business. Other French mercenaries include the late Frog-Man (Francois LeBlanc) of the Ani-Men; former Avenger the Swordsman (Jacques DuQuesne); the cyborg Rapido (Roussel Dupont); French NATO engineer Cyclone (André Gerard), slain by the Scourge of the Underworld, and his successor Cyclone (Pierce Fresson); and the winged Peregrine (Alain Racine). French criminals include: Darkforce manipulator Ecstasy (Renee Deladier); the petrifying Grey Gargoyle (Paul Pierre Duval); Diadem (Luciane D'Hiver), foe of Shang-Chi; Poodle (Clémence Dautry) of the Litter; L'Empereur du Monde Souterrain; and the armored Commanda (Lady Catherine D'Antan). Khor the Black Sorcerer was a 13th century mage banished for use of black magic, who found his way to the Antarctic's Savage Land. Other French sorcerers include the 17th century LaVoisin (Catherine DeShayes), who slew King Louis XIV; her modern day namesake and alleged reincarnation, who bore Hellstorm (Daimon Hellstrom)'s child; the 18th century necromancer Mauvais, who emigrated to Canada and battled the Inuit gods; and Margali Szardos, sorceress of the Winding Way. The 18th century sculptor Jacques DuBois battled Dracula and was transformed into a living statue. Tempest (Nicolette Giroux) was transformed by the mystical entity Watoomb into his Exemplar, while Martyr (Yvette Diamonde) was transformed by the Ruined, retaining her powers even after they were repelled. Exposure to radioactive isotopes turned the scientist Henri Sorel first into Radion the Atomic Man; now cured, he works for Project:

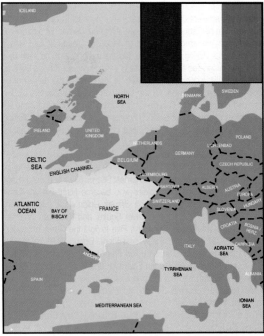

PEGASUS. Drawn to life beneath the sea, Peter Maher had American Dr. Simon Bondy surgically give him gills. Obsessed with revenge against the Atlantean Namor, marine biologist Jacqueline Trufaut briefly gained aquatic powers and mermaid form by utilizing Neptune's trident. French super heroes include the telepath Nuage (Silvie Rouge) and former SHIELD agent Tiger (Hughes Aït-Kaci), both members of Euroforce; Tricolore of the Super Heroes of Europe; the psychic Gemini-member Mandala (Iman Dashire); and les Héros de Paris, whose French-born members include the indestructible Adamantine, the vengeful le Comte de Nuit, the restless spirit Détective Fantôme, gunslinger le Cowboy, the illuminating la Lumiére Bleue, scientific genius le Docteur Q, and speedster le Vent.

PROMINENT CITIZENS: In the 6th century Lancelot du Lac joined the Knights of the Round Table at Camelot. In the modern day, the Bowman, an ally of Iron Fist, claims to be Lancelot, paying penance for his past sins. In the 17th century the Frères de la Côte (Brothers of the Coast) were a pirate confederation from Tortuga; their members included Michel le Basque, François L'Ollonais (Jean David Nau), Monbars l'Exterminateur, Vent-en-Panne and the bitter enemies Captain Tyger and Boute Fou. The 19th century swordsman le Sabre (Gilles Follet) traveled to America and battled the gunslinging Rawhide Kid (Johnny Bart). In the 1920s Merriem Drew inherited land in Transia, traveling there with her English husband Jonathon and daughter Jessica, only to be slain by a werewolf. During WWII, ace pilot and swordsman Lt. Rene D'Auvergne flew alongside Captain K-4's Sky Devils, while resistance fighter Jacques Dernier assisted the Howling Commandos behind enemy lines, the nun Sister Angelique aided the Deadly Dozen, and Jacques LaRocque was a member of the Leatherneck Raiders. Former mercenary Jean Paul DuChamp is a close ally of Moon Knight. Amongst France's other mercenaries are Time Bomb (Louis Joubert) of Hardcase's Harriers, Punisher foe Armand Chauffard, and Colonel Jean Romily, unwilling agent of the insane General Kriegkopf. French assassins include the strangler Garrote (Léopold Brun), the crime czar Pierre Saint Cyr, le Concierge of the European Emissaries of Evil, and Yves Chevrier who died fleeing from Silver Sable and the Black Widow. Intelligence operatives include Reno of Deuxieme Bureau, the French Secret Service; François Borillon, director of EuroMind; the 1920s "Frenchman" who fought a running battle with Dracula; and Alexander Devereaux of the Konsortium, which sought to destroy Russia. Amongst France's more notable thieves were Genevieve Darceneaux, who fell in love with Gambit but was slain by Sabretooth, and jewel thief Paul Dumas, who partnered himself with the amnesiac Inhuman Medusa. Claude Trufaut was a French tourist visiting the UN who had the misfortune to be slain by a bullet that ricocheted off Namor's chest, while Professor Francis LaFarge was a scientist kidnapped along with his daughter at the behest of Dr. Doom, and forced to work for the Latverian tyrant. Dr. Claudia DuBois assisted an undercover Daredevil in thwarting the Kingpin's plans to sell the names of undercover SHIELD agents to the highest bidder. Olympic bobsledder Claude LeBron was pitted in a contest against the Outcast Digger by the Netherworld's Queen Kala. Henri-Désiré Landru is a serial killer who now runs a magic shop in the Bizaar at the End of Unreason.

SUPERHUMAN RESIDENTS: During WWI Isaac Christians, the future Gargoyle, served in France, as did Ernest St. Ives (Deadly Ernest), Hugo Danner, and the Canadian soldier who became Night Raven. Native hero Crimson Cavalier allied with Britons Union Jack (Montgomery, Lord Falsworth), Sir Steel and Silver Squire, and American Phantom Eagle (Karl Kaufman) as Freedom's Five to fight the German invaders on French soil; Phantom Eagle died there. During WWII, numerous foreign heroes operated in occupied France, including three different Destroyers (Keen Marlow, Brian Falsworth and Roger Aubrey), Citizen V (John Watkins), and the Human Meteor (Duke O'Dowd); when the Allies invaded occupied Europe innumerable heroes joined in the liberation. Super Soldier Fantomex (Charlie-Cluster 7) passed himself off as a French native whilst living there. Banshee (Sean Cassidy), Husk (Paige Guthrie), Jubilee (Jubilation Lee), M (Monet St. Croix), Multiple Man (Jamie Madrox), Blob (Fred Dukes), Avalanche (Dominic Petros), Sunpyre (Leyu Yoshida), Fever Pitch, Radius (Jared Corbo), Surge (a disguised Mystique) and Mastermind (Martinique Jason) were all based in Paris while working for X-Corps. M and Multiple Man subsequently joined X-Corporation's Parisian branch, alongside Cannonball (Sam Guthrie), Darkstar (Laynia Petrovna), Rictor (Julio Richter), Sabra (Ruth bat-Seraph) and Siryn (Theresa Rourke). Anaïs of les Héros de Paris is the exiled queen of a Saharan cat civilization. CIA agent Brad Bentley went rogue, and became Surrender Monkey (Edouard Pompidou), a "mutant" member of Euro-Trash. British mage Julian, Lord Phyffe, resided in France prior to his death, and the French Riviera was home to Baron Brimstone (Walther Theodoric). Immortal sorcerers Comte Saint Germain and Cagliostro also called France home in years past, while the temporally displaced Prester John was an advisor to the Frankish king Charles the Simple back in 911 AD. Criminals who have based themselves in France include Fu Manchu and his son Moving Shadow, and cyborg British drug lord Carlton Velcro. Ex-CIA agent James Lardner was unwillingly transformed into the cyborg Cobra while in France. Harlan Ryker, Mainframe, Ben Jacobs, Stanley Cross, Dr. Hu and Dr. Kimble also used France as a base for their Cyberwarrior program. Other superhumans who have called France home include exiled Narobian leader Zanda, Samantha Destine, and Daredevil (Matt Murdock); the Thing (Ben Grimm) moved to France rather than fight in the super hero Civil War. Raptor (Gary Wilton, Jr) attempted to flee there too. Dracula's daughter Lilith resided in France at the time Dr. Strange destroyed all of Earth's vampires.

DOMESTIC CRIME: While not actually illegal, the somewhat suspect Church of the Naked Truth and its successors the Ironists and Sensitivists are based in France. Operation: Cobra committed illegal mind control experiments from their French base until Moon Knight (Marc Spector) stopped them. The Bartovian Liberation Front are terrorists who demand their country's independence from the rest of France.

INTERNATIONAL CRIME: Drug dealer Christophe Marat was part of an international drug ring until he was slain by the Punisher and Clansman (Duncan Ferguson). New York's Kingpin of Crime (Wilson Fisk) sought to create a European crime syndicate under his control, assassinating French criminal Phillipe Delon as part of his plans and targeting the Channel Tunnel, and later sent his Emissaries of Evil against an undercover Daredevil. One branch of Nebulon's Celestial Mind Control Movement was in Paris, as was the One World Church, which planned to turn the entire world's population blue. France has been targeted by the Headmen, who plotted to shrink Paris' citizens, and Kang the Conqueror's forces. Criminal organizations such as Hydra and IDIC (International Data Integration Control) have operated in France, and the Super Sentinel Huntsman was deliberately let loose in France by its creators, the "World," as a test of its abilities.

HISTORY: Humans settled in France at least 30,000 years ago; around 2500 BC the Celts immigrated in from central Europe, dominating the region until the Roman Empire spread, conquering all of Gaul (as the Romans knew it) by 52 BC, the same year Lutetia, later called Paris, was founded. With the Empire's fall, by the late 5th century the Frankish king Clovis I had conquered much of Gaul. Around 840 AD the Carolingian Empire, which had grown from Clovis' kingdom, split. Charles the Bald took Western Francia, which in 987 became France. Between the late 11th and early 13th centuries France sent Crusaders to the Holy Lands at the pope's behest. Meanwhile marriages of noble houses led to rival claimants to the thrones of England and France, leading to centuries of intermittent war between the nations. During the 17th century the French nobility became increasingly seen as extravagant and uncaring by the wider populace, and unrest slowly grew, finally exploding into the French Revolution in 1789. In 1799 General Napoléon Bonaparte became the new French ruler, leading the country to conquer much of Europe before he was finally defeated in 1815. France briefly returned to being a monarchy, but in 1848 Bonaparte's nephew Louis Napoléon became president of the Second Republic, proclaiming himself emperor a few years later. With his exile in 1871, the Third Republic began. The Germans invaded France during both world wars, but in each case were eventually defeated by Allied forces. In the post-war era, France has become one of the wealthiest European nations, and a driving force towards closer European union.

Art by Mike McKone

OFFICIAL NAME: Federal Republic of Germany (Bundesrepublik Deutschland)

POPULATION: 82,400,000

CAPITAL CITY: Berlin

PLACES OF INTEREST: Köln (Cologne) Cathedral, Colditz Castle, Heidelberg University, Neuschwanstein Castle, Castle Frankenstein, Worldengine

GOVERNMENT: Democratic federal republic

MAJOR LANGUAGES: German

MONETARY UNIT: Euro, formerly Deutschmark

MAJOR RESOURCES: Coal, iron ore, machinery, beer, vehicles, textiles.

NATIONAL DEFENSE: Bundeswehr (Federal Armed Forces): Heer (Army), Deutsche Marine (Navy), Luftwaffe (Airforce), Streitkraeftebasis (Joint Service Support Command), Zentraler Sanitaetsdienst (Central Medical Service). Germany's national super-hero team is the Helden-Liga (Heroes League, aka Schutz Heiliggruppe).

INTERNATIONAL RELATIONS: Germany is a member of the United Nations, UNESCO, NATO, Interpol, SHIELD and World Health Organization.

EXTRATERRESTRIAL RELATIONS: Early in World War II four Axi-Tun crash landed into a German mountainside; three fell under Brain Drain's control, who named them Brunnhilde, Donar, Froh and Loga after the Norse gods, and set them against the Allies' Invaders. The fourth, Hilda (Brunnhilde), destroyed both herself and her fellows to free them from Nazi control. Around 1944 a Gnobian ship crashed near Gruenstadt; normally a peaceful race, the survivors were infected with Baron Strucker's madness, and when revived from suspended animation in recent times they became Strucker's Death's Head Squadron. One Gnobian, Lump, escaped the insanity, and helped cure his fellows long enough for the Gnobian mother to commit suicide, taking her damaged children with her.

NONHUMAN POPULATION: The Nazis created several robots to send against the Allies, including the synthezoid Gremlins; the nonsentient Firebrand Squadron, duplicates of the American Human Torch (Jim Hammond); Arnim Zola's Nazi X; and numerous Sleepers hidden away to activate and spread devastation should the Nazi regime be defeated. Verminus Rex was the prince of the ratlike Short Teeth; after being slain during World War I, he became a Spirit of Vengeance. The famous Frankenstein's Monster was created in Ingolstadt, Bavaria by 18th century scientist Victor Frankenstein. Generations later Victor's ancestor Basil Frankenstein created another Monster in the Swiss Castle Frankenstein as a Nazi weapon, but it was destroyed by the Invaders. The Hidden Ones, an off-shoot from the Inhumans, were targeted by the Nazi's Loki Project, but escaped and went into hiding. During Communist rule, East German scientists created the Beasts of Berlin, intellectually enhanced gorillas.

DOMESTIC SUPERHUMANS: In the 16th century occultist Baron (Robert) von Staler fought Puritan adventurer Solomon Kane. Sorcerer Viscount Henrich Krowler helped Hitler rise to power between the wars. During WWII the Nazis produced many superhumans to fight their cause, including: the Blitzkrieg Squad's Colonel Fritz Klaue; the Masked Raider (Dirk Mehler), slain by the Blazing Skull; the chameleonic Agent of 1000 Faces; the saboteur Armless Tiger Man (Gustav Hertz); the aviator Skyshark (Captain Schleigal); the Face (Colonel Eisen), slain by the Warsaw Golem; the explosive General Grüber Brinkhaus; the psychic Otto Weiss; Sky-Wolves foes General Skul and the armored Steel Kommando; the cyborg Planner (Hendrich Von Wilhelm Innsbruck); Young Allies foe the Mad Mechanic (Otto Briefer); the combat-suited Karl Stryker, whose defeat his son Viktor Stryker would try to avenge decades later; Namor's skull-faced foe the Cobra (Dietmar Stock); Namor's clone N2; the snake-limbed Python (Emil Cullen); the winged Vulture (Ottokar Meltzer); and Komtur (Franz Gerhardt), the Teutonic Knight. Many prominent Nazis remain active into recent times, amongst them the Fuhrer Adolf Hitler of Austria, who thanks to Swiss geneticist Arnim Zola now moves from one clone body to the next as the Hate-Monger;

Heinrich Himmler, resurrected by Satannish as the Lethal Legion's Zyklon; the Red Skull (Johann Shmidt), arch foe of Captain America; scientist Baron (Heinrich) Zemo, who formed the Masters of Evil; Baron (Wolfgang) Strucker, who founded Hydra; Captain Axis (Otto Kronsteig), who escaped first to Latveria and then the Microverse; the cyborg Geist (Nikolaus Geist); Warrior Woman (Julia Rätsel), now a member of Axis Mundi; Swarm (Fritz von Meyer), now composed of bees; Lyle Dekker, who transferred his mind into the Ameridroid; the Brain (Otto von Schmittsder), who survived execution as a disembodied head; the sorcerer Thule; the gestalt spy Agent Axis (German component Berthold Volker); the sentient ape Doctorangutan; and Brain Drain (Werner Schmidt). Whisper (Karl Reifschneider) was a former Nazi guard at Auschwitz who swore never to allow mutants to be similarly persecuted; however Magneto refused to believe he had repented his past, and slew him. Though not a Nazi, patriot Iron Cross (Helmut Gruler) fought for Germany during the war; but afterwards joined Allied heroes in forming the V-Battalion's Penance Council. The current Baron Zemo, Helmut, is the son of Heinrich; a longtime Captain America foe, he gradually became more altruistic during his association with the Thunderbolts; the Baroness (Heike Zemo), has claimed to be a reincarnation of Heinrich, Baron Zemo. Neo-Nazi Max Lohmer recently followed in his great-uncle Wilhelm's footsteps to become Master Man; meanwhile Axl Nacht used the Master Man formula to become Axis Mundi's Gotteskrieger. Doppelganger (Dr. Wolfgang Heinrich) was genetically engineered by his Nazi father to copy other superhumans' powers; as an adult he ran the Eastern Bloc's mutant vivisection program until X-Factor intervened. Watchlord (Pieter Altmann) sought vengeance on the Russians for his father's wartime death. The supposedly immortal Johann Faustus was slain by Mortigan Goth's renegade soul; Johann's similarly immortal wife Marguerite escaped. German criminals include Rattler (Gustav Krueger) of the Serpent Society; Libra (Gustav Brandt) of the Zodiac; mutant assassin the Wall (Günter Gross); Emplate's servant Bulwark (Oswald Boeglin); the demonic Stonecold (Johann Bessler); the size-altering thief Eric Wolton; and the Litter's Dane (Jan Rader). Modern German heroes include the mutant Maverick (Christoph Nord); the X-Man Nightcrawler (Kurt Wagner); Dachs (Patrick Kurtz) and Bundesadler (Sigismund Bismarck), slain by Morlun; the armored Saberbat (Valentina Topolev); EuroForce's Key (Geyr Kluge); the Pantheon's invulnerable Achilles;

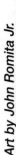
Art by John Romita Jr.

Adler Klaus; the bomber Fiddler (Ulrich Kuster); Field Marshall Erwin Rommel, the Desert Fox; soldier Joseph Heinrich Gerhardt, whose soul Hellstorm helped reach Heaven; sadistic doctor Max Sweikart and his assistant Lola Steimle; Gestapo Major Rudolph Krueger; Devil's Island commander Major Johann Strasser; Red Skull agent Major Richard Uberhart; the spy Sando (Wolfgang von Krantz); boxer Karl Schroeder; the underwater Lightning Squad sent to stop Namor; Oberstleutnant Erik Lonnroth, snatched forward in time to battle Harald Jaekelsson's Vikings; V2 base commander Baron Johann von Braun; plane designer Kurt Steinem; Camp 13 commandant Captain Alban Schnitzler; Young Avenger foe Eric von Himmel; Captain Terror's enemies Black Claw (Fritz Sternberg) and Dr. Leech (Emil Hansen); Dhaka tribe leader Kuoli (Kurt Mueller); poisoner the Ring (Hans Reimann); Namor foe Count Otto von Remden; Major Liberty enemy Heinrich Tode; the Ringmaster of Death (Fritz Tiboldt) and his Circus of Crime; and Destroyer opponents Erwin Krause, Dr. Dragon (Leonard Schaefer), Heinrich Bungler, and Hauptmann Albert Schnagel. Amongst the Nazis who escaped Germany are Franz Gruber, Baron (Heinrich) Zemo's helper; Zemo's assistant Klaus "Kenneth" Sturdy, who empowered the Ani-Men and Count Nefaria; the founders of Matrix 8; the Red Skull's servants Wolfgang Brenner and Horst Lederer; Hydra's Ivan Trefkov; the reformed Wilhelm von Schmidt, who raised the Gnobian Lump; Dr. Vincent Fishler, who experimented on Ben Beckley; the cyborg Dr. Friederich Krause, who maintained Master Man's hibernation; Dr. Doom's servants Gert and Gustav Hauptmann; the Red Skull's Exiles Franz Cadavus, Eric Gruning, and Jurgen "Iron Hand" Hauptmann; Klaus Mendelhaus, the Butcher of Diebenwald; fake psychic detective Mycroft (Miles von Croft); terrorist leader Emil Stein; scientist Luther von Eisenbluth; Yellow Claw servant Fritz von Voltzmann; Baron von Blitzschlag, now part of the USA's Initiative; and Dominic Fortune's foe Wolfgang Heinrich von Lundt, who took the alias Simon Steele. Not all Germans agreed with the Nazis: Oskar Kessler, Coral Liebowitz and Ilsa Koenig were German anti-Nazi resistance fighters; both Eric Koenig and Hans Klaus joined the Howling Commandos; scientists Herman Berg and Hans Stiller refused to hand over devastating inventions; and orphans Maxie Stein, Gus Weber, Hans Brauer, Warren Zumwald and Kurt Erzberger became the Victory Boys. In the 1950s German adventurer Franz Heinrich accompanied Venus to seek the Fountain of Youth on Mars, while Dr. Karl Mantz sought to prolong life by exploding the "cosmic atom." Neo-Nazis include: Wilhelm Bucher, who fought Shang-Chi; and Howard the Duck's foe, Dr. Reich. In recent years Luther Mannheim developed a lethal poison for the Terror Alliance, while Hermann Schreck designed the mercenary Cossack's blindness weapon. After soldier Ute Eiskalt was slain by Magneto, his mercenary brother Adrian Eiskalt sought vengeance. Other notable modern day Germans include: Werner von Strucker, son of Baron Strucker; Satanist Elsbeth von Strucker, Baron Strucker's 3rd wife; members of Nightcrawler's circus, der Jahrmacht, such as fire-breather Feuer Langhagen, the pyrokinetic Jutta, contortionist Gummi, strong man Haus, conjoined twins Kirkegaard, sorceress Jimaine Szardos and her late brother Stefan; criminal Mother Matrix (Barbara Gruber); former Thunderbolt Man-Killer (Katrina van Horne); Alexander van Tilberg, drug-addicted German ambassador to the USA; actor Arnold Schwarzburger, star of the Arkon movies; football player Hans Schulmann of the Head Hunters; and the anarchist spammer Sour Kraut (Gunther Herschein), slain by the Façade virus.

Freiheitskämpfer/Vormund (Markus Ettlinger), leader of Helden-Liga; his late ally Blitzkrieger (Franz Mittelstaedt); and Franz's cousin Courier (Hans Mittlesteadt). The Isolationist (Josef Huber) uncontrollably copies the powers of all Earth's mutants at once. German vampires include Lyza Strang, Blade's archfoe Deacon Frost, and Baroness Blood's servants Grausum and Wampyr.

PROMINENT CITIZENS: In 1480 Harbin Zemo stood alone against Slav raiders, his bravery earning him a baronet. His descendants, the infamous Barons Zemo include Hademar, Heller, Herbert, Helmuth, Hackett, Hartwig, Hilliard, Hoffman, Hobart, Herman, Heinrich and Helmut, the current Baron. 15th century Teutonic knight Frank von Frankenstein was impaled by the pre-vampire Vlad Tepes. During WWI, foes of the Phantom Eagle included dirigible commander General Heinrich von Ronstadt, pilot Captain Verner Carlson and Hermann von Reitberger, the Eagle's killer.

During the 19th century, an unidentified colonel took refuge in Castle Frankenstein and formed a small army out of mentally drained locals, but his plans for conquest were stopped by the Monster. Sara Krowler Mordo was the daughter of sorcerer Viscount Krowler; she slew him, only to be murdered by her son Karl, Baron Mordo. After the Nazis came to power, Jewish scientist Dr. Abraham Erskine fled to the US rather than let his nearly completed Super Soldier formula fall into Nazi hands. He was given the codename Josef Reinstein, but was slain by Nazi Heinz Kruger moments after empowering Steve Rogers. Erskine's colleague Wilfred Nagel defected to the US soon after, taking up his research and the Reinstein codename, but was similarly slain. Meanwhile Professor Eric Schmidt refused to hand over his successful variant of the formula, instead administering it to American Keen Marlow and Briton Brian Falsworth. Dr. Raymond Koch and Colonel Krieghund continued working separately to crack the formula for Nazi Germany. SS Major Albrecht Kerfoot stole a copy of Erskine's formula before he died, but was slain before he could deliver it; the copy would later be found by the 1950s Captain America. Other Nazi scientists include Dr. Jurgen Enderle, who built General Klaue's bionic hand and Dr. Franz Schneider, who designed Iron Cross' armor. Additional prominent Nazis include the Blitzkrieg Squad (General Klaue, Ernst Mueller, Fritz von Sydow, Ludwig Schroeder, Manfred Adler, Otto Rabe and Siegfried Farber), German counterparts to the Allied Howling Commandos; the subversive Reaper (Gunther Strauss); Major Manfred Baumin of the Sobibor Death Camp and his mentor General Reinhard Heydrich; Miss America foe, the Pinheaded Killer (Stefan Halpern); spymaster Baron Boche (Ulbrecht Arzt); Eva Braun's bodyguard Colonel Bryon Kritzberg; torturer Dr. Agony (Conrad Meer); viral weapon creator Dr.

SUPERHUMAN RESIDENTS: During WWII foreign traitors who allied with the Nazis included scientist Cedric Rawlings; Atlantean U-Man (Meranno); the vampire Baron Blood (John Falsworth); American Bundhist Master Man (Wilhelm Lohmer); External mutant Crule; Mys-Tech's Algernon Crowe; and geneticist Mr. Sinister (Nathaniel Essex). Anti-German resistance fighters Citizen V (John Watkins) and the three Destroyers (Keen Marlow, Brian Falsworth and Roger Aubrey) operated across occupied Europe, including within Germany. In more recent times the Baroness' White Ninja, the assassin Black Swan, and the hero killer Zeitgeist (Larry Elker) have all called Germany home. A dozen WWII US heroes (the Blue Blade, Black Widow (Claire Voyant) Captain

Wonder, Dynamic Man, the robot Electro, Fiery Mask, Laughing Mask, Master Mind Excello, Mister E, the Phantom Reporter, Rockman and the Witness) were captured during the Allied invasion of Berlin and cryogenically frozen, only being discovered and released decades later in the modern era.

DOMESTIC CRIME: Germany has a comparatively low crime rate. Numerous thieves through the decades have sought the mysterious, vanishing Momentary Princess gem. The mercenary Sniper (Rich van Burien) tried to steal an Apache antitank helicopter from a war games demonstration, but was stopped by the Punisher (Frank Castle). Former Nazi Emil Stein led the terrorist group DANTE.

INTERNATIONAL CRIME: Nazi war crimes include the Super Soldier experiments carried out at Schwarzbitte Concentration Camp, and the turning of American pilot Michael Kramer into the plague-carrying Judas Man. The kidnapped Ivan Petrovitch was brought to West Germany for training, tricked by his Soviet masters into thinking his captors were Westerners before being "rescued" by Russian agents. One of Europe's biggest drug distributors was Hans-Dieter Flurgen, until he was slain by the Punisher and the Clansman (Duncan Ferguson). The Russian assassin the Confessor sometimes operates inside Germany, as does the mercenary Agent Orange (Roger Goshaw).

HISTORY: Around the 2nd century BC Germanic tribes such as the Franks, Saxons, Teutons, Suevi, Cherusci, Swabians, Goths, Alamani and Bavarians migrated into an area of northern Europe previously held by the Celts, soon becoming the dominant culture and clashing with the neighboring Roman Empire, attacking Gaul and repelling Roman advances into the regions east of the Rhine. As the Roman Empire declined, these tribes began whittling away at its territory, and by the 5th century AD, they occupied much of the Western Roman Empire. Under Charlemagne the Frankish tribe conquered much of western Europe; around 840 AD the Empire was split between Charlemagne's grandchildren, with Louis the German taking East Francia; over the next couple of centuries this would become the Kingdom of Germany. In 936 AD Otto the Great was crowned, and after expanding his domain through conquest, in 962 he was crowned the Holy Roman Emperor by Pope John XII in return for his assistance against Berengar of Ivrea, who had occupied the northern papal states. As centuries passed the Empire became a loose confederation of smaller states run by princes who elected the emperor, until Albert of Habsburg assumed the throne in 1438; his line would rule until the Empire was dissolved during the Napoleonic Wars in 1806. Triggered by a dispute over claims to the

Bohemian throne, Germany was further devastated by the Thirty Years War (1618-1648), and in its aftermath the Empire had shattered into hundreds of small principalities. In 1862 Otto von Bismarck became minister-president of Prussia, and swiftly set about unifying Germany; after defeating Denmark in 1864 and Austria in 1866, he formed the North German Confederation; a final war against France in 1870-1871 allowed Bismarck to pronounce Prussia's King Wilhelm I as Emperor of the Second German Reich (Empire) on January 18, 1871. However when Wilhelm I died, his son Wilhelm II lost little time in dismissing Bismarck, before setting Germany on a campaign of intense colonialism. Tensions between the European powers saw mutual defense treaties drawn up, and gradually Europe formed into two camps, with Germany, Italy and Austria-Hungary on one side (the Triple Alliance), and France, Russia and the UK on the other (the Triple Entente); each country also had treaties with some of the smaller European nations. Thus, when Austria-Hungary declared war on Serbia in 1914, the Russians mobilized in Serbia's defense; believing that they could not fight a war on two fronts (France to the west, Russia to the east), Germany's pre-prepared Schlieffen Plan saw them launch an attack on France first, and since the Franco-German border was heavily defended, they went through neutral Belgium, bringing Belgium's ally Britain into the war. After four years Germany was defeated, and Wilhelm II went into exile; Germany became a republic. Hammered by punitive post-war reparations, Germany's economy collapsed; humiliation at being forced to accept full responsibility for the war added to the German citizenry's resentment, leaving the country ripe for the Austrian demagogue Adolf Hitler to come to power with promises of restoring Germany to her "rightful" position, and laying the blame for Germany's earlier downfall at scapegoats such as the Jews. Hitler led Germany to aggressively expand its territories, with the invasion of Poland in 1939 finally triggering the Second World War, a war which saw the first large scale use of superhuman combatants. Initially the German blitzkrieg overran much of Europe, but the Allies fought back, and in 1945, after the American Human Torch (Jim Hammond) slew Hitler, Germany surrendered. Germany was occupied by the Allies, who split the country into four zones; while the US, Britain and France established the Federal Republic of Germany in 1949 and gave it full independence in 1954, the Russians continued to control the new Democratic Republic of Germany as a satellite state. This division increased with the erection of the Berlin Wall in 1961, splitting the former German capital. With the collapse of the Soviet Communist government, the Berlin Wall was pulled down in 1989, and in 1990 Germany was united again.

Art by Mark Brooks

GREECE

OFFICIAL NAME: Hellenic Republic (Elliniki Dimokratía)
POPULATION: 10,706,000
CAPITAL CITY: Athens
PLACES OF INTEREST: The Acropolis, Dodecanese Islands, Ionian Islands, Kalkhimithia, Kirinos, Kyrinos, Mount Olympus, Olympia, the Parthenon, Saronic Gulf Islands
GOVERNMENT: Parliamentary republic
MAJOR LANGUAGES: Greek
MONETARY UNIT: Euro
MAJOR RESOURCES: Food and beverages (tomatoes, olives, grapes, wheat, wine), manufactured goods, petroleum products, chemicals, textiles
NATIONAL DEFENSE: Hellenic Army, Hellenic Navy, Hellenic Air Force
INTERNATIONAL RELATIONS: Greece holds membership in the United Nations, UNESCO, Council of Europe, International Criminal Court, International Chamber of Commerce, Interpol, NATO, Southeast European Cooperative Initiative, and World Health Organization, and is a member nation of SHIELD.
EXTRATERRESTRIAL RELATIONS: Scouts of the A-Chiltarian race once established a giant robot Cyclops to capture passing ships, but they were driven from Earth by Ant-Man (Henry Pym) and the Wasp (Janet Van Dyne). The abstract entity Eternity once shared its existence with Greek national Socrates Carvopolis, and ultimately absorbed Carvopolis into its being.
NONHUMAN POPULATION: The Eternals dwell in the mountainous city of Olympia, their people's capital. Many of the Olympian gods have lived amongst the people of Greece over the centuries. Ares has recently joined the Avengers.
DOMESTIC SUPERHUMANS: Although he has dual citizenship in Olympus, Hercules, the demigod son of the Olympian ruler Zeus, was born in Thebes, Greece circa 1000 BC. Centuries ago, Iskelior was born on the Greek Isle of Lixos; but her magician father placed her in an alternate dimension for her own safety where she remained for centuries, occasionally offering sanctuary to Earth natives. The international assassin Elektra Natchios, daughter of slain Greek Ambassador Hugo Kostas Natchios, possesses limited telekinetic and telepathic abilities derived from her extensive martial arts training. The vibratory-wave-producing mutant terrorist and former U.S. government agent Avalanche (Dominikos Ioannis Petrakis, later anglicized to "Dominic Janos Petros") was born in the coastal town of Agios Nikólaos, Lasithi prefecture, on the island of Crete. The woman known as Oracle serves as Greece's representative on the Super Heroes of Europe. Born in the impoverished slums of Athens, Greek business magnate Mordecai Midas was driven by an almost psychotic desire to become the world's wealthiest man. Accumulating great wealth as well as Midas International headquartered on an island in the Aegean Sea, Midas sought to acquire Stark Industries, bringing him into conflict with Iron Man (Tony Stark) on several occasions.

The geneticist Dr. Zeus once sought to revive the myth and magic of Ancient Greece by using genetic restoration to recreate many of the creatures of Greek mythology from his lab in Crete. When confronted by Spider-Man (Peter Parker) and Hercules, Dr. Zeus used his gorgon clone to turn himself to stone once he realized he displeased the legendary Hercules.

PROMINENT CITIZENS: Peter Kazantis, a relative of the Greek royal family, was regarded as a national hero and was instrumental in unifying the Greek Resistance during the Axis occupation of World War II.

SUPERHUMAN RESIDENTS: The Order of the Askani (Brother Caesar, Brother Virgil, and Sister Sophia) established a monastery on the Isle of Syrna in the Dodecanese island group of the Aegean Sea after their founder Ch'vayre went missing. The Order, which was dedicated to seeing that the time-displaced mutant Cable (Nathan Summers) was prepared for his destiny-fulfilling battle against Apocalypse (En Sabah Nur), gave Cable the the Psimitar, an Askani weapon that harnesses the telekinetic power of its bearer.

DOMESTIC CRIME: Greece serves as a gateway to Europe for drug traffickers smuggling their goods from the Middle East and Southwest Asia to the West. As a result, money laundering related to drug trafficking and organized crime is prevalent.

INTERNATIONAL CRIME: Amber D'Alexis and Scorpio (Mikel Fury) formerly ran their terrorist organization Swift Sword from an uninhabited island in the Cyclades. The terrorist organization Hydra constructed a complex in the city of Lamia, where a Hydra agent codenamed "Number 16" orchestrated the kidnapping of spies from around the world, torturing them, and then selling the extracted intelligence to the highest bidder, until the operation was shut down by SHIELD's Nick Fury.

HISTORY: The summit of Mount Olympus, Greece's highest mountain, boasts a dimensional nexus that connects Earth with the small otherdimensional planetary body known as Olympus, home of the Olympian pantheon. At the end of the Hyborian Age (approximately 8000 BC), the Olympians sought worshippers on Earth and began interacting with the inhabitants of Ancient Greece from atop Mount Olympus. During the Trojan War, which pitted the Mycenaean Greeks against the Trojans of Asia Minor in the 12th century BC, Olympians assisted both sides of the conflict. Zeus, ruler of the Olympians, often descended to Earth and had affairs with mortal women.

After Titanos, the first city of the superhuman Eternal race on Earth, was destroyed in an explosion of cosmic energy resulting from a failed experiment by the Eternal leader Kronos, Kronos' son and successor Zuras directed the construction of the new city of Olympia in a hidden valley in an undisclosed location among the mountains of northern Greece. For millennia, it served as the home of the Olympian Eternals, concealed from detection by ordinary human beings using advanced Eternal technology.

Greece was eventually absorbed into the Roman Empire in the 2nd and 1st centuries BC, and the Romans began worshiping many of the Olympian gods under different names. When the Roman Empire divided in the 4th century AD, Greece became part of the Eastern Roman (Byzantine) Empire headquartered in Constantinople. With the exception of Poseidon, who still actively watches over the Atlanteans, Zeus and the Olympians gradually withdrew from Earth over the centuries. In approximately 1460, Greece was captured by the Ottoman Turks, who absorbed the nation into the Ottoman Empire. The Greeks rebelled against Turkish rule in 1821 and finally won their independence in 1827. Although the European nations who supported Greece's bid for independence sponsored monarchy and placed a German prince on the Greek throne, the prince was deposed in a revolt and a Danish prince succeeded to the throne.

In 1940, Italy led an unsuccessful invasion of Greece, causing Italy's nationalist leader Benito Mussolini to persuade his ally Adolf Hitler to direct Nazi Germany's powerful military into the southern Balkans. Following a German blitzkrieg, by May 1941, Greece was under joint military occupation by three Axis powers: Nazi Germany, Italy, and Bulgaria. Many of Greece's powerful citizens and political leaders, such as Peter Kazantis, a relative of the Greek royal family, fled the country and became exiles. Although some Greeks supported the Axis as a Nazi puppet regime was established in Athens, many Greek nationalists fled to the hills and founded what came to be known as the Greek Resistance, a loosely affiliated alliance of guerilla armies dedicated to defeating the Axis occupation. However, the guerilla factions were uncoordinated, disorganized, and weakened by dissension. The US military arranged to have the exiled Peter Kazantis transported back into Greece where it was hoped he would unite the various factions of the Greek Resistance against the Axis occupation. Captain Sam Sawyer of the US Army charged Sergeant Nick Fury and his Howling Commandos to escort Kazantis to the Greek Resistance. Kazantis and the Howling Commandos secretly met with Michael Skouras, the leader of one powerful faction of Greek partisans within the Nazi occupation zone outside Athens. Although Kazantis and the Howling Commandos were briefly captured by the Nazis, they soon escaped and Kazantis was reunited with the Resistance. The British military, who had failed to prevent the Axis conquest of Greece in 1941, continued to provide support to the Greek Resistance. The British sent Corporal Logan (later Wolverine) from the Canadian Army to teach the Greeks how to attack Nazi forces using guerilla tactics. After years of struggle against the various factions within the Greek Resistance, the Germans finally retreated from the country in 1944.

Greece next entered into a period of political instability, with several failed governments, a civil war, and a military dictatorship, which ruled from 1967 to 1974. When the dictatorship attempted to intervene on the island of Cyprus, to which Greece and Turkey both laid claim, Turkey invaded the island and the Greek military regime soon collapsed. Greece was then formally established as a parliamentary republic upon the promulgation of a new constitution in 1975.

Approximately a decade ago, in New York City, Greek Ambassador Hugo Natchios was killed when a team of six terrorists kidnapped him and his daughter Elektra, who had moved to New York City to attend Columbia University. Natchios' personal bodyguard Athos, who lost his left eye and leg in the attack, was unable to save his employer, although Elektra survived. With Hugo and Christina Natchios dead and Orestez Nathcios in a self-imposed exile, young Elektra inherited her family's estate in Greece and continued to employ the staff, including Athos. Several years later, the last remaining terrorist was captured by Athos and the staff of the Natchios estate, but Elektra asked that he be set free.

The villainous alchemist Diablo unleashed into the atmosphere a chemical from the gamma-irradiated soil of Middletown, USA, which he spread over the small Greek city of Kalkhimithia, transforming its citizens into gamma-irradiated, Hulk-like monsters. As the Avengers attempted to contain the rampaging Kalkhimithians, Yellowjacket (Henry Pym) discovered that all the Kalkhimithians were similar on a cellular level and could be merged. The Avengers forced the Kalkhimithians to combine into one giant creature, but the heroes' subsequent attempt to shrink it with Pym Particles failed. They then enlisted Bruce Banner who, as the "Professor" Hulk, was aided by the Scarlet Witch's hex in merging with the giant beast, seizing control of the Kalkhimithians' communal mind and forcing the individual Kalkhimithians to return to their normal selves.

Today, the many Greek isles that dot the Mediterranean and Aegean Seas are popular tourist attractions. Shortly after her transformation into Phoenix, Jean Grey vacationed on the Isle of Kirinos in the Cyclades, a Greek island group in the Aegean Sea, where her fragile psyche was corrupted by Mastermind (Jason Wyngarde) of the Hellfire Club. Later, the freelance pilot Cylla Markham crashed her plane into the Aegean Sea while taking off from Kyrinos after the Fenris twins (Andrea & Andreas von Strucker) fired a rocket at her. While in intensive care, Markham was approached by Donald Pierce of the cybernetic Reavers, who convinced her to join the Reavers in exchange for enhancing her with cybernetic body parts.

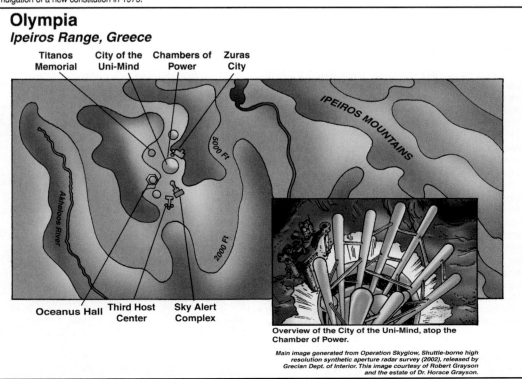

Olympia
Ipeiros Range, Greece

Titanos Memorial   City of the Uni-Mind   Chambers of Power   Zuras City

IPEIROS MOUNTAINS

5000 Ft

2000 Ft

Akheloos River

Oceanus Hall   Third Host Center   Sky Alert Complex

Overview of the City of the Uni-Mind, atop the Chamber of Power.

Main image generated from Operation Skyglow, Shuttle-borne high resolution synthetic aperture radar survey (2002), released by Grecian Dept. of Interior. This image courtesy of Robert Grayson and the estate of Dr. Horace Grayson.

OFFICIAL NAME: Republic of Hungary (Magyar Köztársaság)
POPULATION: 9,981,000
CAPITAL CITY: Budapest
PLACES OF INTEREST: Blasar Court, Bratislava prison, Buda Castle, Debrecen, Miskolc, Vajdahunyad Castle
GOVERNMENT: Parliamentary democracy
MAJOR LANGUAGES: Hungarian
MONETARY UNIT: Forint
MAJOR RESOURCES: Bauxite, coal, natural gas
NATIONAL DEFENSE: Hungary is defended by Land Forces (Magyar Honvedseg), the Border Guard and its Air Force (Magyar Legiero). The country formerly employed the superhuman People's Defense Force.
INTERNATIONAL RELATIONS: Hungary is a member of the European Union, North Atlantic Treaty Organization, United Nations and World Trade Organization. Hungary has a close economic partner in Germany. Hungary has unfriendly relations with Latveria, and has made at least one attempt at annexing the country while Dr. Doom was absent.
EXTRATERRESTRIAL RELATIONS: None known.
NONHUMAN POPULATION: The Beasts of Berlin (an army of gorillas altered to receive human-level intelligence) and Scarlet Beetles (insects mutated to the size and intellect of humans) were formerly stationed in Hungary as part of the People's Defense Force.
DOMESTIC SUPERHUMANS: Hungary has various instances of vampire and werewolf attacks. At one point, the vampires had grown so numerous that Dr. Karl Gottfried fashioned an artificial creature that could feed on vampires as they fed on humans; tragically, Dr. Gottfried and his creation were killed by fearful locals. Some Hungarian werewolves can be driven into bloodlust by contact with water. The international nihilist the Viper (also known as Madame Hydra) was born in Hungary, and evidently lost her family during a conflict in the country. The super-villain Blizzard (Gregor Shapanka) was born in Hungary, but became notorious in the USA, where he ultimately perished at the hands of Iron Man 2020. The half-Hungarian mutant terrorist Marcus Tsung was active internationally until his death at the hands of Romany Wisdom. The heroic Dimensional Man was born to Hungarian parents who immigrated to the USA.
PROMINENT CITIZENS: In the 15th century, Vlad Dracul of Transylvania was forced into a marriage with the Hungarian Zofia; Zofia eventually took her own life, but her daughter Lilith went on to oppose Dracula across

the centuries, both as vampires. The 17th century Countess Elizabeth Bathory committed a string of atrocities, killing virgins so that she could bathe in their blood in the hopes of regaining her youth. Two of the most famous of all Hungarians are the 19th century composer Franz Liszt and 20th century composer Bela Bartok. Famous Hungarian performers of the 20th century included magician Harry Houdini, actor Peter Lorre and actress sisters Eva and Zsa Zsa Gabor. In the 1950s, some parts of Hungary were threatened by the witch Anna Nikhail. Maria Troyvana was the daughter of a geneticist, and while in the USA married Henry Pym, but while the couple were on vacation in Hungary, she was kidnapped and murdered.
SUPERHUMAN RESIDENTS: During a period when he had gone insane, the mutant Quicksilver (Pietro Maximoff) became an ally of Hungary's People's Defense Force and provided useful data for equipping Bratislava prison and the military with the means to contain and combat superhumans. Other members of the People's Defense Force included the gas-gun-wielding Madame X; el Toro, whose helmet was affixed with poisoned horns; and the Voice, who can control people's actions through his speech. The People's Defense Force also made use of Olinka Barankova, who later became the AIM agent MODAM.
DOMESTIC CRIME: Hungary is a significant point of transit in drug trafficking. The demon-worshiping cult called the Enclave has recruited some of its members from Hungary.
INTERNATIONAL CRIME: The vampire Dracula has been active in Hungary at various points throughout his history. The country has faced attacks from the terrorist organization DANTE. The corrupt Wild Pack leader Silver Wolf (Andreas Vadas) placed one of his agents in Budapest, where he was found by Silver Sable and Dominic Fortune.
HISTORY: Hungary was founded in 1000 AD; in 1867, it formed a dual-monarchy with Austria, becoming Austra-Hungary until the end of World War I in 1918. The Kingdom of Hungary endured until World War II, in which Hungary was a major ally of Nazi Germany, much to the detriment of its indigenous populations of Jews and Roma ("gypsies"). After defecting from the Nazis in 1944, Hungary was occupied by them instead. After being released from the Nazis, Hungary was instead occupied by the USSR as a satellite state, but finally achieved independence again in 1989.

Art by Al Milgrom

OFFICIAL NAME: Republic of Ireland (Eire)
POPULATION: 4,110,000
CAPITAL CITY: Dublin
PLACES OF INTEREST: Cassidy Keep (near Dal'roon, County Mayo), the Blarney Stone in Blarney Castle, Rock of Cashel, General Post Office (O'Connell Street, Dublin)
GOVERNMENT: Democratic republic
MAJOR LANGUAGES: English and Gaelige (Irish Gaelic)
MONETARY UNIT: Euro; formerly punt Éireannach (Irish pound)
MAJOR RESOURCES: Computers, chemicals, pharmaceuticals, agriculture, Guinness, tourism
NATIONAL DEFENSE: Irish Defense Forces (Oglaigh na h-Eireann)
INTERNATIONAL RELATIONS: Ireland is a member of the United Nations, UNESCO, Interpol, World Health Organization and European Union. Despite past history, tensions between Ireland and the UK have waned, and in the modern day they cooperate trying to solve the problems of Northern Ireland.
EXTRATERRESTRIAL RELATIONS: When the sorcerer Yandroth unleashed numerous alien and extradimensional menaces on Earth, Ireland was attacked by the Phalanx, transforming many unfortunates into Vi-Locks. The Kinsmen and American hero Lectronn slowed their progress, until the aliens and Vi-Locks departed with Yandroth's defeat.
NONHUMAN POPULATION: The Tuatha de Danaan, or Celtic gods, view Ireland and Scotland as their domains. Their leader is Dagda; Babd and Morrigan both empowered Anthony Ludgate shortly before his demise; Bodb Derg is the Red Lord worshipped by the Bane; Caber and Leir have assisted foreign gods Hercules and Thor in the defense of Asgard against Seth, Surtur and Ymir; Cerunnos, Morrigan and Taranis empowered the mage Kyllian; Nuadhu has represented the Danaans during meetings of pantheonic godheads; in ancient times Scathach approached a recently orphaned girl, who vowed to the goddess she would only ever love a man who could defeat her in battle. The Danaans' eternal foes are the Fomor, whom the gods drove from Ireland into a darkened realm beyond Avalon; around the 12th century Balor, Bres, Cethlann, Dulb, Elathan, Indech and Tethra escaped this prison to attack Avalon, but the Druid Amergin summoned the 21st century's Avengers, who defeated them. Bres escaped forward in time to the modern day, but was captured and imprisoned at Project: PEGASUS. Ireland is also home to Leprechauns, including Donal O'Braidagh, Kelson and Padraic of the Cassidy Keep Families, and "Wee One" of the Kinsmen. Another Kinsman, Dyke, claims she is the last Nereid, or water nymph, and the Kinsman Highlander may be a kind of earth elemental. Irish vampires include Siobhan MacDermott, former lover of Baron Blood (John Falsworth).
DOMESTIC SUPERHUMANS: Local mutants include the criminal Black Tom Cassidy; Plasma (Leila O'Toole), the Cult of the Living Pharaoh's leader; the late Banshee (Sean Cassidy), X-Man; Siryn (Theresa Cassidy), Banshee's daughter; Teleplex of the Kinsmen; the half-Argentinian mercenary Stealth (Carlos McNally); X-Force's St. Anna; and reptilian Acolyte Seamus Mellancamp. In the 12th century the Danaan changed Bridgit O'Hare into Sea Witch. A seeming imposter of Nuada of the Silver Hand recently fought Bridgit's Young Gods. The Kinsmen, recruited by the Irish government, include the previously mentioned Wee One, Dyke, Highlander and Teleplex, as well as the brawler Rapscallion and Boulder, who uses a magical rock provided by Wee One. The luck-manipulating Shamrock (Molly Fitzgerald) is arguably Ireland's most recognizable hero. Another Shamrock was Ireland's member of the Super-Heroes of Europe, until he was slain by the Void. The Kestral Key of Krakkan changed Bridget Malone into the Exemplar Conquest, while the cursed Ebony Blade transformed Sean Dolan into the murderous Bloodwraith.
PROMINENT CITIZENS: Mr. McFadden is the government coordinator for the Kinsmen. The perpetually reincarnating Dracula-foe the Forever Man was the Irish-born Patrick O'Reilly in one life. Centuries ago, Red Lucy Keough was a pirate queen, raiding Spanish clippers. Cormac the Sword-Master of Otherworld's Evil Walkers may once have been the

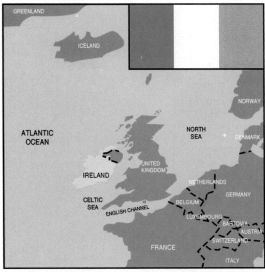

Irish hero Cormac, son of Conchabar Mac Nessa, before Necromon corrupted him.
SUPERHUMAN RESIDENTS: X-Man (Nate Grey) briefly stayed in Dublin. Amergin, High Druid of Avalon, came to Ireland as a young boy with his father, Milesius.
DOMESTIC CRIME: Ireland has historically had a low crime rate, although incidents of muggings and theft have increased in recent years. The Kinsmen and other native super heroes have encouraged most of Ireland's native super-villains to seek easier pickings overseas.
INTERNATIONAL CRIME: During the worst of the "Troubles" in the North, the IRA and other Republican groups used the relatively open border to evade the authorities on both sides. One of the most murderous of IRA killers, the Gael (Paddy O'Hanlon), went freelance, but was captured in the USA by Daredevil (Matthew Murdock).
HISTORY: Humans lived in Ireland as early as 8000 BC, with the Celts becoming resident around 500 BC; during this period battles between the Tuatha Da Danaan and Fomor were common, the latter's defeat enabling mankind to claim the lands. By the first few centuries AD, Hibernia was a land of several kingdoms, with a nominal high king, but internal feuds were common. Missionaries such as St. Patrick brought Christianity in the 5th century, but the end of the 8th century saw the arrival of less welcome visitors, the Vikings. By the middle of the 9th century, Viking settlements had sprung up along the coast; but by 955 AD they ended their raiding, instead trading and allying with rival Irish clans. In the late 10th century, Brian Boru established himself as Ard Ri (High King) of Ireland by force of arms. In 1166 AD the deposed King of Leinster, Dermot MacMurrough asked English, Norman and Welsh aristocrats to help him regain his throne from High King Connacht Rory O'Connor; fearing this would create a rival Norman kingdom, King Henry II of England used a papal bull granting him sovereignty over Ireland as an excuse to invade; in 1174 the Irish High King was forced to accept Henry as his overlord. However for centuries English control was mostly restricted to the area around Dublin, the Pale, and what lay beyond the Pale was only nominally under their control. In the 15th century, England again asserted dominance, but it was England's change into a Protestant republic under Cromwell that saw the worst incursion; with Ireland both Catholic and Royalist allies, Cromwell led a re-conquest in 1649, killing perhaps a third of the population. In 1801 the Act of Union made Ireland a component of the United Kingdom, but in 1916 a failed Easter Rising led to the establishment of the Irish Free State in 1921; the largely Protestant Northern Ireland opted out of the Free State, choosing to remain in the UK. Ireland remained neutral through World War II, although thousands of Irish volunteers joined the British armed forces; in 1949 the Free State became a Republic.

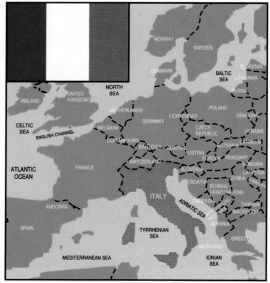

OFFICIAL NAME: Italian Republic (Repubblica Italiana)

POPULATION: 58,147,000

CAPITAL CITY: Rome

PLACES OF INTEREST: Vatican, Colosseum, Mt. Vesuvius, Venice's canals

GOVERNMENT: Democratic republic

MAJOR LANGUAGES: Italian is the official language; there are regions where German, French and Slovene are commonly spoken.

MONETARY UNIT: Euro; formerly Italian lira

MAJOR RESOURCES: Designer clothing, food products, luxury vehicles, tourism, iron and steel.

NATIONAL DEFENSE: Army (Esercito Italiano, EI), Navy (Marina Militare Italiana, MMI), Air Force (Aeronautica Militare Italiana, AMI), Carabinieri Corps (Corpo dei Carabinieri, CC)

INTERNATIONAL RELATIONS: Italy belongs to the United Nations, European Union, Council of Europe, NATO, G-8, Interpol and UNESCO. It contributes troops to SHIELD, which maintains bases in several Italian cities.

EXTRATERRESTRIAL RELATIONS: A coalition of intergalactic warlords once threatened the KGB, who in turn pressured the Italian Maggia into blackmailing a Florida-corporation, as part of a chain of incidents designed to bankrupt Earth's economy.

NONHUMAN POPULATION: Though more commonly associate with Greece, the Olympian gods were active in Italy during Roman times. The Sirens were imprisoned by Demeter on Anthemoessa. Some Cat People lived in Italy, before being banished to the Land Within. The Ancient vampire Saracen and his servant Boy resided beneath the Vatican. Their demonic servant the Reaper was summoned to Earth via an ancient crypt beneath the Colosseum. Rome also houses a N'Garai cairn.

DOMESTIC SUPERHUMANS: Past times Italian superhumans include the Sibylline Sisterhood prophetesses; the last Roman Emperor, Tyrannus (Romulus Augustulus); 13th century sorcerer and now demon Belasco; notorious 15th century poisoner Lucrezia Borgia, now reborn as Satannish's minion Cyana; 17th century alchemist Comte Alvise Gianus, who awoke in the modern day to menace Venice and battle Spider-Man; and immortal sorcerer Cagliostro, reportedly a Sicilian. Modern superhumans include Maggia leaders Silvermane (Silvio Manfredi), Count Luchino Nefaria and his daughter Giulietta (Madame Masque); mutants Marco Delgado, Francisco Milan and Carmella Unuscione, all Acolytes of Magneto; the silent Omerta; Angelo Unuscione, the mutant criminal Unus the Untouchable; "Mike" Silver, aka Argento of Euroforce; the mob assassin Silencer; AIM operatives Child One and Mr. Illusion; the Vatican agent Stigmata; and the Black Knight, imitator of Merlin's champion and agent of a rogue Vatican faction.

PROMINENT CITIZENS: Italy has spawned many magicians: the Roman Orphelus; the 13th century Ebrok, Orann and Yanthon may have been Italians, like their associate Belasco; the 17th century's Giuseppe Balsamo, aka Cagliostro, whose name was later usurped by a much older sorcerer; and the modern day Count Tancredo Carrezi, an ally of Dr. Strange. Other prominent Italians include: World War II Partisan leader and Leatherneck Raiders ally General Theresa Cimmetta; AIM leader Monica Rappaccini; WWII war criminal Baldini of the Exiles; the late Enzo Ferrara, Vatican archivist and vampire hunter; Contessa Valentina Allegra de la Fontaine of SHIELD; Victoria Montesi of the Darkhold Reedemers; and the brothers Ernesto and Luigi Gambonnos, acrobatic members of the Circus of Crime.

SUPERHUMAN RESIDENTS: The immortal Neanderthal Cole lived in Italy during Roman times; other immortals, such as Ulysses Bloodstone, Merlin Demonspawn and the vampire Lord Ruthven, have also called Italy home. The Berserker worked with the Roman legions until buried during the Vesuvius eruption. Wonder Man (Simon Williams) resided in Italy while filming "Guns of the Gunmen", and the mutant thief Gambit has visited Italy a number of times. Hellfire Club Black King Sebastian Shaw lay low in Venice for a time, and the young sorcerer Jinx (William Hastings) is believed to now reside in the Vatican. The international superteam Gemini is based in Italy.

DOMESTIC CRIME: Italy is home to the Mafia and the Maggia; in the 1920s Roman gangster Nick Diablo fought Dracula, while WWII mobster Lo Parino clashed with the Howling Commandos, and in modern times Elio Bessucho heads a Sicilian crime family which fought arms dealer Rocco Castiglione and his nephew the Punisher (Frank Castle). AIM, Hydra and the Leader (Sam Sterns) each maintain Italian bases; an AIM attack on Milan was stopped by Gemini. The Vatican has been the target of repeated assaults by those seeking artifacts housed within, including the demons Diabolique and Olivier Stoker, and the vampires Varnae and Dracula.

INTERNATIONAL CRIME: Nazi superspy Agent Axis was created by merging Italy's greatest spy with Germany's and Japan's. The assassin Sata and professional thief Asp (Richard Hunter) have operated out of Italy, while the Russian assassin Confessor battled the mercenary Maverick in Venice. The Mafia and Maggia have both spread their influence worldwide. Mafia contract killer Suspiria has worked both against and with the vigilante Punisher. Italy was the spawning ground of the terrorist Red Brigade in the 1970s.

HISTORY: Around the 11th century BC, the Greek demigod Aeneas and his men, including the Eternal "Hero," conquered Latium in what is now Italy, laying the foundations for the later Roman Empire. Greek and Etruscan influence in the region waxed and waned from the 9th century BC to the 5th, with Rome becoming dominant thereafter, gradually unifying Italy by conquest and colonization. The Roman Republic spread out across much of Europe, especially under Consul (and later Dictator) Julius Caesar's leadership. After his assassination in 44 BC, his foster son Augustus battled for control of Rome, and in 27 BC proclaimed himself Rome's first emperor. After the Empire's capital moved to Constantinople, Italy became part of the Western Roman Empire, but when the last emperor, Romulus Augustulus was deposed, the Western Empire ended, and Italy soon fractured into smaller kingdoms. By the 12th century a number of city-states had arisen. From the 14th century an intellectual renaissance overtook much of the country, spawning thinkers such as Leonardo da Vinci and Niccolò Machiavelli; then, during the 19th century Giuseppe Garibaldi and Camillo Benso brought about Italian unification. In 1922, following a post-World War I period of financial depression, Benito Mussolini's Fascists came to power, soon establishing a dictatorship; an alliance with Nazi Germany followed, and during WWII, Italy was one of the Axis powers. Shortly after the war ended, Italy became a republic; however Italy remains politically and economically unstable, not least because of the influence of crime families such as the Mafia.

OFFICIAL NAME: Kingdom of Latveria (Königruch Latverien)
POPULATION: 500,000
CAPITAL CITY: Doomstadt
PLACES OF INTEREST: Boars' Vale, Castle Doom, Citadel of Doom, Doom Falls, Doomsport airport, Doomsburg, Doomsdale, Doomsvale, Doomton, Doomwood Forest, Draken River, the Folding City, Klyne River, Mount Sorcista, Mount Victorum, Viscayin Mountains, Werner Academy
GOVERNMENT: Dictatorship
MAJOR LANGUAGES: Latverian, German, Hungarian, Romany
MONETARY UNIT: Latverian franc
MAJOR RESOURCES: Iron ore, nuclear power, robotics, electronics, time travel, machinery
NATIONAL DEFENSE: The Latverian Armed Forces comprises both Ground Forces and Air Force; they number 2,000 men and approximately 500 Servo-Guard robots. The country has also possessed a variety of orbital satellite weaponry.
INTERNATIONAL RELATIONS: Member of the United Nations, close ally of Symkaria; have treaties with Atlantis, Canada, France, USA and Wakanda. Have a history of hostilities with SHIELD, Germany and Hungary.
EXTRATERRESTRIAL RELATIONS: Dr. Doom's all-consuming quest for power has caused him to bring several extraterrestrials into Latveria in the hopes of claiming their power; victims have included the Silver Surfer (Norrin Radd), ex-herald of Galactus, and the energy being known as the Hunger. Doom has also contested with the Faceless One, a member of the Kt'kn race who has aided Prince Rudolfo in organizing resistance against him. The demon Mephisto has entered Latveria on several occasions to battle Doom for the soul of Cynthia von Doom. Doom formerly ruled the duplicate planet of Counter-Earth concurrent to his rule of Latveria, resulting in some turmoil when Counter-Earth's Young Allies threatened to drop nerve gas on Latveria in retaliation against Doom. Doom's castle was briefly usurped by a duplicate ("doppelganger") of himself created in the Dimension of Manifestations by the Magus.
NONHUMAN POPULATION: Latveria features an immense population of robots, all the design of Dr. Doom; although they are not recognized as sentient beings by their maker, one creation called the Doomsman was able to evolve past his programming, and as Andro has since led rebellions against Doom in attempts to liberate his robotic brethren. Most of Doom's robots are of the Servo-Guard model, specially designed to enforce curfews, guard Doom's castles, examine illegal incursions and engage hostiles. Doom's Killer Robots are his most powerful model, originally numbering at one dozen, and capable of leveling an entire town if so needed. Doom's so-called "Doombots" are his personal robot imposters, programmed to believe themselves to be the true Dr. Doom, except when in their master's presence; many of these Doombots have been employed in overseas matters that Doom did not wish to involve himself in, and faulty programming has caused many to turn rogue, such as the Mechadoom model who sought to evolve beyond its programming as the Doomsman had. Doom also employs a variety of robot drones for simple labor, select combat models called Pacifiers, and specialized models for aerial and underwater combat situations. The might of Doom's robot army seems to render most of his human armed forces superfluous. Local legends in Latveria refer to a demonic creature called Darkoth, upon which Doom based his superhuman agent Desmond Pitt. Doom once created a clone of himself invested with the powers of the Fantastic Four; "Victor von Doom II" lived only briefly before being executed by Doom himself.
DOMESTIC SUPERHUMANS: Dr. Doom (Victor von Doom), monarch of Latveria is an inventive genius and scholar of the mystic arts; despite numerous attempts at unseating him, Doom has resumed leadership of Latveria time and again. Kristoff Vernard was orphaned during the civil unrest caused by Prince Zorba's reign, and became Doom's ward; for a time, Kristoff believed himself to be Doom, and ruled Latveria in his stead. Dreadknight (Bram Velsing) was a former scientist of Doom's whose mask was fused to his face as punishment for his ambitions; the Dreadknight has made some attempts to rule Latveria for himself.

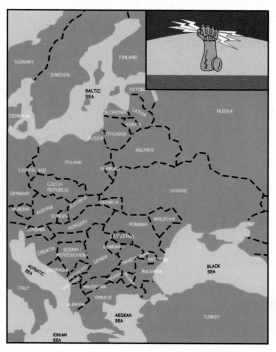

The psychic Psi-Borg (Fionna Wyman) served as a double agent within SHIELD for Hydra, but was killed soon after being found out. The Exalted One is ruler of the Folding City, an experiment in space/time begun by Doom that left the entire complex phased outside normal perception and interaction. The sorceress Pandemonia lives on Mount Sorcista.
PROMINENT CITIZENS: Werner von Doom was a talented doctor of the Zefiro tribe, and father of Victor von Doom; he gave his life helping to protect his son from the forces of King Vladimir; Victor named the Werner Academy after his father. Cynthia von Doom was Victor's mother and had been a mystic, dying after making an unfortunate pact with Mephisto; Doom spent decades of his life seeking the means to rescue her soul from Mephisto's clutches. Boris, Doom's Zefiro guardian since childhood is the monarch's closest confidant. In his childhood, Doom loved Valeria, a fellow Zefiro; he eventually sacrificed her to the Haazareth demons to increase his mystical powers. Djordji Zindelo Hungaros was the Zefiro mystic who trained Cynthia von Doom. Ambassador Jakob Gorzenko has served as Latveria's chief representative to the USA; during his rule, Prince Zorba installed Arturo Frazen as ambassador. Another Latverian agent in the USA is Hans Stutgart. Doom's chief scientists have included Fydor Gittelsohn, Otto Kronsteig and the brothers Gustav and Gert Hauptmann, all deceased. One of Doom's most important employees is the Editor, whose task is to rewrite Latveria's history to conform with Doom's worldview. Stanislaus and Grigori Mengochuzcraus ("the Mengo Brothers") are a pair of international mercenaries. Lucia von Bardas was briefly installed as Latveria's prime minister during one of Doom's absences, but after Nick Fury learned that she was funding the activities of super-villains, he led an unsanctioned team into Latveria to destroy her. From the 16th to 19th centuries the Kroft family (including Wilhelm, Stefan, Leo, Oscar, Pietro and Kurt Kroft) served as local vampire hunters, helping to drive the creatures from Latveria's borders. The royalty of Latveria prior to Doom's rule included King Rudolfo I, Baron Karl Haasen (14th century), Baron Karl Haasen III, Vlad Draasen (15th century), King Stefan I, Count Sabbat (16th century), and in recent years King Vladimir Vassily Gonereo Tristian Mangegi Fortunov, his sons Princes Rudolfo and Zorba, and Vladimir's illegitimate grandson Dmitri Fortunov.
SUPERHUMAN RESIDENTS: Nathaniel Richards, claiming to be the father of Kristoff Vernard, once claimed the throne of Latveria on Kristoff's

behalf; he vacated the throne when Doom returned. The mutant Stryfe briefly served as prime minister during one of Dr. Doom's absences, using Doombots to help mask Doom's disappearance. Latveria has been infested at various times by vampires, including Lucas Cross and Dracula.

DOMESTIC CRIME: Crimes ranging from petty theft to murder are virtually unheard of in Latveria; however, Dr. Doom has repeatedly abused his powers to inflict misery and death upon his own subjects. Various grassroots movements to overthrow Doom have been attempted from within his own citizenry, including those of Princes Rudolfo & Zorba, Andro, and Dmitri Fortunov.

INTERNATIONAL CRIME: On two occasions, the Red Skull (Johann Shmidt) has been able to briefly occupy Latveria, but these coups were undone within days. The Fantastic Four once occupied Latveria, but surrendered the country in the face of mounting international pressure. The Shroud (Maximillian Coleridge) attempted to kill Dr. Doom in his earliest adventure as a crimefighter. The Circus of Crime have traveled peacefully through Latveria. The Roxxon Oil Corporation once financed an attempt by the Dreadknight to conquer Latveria.

FIRST APPEARANCE: Fantastic Four Annual #2 (1964)

HISTORY: Called "the jewel of the Balkans," Latveria is a strong, self-sufficient country that seldom interacts with its neighbors; the country's motto is "We master all that lies before." For over 600 years, Latveria was ruled by the Haasen bloodline, based from Haasenstadt (now Doomstadt). Latveria was originally founded in the 14th century in territory captured from Transylvania by Rudolfo and Karl Haasen. Rudolfo was the first king of Latveria, but after the death of Karl Haasen III in 1447, Vlad Draasen ascended to the throne, and his difficult rule divided the country until 1544, when the Bolgorad Treaties finally restored the Haasen bloodline to the throne. In 1588, King Stefan I and Count Sabbat began construction of a castle (now Castle Doom), and a second was constructed in 1593 (now the Citadel of Doom). During World War II, Latveria forged an alliance with Symkaria to resist the forces of invading Nazi Germany led by Baron Wolfgang von Strucker; the ultimate success of this shared struggle has left a strong bond between the two nations. In recent years, King Vladimir Fortunov imposed a tyrannical rule that was especially harsh

to the Romany ("gypsies") who lived in Latveria's borders. Cynthia von Doom, a mystic of the Zefiro tribe, once made a pact with the demon Mephisto in an attempt to gain vengeance for her people, but only lost her own soul. When King Vladimir's wife was near death, he summoned Werner von Doom, a Zefiro healer. The king's wife was too far gone for Werner to save her, but the king, mad with grief, blamed Werner and sought his death. Werner died sheltering his son Victor from the king's forces, and placed Victor in the custody of his friend Boris before passing away. Victor was determined to avenge his parents, and studied both science and magic for the means to oppose King Vladimir. While attending university in the USA, Victor was horribly scarred in an accident, and returned to Latveria garbed in armor. Killing King Vladimir and employing a robot of Prince Rudolfo to hand him the crown, Doom has been de facto ruler of Latveria ever since.

Doom's rule has been interrupted by King Vladimir's son Zorba who tried to bring democracy to Latveria, only to plunge his nation into war before finally being ousted by Doom. Doom's ward Kristoff Vernard also claimed the throne while believing himself to be Doom, and the outsiders Nathaniel Richards and Stryfe both laid claim during absences of Doom's. The USA helped back Lucia von Bardas as prime minister, but she was forcibly removed by an unauthorized team led by Nick Fury. Latveria has expanded its borders to include Slokovia, a neighbor which was divided by religious strife when its people began to worship the Asgardian god Thor; when the country's rulers were overthrown, Doom quietly annexed the country. Latveria remains in Doom's thrall, its people content and happy with their lot in life, perpetually aware of the punishments awaiting those who dissent.

ZEFIRO

Latveria

Doomstadt, capital city and seat of the Kingdom of Dr. Victor von Doom.

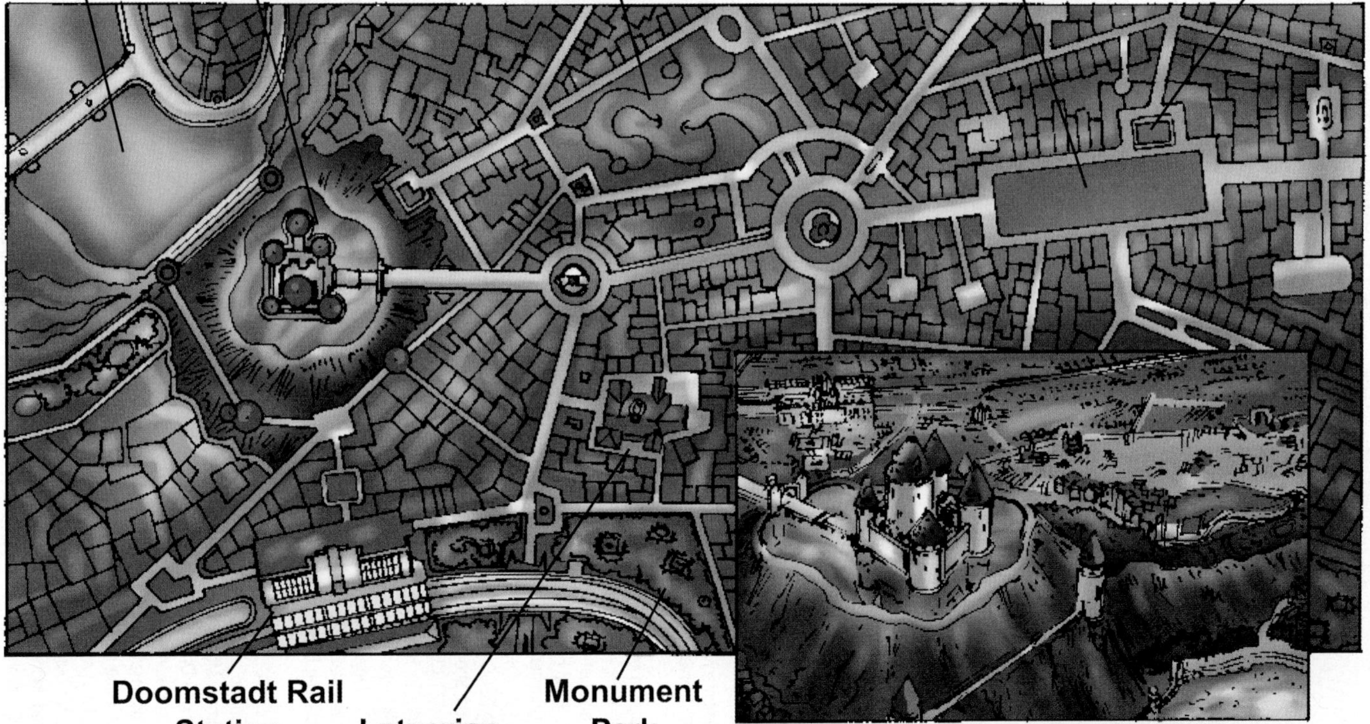

Doom Lake

Castle von Doom

Kron Victory Sward

Cynthia von Doom Memorial Park

Doomstadt Rathauz

Doomstadt Rail Station

Latverian Academy of the Sciences

Monument Park

Scenic overview of Castle von Doom showing the ancient drawbridge and moat. The castle looks over the old town of Doomstadt, various monuments to His Majesty and His family are visible. The twin churches, St. Peter and St. Blaise are seen on the Heroic Andrew Boulevard.

—Image courtesy the Latverian Board of Tourism

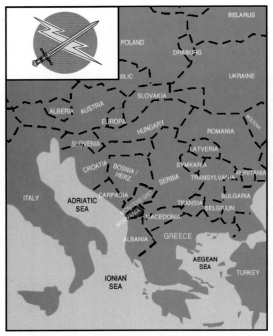

OFFICIAL NAME: Republic of Morvania (Republica Moravania)
POPULATION: 685,000
CAPITAL CITY: Morstrava
PLACES OF INTEREST: Imperial Castle, Morstrava; Old City; Vastopol
GOVERNMENT: Parliamentary democracy
MAJOR LANGUAGES: Morvanian (official), Czech, Slovak, Serbian, Albanian, Croatian
MONETARY UNIT: Moravian lek
MAJOR RESOURCES: Vehicles, machinery and electrical equipment, base metals, chemicals and minerals, plastics
NATIONAL DEFENSE: Land Forces Command (Army), Naval Forces Command, Air Defense Command, Logistics Command
INTERNATIONAL RELATIONS: Morvania holds membership in the United Nations, UNESCO, the World Trade Organization, the International Criminal Court, and Interpol.
EXTRATERRESTRIAL RELATIONS: None documented.
NONHUMAN POPULATION: None documented.
DOMESTIC SUPERHUMANS: None documented.
PROMINENT CITIZENS: Václav Draxon (deceased), former Supreme Dictator of Morvania. Isaac Maisel, former leader of the underground resistance movement opposing Draxon's regime/architect of Morvania's current political system.
SUPERHUMAN RESIDENTS: None documented.
DOMESTIC CRIME: Due to a constant military presence on nearly every village street corner, Morvania's crime rates were very low under the regime of General Draxon. Once Draxon's dictatorship was overthrown, crime rates temporarily surged in a period of social upheaval prior to the official establishment of Morvania's current parliamentary democracy. However, the crime rate has since stabilized as Morvania's new governmental institutions have gained credibility and legitimacy.
INTERNATIONAL CRIME: During the dictatorship of General Draxon, many nations considered Morvania a rogue entity. Membership in the UN was temporarily revoked due to several members of the Security Council refusing to acknowledge the legitimacy of the Draxon government. However, no trade embargoes were placed upon the country and Draxon's government continued to conduct business with many international corporations. Morvania was reinstated to the UN shortly after Draxon's overthrow.

FIRST APPEARANCE: Incredible Hulk #133 (1970)
HISTORY: The modern-day nation of Morvania traces its earliest roots back to the empire of Great Moravia, which stretched across Central Europe from 833 to the 10th century AD. After Great Moravia was overrun by nomadic Magyar invaders from the Kingdom of Hungary in the early 10th century, an aristocratic family established the independent Kingdom of Morvania on the Mediterranean Sea, just to the southwest of the failing empire. During the Middle Ages, the royal family of Morvania created the Imperial Amulet as a physical symbol of their power. The Imperial Amulet was passed down through the generations, and the subjects of Morvania came to unquestioningly view the possessor of the Amulet as Morvania's rightful ruler. Morvanian tradition held that only one who slays the current bearer of the Imperial Amulet could break the familial chain of secession and become the kingdom's ruler.

When Adolf Hitler established a "protectorate" over Czech lands in 1939, many inhabitants of Prague's Jewish communities fled south of the Czechoslovakian border into Morvania and settled alongside the nation's mostly Christian, peasant population. The Jewish refugee population brought their traditions and folktales with them, such as the legend of the Golem: Judah Loew ben Bezalel (1525-1609), a leading rabbi in Prague, was believed to have created a monstrous Golem from clay that came to life and protected Prague's Jewish community from harm (the refugees also adapted the legend for Morvania, adding that that Golem was responsible for creating the Imperial Amulet). Miraculously, the sovereignty of the Morvanian throne was not disturbed by Nazi Germany or the Soviet Union in the mid-20th century.

Václav Draxon, born into one of Morvania's many rural peasant families, enlisted as a soldier in Morvania's small Royal Army as an adolescent. He eventually became the army's highest-ranking general and, after increasing the size and influence of the armed forces, seized power in recent years. By killing the reigning King of Morvania and wresting the Imperial Amulet from his grasp, General Draxon named himself the nation's new Supreme Dictator and moved into the towering iron and stone Imperial Castle that sits on a mountaintop in Morvania's capital. Ruling through force and cruelty, Draxon ordered his army to raze Morvania's Old City when a peasant revolt erupted there, and decreed that the ruins of Old City would stay forever unrestored as a monument to the peasants' folly. Draxon, who fancied himself as one who would succeed at conquering Europe where Napoleon Bonaparte and Adolf Hitler previously failed, plotted to invade his neighboring Mediterranean nations, then the rest of Europe, and finally the world. In preparation for his planned conquests, he ordered parts from United States munitions manufacturers to construct the War-Tower of Draxon, a gigantic, seemingly indestructible, armored combat vehicle. However, the Hulk (Bruce Banner) inadvertently stowed away on the last shipment of instruments needed for the War-Tower's completion. Upon discovering the Hulk's presence, Draxon offered him the chance to assist in his conquest of Europe and ordered his army to attack the Hulk upon his refusal to aid Draxon. The Hulk was eventually located by Isaac Maisel, a descendant of Jewish immigrants from Prague and the leader of the underground resistance movement opposing Draxon's rule. Inspired by the legend of the Golem, Maisel attempted to persuade the Hulk to aid the resistance movement in overthrowing Draxon. Hulk was eventually convinced to oppose Draxon as the Imperial Army attacked the resistance movement. Draxon was killed aboard his War-Tower when the Hulk caused the armored vehicle to explode. Maisel then seized the Imperial Amulet from Draxon's body and offered it to the Hulk, declaring him Morvania's new king; but Hulk crushed the amulet and left the country, inspiring the resistance to institute a more democratic form of government.

OFFICIAL NAME: Kingdom of Norway (Kongeriket Norge)
POPULATION: 4,628,000
CAPITAL CITY: Oslo
PLACES OF INTEREST: Lakstad
GOVERNMENT: Democratic constitutional monarchy
MAJOR LANGUAGES: Bokmal Norwegian (official), Nynorsk Norwegian (official), small Sami- and Finnish-speaking minorities; note — Sami is official in 6 municipalities
MONETARY UNIT: Norwegian krone
MAJOR RESOURCES: Natural gas, oil, fishing, pulp and paper, minerals, forestry, shipping, hydropower. Norway has the third largest oil reserves on Earth, after Saudi Arabia and Russia.
NATIONAL DEFENSE: Norwegian Army (Haeren), Royal Norwegian Navy (Kongelige Norske Sjoeforsvaret, RNoN), Royal Norwegian Air Force (Kongelige Norske Luftforsvaret, RNoAF), Home Guard (Heimevernet, HV)
INTERNATIONAL RELATIONS: Norway belongs to the United Nations, UNESCO, Interpol, World Health Organization and NATO. A 1994 referendum saw Norway opt to stay out of the European Union, but they still contribute to its budget as a member of the European Economic Area.
EXTRATERRESTRIAL RELATIONS: A little over a decade ago a Kronan invasion force tried to establish a beachhead in Norway, but were driven off by the Asgardian Thor.
NONHUMAN POPULATION: Over the centuries the Norse Gods have been very active in Norway, particularly Thor, Loki, the Valkyries and Tyr. Other Asgardian races such as the Trolls, Jotun (giants), dwarves and elves have all visited Norway on numerous occasions. The Godstorm was a sentient Asgardian storm that Loki convinced centuries ago to attack Thor; imprisoned beneath the ocean for its impudence, it was freed in recent years by a Norwegian oil platform's drilling.
DOMESTIC SUPERHUMANS: The murderous 11th century Viking raider Harald Jaekelsson and his crew were cursed by the sage of Lakstad village to sale for a thousand years under a runestone blood curse before they reached land again; they finally reached harbor in the modern day, where they battled the Avengers, Dr. Strange, and the sage's descendants; the raiders were slain, and the undying Jaekelsson was ripped limb from limb, then hurled into orbit. The trickster god Loki transformed insane terrorist Knut Caine into an avatar of himself; though Caine believed himself to be Loki, the press dubbed him the Mad Viking. Caine, in turn, empowered the kidnapped Effie Pedersen as his "daughter" Hel; with Caine's demise, Effie returned to normal.
PROMINENT CITIZENS: In 200 AD, the Viking Wulfhere was slain by a time-travelling King Kull. Circa 1100 AD, Norwegian explorer and surgeon Dr. Knute Svenson discovered Kallusian extraterrestrials hiding from their Yirbek foes beneath the Arctic ice; he was rescued by the Avengers, who had come seeking his surgical expertise. Brom Anders was the head of a deep sea mining expedition, which unwittingly released the imprisoned Godstorm from beneath the sea. Eilif Dragonslayer was the last member of a hidden Viking colony who continued to worship the Norse gods into the present day; an elderly man, he died assisting Thor in battling the dragon Fafnir, thus becoming the last human to earn the right to enter Valhalla.
SUPERHUMAN RESIDENTS: In 1940 the ghost John Kowalski temporarily took over the corpse of deceased German soldier David Mueller, and assisted local Norwegian Jews escaping from Skalsø. The Thunderbolts formerly kept a headquarters near Norway upon an island in the North Sea.
DOMESTIC CRIME: Norway has a relatively low crime rate. There are a handful of illegal cults dedicated to some of the less palatable sections of Norse mythology, such as the sect that attempted to use the Amulet of Surtur to revive the fire giant.
INTERNATIONAL CRIME: While comparatively few Norwegian mortals seem to break the laws of other countries, the Asgardians have shown much less respect for international legislature. Loki and the Enchantress (Amora) in particular are guilty of multiple cases of

granting superhuman abilities to criminals and murder, amongst a multitude of lesser offenses.
HISTORY: Norway is believed to have been settled more than 10,000 years ago, as the last Ice Age ended and hunters followed the herds north to newly uncovered pastures. These settlers brought with them their gods, as rugged and changeable as the new land their inhabited. Historical records of early Nóregr (apparently from "norð vegr," the north way) are limited; the inhabitants belonged to independent clans, finally united through force by Harold Haarfager (Fair-Hair) in 872 AD. Norse sailors who went forth to explore, trade with and raid other countries were called Vikings, a name their victims often applied to all Norsemen. The boisterous and immature thunder god Thor would often accompany raiding parties, reveling in the adventure, but after witnessing the aftermath of their sacking of a monastery, Thor found such trips less palatable. Ironically, after a couple of centuries raiding, the Vikings converted to Christianity, and the Asgardians withdrew from regular involvement with men. In 1319 the crowns of Norway and neighboring Sweden became intertwined, when 3-year-old Magnus Eriksson of Sweden became first in line for both thrones, but it proved an uneasy union, with the crowns briefly splitting again, only to reunite a few decades later, when Eric of Pomerania was crowned King of Norway, Sweden and Denmark. While Sweden soon split off again, Norway and Denmark remained combined, and by 1586 Norway had become part of the Danish Kingdom, remaining so until split apart in 1814 as a result of the Napoleonic wars, and reluctantly entered into union with Sweden once more. In 1905 Norway regained its independence. Norway declared neutrality in both world wars, but the Nazis still invaded in 1940; the USA's Howling Commandos undertook several missions behind enemy lines in occupied Norway. After the war Norway decided to invest in shared security rather than neutrality, and in 1949 became a NATO member. Though recent years have seen the Asgardians increase their visits to Earth once more, Norway seems to have largely avoided the superhuman strife that has afflicted much of the rest of the world.

OFFICIAL NAME: Republic of Poland (Rzeczpospolita Polska)

POPULATION: 38,536,000

CAPITAL CITY: Warsaw

PLACES OF INTEREST: Krakow, Szczecin

GOVERNMENT: Republic

MAJOR LANGUAGES: Polish

MONETARY UNIT: Zloty

MAJOR RESOURCES: Coal, sulfur, copper, natural gas, silver, lead, salt and amber.

NATIONAL DEFENSE: Armed Forces of the Polish Republic (Sily Zbrojne Rzeczypospolitej Polskiej), including Land Forces, Navy and Air Force, together comprising 215,000 active members.

INTERNATIONAL RELATIONS: Member of the Council of Europe, European Union, Interpol, the North Atlantic Treaty Organization, UNESCO, the United Nations and the World Trade Organization, participated in the Pan-European Conference on Superhuman Affairs.

EXTRATERRESTRIAL RELATIONS: The gaseous entity Gor-Kill ("the Living Demon") once attempted to destroy a dam in Krakow, but was driven off by local Hans Grubnik. Residents of Krakow were unaware of Grubnik's heroism.

NONHUMAN POPULATION: None known.

DOMESTIC SUPERHUMANS: Poland's eminent hero is Prodigy, a youthful genius who can take control of electronic devices; Prodigy represented Poland in the Pan-European Conference on Superhuman Affairs. The notorious mutant activist Magneto (Erik Lehnsherr) is believed to have been born in Poland, and met his wife Magda while being incarcerated in a Nazi camp during World War II; Magda died shortly after giving birth to their children Pietro and Wanda Maximoff in Transia, and Magneto has gone on to become the face of mutant supremacy, despite temporary periods where he served as one of the X-Men. The mutant criminal Bloodlust (Beatta Dubiel) served in the Femme Fatales, but lost her powers due to the events of "M-Day." During World War II, Jewish scholar Jacob Goldstein became the heroic Golem, using his powers to combat the Nazis in Warsaw alongside the Invaders. Meyer Banciewicz developed mutant abilities during the war, and later

emigrated to the USA. Dr. Rueben Jabokwitz collaborated with the Nazis during the war to develop biological weapons, and was killed by Isadore "Izzy" Cohen of the Howling Commandos.

PROMINENT CITIZENS: During World War II, scientist Johann Goldstein (brother of Jacob) was forced to design and operate the Blue Bullet armor, battling the Invaders in that identity; he later died resisting the Nazis. After a superlative US military career, John Kowalski was exiled back to his birthplace of Poland over charges of espionage; Kowalski arrived in 1939, just as the country was invaded by Germany; ignoring a chance to warn his people about the invasion, Kowalski was cursed so that after his death, he would inhabit the body of another person until they died; Kowalski continued to suffer this curse up until recent years, when he was finally permitted to train a successor. The famous geneticist Wladyslav Shinski became one of the super-intellectuals comprising the Enclave, and participated in the creation of beings such as Adam Warlock and Kismet. Polish citizen Sergei Radek is currently an agent of SHIELD. Costume designer Leo Zelinksy emigrated to the USA.

SUPERHUMAN RESIDENTS: In 1942, James Howlett (later the hero Wolverine) was incarcerated in the Nazi-run Sobibor Death Camp. The heroic Citizen V (John Watkins) and his V Battalion were active in Poland during the war.

DOMESTIC CRIME: Poland has recurring issues with drug production and smuggling through their borders.

INTERNATIONAL CRIME: During World War II, the Nazi officer known as the Face helped occupy Warsaw, but was killed battling the Invaders and the Golem. The terrorist forces of Fenris once assaulted the Szczecin military compound, framing the mutant X-Men for the crime. The terrorist group ULTIMATUM has recruited some of their agents from Poland such as Vladimir Korda of Krakow, an agent who died at the hands of Captain America (Steve Rogers).

HISTORY: Poland came into existence as a state in 966 AD, soon becoming the Kingdom of Poland in 1025. From 1569 to 1795 it was merged with Lithuania as the Polish-Lithuanian Commonwealth. Thereafter, Poland was divided up between Russia, Prussia and Austria. Poland regained its independence in 1918, but was quickly conquered and occupied in 1939; many of its citizens were exterminated by the Nazi forces, and in 1944 resistance forces in Warsaw put up a pitched campaign against their occupiers. After World War II, Poland was occupied by the USSR, and did not regain its independence until 1989; Poland's struggle against the USSR was instrumental in the collapse of the Soviet Union.

SOBIBOR DEATH CAMP, CIRCA 1942

Art by Kaare Andrews

OFFICIAL NAME: Romania
POPULATION: 22,303,000
CAPITAL CITY: Bucharest
PLACES OF INTEREST: Bistrita, Castle Dracula, Castle Frankenstein, Castle Mordo, Medias, Moldavia, Ploesti, Russoff Castle, Russoff Manor, Sibiu, Transylvania, Wallachia
GOVERNMENT: Republic
MAJOR LANGUAGES: Romanian, Hungarian, German
MONETARY UNIT: Leu
MAJOR RESOURCES: Petroleum, timber, natural gas, coal, iron ore, salt and hydropower.
NATIONAL DEFENSE: The Romanian Armed Forces are comprised of Land Forces, Naval Forces, and the Air Force, with 90,000 members in service.
INTERNATIONAL RELATIONS: Member of the European Union, Interpol, the North Atlantic Treaty Organization, UNESCO, the United Nations and the World Trade Organization. Have boundary issues with the Ukraine.
EXTRATERRESTRIAL RELATIONS: In 1961, Transylvania was invaded by a band of extraterrestrials claiming to be "Martians," but Vandoom's Monster drove them away; also in 1961, an immobile extraterrestrial scout called "the Glop" was awakened by a special paint and threatened to summon an invasion force, but it returned to immobility when the paint was removed. Spragg, "the living hill" was once based in Transylvania, but was expelled by Professor Bob Roberston.
NONHUMAN POPULATION: In 1960, the amoeba creature Sporr was created at Castle Frankenstein, but was ultimately destroyed by its creator. Vandoom's Monster is a giant wax statue, which was inexplicably brought to life in 1961; it has since relocated to Monster Island under the custody of the Mole Man (Harvey Rupert Elder).
DOMESTIC SUPERHUMANS: The vampire Dracula was born Vlad Dracul, and fought for Wallachia against the Ottoman Empire in the 15th century; after becoming a vampire, Dracula continued to rule from Castle Dracula, raising armies of vampires in the area and enslaving human servants; Dracula continues to operate from Castle Dracula on the occasion, and maintains an army of faithful vampires in Transylvania. Dracula's rule was briefly usurped by the vampire Torgo, and Dracula's daughter Lilith has repeatedly sought her father's destruction. Nimrod, a chief follower of Varnae in the 15th century, was based in Transylvania. Baron Karl Amadeus Mordo is a powerful sorcerer and one-time pupil of the Ancient One; many members of Mordo's family have also been mystics, including his grandfather Heinrich Krowler, his wife Lilia

and his daughter Astrid Mordo; Castle Mordo is their ancestral home. Lilia was descended from Miarka, a Romany mystic of the 19th century. Skein (Sybil Dvorak), also known as Gypsy Moth is a mutant criminal who has served in the Masters of Evil. The Russoff/Russell family lived in Transylvania for part of their lives; Jack Russell became a Werewolf later in life, while his sister Lissa was released from the family curse; their grandmother Maria Russoff was a Romany mystic. 19th century Countess Cynthia "Absynthia" von Mort obtained power over life and death from Diablo in a vain effort to resurrect her dead husband, Count Victor von Mort. The vampire-like killer Bloodbath (Mordechai Kovax) was the son of a Transylvanian woman with a rare blood disease.

Art by Howard Chaykin

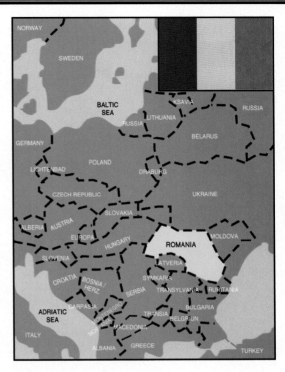

PROMINENT CITIZENS: Ludwig Vandoom was a wax museum owner, son of Heinrich Vandoom; Ludwig created Vandoom's Monster. Georg Odekirk helped forge papers for Magneto (Erik Lehnsherr) at one point in his career, only to be later killed by Magneto to cover his tracks. Viktor Benzel helped Lilith in her struggle against Dracula, only to be killed by Dracula himself.
SUPERHUMAN RESIDENTS: The mad alchemist Diablo operated in Transylvania during the 19th century, and was entombed within his citadel until recent years. Diablo's lover Gilded Lily (Lillian von Loont) also lived in Transylvania for a time. Members of the international sect of heroic vampires called the Mortuus Invitus have been active in Bucharest.
DOMESTIC CRIME: Romania is a major transit point in the international drug trade. Transylvania has one of the world's highest instances of vampire attacks. A local racketeer nicknamed "Bear" was involved in a plot to consolidate European crime through the Chunnel, but was killed by the Punisher (Frank Castle).
INTERNATIONAL CRIME: The vampire Nocturne once made an attempt to release Diablo from his prison. The mutant Apocalypse and his Riders of the Storm clashed with Wallachia's armies in the 15th century.
HISTORY: Romania was formed by the merging of Moldavia and Wallachia in 1859; they were later joined by Transylvania in 1918. In the 15th century, Vlad Dracul was prince of Wallachia, and became notorious in battle against the Ottoman Empire for disposing of his enemies by placing their bodies atop immense pikes, earning him the moniker "Vlad the Impaler." In 1459, Dracula was captured by Turac and placed in the care of the Romany ("gypsy") Lianda, a vampire serving the lord Varnae; Lianda made Dracula a vampire, and he soon cut a new bloody path through the area, claiming Castle Dracula in Transylvania as his main base of operations, and turning his supernatural might against his enemies. Eventually chosen as Varnae's successor, he consolidated his power as the lord of Earth's vampires, a title held to the present day. During World War II, Dracula helped defend his region against the invading Nazi forces, even as Romania itself allied to the Nazi cause in order to fight the USSR. In recent years, Castle Dracula has been renovated into a tourist locale, but this has not prevented Dracula from continuing to use the location as a secret base of operations.

OFFICIAL NAME: Republic of Rumekistan (Republika Rumekistan)
POPULATION: Indeterminate
CAPITAL CITY: Barjñov
PLACES OF INTEREST: Barjñov Capitol Plaza, Barjñov Harbor, Tenyan Foothills
GOVERNMENT: Democratic republic; formerly dictatorship
MAJOR LANGUAGES: Rumeki
MONETARY UNIT: Rumeki Ruble
MAJOR RESOURCES: Indeterminate
NATIONAL DEFENSE: Rumeki Security Force
INTERNATIONAL RELATIONS: Rumekistan's government has signed military alliances with 4 neighboring countries and trade pacts with 12 other nations.
EXTRATERRESTRIAL RELATIONS: None known
NONHUMAN POPULATION: None known
DOMESTIC SUPERHUMANS: None known
PROMINENT CITIZENS: Nenad Petrovic was a history professor turned resistance leader before he was captured, incarcerated, and ultimately killed by Flag-Smasher's Silent Guard. Michael Straka was a captain in ULTIMATUM's occupying force before joining President Cable's efforts to rebuild the nation.
SUPERHUMAN RESIDENTS: Former President Pro Tem Nathan Summers was also known as the mutant soldier Cable of the X-Men.
DOMESTIC CRIME: Since the overthrow of Flag-Smasher, local crime has taken a sharp decline.
INTERNATIONAL CRIME: Rumekistan was once ruled by Flag-Smasher, leader of the terrorist group ULTIMATUM. He was opposed by the Rumekistan Resistance Movement who, in turn, were aided by the Canadian mercenary Deadpool. Flag-Smasher was later assassinated by the mercenary Domino. The mercenary Six Pack once briefly disrupted Barjñov's electricity supply.
FIRST APPEARANCE: Citizen V and the V-Battalion: The Everlasting #1 (2002)
HISTORY: After seceding from the former Soviet Union, the nation of Rumekistan was torn by sectarian and religious strife for many years. Seizing the opportunity, the anarchist Flag-Smasher and his ULTIMATUM (Underground Liberated Totally Integrated Mobile Army To Unite Mankind) terrorist group sought to invade the country. During the ensuing anarchy, the V-Battalion's operative Citizen V brokered a deal with Flag-Smasher, allowing him to accomplish a bloodless coup of the country by using the V-Battalion's Vanguard ship to induce sleep in the populace. The Rumeki people awoke to find themselves with a new ruler who soon proved to be even more ruthless than his predecessor, creating a military state where there were no prohibitions on alcohol or narcotics yet the teaching of history was banned due to its promoting misguided nationalism. Seeking to liberate Rumekistan from ULTIMATUM's control, the mutant soldier Cable allied with Citizen V to overthrow Flag-Smasher. He hired the mercenary Deadpool to work with the Rumekistan Resistance Movement; however, Flag-Smasher was assassinated by the mutant mercenary Domino. Cable quickly took control and, after being accepted by the Rumeki people as president pro tempore until the country could support free elections (and set a date for them in 6 months time), he began working to rebuild the shattered nation, starting by improving the infrastructure of the capital and outlying suburbs first to facilitate the rapid creation of new jobs. He signed military alliances with 4 neighboring countries and trade pacts with 12 other nations. Cable later met with the US president after the initiation of the Superhuman Registration Act saw America's super heroes divided in a "civil war." After Cable was forced to return to his South Pacific island Providence to deal with an act of sabotage, the spy agency SHIELD dispatched the mercenary Six Pack to Rumekistan to foment chaos in an effort to tarnish Cable's reputation. Despite their initial success in causing a massive power outage in the capital Barjñov, Cable soon restored power to the city, defeated the Six Pack, and repaired his reputation. When Cable seemingly died shortly afterward, a statue was raised in his honor in Barjñov.

Art by Dave Ross

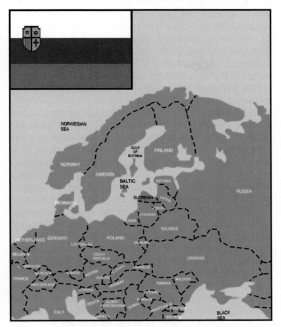

OFFICIAL NAME: Republic of Slorenia (Republica Slorenijas)
POPULATION: 1; formerly 752,364
CAPITAL CITY: Tblunka
PLACES OF INTEREST: None; formerly Karnu National Park, Tblunka's Freedom Monument, Dunrâle Palace, Winter Palace
GOVERNMENT: None; formerly dictatorship
MAJOR LANGUAGES: Current inhabitant speaks English, Irish Gaelic; former population spoke Slorenian, Latvian, Russian
MONETARY UNIT: None; formerly Slorenian lita
MAJOR RESOURCES: Limestone, wood, hydropower
NATIONAL DEFENSE: Bloodwraith currently protects Slorenia from any intruders; Ultron defended Slorenia with robotic drones and necro-cyborgs; prior to his incursion, Slorenian Armed Forces, including Targoth troops.
INTERNATIONAL RELATIONS: Slorenia was formerly a member of the United Nations, UNESCO, World Health Organization and Interpol (the last only nominally). Slorenia is currently a quarantined country, closed off to any visitors while the Bloodwraith is trapped there.
EXTRATERRESTRIAL RELATIONS: The Homodur Century and Rigellian Recorder both visited Slorenia during Force Works' missions there.
NONHUMAN POPULATION: Volkhvy and Ember were supernatural entities, respectively mystic champions of the Slorenes and Dudaks. Each would possess a suitable host from the race they represented, and could drain energy from the other. Volkhvy eventually abandoned changing hosts, secretly running the country behind the scenes whilst sustaining himself by draining captive Dudaks' life energies through the "Program." Ember remained dormant through much of Communist rule, the triptych which housed him secured away in the Slorenian Winter Palace's vaults, but was revived in recent times when Dudak historian Pavel Chenklo discovered the triptych. Volkhvy's rule was brought to an end by Ember, who drained him to destruction, at least temporarily. Ember was subsequently destroyed by U.S.Agent, but rose again to battle Ultron, only to fall almost immediately. With their people slaughtered, it may be that both entities are now permanently destroyed; however, when Bloodwraith absorbed the essences of Slorenia's dead, he may have combined his own mystic energies with either or both Volkhvy and Ember, contributing to the vast power increase Bloodwraith demonstrated. It is unknown what, if any, connection Volkhvy had to Volkh, shapeshifting folk hero of Russian byliny.

Through genetic manipulation prisoners were transformed into the Targoth ("Brutal Ones"), zombie-like brutes of limited intellect but great strength and durability; they were mainly used for capturing the Dudaks to feed Volkhvy and ethnic cleansing of same. Targoth were later deployed against Ultron, who swiftly destroyed them. After Ultron slaughtered the Slorenians, he turned their corpses into "necro-cyborgs," which he used to slaughter UN forces sent to retake the country; it is believed all of the necro-cyborgs were destroyed when Ultron was defeated.

DOMESTIC SUPERHUMANS: Locomotive Breath (Laslo Magzel) was an apparently immortal Slorenian mutant with an innate genius for invention; over the years he worked with various world governments, including Volkhvy's, and he designed the Program which drained life energies to sustain Volkhvy, and apparently, less often, himself. To stave off boredom he joined the thrill-seeking Rush Club, designing them powered armor, but upon learning that he would be denied access to the Program due to Slorenia's civil war, he tricked War Machine into assisting him in breaching the Slorenian Winter Palace, hoping to use Ember's triptych as a new power source. Instead the triptych overloaded him, seeming to either slay him or turn him into Ember's new host.

PROMINENT CITIZENS: Dudak historian Pavel Chenklo discovered Ember's triptych in the vaults of Slorenia's Winter Palace, and became the entity's new host; while battling Force Works, Ember's energies drained to the extent where he reverted to being Chenklo again. Shortly afterwards he was apparently slain when Black Brigade fired on him, causing the floor under him to collapse. Juris Boshlovor was the spokesman and public leader of the Tabissara ("Elevenfold"), Slorenia's 10 man ruling council; in truth he was subservient to Volkhvy, the secret 11th council member. He courted Tony Stark hoping to convince him to establish a trade agreement between Stark Enterprises and Slorenia. After Volkhvy's destruction, the Tabissara were replaced by a new government. Dr. Irena Renko was an expert on Slorenian history and folklore.

SUPERHUMAN RESIDENTS: Black Brigade was a Russian cyborg, a former Red Army operative assigned to Slorenia and equipped with armor designed by Locomotive Breath; when the Soviets withdrew from Slorenia, Black Brigade remained, working as a government enforcer. When Ember reappeared, Black Brigade was assigned to destroy him, and he slew Ember's human host, Pavel Chenklo. He apparently died battling Ultron.

Sean Dolan was the Irish former squire of the Black Knight (Dane Whitman), who had been previously overcome by the curse of the Ebony Blade and transformed into the murderous Bloodwraith. Wrongly believed cured, he joined the UN/SHIELD relief effort clearing the corpses and rubble in post-Ultron Slorenia; while he genuinely wished to do something positive with his life, his decision to visit the devastated country was influenced subconsciously by the Blade. Drawn to unsheathe it on Slorenian soil, the soul-eating Blade absorbed the restless spirits of Slorenia's murdered population, and perhaps the conflicting mystic energies of Volkhvy and Ember too; Dolan transformed into the Bloodwraith once more, the energies absorbed causing him to grow to Brobdingnagian proportions, and he slaughtered many of the relief workers. Wanting the entire world to share the murdered Slorenia's pain, Bloodwraith marched towards neighboring territories, but was intercepted by the Avengers; finding him too powerful to overcome, the Scarlet Witch bound Bloodwraith to the land so that he could not pass beyond Slorenia's borders. He currently remains trapped there, a vengeful god waiting for the opportunity to escape.

DOMESTIC CRIME: Under Volkhvy, regular crime was minimal, as suspected criminals were simply rounded up and turned into Targoth without the benefit of trial or appeal. The reappearance of Ember and the ensuing civil unrest he triggered saw crime rates increase as Dudak rebel forces committed robberies to fund their rebellion and acts of terrorism against the incumbent regime. The Tabissara regime instigated a program of ethnic cleansing against the minority Dudak people.

INTERNATIONAL CRIME: None. Before the population was slain, a small amount of smuggling persisted, in spite of the harsh punishments meted out if the perpetrators were caught. After Volkhvy's overthrow, groups such as the Russian mob began to make significant inroads into the country, and AIM became involved with the new government, learning the Targoth-creation process from them, but all these activities abruptly ended with Ultron's arrival. The would-be terrorists, the Popular Front for Slorenian Sovereignty, made one attempt at world recognition, hijacking a New York to LA flight, only to be swiftly overpowered by passengers Wonder Man (Simon Williams) and Beast (Hank McCoy).

FIRST APPEARANCE: Force Works #4 (1994)

HISTORY: Humans have lived in what would become Slorenia since at least 9000 BC, with the ancestors of the Dudak, a Finnic people, believed to have arrived some time around 4000 BC. Circa 2000 BC the proto-Balts, including what would become the Slorene people, migrated into the region. Initially the relationship between the immigrants and established population was remarkably peaceable, but within a few hundred years tensions flared up over Slorenes driving Dudaks off the best farming land. Around 1200 BC the first stories of angry gods fighting for either side appear in the local sagas, entities identified in modern times as Ember and Volkhvy. While their neighbors grew rich as trading crossroads, travelers largely shunned the Slorene territory, scared off by the unrest and reports of demons. As each entity gained dominance in turn and temporarily destroyed the other, Slorenia/Dudakmaa (the name depending on which ethnic group was in control) went through periods of relative stability, though at any given time the dominant faction would persecute their rival. Despite the stories of Slorenia's supernatural defenders, it endured regular raids from the Couronians ("Baltic Vikings") during the 12th and 13th centuries, their external attacks ironically bringing about unprecedented cooperation between the Dudak and Slorene factions. The country's strategic geographic location saw other neighbors attempt invasions too; while some achieved brief occupations, all were eventually repelled as Ember and Volkhvy shifted their focus from attacking each other's people to attacking the interlopers. At some point however when Ember was temporarily destroyed, Volkhvy made a deal with an ageless mutant Laslo Magzel; Magzel designed a machine, the Program, which could drain life forces, sustaining Volkhvy so that he did not need to relinquish his host form. This advantage allowed Volkhvy to change tactics; unbothered whether Slorenes or foreign powers were nominally in power, he took control of Slorenia from behind the scenes, and had the triptych, which housed Ember's spirit, hidden away in the Slorenian Winter Palace's vaults, where it could not connect with a Dudak host.

In the 18th century the Russian Empire's expansionist plans triggered the Great Northern War, and by the end of the century Slorenia was under Russian rule. Industrialization spread swiftly, but living conditions for peasants of all ethnic groups worsened. During the World War I, Slorenes and Dudaks fought on the Tsarist Russian side, with pride in their forces triggering a surge in Slorenian nationalism. In January of 1918, hoping to take advantage of Russian post-revolutionary turmoil, Slorenia declared independence; however the Red Army swiftly moved, declaring it under Soviet rule. Two years of fighting followed, at the end of which Russia acknowledged Slorenia's sovereignty, promising to give up any claim to the country for all time; this proved to be a hollow pledge. In 1921, Slorenia joined the League of Nations, that era's most prominent international organization. The period between the wars was spent rebuilding a shattered economy, which Volkhvy did through ruthless exploitation of the Dudak minority, forced labor being cheap. However both Hitler and Stalin viewed the Baltic countries as theirs by right, and in 1939 the Soviet Union and Nazi Germany signed a non-aggression treaty, the Molotov-Ribbentrop Pact, which included a secret clause discussing the division of Eastern Europe between them; Slorenia was assigned to the Soviets. With this in place, Germany invaded Poland, triggering World War II, and the Soviet Union moved on the Baltic States. Moscow issued an ultimatum to Slorenia, forcing it into a "mutual assistance" treaty, which permitted 20,000 Red Army troops to be garrisoned in bases within Slorenia, more soldiers than

were in Slorenia's own army. In mid-1940 the Soviet press alleged unsubstantiated anti-Russian activities from the Baltic states, a pretext for further Soviet build-up within Slorenia, and by the end of the year the Soviets seized complete control, with a Soviet puppet parliament voting to make Slorenia part of the USSR. However in 1941, Slorenia was invaded by the Nazis, becoming part of Germany's Reichskomissariat Ostland. Throughout each occupation, Volkhvy remained quietly in the background, content to be a spider in the web controlling whichever group was in power, happily shipping Dudaks out to concentration camps alongside Slorenia's tiny Jewish population. In mid-1944 the Soviet Army reclaimed Slorenia, and it would remain part of the Soviet Union until the collapse of communism; ironically during this period the Dudaks found Slorene persecution lessened, as Volkhvy limited his activities for fear of drawing Moscow's notice. In 1991 Slorenia declared independence, with the Tabissara assuming control of the country. With persecution of the Dudaks again becoming prevalent, civil unrest increased, becoming full-scale civil war after Ember was revived. Intervention by the American team Force Works eventually led to the downfall of Volkhvy, Ember and the Tabissara, and the creation of a new regime that promised to respect human rights. However soon afterwards Ultron moved on Slorenia, intending to make it his new base; he sealed off the border, and his robot army methodically moved inwards, slaughtering everything; within 3 hours he had slain the entire population. The Avengers led a UN army that destroyed him, but Slorenia was devastated. Relief agencies moved in to bury the dead and attempt to rebuild, with Slorenians who had been overseas coming home hoping they might be able to eventually repopulate their shattered country. Unfortunately the vengeful souls of the dead were absorbed into the mystic Bloodwraith, driving the relief workers out; with his rage now contained within the dead country, there seems no hope of ever rebuilding.

OFFICIAL NAME: Kingdom of Spain (Reino de España)
POPULATION: 40,448,191
CAPITAL CITY: Madrid
PLACES OF INTEREST: Valle de los Caídos; Altamira; Alhambra; Seville Cathedral
GOVERNMENT: Democratic parliamentary monarchy
MAJOR LANGUAGES: Castilian Spanish; Catalan, Galician and Basque are all official languages in certain regions
MONETARY UNIT: Euro; formerly Spanish pesetas
MAJOR RESOURCES: Coal, iron, motor vehicles, tourism
NATIONAL DEFENSE: Spanish Armed Forces: Army (Ejercito de Tierra), Spanish Navy (Armada Espanola, AE), Spanish Air Force (Ejercito del Aire Espanola, EdA)
INTERNATIONAL RELATIONS: Spain is a member of the United Nations, UNESCO, NATO, Interpol, World Health Organization and European Union. SHIELD maintains a presence in Spain, as does the related research agency EuroMind. Spain and the UK continue to differ over the future of British-run Gibraltar, and Portugal does not recognize Spanish sovereignty over Olivenza, but otherwise remains on reasonably cordial terms with both countries.
EXTRATERRESTRIAL RELATIONS: A Skrull ship crash-landed in Spain several centuries ago, around the time of the Inquisition; the superstitious locals disposed of the ship and corpses by dropping them into a deep gorge.
NONHUMAN POPULATION: In the 13th century BC the Greek demigod Geryon was king of Erytheia, now part of modern Spain. There are Moloid Subterranean colonies beneath Spain. During the Inquisition, captured Inhumans were dropped down a deep gorge. Unable to escape the caverns, the survivors became cannibals, degenerating into mutated shapeshifters when they devoured Skrull corpses dropped into the gorge.
Frederico Valencia was a Spanish vampire turned in 1492 just before he was due to sail on the Santa Maria with Columbus.
DOMESTIC SUPERHUMANS: The criminal alchemist Esteban Diablo was born in 9th century Spain; having sold his soul to Mephisto, the Brass Bishop (Benedicto de vica Severtes) sought to renege on the deal, hiding his soul within mystical armor. Spanish mutants include Empath (Manuel de la Rocha) of the Hellions, the External Gideon, Picaro (Antonio Rey) of Euroforce, the Acolyte Static (Gianna Carina Esperanza), the crimelord Conquistador (Miguel Provenza), and the crimefighting el Aguila (Alejandro Montoya); in the wake of "M-Day," Aguila and Conquistador are reportedly depowered, Empath retains his abilities, and the others' fates are undisclosed. The Spider Society and Sisterhood of the Wasp both originated in ancient Spain.
PROMINENT CITIZENS: The Order of Deacons banished Diablo from Spain in the 9th century; their only known modern day survivor is Blanca del Hierro. Allegedly immortal, the magician Comte Saint Germain is reputed to be of Spanish birth. The 15th century warrior Vargas tried to keep Dracula out of Spain; his modern day namesake came into conflict with the X-Men. Unidentified Spanish explorers founded the hidden la Hacienda by the Fountain of Youth in the Florida swamps. Alejandro Montoya's ancestor Paco was el Aguila in the 1880s. Manuel Elongato was once Spain's premier bullfighter, el Supremo, but after being disgraced in the ring, he used his skills to commit crimes as the Matador. Fire-Eater (Tomas Ramirez) is a member of the Circus of Crime. Scientist Carlo Zota is one of the criminal Enclave.
SUPERHUMAN RESIDENTS: During the 12th century Aelfric the Mad Monk lived in the Abbey of St. Michael. Kay Destine, aka Cuckoo, inhabited the body of a dead Spanish nobleman in 1519 AD so that she and her sister Gracie could accompany Pizarro's Conquistadores to the New World; in modern times, now the fashion designer Kay Cera, Cuckoo spent much of her time in Barcelona, until her body was slain by Lenz's offspring. Captain Terror (Dan Kane), Eugene Judd and Logan (James Howlett) were all active during the Spanish Civil War. After being framed, Euroforce were last seen regrouping in Spain.
DOMESTIC CRIME: Spain's crime rate has been about average for

a Western country, but has recently begun to reduce, in no small part due to the Guardia Civil's Action Force, a well-equipped and trained taskforce led by Diego Sandival. Roc was a highly successful Madrid-based assassin until he was killed by the Punisher (Frank Castle). Paco Cardenas headed a crime syndicate in northern Spain, but was slain by his own nephew on the Kingpin (Wilson Fisk)'s orders.
INTERNATIONAL CRIME: Foreign pirates such as the 16th century Red Lucy Keough and the 17th century Captain Tyger targeted Spanish ships in centuries past. During the Spanish Civil War the Gentleman (Gustav Fiers) sold arms to both sides. The American Kingpin sought to create a European crime syndicate, sending Snakebite, Rapido (Roussel Dupont) and Batroc to Spain to eliminate the uncooperative Paco Cardenas. The thief known as the Asp (Rich Harper) was, for a time, based in Spain.
HISTORY: Humanity's presence in Spain dates back to at least 30,000 BC. Over subsequent centuries Iberians, Celts, Phoenicians, Greeks and Carthaginians colonized the region; eventually Rome invaded, turning it into their province Hispania. Goths invaded circa 410 AD, holding the region until 711 AD, when Moor forces crossed from Africa, laying claim to the south of the country, the renamed Al-Andalus. Internal strife eventually weakened the Moorish caliphates, allowing the Christian northern kingdoms to slowly regain territory; the last caliphate, Granada, fell to King Ferdinand "the Catholic" in 1492, reuniting Spain as a country. The same year Ferdinand and his wife Isabella issued the Alhambra Decree, ordering the expulsion of all Jews and Muslims from Spain; many converted, but suspicious that they were not sincere in their faith change, Ferdinand set up an Inquisition. Meanwhile Spain grew rich on gold and silver from the newly discovered Americas. Spain warred with its neighbors over the next few centuries, gaining and then losing an empire overseas. An economic crisis in the 1920s led to a military dictatorship until 1930; elections in 1931 brought the Republican left to power, and the King went into exile, but in 1936 Civil War broke out. General Franco's Nationalists gained control by 1939, but despite having been supported by Nazi Germany and Fascist Italy, Franco kept Spain neutral during World War II. Franco restored the monarchy in 1969, and after his death in 1975 Spain became a constitutional monarchy.

SWEDEN

OFFICIAL NAME: Kingdom of Sweden (Konungariket Sverige)
POPULATION: 9,031,000
CAPITAL CITY: Stockholm
PLACES OF INTEREST: Karlskrona, Vasa Museum, Visby, Ice Palace
GOVERNMENT: Democratic constitutional monarchy
MAJOR LANGUAGES: Swedish, small Sami- and Finnish-speaking minorities
MONETARY UNIT: Swedish krona
MAJOR RESOURCES: Telecommunications, motor vehicles, iron and steel, wood pulp and paper products, hydroelectrics
NATIONAL DEFENSE: Swedish Armed Forces (Forsvarsmakten): Army (Armen), Royal Swedish Navy (Marinen), Swedish Air Force (Svenska Flygvapnet)
INTERNATIONAL RELATIONS: In 1397 Sweden, Norway and Denmark formed the Kalmar Union, largely to protect themselves from the growing influence of the Germanic Hanseatic League. In modern times Sweden is a member of the Council of Europe, the Nordic Council, Interpol, the United Nations, UNESCO and World Health Organization. It joined the European Union in 1995, but rejected adopting the unified currency, the euro.
EXTRATERRESTRIAL RELATIONS: None known
NONHUMAN POPULATION: Sweden is reputedly the home of various monstrous races, such as trolls, giants, Tomte (elf-like creatures), Lyktgubbar (jack o' lanterns), faeries, nymphs and sprites. While no verified encounter with these has been recorded, it is possible some of these legendary creatures hail from Asgard. Despite being more commonly associated with neighboring Norway, the Asgardians were also worshipped and active in Sweden.
DOMESTIC SUPERHUMANS: Stockholm is home to the triclops mutant Ankhi Gottberg, though she is believed to be depowered in the wake of "M-Day." Heat-manipulator Magma is a respected senior member of the Super-Heroes of Europe (SHE). Swedish genius and electrical engineer Dr. Jan Maarshall worked alongside fellow scientific giants in the US-based Nest, before being transformed into the energy being Yama Dharma, and departing for the stars with his similarly empowered colleagues.
PROMINENT CITIZENS: Historically, Beowulf, King of the Götar (or Geats), who fought the monster Grendel in nearby Denmark, may be the most famous of Sweden's people; though he pre-dates Sweden's formation, Götaland lies in what is now southern Sweden. However it is unclear if Beowulf truly lived, as two immortal adventurers, Ulysses Bloodstone and the Forgotten One of the Eternals both claim to have used the name. Another famous historical Swede was chemist Alfred Nobel, inventor of dynamite, and namesake of the Nobel Prize. Swedish diplomat Max Lindstrom was assigned to be the Atlantean monarch Namor's personal liaison to the UN when Namor sought to enter his kingdom into that august body in recent years. Less distinguished, Bruce Olafson is the Strong Man of the infamous Circus of Crime.
SUPERHUMAN RESIDENTS: None identified
DOMESTIC CRIME: Sweden has a low, but slowly growing, crime rate, much of it connected to drug abuse.
INTERNATIONAL CRIME: In the armored form of Crucible, Enclave criminal scientist Maris Morlak brought kidnap victims Isabel Aguirre and Gordon Clay to Sweden, where he threatened them into his service, before then attacking a Swedish scientific symposium, bringing him into conflict with the visiting Mr. Fantastic (Reed Richards) and the Thing (Ben Grimm).
HISTORY: Archaeological evidence suggests Sweden has been inhabited by humans since at least 3300 BC, and possibly much earlier. The Roman historian Tacitus wrote of the Suiones, a powerful tribe with a single ruler, inhabiting the region in 98AD, but the exact dates the Swedish kingdom was formed remain lost in time. Tales of Beowulf mention wars between the legendary king's Götaland (in modern times, southern Sweden) and the Swedish kingdom, Svealand, to the north. From the 8th century AD Swedish Vikings spread outwards, their trading and raiding expeditions traveling mostly to the south and east, unlike their Norwegian and Danish counterparts who went west; they reached as far as the Byzantine Empire capital Constantinople (modern day Istanbul). Historical records recognize Erik the Victorious, who assumed the combined throne of Svealand and Götaland, as the first Swedish king, although sagas and myths name much earlier monarchs. Unlike most kingdoms, the Swedish king was elected by an aristocrat council, not inherited, leading to frequent political instability, until Gustav Vasa established himself as absolute monarch in 1523. Taking advantage of overseas strife, Sweden's influence grew through trade and military might, becoming one of the great powers of Europe between 1611 and 1718, a period during which Sweden was almost constantly at war. At its peak, the Swedish Empire encompassed Finland, Estonia, Latvia, Ingria, Trondhjem (in modern Norway) and parts of northern Germany. However defending the extended borders eventually proved too costly, and the end of the Empire weakened the monarchy for decades. In 1810, the French Jean Baptiste Bernadotte, formerly one of Napoleon's field marshals, was elected crown prince of Sweden and adopted by the aging monarch Karl XIII shortly afterwards; renamed Karl XIV Johan, he led his adopted homeland against his former commander, and won Norway from its Danish rulers. In 1818 he was elected king of both Sweden and Norway, a union that lasted until 1905. Sweden declared itself neutral during World War I and II, and despite the Nazis occupying neighboring Norway during the latter conflict, they never attacked Sweden. In the post war era, Sweden has remained consistently neutral, avoiding participation in any wars, and maintaining a steady economy, finally joining the EU in 1995; it has similarly avoided much of the super-powered conflict, which has afflicted the rest of the globe.

Art by Charlie Adlard

OFFICIAL NAME: Swiss Confederation (Schweizerische Eidgenossenschaft [German], Confédération suisse [French], Confederazione Svizzera [Italian], Confederazuin svizra [Romansh])

POPULATION: 7,523,000

CAPITAL CITY: Bern

PLACES OF INTEREST: Castle Frankenstein, Castle Zola, Geneva, Hawk Eyrie, the Matterhorn, the Swiss Alps, Zurich

GOVERNMENT: Democratic republic

MAJOR LANGUAGES: French, German, Italian, Romansh

MONETARY UNIT: Swiss franc

MAJOR RESOURCES: Nuclear energy, watchmaking, banking, merchant marine, chocolate

NATIONAL DEFENSE: Swiss Armed Forces, includes Army and Air Force.

INTERNATIONAL RELATIONS: Switzerland was host of the Pan-European Conference on Superhuman Affairs, the Geneva Conventions which outline the standards for international law and humanitarian treatment, holds membership in the United Nations, UNESCO, Council of Europe, the International Criminal Court, and Interpol, and has cooperated with Alpha Flight, MI-6, SHIELD, and the X-Corps. The Red Cross was founded in Switzerland and is headquartered in Geneva.

EXTRATERRESTRIAL RELATIONS: Switzerland was visited by Hargen the Measurer, a representative of the Celestials' Fourth Host. The country was briefly invaded by the Phalanx, but were driven out after their defeat by the X-Men.

NONHUMAN POPULATION: Various genetic experiments of Arnim Zola (no legal status).

DOMESTIC SUPERHUMANS: Switzerland's best-known hero is Weisse Kreuz, a member of the Super-Heroes of Europe. The Psight Corporation, a superhuman genetic research firm, is based in Geneva. Also native to Switzerland are the mutants Madame la Farge, a telepath, and Neophyte (Simon Hall), one of Magneto's Acolytes (mutant status post "M-Day" not known). Local scientist Hans Feldstadt once transformed himself into a gamma-powered mutate, ultimately dying in battle with the Hulk.

PROMINENT CITIZENS: Nora Queen, a former Asgardian, founded the Praxis corporation from a base in the Alps. The von Frankenstein family have lived in and around Castle Frankenstein since the 18th century. Although the original Frankenstein's Monster first came to life under Victor Frankenstein's care in Germany, the creature wandered through Switzerland in the centuries that followed, clashing with his creator's various descendants. The modern-day Veronica and Victoria Frankenstein still live in Switzerland; Veronica is a surgeon, while Victoria cares for the various misshapen creatures ("the Children") her ancestors

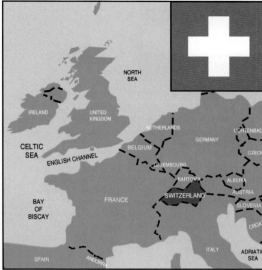

created. The creature has also attracted a number of enemies, such as mad scientist Walston Kraft. Jurist Gustave Roch Uderzo served in one of the attempts to try Magneto in the World Court.

SUPERHUMAN RESIDENTS: Cable (Nathan Summers), Maurice Fortuit of the Destine family, and former STRIKE agent Alison Double have each maintained chalets in the Alps. Quicksilver and the Scarlet Witch briefly lived in the Alps before joining the Avengers. M (Monet St. Croix) briefly attended a Swiss boarding school. X-Man (Nate Grey) spent some of his time in Switzerland, occasionally accompanied by his lovers Threnody and Madelyne Pryor.

DOMESTIC CRIME: Although Switzerland has a low crime rate, it has proved an attractive hiding place for many super-villains. Mad geneticist Arnim Zola dwells in Castle Zola in the Weisshorn Mountains. Many of Zola's creations such as Doughboy were brought to life on his property, and he has provided shelter to his employer the Red Skull and other confederates. The original Flag-Smasher was born in Switzerland, recruited many operatives for ULTIMATUM from his homeland, and had ULTIMATUM bases within Switzerland's border. The vampire Arthur de la Courte ran a boarding school where he fed upon his students, until M destroyed him.

INTERNATIONAL CRIME: During World War II, the Nazi agent the Planner (Hendrich von Wilhelm Innsbruck) was based in Switzerland at the Hawk Eyrie castle. Many Nazi war criminals have sought shelter in Switzerland, including Brain Drain and Master Man (Wilhelm Lohmer). The Hellfire Club has bases within Switzerland, and the Shaw family owns a chalet in the Alps. Exodus lay dormant in the Alps for 800 years before being awakened in modern times by Magneto. Nicodemus of the Externals was based in the Alps; Apocalypse maintained one of his hibernation chambers in Switzerland as well. Other criminals who have had property or mercenary interests in Switzerland include Deadpool, Dr. Doom (Victor von Doom), Richard Fisk, Future Man, Dr. Killebrew, the Kingpin (Wilson Fisk), Mr. Kline, Madame Death, the Mandarin, Marduk (Zoltan Nestor), Stewart Montenegro, Mystique, Sabretooth, Marco Sanzionare, the Si-Fan, Emil Stein, and Tombstone.

HISTORY: Founded in 1291, Switzerland has a long-established neutrality. This neutrality has prevented the country from participating in many international ventures and from building up a military force comparable to its neighbors, but it has also kept the country free from many battles, including World War II. Switzerland is best known for their banking services, which offer their clients complete privacy; unfortunately, this has resulted in many white-collar criminals taking advantage of the Swiss banks in order to finance their operations. The Swiss Alps and mountain ranges, which include the Matterhorn, attract many tourists, and the country has a lively skiing industry.

Art by Ron Wilson

CASTLE ZOLA

OFFICIAL NAME: Kingdom of Symkaria (Symkrija Kiralysog)
POPULATION: 1,500,000
CAPITAL CITY: Aniana
PLACES OF INTEREST: Castle Sable, Castle Hargenhoff, Castle Masada, Draken River (Latverian border), Eptrios, Kronlia, Mount Balba, Sergeikan Caverns, Raven's Copse, Ryork River, Sergeikan Caverns, St. Eboar, University of Aniana, Viscayin Mountains, Wild Pack Headquarters (Aniana)
GOVERNMENT: Parliamentary monarchy
MAJOR LANGUAGES: Symkarian, Hungarian
MONETARY UNIT: Symkarian franc
MAJOR RESOURCES: Mercenaries, coal, iron ore, machinery, nuclear power, watchmaking, toys, car & jet manufacturing
NATIONAL DEFENSE: Symkarian Armed Forces, including Ground Forces and Air Force, together numbering 2,000 active members. Additionally, the Wild Pack is an international mercenary force handpicked by Silver Sable and often employed for national security.
INTERNATIONAL RELATIONS: Member of the European Union, Interpol, UNESCO, the United Nations and the World Trade Organization. Close ally of Belgriun, Bosqueverde, France, Latveria, Mexico, Norway, Russia, UK, USA (including Wild Pack mercenary operations for the CIA)

and Wakanda. The Wild Pack's mercenary operations have occasionally set Symkaria at odds with Russia.
EXTRATERRESTRIAL RELATIONS: A white hole once formed overtop Castle Masada, generated from the duplicate planet Counter-Earth; although the efforts of the Thunderbolts sealed the rift, Castle Masada was destroyed.
NONHUMAN POPULATION: None known.
DOMESTIC SUPERHUMANS: None known.
PROMINENT CITIZENS: During World War I, the country was ruled by King Petrio; in World War II, his descendant King Phillip ruled. Their descendant King Stefan is the current ruler; Stefan's wife Queen Vivian was tragically slain by Sabretooth. The current prime minister is Alphonse Gallatik; his predecessor, Klaus Limka was ousted after being discovered to have collaborated in the death of Queen Vivian. Scientist Wolfgang Hessler was once sought by the Master of the World. One-time intelligence minister Ernst Sablinova founded the Nazi hunting Wild Pack, but he has since retired, too aged to continue field work; his wife Anastasia was an unfortunate casualty at the hands of war criminal Ivan Trefkov. Ernst's brother Fritz defected from the Wild Pack to the terrorist Genesis Coalition organization, ultimately dying in battle with the Wild Pack. Ernst's daughter Silver Sable (Silver Sablinova) has been the leader of the Wild Pack in recent years. Sable's niece Anna and uncle Mortimer usually live in the USA. When Sable handed leadership of the Wild Pack to Andreas Vadas, he took the alias of "Silver Wolf" and corrupted the Wild Pack until he was finally killed by Sable. Lorna Kleinfeldt is one of Sable's top aides, and helps monitor operations from the embassy in New York. Other members of the Wild Pack have included Joannes Boros and Artur Sobczak. Ambassador Fyotr Jannsens represents Symkaria for Latveria.
SUPERHUMAN RESIDENTS: A number of superhumans in the employ of Silver Sable have dwelt in Symkaria for extended periods, including Battlestar (Lemar Hoskins), Fin, Lightbright (Obax Majid), Madcap, Man-Eater, Paladin, and the Sandman (William Baker). Since the 1950s, Symkaria has served as the central base of operations for the V-Battalion, out of Castle Masada; members stationed in Symkaria have included Citizen V (John Watkins, Jr.), Citizen V (John Watkins III), Fred Davis, the Destroyer (Roger Aubrey), Goldfire (Ameiko Sabuki), Jim Hammond, the Human Top (David Mitchell), Iron Cross (Helmut Gruler), Isadora Martinez, Nuklo (Robert Frank, Jr.), the Silver Scorpion (Elizabeth Barstow), Andrea Sterman and Topspin (Darren Mitchell). The team also employed the massive Vanguard carrier vessel, but both it and Castle Masada were destroyed by a white hole; it is not known if Castle Masada will be rebuilt.
DOMESTIC CRIME: The Crimson Cowl (Justine Hammer) formerly

CASTLE SABLE

operated from Symkaria, abusing her friendship with Silver Sable to avoid prosecution for her acts of terrorism and extortion; she also sheltered members of the Masters of Evil, including Black Mamba (Tanya Sealy), Hydro-Man (Morris Bench) and Machinesmith (Samuel Saxon). The Erganoff Brothers are a minor nuisance to the country, using their front as clockmakers to smuggle illegal goods in and out of Symkaria.

INTERNATIONAL CRIME: The mutant killer Sabretooth assassinated Prime Minister Limka while ULTIMATUM inflicted a terrible tragedy upon the nation by killing Queen Vivian, all part of a plot by the Red Skull (Johann Shmidt) to destabilize relations between Symkaria and the USA. The Master of the World once kidnapped Wolfgang Hessler to use in his Compound Omega viral sterilization project. Other attempts to undermine the country's national security have been made by the Genesis Coalition, the Life Foundation, the Authority (Tito Mendez), and Silver Sable's ex-husband the Foreigner.

FIRST APPEARANCE: Amazing Spider-Man #265 (1985)

HISTORY: Symkaria is traditionally a monarchical country, the bloodline of whose kings reaches back 300 years, although the monarchy today serves as a figurehead. During World War I, the tiny Balkan country was nearly absorbed by its neighbors, but instead carved out its independence. Again threatened in World War II, Symkaria joined forces with its neighbor Latveria; though the country was occupied in Eptrios, through cooperation they avoided total conquest by the Nazi forces, but paid with the lives of 1200 citizens. Likewise, in the postwar years they prevented absorption into the USSR. Ever mindful of the sacrifices their people made, Symkaria positioned itself as one of the premiere Nazi hunters. For their assistance in hunting war criminals, the V-Battalion have been welcome in Symkaria since the 1950s, and given Castle Masada to serve as their central base of operations. Ernst Sablinova helped establish Symkaria's greatest effort in hunting war criminals, the Wild Pack. In addition to hunting fugitive Nazis, the Wild Pack branched out over the years to accept contracts from any government or individual, performing missions varying from security to hostage rescues to munitions raids. Before long, the Wild Pack was providing more capital for the country than any single other endeavor. As a sign of Symkaria's gratitude, the Sablinova family were given Castle Sable to serve as their home. When Ernst was lost on a mission and believed dead, his daughter Silver Sable assumed command of the Wild Pack. Driven by her mother's death and her father's emotional distance, Sable has proved herself a harsh, pragmatic leader. Sable expanded the Wild Pack via Silver Sable International, and has hired costumed heroes such as Hawkeye (Clint Barton), le Peregrine (Alain Racine), the Prowler (Hobie Brown), Rocket

CASTLE MASADA & VANGUARD

Art by Manuel Garcia

Racer (Robert Farrell), Spider-Man (Peter Parker) and the Will O' the Wisp (Jackson Arvad). She also developed additional teams such as the Intruders and Outlaws. Although Sable's missions have occasionally threatened engulfing Symkaria, the country remains grateful to the Wild Pack for their services and prestige. Sable's most unfortunate indiscretion was marrying the Foreigner, who proved to be an assassin; although they have been divorced for years, the Foreigner has made repeated attempts on Sable's life, damaged her professional reputation and constantly undermines Symkarian security. Symkaria was once nearly plunged into war with the USA when the Red Skull hired Sabretooth to assassinate Prime Minister Klaus Limka and the terrorists ULTIMATUM to kill Queen Vivian, implicating the CIA in the deed; through the efforts of Spider-Man, evidence was obtained to prevent a war. Sable has helped to maintain Symkaria's close relationship with Latveria by attending an annual dinner with monarch Victor von Doom. Sable eventually discovered that her father was alive and returned him to Symkaria, but he has remained mostly inactive. Silver Sable recently took a leave of absence from the Wild Pack, and her successor Andreas Vadas corrupted the organization's purpose, funding an operation to create sleeper agents of unsuspecting people around the Earth. With the help of the enigmatic Dominic Fortune, Sable was able to best and kill Vadas. She and Fortune investigated establishing a business of their own. The future of the Wild Pack is uncertain.

WILD PACK HQ

Art by John Burns

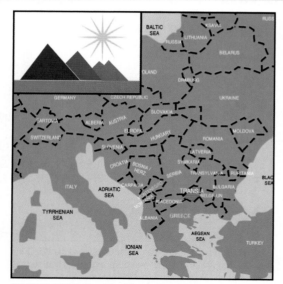

OFFICIAL NAME: Republic of Transia (Republik Transien)

POPULATION: 20,000

CAPITAL CITY: East Transia

PLACES OF INTEREST: Citadel of Science, Dragorin, Mount Wundagore

GOVERNMENT: Constitutional democracy

MAJOR LANGUAGES: German, Hungarian, Symkarian

MONETARY UNIT: Trans

MAJOR RESOURCES: Coal, iron ore, toys, uranium, timber, petroleum, salt, natural gas

NATIONAL DEFENSE: None; Mount Wundagore is defended by the Knights of Wundagore.

INTERNATIONAL RELATIONS: Member of the European Union, UNESCO, the United Nations and the World Trade Organization.

EXTRATERRESTRIAL RELATIONS: The elder god demon Chthon was bound to Mount Wundagore by Morgan le Fay, and the presence of its evil can be felt within the mountain's clay and wood, which can be used as a sort of sympathetic magic by forming images of people and then manipulating them from a distance; the Puppet Master has made use of this clay, while Django Maximoff has used the wood; Chthon remains ever watchful for the means to escape its imprisonment.

NONHUMAN POPULATION: In 1928, subterranean slaves were employed by Herbert Wyndham in order to create his Citadel of Science at Mount Wundagore; these slaves were of the same stock known as "Moloids," which went on to follow the Mole Man (Harvey Rupert Elder). Since the 1930s, various New Men have lived at Mount Wundagore, primarily at the Citadel of Science; each New Man is an animal mutated by the High Evolutionary to possess human-level consciousness. Many of the New Men serve as the Knights of Wundagore, an order of warriors educated to follow medieval codes of honor; the many knights include the cat man Count Tagar, pig man Sir Porga, dog man Lord Churchill, dolphin man Lord Dephis, ferret man Sir Ferret, alligator man Lord Gator, goat man Sir Gote, pig man Sir Hogg, porcupine man Sir Hystrix, leopard man Sir Lepard, lion man Sir Lyan, ocelot man Sir Ossilot, panther man Sir Panther, puma man Sir Puma, sheep man Sir Ram, horse man Lord Steed, tiger man Lord Tyger, bear woman Lady Ursula, bear man Sir Ursus, rat woman Lady Vermin and wolf man Sir Wulf. Even during periods where the majority of New Men were based elsewhere, New Men such as the cow woman Bova and the Cult of the Jackal have remained at Mount Wundagore.

DOMESTIC SUPERHUMANS: The twins Quicksilver (Pietro Maximoff) and the Scarlet Witch (Wanda Maximoff) were born on Mount Wundagore at the Citadel of Science, and were raised by the Romany couple Django and Marya Maximoff, eventually becoming minions of Mangeto in the Brotherhood of Evil Mutants, but later heroes in the Avengers. Spider-Woman (Jessica Drew) was brought up on Mount Wundagore by the High Evolutionary and for a time believed that she was one of the New Men. The mutant Pavane made a long study of Quicksilver and the Scarlet Witch's powers before relocating to the USA; his power status following "M-Day" is not known.

PROMINENT CITIZENS: The Romany couple Django and Marya Maximoff raised Pietro and Wanda as their own children, replacing their dead children Mateo and Ana; both are now deceased.

SUPERHUMAN RESIDENTS: The High Evolutionary (Herbert Wyndham) has lived at the Citadel of Science on and off since 1928, perfecting his New Men and other experiments. The Jackal (Miles Warren) was once his assistant, but was eventually dismissed. The sorcerer Magnus lived at Mount Wundagore for a time to aid the High Evolutionary against Chthon. Gregor Russoff, a werewolf, was manipulated into nearly releasing Chthon, and was slain by the demon. The sorcerer Modred lived on Mount Wundagore with Bova during the time when he had gone insane.

DOMESTIC CRIME: The presence of the High Evolutionary and his New Men at Mount Wundagore has resulted in some bands of raiding parties being formed in attempts to kidnap New Men and steal their advanced technology. Some of the New Men have turned rogue, including the wolf man Man-Beast who has created New Men of his own to serve him while opposing the High Evolutionary on Counter-Earth, the cat man Tabur who waged war against the Cat People and the mongoose man Mongoose who has become an international criminal serving the death god Seth.

INTERNATIONAL CRIME: Mount Wundagore has faced repeated attacks by forces of the Acolytes, mutants who worship Magneto and regard the birthplace of his offspring as sacred ground. The Knights of Wundagore have also faced off an invasion by the Genesis Coalition.

FIRST APPEARANCE: (unidentified) Avengers #31 (1966); (named) Thor #133 (1966)

HISTORY: Transia was once part of Wallachia, but broke off on its own in 1857 when Wallachia merged with Moldavia and Romania. In the country's distant past, the demon Chthon had been bound to Mount Wundagore by Morgan le Fay wielding the Darkhold. Mount Wundagore became the site of the High Evolutionary's Citadel of Science in 1928, thanks to the patronage of the Inhuman geneticist Phaeder. The High Evolutionary used the solitude to develop his race of New Men. Alerted to the threat of Chthon by the sorcerer Magnus, the High Evolutionary trained his New Men to become the Knights of Wundagore. On the evening that the wandering Magda gave birth to twin children on Mount Wundagore, Chthon attempted to escape its confines, only to be driven back by Magnus and the Knights. The twin children were given to a Romany ("gypsy") couple to raise as their own, and eventually became the heroic Quicksilver and Scarlet Witch. The High Evolutionary has attempted to relocate his New Men to safer locations, but each time has inevitably returned them to their first home.

Art by Alex Maleev

The Citadel of Science of Mount Wundagore
Transian Mountain Range, Transia

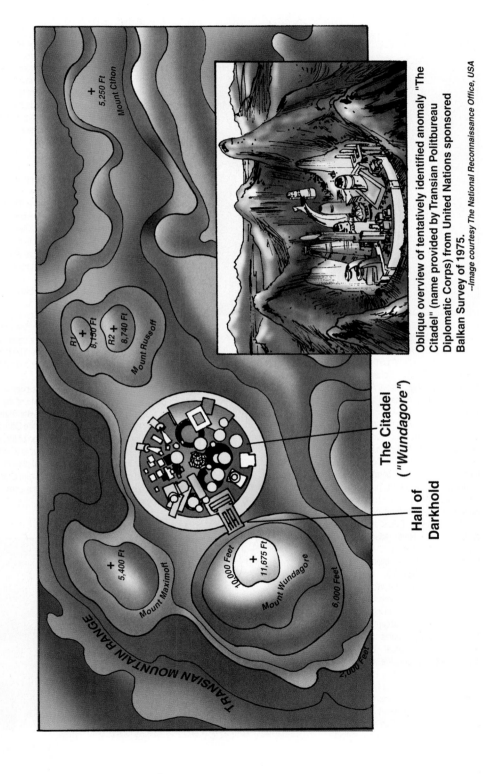

Mount Cthon
5,250 Ft

R1
8,150 Ft

R2
8,740 Ft

Mount Russoff

5,400 Ft

Mount Maximoff

10,000 Feet

11,675 Ft

Mount Wundagore

6,000 Feet

2,000 Feet

TRANSIAN MOUNTAIN RANGE

The Citadel
(*"Wundagore"*)

Hall of
Darkhold

Oblique overview of tentatively identified anomaly "The Citadel" (name provided by Transian Politbureau Diplomatic Corps) from United Nations sponsored Balkan Survey of 1975.

--Image courtesy The National Reconnaissance Office, USA

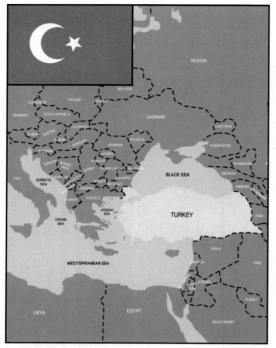

OFFICIAL NAME: Republic of Turkey (Türkiye Cumhuriyeti)

POPULATION: 70,413,000

CAPITAL CITY: Ankara

PLACES OF INTEREST: Basilica Cistern, Church of Antioch, Dolmabahce Palace, Ephesus, the Grand Bazaar, Hagia Sophia, Istanbul, Mount Agri, Mount Ararat, Pera Palas, Sea of Marmara, Sultan Ahmed Mosque, Topkapi Palace, Troy, formerly the Wellspring of All Things

GOVERNMENT: Republican parliamentary democracy

MAJOR LANGUAGES: Turkish, Kurdish, Dimli, Azeri, Kabardian

MONETARY UNIT: Turkish lira

MAJOR RESOURCES: Coal, iron ore, copper, chromium, antimony, mercury, gold, barite, borate, celestite, energy, feldspar, limestone, magnesite, marble, perlite, pumice, sulfur, clay and hydropower.

NATIONAL DEFENSE: The Turkish Armed Forces, including Army, Navy, Air Force, Gendarmerie and Coast Guard.

INTERNATIONAL RELATIONS: Turkey is a member of the Council of Europe, the North Atlantic Treaty Organization, the Organization of the Islamic Conference, UNESCO, the United Nations and the World Trade Organization. Turkey has applied to the European Union, but has yet to be accepted. Turkey partially occupies the Greek isle of Cyprus. The country also has disputes with Armenia, Iraq and Syria.

EXTRATERRESTRIAL RELATIONS: Turkey was the scene of a battle between the extradimensional New Son and the mutant hero Gambit (Remy LeBeau).

NONHUMAN POPULATION: None known.

DOMESTIC SUPERHUMANS: The heroic Flying Carpet represents Turkey as a member of the Super-Heroes of Europe. The mystic Turham Barim is an associate of Sorcerer Supreme Dr. Strange.

PROMINENT CITIZENS: In the 15th century, the warrior Turac was an opponent of Wallachia, and led forces of the Ottoman Empire against Vlad Dracul, taking him prisoner; it was while under Turac's care that Dracul was transformed into a vampire; Dracula turned Turac into a vampire as well, and he was finally slain by his daughter Elianne; Elianne obtained an extended lifespan from the demonic N'Garai, and pursued Dracula for centuries, finally perishing in recent times. Important Turkish leaders such as Sultan Murad and Baron Korda became early victims of Dracula after he claimed the throne of Transylvania. Intelligence director Mehmet Kemel was transformed into a dinosaur-like creature by Count Nefaria while on a mission to the Savage Land.

SUPERHUMAN RESIDENTS: The Pakistani mystic Taboo was formerly active in Istanbul.

DOMESTIC CRIME: In 1948, the rebellious Amouzecar conspired with Prime Minister Amin Yusef to murder members of his own cabinet; Yusef's daughter Magda summoned the heroic Namora to her father's aid, unaware of his involvement, and Namora eventually revealed Yusef's guilt. The Brotherhood of the Wellspring were stationed in Constantinople until the Wellspring location there was sealed. In recent decades, Turkey has been in combat with the People's Congress of Kurdistan. Turkey has been used for the trafficking of various narcotics, including heroin, morphine and opium.

INTERNATIONAL CRIME: Mongolian crimelord Ulan Bator and his American ally Peg-Leg Martin attempted to hide in Turkey, but were found by their foe the Eternal Brain (William Carmody). Turkey was once assaulted by the Void, the villainous aspect of the hero Sentry (Robert Reynolds). The Mutant Liberation Front stole a tapestry from Istanbul to assist Stryfe in his quest to destroy Apocalypse. The terrorist faction Swift Sword has been active in Turkey, employing Scorpio (Mikel Fury) as one of their operatives.

HISTORY: The country of modern Turkey has been a major force in the world for centuries. The ancient city of Troy where the great Trojan War was fought around 11-13th century BC lies within Turkey's border. After being settled by the Turkish peoples for ages, the Ottoman Empire arose in the 13th century, and made the country one of the most powerful on Earth. In the 15th century, the empire was at war with Wallachia, and the Turkish leader Turac had the misfortune of playing a principle role in the transformation of Vlad Dracul into the vampire Dracula. Dracula was the repeated foe of the Ottoman Empire in the centuries that followed. Modern Turkey came into existence in 1923.

Art by Tom Grummett

OFFICIAL NAME: United Kingdom of Great Britain and Northern Ireland
POPULATION: 60,776,000
CAPITAL CITY: London is the English and UK capital; Cardiff, Edinburgh and Belfast are the capitals of Wales, Scotland and Northern Ireland respectively.
PLACES OF INTEREST: Braddock Manor, Buckingham Palace, Camelot, Darkmoor, Giants Causeway, Garrett Castle, Greymoor Castle, Hadrian's Wall, Loch Fear, Loch Ness, Muir Island, Stonehenge, Stormhaven, the World
GOVERNMENT: Democratic constitutional monarchy
MAJOR LANGUAGES: English, Welsh, Scottish Gaelic
MONETARY UNIT: British pound
MAJOR RESOURCES: Natural oil and gas, coal, iron, nuclear power, manufactured goods, electronics and communications equipment.
NATIONAL DEFENSE: British Army, Royal Navy, Royal Air Force
INTERNATIONAL RELATIONS: The UK is a United Nations Security Council permanent member, and belongs to UNESCO, the European Union, G-8, Interpol, SHIELD, NATO and World Health Organization. It has ongoing disputes with Spain over Gibraltar and Argentina over the Falkland Islands. It has recently twice gone to war with Otherworld.
EXTRATERRESTRIAL RELATIONS: During Arthurian times the Dragon of the Moon and renegade Makluans attacked England. Centuries later an unidentified alien scout landed beneath Loch Ness. In the 1960s, Skrull agents impersonated the Beatles, then went native; Skrull John is now a member of MI-13. The Free Kree Liberation Army also visited the UK around this time. The Galadorian Rom banished Dire Wraiths in the UK. The Mephistoid Butcher, Shi'ar Deathcry and T'Kyll Alabar, and Kree Lunatic Legion battled one another in Scotland. The rock-encased Shambler was released in England. Many alien visitors, including the Uncreated, Phalanx and Brood, were collected by Black Air for study at the Dream Nails compound. The Brood Queen Hannah Conover was treated on Muir Island for a time. The techno-organic Warlock and Shi'ar Cerise were both UK residents during their time with Excalibur, and Galactus has visited Excalibur's lighthouse. Extradimensional Martians from Reality-691 recently attempted invasion, as did the Skrulls; in both cases the forces of MI-13 and Britain's native superhumans were instrumental in repelling them. During the latter incursion, JIC Chief Sir Mortimer Grimsdale was exposed as a Skrull imposter and slain.
NONHUMAN POPULATION: The UK has been home to numerous mystic races and individuals, many of whom now reside on Otherworld. Amongst them are the Tuatha De Danaan (Celtic Gods), notably Bodb Derg, the Bane's Red Lord; the Green Knight; the Fomor (Balor, Bres, Cethlann, Dulb, Elathan, Indech, Tethra); trolls and goblins (Gagol, Croglin, Bogweed, Hornwort, Gog and Magog); elves (Buckthorn, Jackdaw, Moondog, Sundog, Telesti); dragons (Ashtoroth, Kharad Dur, Sarafand, Malcolm Drake and y Ddraig Goch (Dave Griffin, the Welsh Dragon)); Merlyn's giant creation Gargantua; the faerie (including their king, Oberon, and his daughter Tink, now working for MI-13); the Iron Ogre; the stony Ancient One; the Nethergods (Mandrac, Necromon) and their servants, including the White Rider, Nightshade and Wolfsbane; the Washer Woman; Black Annis and Red Cap; the giant Pantagruel and her guardians; Morgan Le Fay's Wicker Man; the demons Beliar and Samhain; the Myth Monster; the lycanthropic Children of Danu; the Shadow Rider's ally Goodfellow; the Lady of the Lake, Niamh; Camelot's sorcerer Merlin and his daughter Roma, and the sorcerers Necrom and Feron; and Merlin's animated armor Black Knight. The Blood's Patriarch and Eternal Interloper have also resided in Britain.

Technological constructs living in the UK include the Sleepers (Tommy, Aftermath and the Second Sleeper); the computer Mastermind; the robot Pendragon Gawain; the Fury; Mys-Tech's Psycho-Warriors; DUCK's Ambassador; Arcade's Merry Maladies (Beastmaniac, Captain Sheepdog, Elmer Strange, Hawky, Rawhide Le Pew, Ringo Gonzales, Thor O. Coyote, Victor the Martian); Widget; and the computer program Mainstream. Killpower (Julius Mullarkey) is a genetically engineered

warrior grown in Mys-Tech's labs, which also produced the fungus creature Sporr, the Mothmen, and indirectly the protoplasmic entity Plasmer. Dinosaur-like monsters live in Loch Ness and Loch Fear, and subhuman Troglodytes in caves beneath Garrett Castle. Sam Wantling is a Child of the Voyager, a fragment of that mystic entity. Extradimensional visitors who stayed in the UK for a time include mercenary groups the Special Executive and their counterparts the Technet (Bodybag, China Doll, Cobweb, Fascination/Scatterbrain, Ferro2, Gatecrasher, Hard-Boiled Henry, Joyboy, Lady Burning Fish, Legion, Numbers, Oxo, Ringtoss, Sextant, Thug, Wardog, Waxworks, Yap, Zeitgeist); Abadon; Warwolves; and saurians from Earth-99476 (Wilbur, Martha, Calvin and Susie Griswald, and Color Sergeant Vaughn).

The Asgardian Troll Associates (Phay, Phee, Phelix, Phiend, Phit, Phlegm, Phlopp, Phopp, Phough, Phumm and Phy) lived beneath London. The Crazy Gang (Tweedledope, Knave, Jester, Red Queen and Executioner) was created from the earth by the reality manipulating Mad Jim Jaspers. The genetically accelerated Dalmatian Dempsey was Herbert Wyndham's first enhanced creature. An unidentified demon is trapped beneath London, and there is a N'Garai cairn in Scotland.
DOMESTIC SUPERHUMANS: Since Arthurian times Merlin has chosen Black Knights to defend the UK; the first eight, including King Arthur's cousin Sir Reginald, were driven insane by the Ebony Blade, before it was given to Sir Percy of Scandia. After Percy's death, he was succeeded by the 7th century Sir Raston, 12th century Eobar Garrington, Bart in the 16th, and the 18th century Sir Nigel. In recent years Nathan Garrett, unworthy to wield the blade, became a villainous Black Knight, before the American Dane Whitman took the name. The half-faerie sorceress Morgan Le Fay plotted Camelot's downfall with Mordred the Evil, and continue their evil to the present day; they empowered the villain Excaliber (Jason "Slappy" Struthers). Mordred was one of the 12 Walkers, men wise in magic and other lore; 5 more turned like him to evil (Balor, Cormac, Gurien, Karadoc and Scartac), while 6 remained good, the Proud Walkers Herne, Voritgen, Gwent, Gamael, Bran, and Gael. Morgan's lover Magnus turned against her, and as a ghost continues to oppose her. The sorcerer Gervasse taught his daughter Janice and her lover Modred magic, until Modred succumbed to the demon Chthon's influence; St. Brendan allied his white magic to Merlin's cause to contain Modred. The legendary blacksmith Wayland is based in Camelot. In 987 AD the Sect of Chasidm (Algernon Crowe, Bronwen Gryffn,

EXCALIBUR'S LIGHTHOUSE

Art by Alan Davis

Ranulph Haldane, Porlock, Rathcoole, Gudrun Tyburn, Ormond Wychwood) sold their souls to the demon Mephisto for immortality; in the modern day they are the villainous Mys-Tech board. In the 11th century, the druid Amergin battled the Fomor; his modern day descendant was the hero Dr. Druid (Anthony Ludgate Druid). During World War I, the heroes Union Jack (Montgomery, Lord Falsworth), Sir Steel and Silver Squire battled the Germans as 3 of Freedom's Five. With the outbreak of World War II, Citizen V (John Watkins) fought in occupied Europe; Brian Falsworth became first the Destroyer and then Union Jack, while his lover Roger Aubrey became Dyna-Mite and then the Destroyer; Brian's sister became the speedster Spitfire. Captain Wings (Roger Dicken), Ghost Girl (Wendy Hunt), Thunderfist (Patrick "Pat" Mason) and Tommy Lightning (Thomas Lovejoy) joined Dyna-Mite and the American Spirit of '76 (William Naslund) to form the UK-based Crusaders. Other British heroes included the pyrokinetic Captain Kerosene (Gulliver Jones) and Captain Midlands (Sid Ridley). In subsequent years Knight Templar (Ian Fitzwilliam-Dare) and Squire fought for justice with the First Line until killed fighting against a Skrull armada.

In recent years Merlin chose Brian Braddock to become Captain Britain, battling foes such as the Reaver (Joshua Stragg), Hurricane (Albert Potter), the crimelord Vixen, Mastermind's pawn Dr. Synne (Christopher Thorn), Lord Hawk (Professor Willard Scott) and his robot falcon, and the biker Highwayman (Ross Horton). Brian's telepathic sister Elisabeth joined STRIKE Psi-Division, becoming telekinetic Tom Lennox's lover. When the crimelord Vixen took over STRIKE, she hired Slaymaster to eliminate the telepaths; Kevin "Dr. Destiny" Mulhearn, Vicki Reppion, Avril Davis, Dennis Rush, Andrew Hornby, Leah Mickleson and Stuart Hattrick were slain, leaving Tom, Betsy and Alison Double the only survivors. Betsy later became Captain Britain and then the X-Man Psylocke. Brian's brother Jamie Braddock is a reality-manipulator, one quarter of the Foursaken (Godfrey Calthrop, Ned Horrocks and Amina Synge). Captain Britain's wife Meggan is a mutant shapeshifter; her father William possesses "crawly dolls." Other British mutants include Micromax (Scott Wright), Kylun (Colin McKay), Pixie (Megan Gwynn), Chamber (Jonothan Starsmore), Peter Wisdom, Wolfsbane (Rahne Sinclair), Toad (Mortimer Toynbee), Guvnor (Andrew Black), Acolyte Spoor (Andrew Hammish Graves), reality manipulators Mad Jim Jaspers (Sir James Jaspers) and Proteus (Kevin MacTaggert), Black Air operatives Scratch and Shine, Bash (Vincent Gardner), Alchemy (Thomas Jones), Lila Cheney, exploder Liam Connaughton, plastic skinned Harry Pizer, pyrokinetic Brigit Shane, the Brotherhood's Bela (Tom Morgan), Bryson Bale, Malon Reeves, Clive Vickers and Fiona Dunn, telekinetic Mary Campbell, Malcolm Reeves, Euro-Trash's Oxford Blue (Preston Allen), Zapper (Colin Smith), teleporter Frederick Slade, Frederick's body-morphing brother Hamilton Slade, and their mother Margaret Slade; firebreathing Jack Starsmore, London Hellfire Club Black Queen Emma Steed and Red Rook "Scribe" (Jane Hampshire), the Scarlet Knights (Squadron Leader Colin Hardy, his father Group Captain Arthur Hardy, mother Lisa Hardy, brothers Edward and Malcolm, and sisters Jennifer and Nell), serial killer John Gideon, and the Alchemist, defender of Britain's mutants.

Merlin gave Time Smasher (Killgore Slaughter) immense power; Brian Braddock gave Lionheart (Kelsey Leigh) Captain Britain's powers, while the extradimensional Albion empowered the Shadow-Captains. The Green Knight has imbued numerous champions with the Pendragon spirit, who latterly came together as the Knights of Pendragon: Albion (Peter Hunter), Ben Gallagher, Grace (Francesca Lexley Grace), Breeze James, Kate McClellan, and the current Union Jack (Joseph Chapman). Mys-Tech has also enhanced a number of individuals, including Ridge (Tim Holloway), Stinger (Blodwen Reese), and Vesper (Raani Jatwinder) of Genetix; Victor Sternwood of Mys-Tech's Q-7 Strikeforce; Bubble, Fractal, Fugue, Karbon and Shrapnel of Tektos; and indirectly the foulmouthed Motormouth (Harley Davidson). They also maintain Warhead teams (Bina, Cesad, Gebu, Hesod, Hod, Kether, Kockmar, Malkuth, Net, Tifaret and Ubu Troops) to procure technology from other realities through wormholes: notable members include Kether Troop's Tigon Liger and Stacy Arnheim, both of whom were later recruited into the extradimensional Dark Guard, and Misha, their troop's psi-scout. STORM agents include the Gene Dogs Cat (Emma Malone), Kestrel (Annie Jones), Panther (Corinne Walton) and Tyr (Marc Devlin). British mages and magic users include Winding Way sorcerers Shrill and Gravemoss; Devil-Slayer's foe Ian Fate; Martina and Regina Wolcroft and their rival Thorne; "Old" Sarah Mumford; Julian, Lord Phyffe and his son Augustine; alchemist Daniel Decyst; Gilded Lily (Lillian von Loont); the Warlock Prime (Sir Nigel Carruthers); Sir Anthony Baskerville; Harriet Homerstone; Alicia Harker; Dark Mairi of the Shore; Alisabeth and Megan Daemon in the 1920s; and Feron of Excalibur. The 12th century Crusader Adam Destine rescued and fell in love with a female djinn; she made him immortal and invulnerable, and over the centuries they have produced several super-powered children, including Albert, Dominic, Florence, Garth, Gracie, Kay, Lance, Maurice, Newton, Pandora, Rory, Sherlock, Thaddeus, Walter, Will and Vincent. To their elders' consternation, the youngest, twins Rory and Pandora have become costumed adventurers, Crimson Crusader and Imp.

Captain Britain's foe Mad Jim Jaspers engulfed Britain in a reality warp; after it ended, several individuals were left distorted and with incredible powers. These Warpies were mostly gathered up by RCX, who trained them as a super-powered army. Known Warpies include RCX's Cherubim (Quill, Lump, Fern, AC-DC, Giggles and the Whirlwind quintet), Seraphim (Cabbage, Cyanide, Oak, Peanut, Weasel), Advocates (Aberdeen Angus, Celery, Mustard, Salt, Shrew), Lodestone, Ocelot, Oak, Beetroot, Syphon, Sponge, Static, Silkworm, Iris, Scope, Sonar, Lens, Scan, Snoop, Ferret, Butane, Pumice, Prune, Wire, the Sky Pilots, and the near mindless Serpents; outside RCX's control are the murderous Silver Death (Calum McGill), the exploding Robert Arnold, and street gang the Parasites (Uncle Lex (James Lexington Christian), Hal, Nettle, Peeping Tom, Ramora, Snap, Spasm, Siren and Moley). Weapon Plus maintained an experimental complex, the World, in London, to produce Super Soldiers: Weapon XIII aka Fantomex (Charlie Cluster-7), Weapon XII (Huntsman / Zona Cluster 6) and Ultimaton (Weapon XV) were created there. The British Super Soldier program produced Dauntless (Alec Dalton), Gog (Owen Llewelyn), Invincible (Joseph Hauer), Dreadnaught (Paul Turner), Victory (Kenneth Wright), Challenger (Oscar Black) and Revenge (Lee Childs). Earlier test subjects, the "Super Squaddies," were used by Empire Chemical Enterprises as Corporate Commandos.

Other British heroes include: the mystically-powered Dark Angel (Shevaun Haldane); the vigilante Crusader (Perseus Ablemarle); the electronic Digitek (Dr Jonathan Bryant); Knight Errant (William Matson); Electro-Man (Robert Tunstall); Spider-Woman (Jessica Drew); Thunderclap (Stanley Johnson); EuroForce cyborg Deep Sight (Jane Melville); Shadow Riders Boot (Steven White), Roadie (Alison Kane), and Grunt (Arnold Coltrane); Doorman (Herbert Isaacs); Gemini members Front (Gabriel Caine), Balance (Debora Crovi), Grip (Brandon Blake), Suede (Nicholas Blake) and Mandala (Iman Dashire); Clansman (Ian Og's ghost possessing Detective Sergeant Duncan Ferguson); the vigilante Outlaw (Nigel Higgins); G-Force (Daniel Jones); vampire slayer Blade (Eric Brooks) and his ally Bible John (John Carik); government agent Jack Smithers; Dragon Circle leader Dafydd ap Iowert; Super Heroes of Europe members Claymore, Red Dragon (Gareth Thomas) and his replacement. Super-powered criminals include: the lycanthropes Pitbull (Kevin Wilson) and Terrier (Monte Devlin) of the Litter; the assassins Knight (Malcolm Knight), Fogg (Matthew Fogg) and Crossbow (Jason Praed); Ripperologist James Ransom; geneticists Mr. Sinister (Nathaniel Essex) and the High Evolutionary (Herbert Wyndham); Plantman (Samuel Smithers); the Plunderer (Parnival Plunder); Bane lord Shadow Wing (Alan Trent); Bane-empowered serial killer Dolph (Colin Snewing); the Exemplar Conquest (Bridget Malone); the cyborg Assassin-8; Endotherm (Tom Wilkins); the Church of Humanity's Mr. Clean (Paul Botham); the Bacillicons (Byte (Grant Vogel), Kay (Lexi Petrezyn), Purge (Mark Paxton)); scientist Jonothon Cayre; AIM spy the Highwayman (David Pennant); Pendragon's foe Magpie; and elemental manipulator Damian Tryp. British mercenaries include: Stealth (Eliza Clare Necker) of the Requiem Sharks; Maximillian Zaran; and Shockwave (Lancaster Sneed). Other British superhumans include Garokk the Petrified Man, the undying Immortalis (Mortigan Goth), the Monster of the Moors (Ronson Slade), the Morlands Monster (Randolph Dering), the unaging Gary Redek (Tom Dekker), the ghosts Duncan Corley and Charles Grey, mutated tramp Sidney Crumb, MI-13 psychic Maureen Raven and Skrull Kill Krew's Moonstomp. Apocalypse's Horseman Famine appears to be scientist Rory Campbell, though he may be the Rory Campbell of another timeline. British vampires include Baron Blood (John Falsworth), his successors Baron Blood (Kenneth Crichton) and Baroness Blood (Lily Cromwell), Christopher Sinclair, Lord Ruthven, Rachel Van Helsing, Varney, Katherine Ainsley-Jones, the Brotherhood of Judas (Dr. Samuel Harkins, Morgana St. Clair) and the Black Baron (Rupert Kemp, Baron Darkmoor). The Silver One and Gideon Harkins were 16th century werewolves.

PROMINENT CITIZENS: During the 1st century AD Arianrhod MacLlanllwyr, her father Donal MacLlanllwyr, and grandmother Rhiannon battled the demon Y'Garon. Camelot's knights included King Arthur and Sirs Galahad, Gareth, Gawain, Kay, Mogard, Percival, Percy and Tristan. The Elizabethan age (late 16th century) was the time of the Puritan adventurer Solomon Kane and immortal occultist John Dee. Memorable Britons during WWII include the Sky Devil Ronald Wolverstone-Clodd; Stan Twimbly of the Terror Squad; General Sir Robert Hunt; the Deadly Dozen's Laurie Livingstone; Howling Commando Percival "Pinky" Pinkerton and his elder brother Reginald; and the traitors Alfie (William Leese), Cedric Rawlings and Sir Percival Hawley (Lord Ha-Ha). Shortly after the war Otherworlder Sir James Braddock took the place of his deceased Earth-616 counterpart.

Ka-Zar (Kevin, Lord Plunder) of the Savage Land, and Avengers butler Edwin Jarvis are two of Britain's best known expatriates, while billionaire Justin Hammer was a longtime rival of Tony Stark. Moira MacTaggert was a world expert on mutations. Oonagh Mullarkey is Mys-Tech's most gifted and least scrupulous scientist; other British scientists include Sidney Fishburne, Jonathon Drew, Hugo Travis, Neil MacKenzie; and Alpha (Hywel Griffin) and his Omegans. The UK's most renowned private detective remains Sherlock Holmes, while notable police detectives include Dai Thomas, psychic Kate Fraser, Inspector George Chelm, Frank Sweeny, Chief Inspector Jack Lamb, Dennis Kitchner, Harold Wisdom and Warren Curzon. Chief Inspector Albert Eccles, forensic scientist Bob Willows, occult detective Constance Johanssen, and Inspector Craig Strangefoot make up Department F66. Serial killer Jack the Ripper was initially the possessed hunchback Tom Malverne; Jack remains the country's most infamous criminal. Both the Mad Slayer (Phillip Durant) and the Ripper (Jacqueline Davenport) emulate him. Other British criminals include assassins Cane (Lorne Quickfall), Sari St. Hubbins and Donald "Shoulders" McGill; druglord Carlton Velcro; crimelord Mario Zampa; Red Skull agent Dr. Keith Ramsey; banker Nigel

Frobisher; Arcade's engineer Mr. Chambers; "Black" Jamie MacAwber; innkeeper Ross McNab; and the terrorist Atheist (Gerard O'Higgins). British soldiers include General Francis Mayhew, Major Jock Gunn and mercenary Hardcase (Harry Malone) of the Harriers. Sir Marcus Grantby-Fox formerly headed the Super Soldier program, with scientists Drs. Arnold Stratton, Bruce McDonald, Simon Ogilvey and Richard Brown (and the Pakistani Dr Jahved Khan) developing the process. STRIKE agents included Commander (now Commodore) Lance Hunter and the traitor Tod Radcliffe. RCX agents include leader Peter (Nigel Orpington-Smythe) and Zebedee, Nicholas, Luke, Maria, Mr. Jordan, Michael, Gabriel and Raphael. Brigadier Theobald "Inky" Blott ran FI-6, with operatives including Lance Corporal Andrew Hodge, George Wallace, Mortimer Clayworth, telepath Sebastian Edwards, and Captains Ray Bodie and William Doyle. Other government agents include Black Air's Threadgold, Michele Scicluna and Ed Culley; WHO's Brigadier Alysande Stuart, her brother Alistaire, Elton Krieger, Blane MacNeil, Caradoc Peel and Hugh Styman; Criminal Intelligence's Arthur Jardine; DUCK's Sam Pritchard; STORM's Eagle (Lars Dinkelbach), Dr. Samuel Merrick and Henry, Lord Winstanely; MI-5's Yorkie Mitchell, Larry Pitman, Duncan O'Neill and Phil Gavin; MI-6's War Yore (Eric Slaughter), James Larner, Mordillo (Simon Bretner), Agent D, Omega Team (Morgan Spetz, Buckman, Calder, Parkins, Slade, Stone, Tumball), Archimedes "Archie" Fogg, Sir Denis Nayland-Smith, Clive Reston, Lyman Leeks, Dr. James Petrie, "Black" Jack Tarr, Carrington Scullers, Trevor Doyle, Melissa Greville, Carl Blevins and Ward Sarsfield; MI-13's Rana Mousabi and quartermaster O; Sir Mortimer Grimsdale, JIC (Joint Intelligence Chiefs) chairman, at some point replaced by a Skrull infiltrator; and Romany Wisdom, head of an unidentified above-top-secret agency. British SHIELD agents include Desmond Boothroyd and Jerry Hunt, while Gemini founder Edwig Caine is a former secret agent.

Banker Courtney Ross is Brian Braddock's former lover. His other friends include Sandy York, housekeeper Emma Collins, and the Scott family (Bob, Joan, Josie and the late Micky). Jacko Tanner was Brian's university rival. Other notable Britons include vampire hunters Quincy Harker, Jason Faust and Noah Tremayne; Megan Daemon's suitor Ian MacInnis; Chamber's former lover Gayle Edgerton; Victoria Bentley; the Hellfire Club's Black King (Quentin Templeton), Red King (Alan Wilson), Red Bishop (Conrad Strathdee) and Angus Munroe; Shang-Chi's apprentice Jonathan Raven; UFO hunter Rupert Halloway; Len Arkwright, master of Ecky Thump; actress Julie Vane; soccer player Bert Bullard; Punisher ally Morgan Sinclair; psychics Mike Hellman, Madame Zelda and Emelia Witherspoon; Fury victim Mrs. Esther McGeary; Hydra foe Alan Desmond; Hellfire Club butler Nicholas Rutledge; oceanographer Vivian Morgan, whom Morgan Le Fay possessed; Amos Starn, possessed by the demon Y'Garon; archaeologists Grant Whittaker and Janet Lyton who uncovered Mordred the Mystic's crypt; Meggan's cellmate Sue Craddock; Gideon Smith, English incarnation of Forever Man; and Genevieve Cross, Will Fanshawe, Roger Loomis and Sian Bowen, who became hosts for the Dragon Circle.

SUPERHUMAN RESIDENTS: During the 1st century AD Marada Starhair visited the British kingdom of Ashrandiar. Around the 6th century the French Knight Lancelot joined the Round Table and Merlin Demonspawn impersonated the true Merlin. The magician Monako received his formal education in England between the world wars. During WWII American Captain Red Ruff flew the Flying Flame against the Nazis, while the American hero Spirit of '76 (William Naslund) joined the

BRADDOCK MANOR

Art by Alan Davis

London-based Crusaders; the Invaders (Bucky (James Barnes), Captain America (Steve Rogers), Namor, Human Torch (Jim Hammond) and Toro (Thomas Raymond)) also used London for a base. Several Nazi agents worked secretly within Britain, including Master Man (Wilhelm Lohmer), Arnim Zola, Baron (Heinrich) Zemo and, reluctantly, Blue Bullet (Jonathon Gold). Muir Island Research Centre has been the home for various foreign mutants, including Banshee (Sean Cassidy), Multiple Man (Jamie Madrox), Siryn (Theresa Rourke), Legion (David Haller), Polaris (Lorna Dane), Havok (Alex Summers), Strong Guy (Guido Carosella), Rogue (Anna-Marie), Forge, Sunder (Mark Hallett), the infantized Brotherhood of Evil Mutants (Magneto, Unus (Gunther Bain), Blob (Fred Dukes) and Lorelei), as well as non-mutants Sharon Friedlander and Tom Corsi. British residents hailing from alternate realities include the hero-killing Fury (at least until it was destroyed), Captain UK (Linda McQuillan), Albion, Saturnyne, Sat-Yr9, Mountjoy, and the Shadow-X team (Angel, Beast, Cyclops, Iceman, Marvel Girl). Other long-term residents include the immortal warrior Black Axe, Elsa Bloodstone, Black Knight (Dane Whitman), the Pantheon's Perseus (Scott Shannon), Victorius (Victor Conrad), the ancient vampire Lamia, the Comte St. Germain, Shang-Chi, Dracula, Hunter Joe, Dredmund Druid, Piecemeal, Excalibur members Nightcrawler (Kurt Wagner), Shadowcat (Kitty Pryde), Colossus (Piotr Rasputin), Phoenix (Rachel Summers), Dazzler (Alison Blaire), Sage, Daytripper (Amanda Sefton), Juggernaut (Cain Marko) and Nocturne (Talia Wagner), Base (Hiro Sokuto), Shift (Clifton Joseph), Tattoo (Tudo Sokuto), Dr. Crocodile (Joshua N'Dingi), assassins Arcade and Slaymaster, and deposed Umbazi dictator Basil Crushstone (the Manipulator).

DOMESTIC CRIME: Britain has a relatively low level of mundane crime, despite crimelords such as Mario Zampa or Mingus Strathcoe, but a growing super-powered crime problem, with Mys-Tech and the Vixen's organization exacerbating things. Numerous agencies have been assigned to handle the problem, including Department F66 (Department of Unusual Death) investigating bizarre murders, and Dai Thomas' Interregional Task Force for general super-crime. STRIKE (Special Tactical Reserve for International Key Emergencies) handled larger scale threats; with its dissolution FI6, Black Air, STORM (Special Task Force Omega Response Mandate), WHO (Weird Happenings Organisation), RCX (Resources Control Executive) and DUCK (Department of Unknown and Covert Knowledge) were formed with different but overlapping remits, unsurprisingly leading to jurisdictional conflicts. RCX absorbed FI6 and WHO, before Black Air seemingly wiped them out; officially dissolved, Black Air went rogue, while its successor, the Department, was renamed MI-13. Presently MI-13, MI-5, MI-6 and ITF share defense duties of the UK, with military backup as required from Armed Forces Paranormal Response.

INTERNATIONAL CRIME: Fu Manchu's Si-Fan have operated from London's Limehouse district for more than a century, and the UK-based Mys-Tech carries out illegal operations around the globe, on alien worlds and other realities. Neo-Nazis Matrix 8 and Axis Mundi have operated in the UK. The alternate reality mercenary Death's Head (Minion) has frequently operated in the UK, not always on legal missions. Madman (Phillip Sterns), the Red Skull (Johann Shmidt) and RAID (Radically Advanced Ideas in Destruction) have all launched attacks on London in recent years, while Viper has threatened to blow it up. AIM also has a British branch.

HISTORY: The British Isles were settled as far back as 14,000 BC. As centuries passed, various groups migrated to the islands, with their gods' aid driving back the monstrous Fomori, and by 55 BC, when Julius Caesar's first Roman expedition arrived in Britannia (their name for the main island) Celtic tribes like the Picts and Caledonians (Caledonia, the future Scotland), the Gaels, Scots and Milesians (Hibernia, the future Ireland), the Silures and Ordovices (the future Wales) and the Ashrandiar, Catuvellauni, Dumnonii and Iceni (the future England) inhabited the isles. In 43 AD, the Romans invaded, and by 79 AD all the south was under their control; the barbarians in the north remained independent, with fortifications such as Hadrian's Wall erected to keep them from raiding the south. Around the start of the 5th century the Romans retreated from Britannia, but some of their former mercenaries, the Germanic Angles, Jutes and Saxons moved on the southern territory, founding several kingdoms. While these Anglo-Saxons spread northward, the Scots migrated to Caledonia. Around this time the kingdom of Camelot briefly stood. In 827 AD Egbert became the first king of England (Angle-Land); in 844 Kenneth MacAlpin became the Scots king. In the 9th century the Norse moved into northern Scotland and western Ireland, and the Danes conquered much of England, adding it to the Danish Empire. In 1014 Brian Boru defeated the Norse in Ireland, and the death of Danish King Canute in 1035 split the Danish Empire. In 1066 William of Normandy led a new invasion, conquering England by 1071; around a century later England's Henry II moved on Scotland and Ireland. Over several centuries the independence of both countries from England would fluctuate back and forth. In the late 13th century Wales fell under English rule, and in 1536 the two countries were officially unified. England meanwhile faced external threats from rival European powers such as France and Spain. In 1603 Scots King James VI was crowned James I of England, uniting the crowns, and in 1606 the Union Flag of Great Britain was adopted for his realm. Civil war broke out in 1642, and in 1649 Britain became a republic with Charles I's execution; Lord Protector Oliver Cromwell became Britain's new ruler. However, two years after his death in 1658 the monarchy was restored. In 1801 Great Britain and Ireland's crowns merged to form the United Kingdom of Great Britain and Ireland. By the mid-19th century the UK was the world's dominant maritime and industrial power with an empire covering over a quarter of the Earth's surface. However the two 20th century world wars saw this gradually come to an end; southern Ireland left the union in 1921, and most of the UK's overseas colonies gained independence by the 1950s. In recent years there has been a surge in the country's superhuman population, while Wales, Northern Ireland and Scotland have all gained regional assemblies or parliaments.

MUIR ISLAND RESEARCH FACILITY

Muir Island
MacTaggart Research Station, Outer Hebrides, United Kingdom

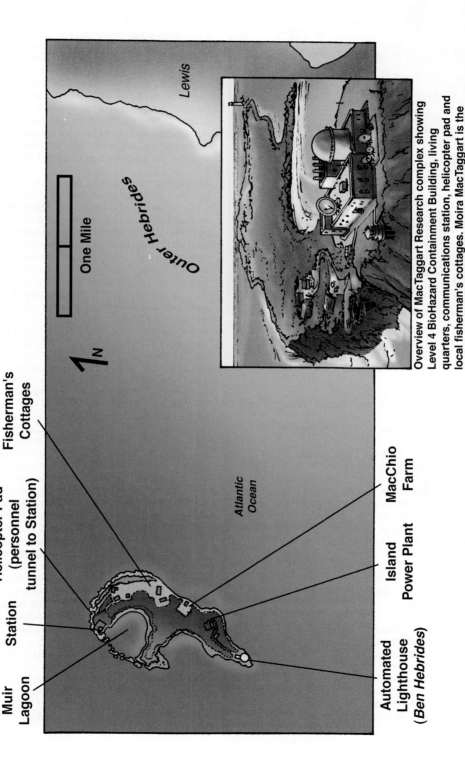

Muir Lagoon

Station

Helicopter Pad
(personnel tunnel to Station)

Fisherman's Cottages

One Mile

N

Outer Hebrides

Lewis

Atlantic Ocean

Automated Lighthouse
(*Ben Hebrides*)

Island Power Plant

MacChio Farm

Overview of MacTaggart Research complex showing Level 4 BioHazard Containment Building, living quarters, communications station, helicopter pad and local fisherman's cottages. Moira MacTaggart is the inventor of the Dynamic Transgenetic Sequencing and Manipulation technique.

--Image courtesy of Center for Disease Control via The State Department of the United States and RCX, LLC, Outer Hebrides, Scotland, United Kingdom

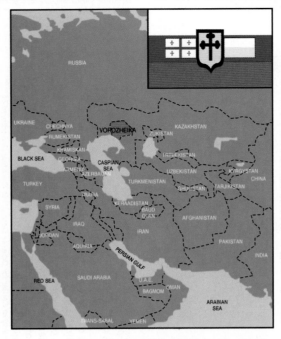

OFFICIAL NAME: Republic of Vorozheika (Vorozheika Respublikata)
POPULATION: 1,100,000
CAPITAL CITY: Krozniev
PLACES OF INTEREST: Vorozheikan Parliament House, Krozniev; Vorozheika National Airport
GOVERNMENT: Federal republic
MAJOR LANGUAGES: Vorozheikan, Russian, Chechen, Georgian
MONETARY UNIT: Vorozheikan maneti
MAJOR RESOURCES: Iron ore, machinery, chemicals; cotton; citrus fruits, tea, wine
NATIONAL DEFENSE: Ground Forces (includes National Guard), Navy, Air and Air Defense Forces
INTERNATIONAL RELATIONS: Vorozheika holds membership in the United Nations, UNESCO, the Commonwealth of Independent States (CIS), and Interpol. Although Vorozheika signed and ratified the Rome Treaty, it formally withdrew from the International Criminal Court soon after Ivan Druig's rise to power.
EXTRATERRESTRIAL RELATIONS: None known.
NONHUMAN POPULATION: Ivan Druig of the Eternals.
DOMESTIC SUPERHUMANS: None known.
PROMINENT CITIZENS: Prime Minister Ivan Druig; Former Prime Minister Ermolai Ivanovich (deceased); Ambassador Danay Leptyuhov; Pavel Prykrish (deceased)
SUPERHUMAN RESIDENTS: None documented.
DOMESTIC CRIME: Following the dissolution of the Soviet Union, the newly independent Vorozheikan republic was plagued by high financial and violent crime rates and widespread government corruption. Although the annual number of violent crimes was greatly reduced during the Prosperity Party's control of Parliament, such crimes became virtually nonexistent since Prime Minister Ivan Druig ascended to power and reinstituted a Soviet KGB-style secret police force while undermining many of Vorozheika's nascent democratic institutions.
INTERNATIONAL CRIME: Although there have been charges that the Vorozheikan government has been cooperating with former members of the Soviet KGB and rogue elements within the Russian state to commit criminal acts abroad, these allegations have yet to be proven in an international tribunal. Similarly, charges of state-sponsored kidnapping have not yet been substantiated.
FIRST APPEARANCE: Eternals #1 (2006)

HISTORY: Once an independent kingdom, Vorozheika was invaded by Russian Soviet forces in the 1920s and incorporated into the Soviet Union as the Vorozheikan Soviet Socialist Republic. Although, like all Soviet socialist republics, Vorozheika was theoretically able to exercise its right to secede from the Soviet Union, the constant presence of Soviet troops and KGB (Committee for State Security) secret police made secession impossible in reality. During this time, Druig, a member of the immortal race known as the Eternals, posed as a human member of the Soviet KGB under the alias "Ivan Druig." Eventually, during his failed attempt to kill the Celestial known as Ziran the Tester using the Celestials' own weapon, Druig was disintegrated by his cousin, the Eternal Ikaris, and his remains were placed inside the extraterrestrial space station known as the Desecration Annex. Upon the collapse of the Soviet Union, Vorozheika established itself as an independent federal republic.

However, when the Eternal Sprite sought to become mortal so that he could enjoy an ordinary life, he manipulated the Dreaming Celestial to refashion all of Earth's Eternals into humans with manufactured memories, ordinary lives and no recollection of who or what they truly were (including Eternals who had previously ceased to function, such as Druig). With no memories of his Eternal physiology, Druig again resumed his life as "Ivan Druig" and was elected to the position of Deputy Prime Minister in the newly established Vorozheikan Parliament. As Deputy Prime Minister, Druig's initiatives attempted to generate international tourism by bringing attention to Vorozheika's plentiful ski slopes and abundance of bears and wolves for hunting, as well as attract the world's most renowned scientists by offering state-of-the-art research facilities. However, unknown to Druig, Prime Minister Ermolai Ivanovich and other members of the rival Prosperity Party disapproved of his former Soviet connections and secretly plotted to remove him from office through assassination. The Prosperity Party even succeeded in secretly turning Druig's trusted aide Pavel Prykrish against him, convincing Prykrish that Druig's connections to the former Soviet regime made him a liability to the current Vorozheikan State. During a social event hosted by Druig at the Vorozheikan Embassy in Manhattan where he planned to kidnap the world's leading mechanical engineers and take them to Vorozheika to develop weapons systems, Russian terrorists hired by the Prosperity Party attacked Deputy Prime Minister Druig, Ambassador Danay Leptyuhov, and their guests. However, due to the fortuitous presence of three other Eternals at the party, Druig's dormant Eternal powers were reawakened and he survived the assassination attempt. Realizing that he could determine the psychological weaknesses and control the minds of others, Druig returned to Vorozheika, where the ruling Prosperity Party had ordered his arrest for traitorous activities. Using his newfound powers, Druig compelled Prime Minister Ivanovich, his chief political rival, to commit suicide and arranged for his supporters to assassinate the Parliament members who had conspired to kill him. Blaming the assassination of his political rivals on Vorozheika's Jewish and Romany ethnic minorities, Druig established a new government with himself as the unchallenged head of state. Prime Minister Druig immediately began to reinstall political institutions reminiscent of the old Soviet Union, such as secret police, to suppress dissidents and keep order.

When Zuras, leader of the Eternals, learned that the Dreaming Celestial would remain in San Francisco to begin a new judgment of Earth, and that its awakening would eventually result in an invasion by the extraterrestrial Horde, Druig agreed to help (in exchange for Zuras vowing to never interfere in Vorozheikan internal affairs). Having consolidated his dictatorship, Druig has used Vorozheika's intelligence network to locate other amnesiac Eternals for him.

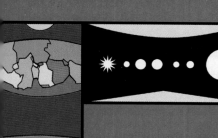

dian
ngland

ast

80° N

Arctic Circle

60°

40°

Tropic of
Cancer

20° N

Equator   80° E

Equator

20° S

Tropic of Capricorn

40°

60°

80°   100°   120°   140°   160°   180°

Meridian

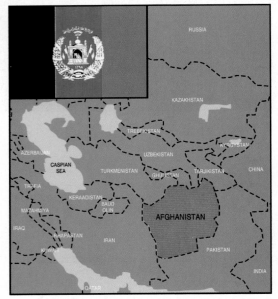

OFFICIAL NAME: Islamic Republic of Afghanistan (Jamhuri-ye Islami-ye Afghanestan)

POPULATION: 31,057,000

CAPITAL CITY: Kabul

PLACES OF INTEREST: Herat, Jalalabad, Kandahar, Mazari Sharif, the Minaret of Jam

GOVERNMENT: Islamic republic

MAJOR LANGUAGES: Afghan Persian, Dari, Pashtu, Uzbek, Turkmen

MONETARY UNIT: Afghani

MAJOR RESOURCES: Opium, wheat, fruit, nuts, wool, mutton, sheepskins, lambskins, textiles, soap, furniture, shoes, fertilizer, cement, carpets, natural gas, coal, copper

NATIONAL DEFENSE: Afghan National Army and Afghan Air Force, together numbering over 4,000,000 members.

INTERNATIONAL RELATIONS: Member of Interpol, the South Asian Association for Regional Cooperation, UNESCO and the United Nations. Presence of the Taliban has resulted in occupation by NATO peacekeeping forces; the USA is assisting in the country's rebuilding. Neighboring country Pakistan seeks to fence and mine its border against Afghanistan. Afghanistan and Russia have an uneasy history, and the country is currently in debt against Russia.

EXTRATERRESTRIAL RELATIONS: When the scientist Arize of the extradimensional "Mojoverse" escaped to Earth, he emerged in Afghanistan, where he wound up in Mujahedeen custody. Mojo dispatched an army of warriors to retrieve him, but they were repelled by the X-Men.

NONHUMAN POPULATION: None known.

DOMESTIC SUPERHUMANS: The mutant Dust (Sooraya Qadir) was kidnapped by slave traders, but rescued by the heroes Fantomex and Wolverine; as a result, she wound up becoming a student at the Xavier Institute, serving in the Hellions and "New X-Men" squads. The Mujahedeen were formerly aided by a Gnostic wizard who once used his powers to control Gargoyle (Isaac Christians) as a weapon against Russia.

PROMINENT CITIZENS: Dust's mother Mirah Qadir currently resides in the Maslak Refugee Camp.

SUPERHUMAN RESIDENTS: The mutant Sage (Tessa) was a bandit in the mountains until an encounter with Charles Xavier led to her becoming one of his X-Men. The Blazing Skull (Mark Todd) spent several years in voluntary confinement within Afghanistan, until he was recruited into the Invaders by the U.S.Agent (John Walker). The mutant villain Stryfe formerly held a base in the Khyber Pass, until its destruction while battling the Six Pack (G.W. Bridge, Cable, Grizzly (Theodore Wincester), Domino, Hammer (Eisenhower Canty), Garrison Kane).

DOMESTIC CRIME: The ritual murderers known as Thugees, members of the Cult of Kali, operated in Afghanistan in centuries past; they are now active as members of the Si-Fan crime cartel. Afghanistan is a major producer of heroin and opium, attracting many illicit activities, including corrupt CIA official Robert Bethel.

INTERNATIONAL CRIME: Afghanistan's uneasy history with Russia has led to a variety of assaults between the two nations. Superhuman Russian agents sent to combat Afghanistan's Mujahedeen include the cyborg Black Brigade; the expert sniper Dragunov (Dima Alekov Kaganitzky); stealth agent Skull-Jacket; SPACs, heavily armored one-man combat suits; and Warborgs, powerful cybernetic super-soldiers. Russian forces in Afghanistan also once encountered the Hulk (Bruce Banner) as he was entering Russian territory. The Canadian adventurer Puck (Eugene Judd) traveled through Afghanistan during his pre-costumed days. X-23 was sent on missions to Afghanistan while under the control of the Facility. The terrorist actions of the Taliban have led to occupation by a coalition of UN forces spearheaded by the USA, and heroes such as X-Statix have journeyed to Afghanistan to combat the Taliban. The Lord of Living Lightning supplied weapons to the Taliban until they were driven out by SHIELD's Howling Commandos unit.

HISTORY: Modern Afghanistan arose from the 1747 alliance of local tribes, and served as a buffer zone in the region between British- and Russian-occupied countries. Afghanistan became independent in 1919, and in 1978 established a communist regime, backed by the USSR. The communist government was fought by the local rebel Mujahideen, who had been supported by anti-communist states, and the USSR finally withdrew in 1989. In 1996, the terrorist Taliban came to power, and attained global notoriety for sheltering the Saudi Arabian Osama bin Laden (a former ally of the Mujahideen), architect of the September 11, 2001 terrorist attacks. The Taliban's government has been overthrown and a democracy installed, but the country remains volatile, and is still occupied by NATO peacekeeping forces.

Art by Clayton Henry

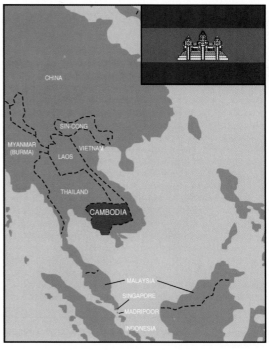

OFFICIAL NAME: Kingdom of Cambodia (Preah Reacheanachakr Kampuchea)

POPULATION: 13,881,000

CAPITAL CITY: Phnom Penh

PLACES OF INTEREST: Angkor Wat, Bokor Hill Station, Sihanoukville. Until recent years, the Temple of the Dragon's Breadth stood for centuries in the jungles of the Plateau Dus Bolovens; this structure housed a conduit to the Wellspring of All Things, extradimensional forces which can grant superhuman abilities.

GOVERNMENT: Multiparty democracy under a constitutional monarchy

MAJOR LANGUAGES: Khmer

MONETARY UNIT: Riel

MAJOR RESOURCES: Oil, gas, timber, gemstones

NATIONAL DEFENSE: Royal Cambodian Armed Forces, which include the Army, Navy and Air Force with membership numbering over 100,000.

INTERNATIONAL RELATIONS: Member of the Association of Southeast Asian Nations, United Nations and World Trade Organization, but have ongoing border disputes with Thailand and Vietnam. Were formerly administered by France from 1863 to 1953, currently have friendly relations. Have received major economic support from Australia, Japan and USA. Good working relations with the Avengers.

EXTRATERRESTRIAL RELATIONS: Invaded by the Axi-Tun Famine, one of the Four Horsemen of Apocalypse, who was ultimately driven out by the Fantastic Four. When Vietnam was briefly phased out of reality by Immortus, the heroes of Force Works observed the effects from Cambodia.

NONHUMAN POPULATION: None known.

DOMESTIC SUPERHUMANS: Formerly Angkor (Father Thommanom), a priest driven insane by exposure to ionic radiation from Wonder Man (Simon Williams); Angkor ultimately perished battling Wonder Man. The sorceress Tai led the forces of the Cult of the Dragon's Breadth, but was ultimately slain by Night Thrasher (Dwayne Taylor). Tai was the mother of the "Daughters of the Dragon," whose ranks included Miyami Chord; Tai's grandchildren included the superhumans Bloodstrike (Eric Conroy), Midnight's Fire, Silhouette, Silk Fever (Ming Li Ng) and Smiling Tiger (Conrad Mack).

PROMINENT CITIZENS: Pol Pot, former dictatorial leader of the Khmer Rogue, now deceased; Chin-Li Yan, a rice farmer; Phimeanakas, a Buddhist priest who relocated to Los Angeles.

SUPERHUMAN RESIDENTS: Alec Dalton, a British expatriate who served in his country's Super Soldiers, was briefly retired near the country's border with Thailand; he was ultimately recalled to duty by the U.S. Agent (John Walker).

DOMESTIC CRIME: The country has recurring issues of prostitution, forced labor, and drug smuggling. Cambodia is part of the so-called "Golden Triangle," named for the trade of opium. Local Khieu Dap was involved in the drug trade alongside former US soldier Cleve Gorman, but both were killed by the Punisher (Frank Castle). Another dealer, a superhuman calling himself "the Warlord" operated an opium trade out of the Golden Triangle until his operations were disrupted by Cloak (Tyrone Johnson) and Dagger (Tandy Bowen).

INTERNATIONAL CRIME: The country was once troubled by the Advisor, who used his powers and influence to inflame hostilities in the area. After the remains of Asteroid M crashed in the Kulen Hills, Magneto and the X-Men came to claim it, resulting in a clash between them and both the Avengers and Soviet Super Soldiers. The assassin Sabretooth (Victor Creed) has also been active in Cambodia.

HISTORY: The country of Cambodia arose from what had originally been the states of Funan and Chenla, becoming the Khmer Empire in the 9th century. Cambodia remained neutral during the neighboring Vietnam War, but in 1975 the communist Khmer Rouge came to power, led by Pol Pot; the resulting waves of genocide were not halted until 1979, and the Khmer Rogue continued operations within the country for years to come. During these years, the country was known as Kampuchea. The country is now led by a prime minister, appointed by the reigning monarch.

For centuries, a cult existed in the Temple of the Dragon's Breadth, carefully concealing the power of the Wellspring of All Things hidden inside, and devoting themselves to the ultimate goal of claiming the well's power. To that end, they instituted a program of selective breeding, until the finest of their women — "the Daughters of the Dragon" — were born. Led by Tai, they were offered as mates to the "Half-Fulls," a squad of US soldiers who discovered the temple by accident. Tai intended for the offspring of the Half-Fulls to act as a ritual sacrifice so that she could claim the wellspring's power. Ultimately Tai was slain by Night Thrasher, and both the temple and wellspring were destroyed.

TEMPLE OF DRAGON'S BREADTH

Art by Mark Bagley

CHINA

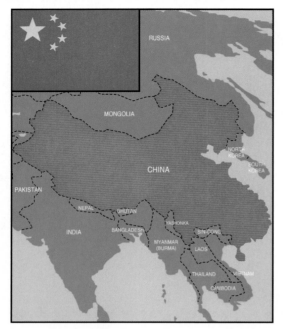

OFFICIAL NAME: People's Republic of China (Zhonghua Renmin Gongheguo)
POPULATION: 1,321,851,000
CAPITAL CITY: Beijing
PLACES OF INTEREST: Feng-Tu, Forbidden City (Beijing), Great Wall, House of Orchids, Mausoleum of the First Qin Emperor, Mogao Caves, Valley of the Dragons, Wellspring of All Things
GOVERNMENT: Communist state
MAJOR LANGUAGES: Mandarin (Putonghua), Yue (Cantonese), Wu (Shanghainese), Minbei (Fuzhou), Minnan (Hokkien-Taiwanese); in Hong Kong English is also widely spoken
MONETARY UNIT: Yuan (CMY), also known as renminbi (RMB); the Special Administrative Regions of Hong Kong and Macau use Hong Kong dollars and pataca respectively
MAJOR RESOURCES: Hydropower, natural gas, coal, iron, oil, plastics, optical and medical equipment; (Hong Kong) electronic equipment, banking
NATIONAL DEFENSE: People's Liberation Army (PLA): Ground Forces, Navy, Air Force, and Second Artillery Corps (strategic missile force); People's Armed Police (PAP); Reserve and Militia Forces
INTERNATIONAL RELATIONS: China is one of the United Nations Security Council's five permanent members. It is also a member of UNESCO, Interpol and World Health Organization. It has several outstanding territorial or boundary disputes with most of its neighbors.

China continues to occupy Tibet and Timbetpal; and remains technically at war with Taiwan (aka the Republic of China), which has yet to formally renounce its claim over the Chinese mainland. Lemurian Deviant forces led by Dulpus and Glomm have attacked China, as have rogue Atlanteans Fathom Five. In past years, China tried to discredit Captain America (Steve Rogers) with Cyril Lucas' propaganda movie and a Life Model Decoy imposter, secretly deposited the radioactive Missing Link and the robotic Thermal Man on American soil, and financed the building of robot dragon Zoga the Unthinkable to attack Japan. Stark International and Roxxon both have branches in Hong Kong, as does the Hellfire Club.

EXTRATERRESTRIAL RELATIONS: A Makluan spaceship crashed in ancient China; one Makluan, Axon-Karr, was slain soon after landing. Centuries later his skeleton was discovered by the Mandarin. Another Makluan, Fin Fang Foom, was placed into hibernation, intermittently reawakening to cause havoc. The remainder hid amongst humanity, assuming the identities Chen Hsu, Chi Chan, Wu Pong and others. Recently they revealed themselves, but were slain by the Mandarin and Iron Man (Tony Stark). Pursuing its opponents the Rajaki, the construct Ultimo crashed into the Valley of the Spirits during the 19th century, and was recently revived by the Mandarin. The Mandarin later used the extraterrestrial Heart of Darkness to transform China back to a pretechnological realm and empower his Avatars. The Kree Lunatic Legion attacked China's Shanxi province. Worldform, Inc. sent the robotic Ramrod to reshape Earth; it dispatched Changer robots to begin the process, one of which went to China.

NONHUMAN POPULATION: The Xian are the Chinese gods. Ho Ti of the Japanese Kami has worked as a Chinese government agent. Mr. Lao is an immortal dragon who advises the Atlas Foundation's Khan. The N'Garai cairn in Hong Kong potentially grants them access from their home dimension. The Gynosii are undead victims of Tsin Hark animated by his necromancy. The All-Devourer, fiercest of all Chinese demons, briefly returned from extradimensional banishment to battle Iron Man (Tony Stark).

DOMESTIC SUPERHUMANS: Many of China's superhumans have been drafted into the government's China Force: while Ox, Rabbit, Rat and Snake remain loyal, Dog, Horse, Monkey, She-Devil, Gold (Zhao Tang) and Silver (Jimon Tang) turned mercenary; the trainees Gold (as Auric) and Silver defected to Canada and joined Gamma Flight, but were killed soon after. Jade Dragon (Dei Guan), the Collective Man (Han, Chang, Lin, Sun, and Ho Tao-Yu) and Nuwa banded together as 3-Peace to end Chinese mutant persecution; the Chinese government reportedly slew any mutants with creative talents, such as instinctual thinkers, and imprisoned others in Feng-Tu. Imprisoned in an asylum, a superhuman patient's split personality emerged as the life-consuming Black Shadow and the altruistic White Shadow. Other mutants include: Lionmane (Lo Chien), who led a pirate attack on Madripoor; Red Army officer Ao Jun, who generates short-lived duplicates of himself; Paradigm, a techno-organic entity created when an unwilling technokinetic Hong Kong youth was injected with Phalanx material; the immortal Saul (Garbha-Hsien),

Art by Ben Oliver

finally slain by Selene; and twin brothers Kuan-Yin Xorn and Shen Xorn, both possessing immense energy powers — Kuan-Yin was imprisoned at Feng-Tu, while Shen was imprisoned in his home village, until both were freed by the X-Men. The Eight Immortals (Chuan Chung Li, Chang Kuo-Lao, Lu Dong-Pin, Tsao Guao-chiu, Tieh Guai Li, Han Hsian Tzu, Lan Tsai Ho, Ho Hsien Ku) assisted the X-Men containing Shen's out-of-control powers. Cybermancer (Suzi Endo) became a Hong Kong super hero after meeting herself from an alternate future. Radioactive Man (Dr. Chen Lu) mutated himself, and now works with the Thunderbolts. Energy thief Goth seemingly died battling the X-Men. Lady Chi is the Serpent Leader of the Triads, possessing a poisonous touch. Sorcerer Tsin Hark sought to banish technology, but Ghost Rider (Danny Ketch) stopped him. Pao Fu (Lian) was a young girl transformed into a Spirit of Vengeance. Taaru the Terrible ruled over a small village until the Valkyrie Brunnhilde defeated him. The Shadow Thief who fought Shang-Chi may have been stage magician Cho Lee. Scientist Dr. Sun's brain was transplanted into a robotic body. Immortal Yi Yang's Dragon Tong has branches worldwide; among its agents were Dragonfire in the 1920s and Ghost Tiger in the 1980s. The Mandarin gained power from Makluan rings and immense intellect; since his apparent death his son Temujin has taken over his father's organization, including his superpowered Avatars (Ancestor, Butterfly, Deluge, Foundry, Lich, Old Woman, Q'Wake, Sickle, Turmoil and Warfist).

PROMINENT CITIZENS: A thousand years ago the warrior monk Kan led rebels in overthrowing the Wizard Kings of Majaedong; his descendant is Dr. Strange's housekeeper, Wong. Nineteenth century brothers Yin and Yang emigrated to the USA, where they battled the Rawhide Kid. During World War II, guerilla Red Fox (Nuy) died assisting the US leatherneck

Raiders fighting the Japanese. WWII traitor General Jun Ching joined the Red Skull's Exiles, and a few years later, when the communists won China's civil war, instead of fleeing with fellow Nationalists to Taiwan, the Warlord (Huang Zhu) joined Hydra and carved out his own empire in the Savage Land. Disgraced General Tai Chen stirred up unrest in the USA as the Sons of the Serpent's Supreme Serpent. China's numerous spies include: Mei-Toy, who assisted Namor in the 1940s against Japan's Dr. Nichi; Shareen, who sought to retrieve the stolen Golden Dragon; Pail, who in retirement assisted former foe Nick Fury against Hydra, but was slain by his turncoat son Weng; and Hu Chen, Colonel Wai Ling and Dr. Chao Yen, who tortured the captive Black Widow (Natasha Romanova). Shang-Chi, the son of Fu Manchu, has worked for MI-6; his half-brother, Moving Shadow, remained loyal to their father, but was slain for failing him. Leiko Wu is a member of Freelance Restorations and Shang-Chi's girlfriend. Chinese mercenaries include: Teng Yun-Suan, Rick Mason's sifu; Cat (Shen Kui), Shadow Slasher (Xi-shan Hao), Skullcrusher (Chao Sima), Kogar (Li-Peng Kai), and Harmony Killdragon. Killdragon's mentor Master Kee fled to America with the orphaned infant Lin Sun, where she grew up to join the Sons of the Tiger. Criminals include: Wild Tiger (Deng Ling-Xiao), who headed Cursed Lotus' drug operations in Hong Kong, and Mandarin agent Madame Macabre and her servant Gogo. Neurological research scientist Dr. Su Yin assisted Tony Stark recovering from spinal injuries. Yellow Claw chose Olympic athlete and scientist Shu Han to be his bride. Wai Chee Yee and Sen Yu are sorcerous associates of Dr. Strange. Seven unidentified sorcerers banished the demon All-Devourer centuries ago; when it returned, one of their descendants, Soo Lin Chu banished it again. When the Mandarin temporarily regressed China to a pretechnological state, ex-politician Chu Lo Yan set himself up as the Warlord Chu. Ambassador General Ping Su was sent to address the UN, but was taken hostage by Dr. Octopus; Leiko Wu's brother David is also a Chinese ambassador. Suwan is the Yellow Claw's niece, and lover of SHIELD agent Jimmy Woo. Juno, an agent of Dr. Sun, managed to temporarily slay Dracula. Ma Yung-Chen is a top Hong Kong martial artist once forced to work for the Yellow Claw.

SUPERHUMAN RESIDENTS: Prester John visited China during his travels, many centuries ago. The sorcerer Cagliostro learned the secrets of the Soul-Takers in China at the start of the 20th century. Adam Destine and Logan (James Howlett) were both active in 1920s China. US Marine John Kowalski was stationed in Ch'Ang-Sha in the 1920s; after his death in 1939, his ghost briefly inhabited Japanese Colonel Sessue Takeda, in charge of the occupying forces. Domino (Neena Thurman) and Risque (Gloria Dolores Munoz) were in X-Corporation's Hong Kong office. African Si-Fan assassin Midnight Sun (M'Nai) grew up in China, training alongside Shang-Chi. The Ru'Tai Pilgrimm hid in China as Colonel Wei.

DOMESTIC CRIME: Hong Kong is home to numerous Tongs (Chinese crime families), and formerly crimelord Lotus Newmark. The Four Winds (East, West, North and South) are a dynasty of assassins from Ningxia Hui. Snakeroot was a ninja cult originally based in Hong Kong.

INTERNATIONAL CRIME: China is a shipping point for much of

Southeast Asia's heroin, and home of secret societies such as the Council of Nine, who plot world domination. Known in the West as the Yellow Claw, Plan Tzu led a worldwide secret society dedicated to perpetuating the Mongol Empire, with agents including biochemist Mai-Pan and scientist William Liu; its most recent incarnation, the Atlas Foundation, is now run by his successor Jimmy Woo. Heading another insidious society, the Celestial Order of the Si-Fan, the supposedly immortal Fu Manchu has clashed repeatedly with Britain's MI-6. Both his son Shang-Chi and daughter Fah Lo Suee have turned against him, though Fah Lo Suee returned to crime, working under the alias Cursed Lotus and distributing drugs across China. Notable Si-Fan operatives include ancient warrior Shaka Kharn, Shadow Stalker, and the Cyber-Ninjas (including Bludgeon, Fist and Katana). The poorly policed South China Sea has served as a base for many pirates and terrorists, including Madame Hydra Six, the Pacific Pirates recruited by Future Man and Madame Death, assassin and former MI-6 operative Mordillo (Simon Bretner), Mordillo's servant Brynocki, munitions magnate Damon Dran, international assassin Arcade, and the Yellow Claw. Brian Argus, founder of the Terror Alliance, plotted mass poisonings from an island near Hong Kong, until Shang-Chi stopped him. The half-Chinese mutant Marcus Tsang ran a crime empire that spanned China, India and Russia. China's top martial artists trained the Russian assassin Ghost-Maker (Grigori Sovchenko). Kang once sent a Macrobot, containing an imprisoned Iron Man, to slay the Chinese heads of state. John Sublime arranged for

Chinese mutants imprisoned at Feng-Tu to be shipped overseas to be harvested for their organs; jailer Ao Jun alleged that this was condoned by the government, as a way of disposing of their unwanted mutant population. Hong Kong-based Shing Fu Xue was a member of the Unity, which sought to monopolise the secrets of a Laos temple, and was prepared to murder to do so. Fong Lee was one of the Council Supreme, a union of cult leaders, but was slain when he failed to acknowledge Damballah as his master. Lady Chi's Triad has exerted its influence as far afield as New York, where it battled Araña. Emil Vachon became one of Hong Kong's most powerful crimelords before being slain by Colleen Wing. The Bane shipped poached African ivory through Hong Kong's House of Orchids.

HISTORY: One of Earth's earliest known civilizations, with a recorded history nearly 5000 years old, China's dynasties go as far back as the 21st century BC's Xia Dynasty. In 221 BC Qin Shi Huang unified much of China under his rule, becoming the first emperor of the Qin Dynasty; during his rule, construction began on a 3000-mile-long wall, a precursor to the modern Great Wall, but his dynasty fell with his death, replaced by the Han dynasty, which lasted until 220 AD. Four centuries of fragmented warlord rule followed, until the Sui dynasty reunified China in 589 AD. Its successor, the Tang Dynasty (618-907 AD) is regarded as a cultural high point in Chinese civilization; around the start of this era a group of Makluans landed in China, most eventually hiding amongst the population. In 1279, possibly with the assistance of the dragon Mr. Lao, Mongolian ruler Kublai Khan conquered the Song Dynasty, which followed Tang, establishing the Yuan Dynasty, the first time China had been ruled by outsiders. The Ming Dynasty overthrew the foreign invaders in 1368, only to fall in turn in 1644 to Manchu invaders from the north; they established China's last Dynasty, Qing, which ruled until 1911. Western trade in the 18th century initially proved favorable to China, with their porcelain, silk and tea in demand, while they wanted little from the Westerners; however the British found a market importing Indian cotton and opium, the latter of which was banned by Imperial decree. Trying to stop the opium trade, in 1839 commissioner Lin Zexu detained all foreigners in Guangzhou and destroyed over 2000 chests of opium; in retaliation Britain declared war, defeating China within 3 years, forcing them to give trade concessions and sign over Hong Kong for the next 150 years. Foreign influence and the weakening Qing rule contributed to increasing unrest, culminating in Sun Yat-sen's Republican Revolution of 1911. Japanese territorial incursions swiftly weakened the Nationalist government, indirectly encouraging the rise of a Communist opposition led by Mao Zedong, and in 1949 a Civil War ended with the Nationalists fleeing to Taiwan and the Communists in power. For decades the Communists maintained a strict control on every aspect of Chinese life, ruthlessly crushing any dissent. Recently China narrowly avoided extinction, when the god Marduk's plan to slay the entire population through manipulation of the Collective Man's powers was thwarted by the V-Battalion.

OFFICIAL NAME: Republic of India (Bharat Ganarajya)
POPULATION: 1,129,866,000
CAPITAL CITY: New Delhi
PLACES OF INTEREST: Taj Mahal, Agra Fort, Golden Temple of Amritsar, Vajrasana in Bodh Gaya, Mahakaleshwar Temple, Red Fort of Delhi, Temple of Light in Lashi
GOVERNMENT: Democratic federal republic
MAJOR LANGUAGES: Hindi; 14 other official languages including Bengali, Telugu, Marathi, Tamil, Urdu, Gujarati, Malayalam, Kannada, Oriya, Punjabi, Assamese, Kashmiri, Sindhi, and Sanskrit. English is widely spoken; Hindustani is common in northern India.
MONETARY UNIT: Indian rupee
MAJOR RESOURCES: Coal, manufactured goods, gems, chemicals.
NATIONAL DEFENSE: Indian Armed Forces
INTERNATIONAL RELATIONS: India belongs to the United Nations, UNESCO, World Health Organization and Interpol. India has cooperated with the Avengers. X-Corporation maintained a Mumbai branch. Relations between India and Pakistan remain tense. China and India have recently made moves to resolve boundary disputes, notably over Kashmir.
EXTRATERRESTRIAL RELATIONS: Prince Wayfinder led a group of disparate aliens, including Agni, Kali, Maya and Yama, in founding a colony in the Indus Valley around 1 million BC, which was subsequently destroyed by Whirldemons. Thousands of years ago the Shining Ones visited, gradually dying out; the Architect is their only survivor. AIM's Indian branch studied a captured Technarch embryo until Deadpool (Wade Wilson) stole it. The Grandmaster (En Dwi Gast) sent Dr. Spectrum (the Skrull Krimonn) to battle Iron Man (Tony Stark) at the Taj Mahal. When New Delhi was briefly transported into the realm of the Brotherhood of the Ankh, the Avenger Triathlon (Delroy Garrett) helped maintain order.
NONHUMAN POPULATION: The Daevas (Hindu gods) watch over India. Demonic Whirldemons were prevalent in prehistoric India. When Eternity took human form, one aspect became the Indian Sai Anand.
DOMESTIC SUPERHUMANS: Indian mutants prior to "M-Day" included Haven (Radha Dastoor) and her brother Monsoon (Aloba Dastoor), who fought X-Factor; Indra (Paras Gavaskar) of Xavier Institute's Alpha Squadron; the X-Men's Thunderbird (Neal Shaara); the Acolyte Vindaloo (Venkat Katragadda); and information broker Black Box (Garabed Bashur). Non-mutant Indian superhumans include: Serpent, a shapeshifter who fought Marvel Boy (Bob Grayson); Calculus (Jawaharal Patel) of the Young Gods; the brothers "Jonathan Tremont," Lord Templar and Pagan, of the Triune Understanding; Agni (Dr. Araman Nila), a radiation scientist transformed by the Nila Pile; Karima Shapandar, turned into an Omega Sentinel; and Star Thief (Ditmal Pirvat), who fought the New Warriors. The sorceress Topaz may also be Indian. Indian vampires have included Adri Nital; Taj, Adri's father, became a vampire hunter, but was eventually turned too.
PROMINENT CITIZENS: Indian mystics include Ghazandi, who trained the trumpeter Trago; Yogi Dakor of the Terrible Trio; High Priest of Kâli Raga-Shah; Vishnu Dass, Isaac Christians' teacher; and Swami Rihva, who battled the Werewolf (Jack Russell). 1870s Indian rebel, the Mahdi, sought power from the gods to drive out the British; because he ordered rather than asking, the Daevas gave him illusionary weapons, and he died in battle. Rajah (Kabir Mahadevu) is a member of the Circus of Crime. Dr. Niral Chandra was a scientist for the sinister Damocles Foundation. Dr. Kavita Rao was a Benetech geneticist who developed a means to neutralize mutant powers.
SUPERHUMAN RESIDENTS: India's mystical reputation has drawn many truth-seekers there, including the sorcerer Taboo; his teacher, Dr. Glitternight; Isaac Christians (Gargoyle) in the 1920s; Nathan Tyler, who became the Lord of Light and founded his own cult; Vincent Trago, who learned to control people through music; and the Sorcerer (Jonathan East), who later built the Synthetic Man. Centuries ago Apocalypse (En Sabah Nur) spent time in India under the name Kali-Ma, and in 1792 Gideon Smith (Forever Man) learned of his perpetual reincarnation while visiting New Delhi. For a while Master Khan's Ninja

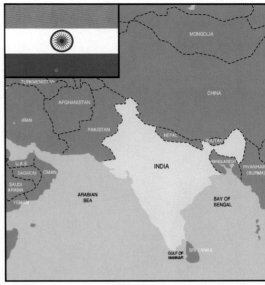

was based in India, as was the Black Lama (King Jerold) and his disciple Raga (George Friedrich), and X-Corporation members Feral (Maria Callasantos), Sunfire (Shiro Yoshida), Thornn (Lucia Callasantos) and Warpath (James Proudstar).
DOMESTIC CRIME: India's crime rate is low, but religious feuds continue between Muslims and Hindu communities. The banned Cult of Kâli remains disturbingly active, despite the Indian government hiring the assassin Deathtoll (Saint Van Sant) to wipe them out. Meltdown and Dr. Neutron plotted to send the Tarapur nuclear plant into meltdown, but were thwarted by Wolverine (James Howlett) and Havok (Alex Summers).
INTERNATIONAL CRIME: India supplies much of the world's opium to various criminal groups. AIM is one of many criminal organizations with Indian branches. Gorilla-Man (Arthur Nagan) of the Headmen plotted to shrink New Delhi's population, but was stopped by the Defenders. The assassin Marcus Tsang's criminal empire encompassed India.
HISTORY: The civilization that grew from the Indus valley is one of the world's oldest; following Prince Wayfinder's city around 1 million BC, permanent human settlements arose by 9000 BC. Approximately 1500 BC Aryan tribes began migrating in, merging with the indigenous inhabitants, and numerous "Great Kingdoms" (Mahajanapadas) formed. Around 321 BC, Chandragupta Maurya founded the Maurya Empire, uniting much of the subcontinent, though it fractured again a few centuries later. Northern India was unified again in the 4th century AD by the Gupta Dynasty, a period later recognized as India's intellectual and cultural Golden Age. From the 8th century Turks and Afghans invaded from the north, bringing the Islamic faith with them. In 1526 the Timurid B bur invaded, establishing the Mughal Dynasty, which ruled most of the subcontinent by 1600. In 1617 the Mughal emperor Jahangir gave the British East India Company permission to trade; regional rulers became increasingly dependent on the Company's financial and military backing. By 1850, while many native princes nominally still ruled, the Company had actual control of most of India. The aftermath of the 1857 Indian Rebellion saw the British government dissolve the Company, administering Indian regions either directly or through treaties with local rulers. Starting in 1920, Mohandas K. Gandhi led a growing, nonviolent campaign for colonial rule to end, eventually winning independence in 1947, though enmity between Hindus and Muslims saw the British partition off Muslim majority areas as separate countries, eventually known as Bangladesh and Pakistan. Racial and religious divides continue to cause problems, with territorial disputes leading to four wars with Pakistan, in 1947, 1965, 1971 and 1999. India became a nuclear power in 1974, ignoring US disapproval; modern day India has the potential to be an economic world power, if it can first overcome the internal problems facing it.

JAPAN

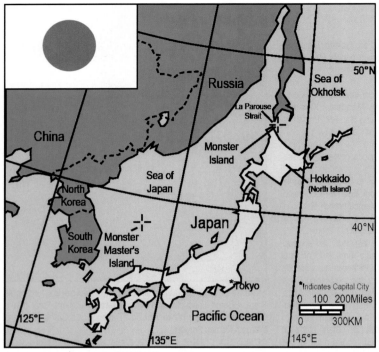

OFFICIAL NAME: Japan (Nihon/Nippon)

POPULATION: 127,433,000

CAPITAL CITY: Tokyo

PLACES OF INTEREST: Cool World Amusement Park, Diet Building (Tokyo), the Arena (Tokyo), Tokyo Giant Monster Museum & Expo Center (Tokyo), Fortress Yashida (Agrashima), Monster Island, Monster Master's Island (within the Liancourt Rocks, Sea of Japan)

GOVERNMENT: Constitutional monarchy with parliamentary government

MAJOR LANGUAGES: Japanese

MONETARY UNIT: Yen

MAJOR RESOURCES: Transport equipment, motor vehicles, semiconductors, electrical machinery, chemicals

NATIONAL DEFENSE: Japanese Defense Agency (JDA)

INTERNATIONAL RELATIONS: Japan holds membership in the United Nations, UNESCO, Organization for Economic Co-operation and Development (OECD), the International Criminal Court (ICC), and Interpol, and has cooperated with Alpha Flight, MI-6, and SHIELD.

EXTRATERRESTRIAL RELATIONS: Approximately 175,000 years ago, members of the Myndai race (the "Followers of Darkness") arrived on Earth and sought to conquer it. They were pursued by members of the Lumina race (the "Followers of Light"), who waged a great war against the Myndai to prevent their conquest. When the Myndai placed themselves in suspended animation so they could conquer Earth in the future, the Lumina created a sanctuary near Japan's Mount Fujimoto and did the same so they could oppose the Myndai upon their return. More recently, Tokyo was decimated by Titannus, a genetically-enhanced Skrull soldier, although Dr. Strange repaired the damage after the alien's defeat.

NONHUMAN POPULATION: Inhabitants of Monster Island; Spider-People; Yiki Onna vampires; Kinitsu-kami; earthbound shinma; tengu

DOMESTIC SUPERHUMANS: The mutant Silver Samurai (Kenuichio Harada) of Clan Yashida is a reformed Yakuza crimelord who was recently hired as the captain of the prime minister's personal security cadre. Otomo is the super-powered mutant descendant of a Japanese scientist who developed a Super Soldier serum in the final days of World War II. Leader of the cybernetic Reavers, Lady Deathstrike (Yuriko Oyama) is the villainous cyborg daughter of the deceased criminal Lord Dark Wind (Professor Kenji Oyama) of Oyama Heavy Industries, who developed the Adamantium-to-bone bonding process. The plasma-powered mutant Sunfire (Shiro Yoshida) once served as Japan's official National Protector until losing his legs to Lady Deathstrike and having them restored by Apocalypse. Big Hero 6 (Baymax, Ebon Samurai, GoGo Tomago, Hiro, Honey Lemon, Sunpyre) is Japan's official super-hero team. Surge (Noriko "Nori" Ashida) is an electricity-absorbing mutant currently attending the Xavier Institute. The vigilante Go-Devil (Fumimaro Ishimori) is an indigenous psionic adept who can actualize the potential energy of his body's molecules for a variety of effects, including emitting explosive energy discharges and converting his body into energy. Gorgon (Tomi Shishido) was a mutant terrorist formerly allied with the Dawn of the White Light and the Hand who briefly usurped control of Hydra before being destroyed by Wolverine. Harvest (Chi Lo) is a human mutate with telepathic control over all forms of vegetation who joined the Young Gods, followers of the Celestials. Lady Lotus is a Japanese psychic who battled the Invaders during WWII as part of the Super-Axis. Base (Hiro Sokuto) of Genetix and Tattoo (Tudo Sokuto) of Tektos are mutant brothers who worked as Yakuza drug runners before they were captured and forced into service by London's Gena-Sys Labs; Steel Vengeance and Steel Wind are sisters who were transformed into motorcycle-riding cyborgs and sent to kill Ghost Rider. The mutant White Ninja is an assassin employed by the Tosei-kai Yakuza clan; Mana and Hana Yanowa are Miko priestesses who served the Shoshei Order, although Hana was corrupted by the shinma-worshipping Clan Ashura and possessed by the demon Ryuki. Decay (Yoshiro Hachiman) was an efficiency expert for Stark/Fujikawa who became the human avatar of Valtorr. Samurai Steel (Yoshida Asano) is a robotics expert and CEO of Asano Robotics who developed a robotic suit of armor to gain vengeance on the U.S. for dropping the atomic bomb during WWII, but he was defeated by Iron Man. Colonel Okada is a member of the JDA who wears a high-tech suit of body armor in combat. Deadline (Dr. Kishi Oramosha) was once a prominent businessman and lecturer at Tokyo University who attempted to unite the nations of the world by threatening to destroy several cities with his solar heat ray before being defeated by Sunfire. Seiji Honda is a young telekinetic mutant able to animate inanimate objects, such as toys.

PROMINENT CITIZENS: Dr. Tamara Hashioka and Dr. Yuriko Takiguchi are scientists specializing in kaiju activity who designed the Behemoth IV Helicarrier and Red Ronin robot; Takashei Otomo is the CEO of Otomocorp/Tempora Corporation, specializing in space exploration, colonization, and terraforming (and formerly affiliated with the Warheads, a team of dimension-hopping agents of the United Kingdom's Mys-Tech Corporation). Kono Sanada is a former sumo wrestler who became an assassin for US munitions magnate Damon Dran. The Oyakata is a former champion sumo wrestler who briefly operated as an assassin for the Yamaguchi-gumi Yakuza clan. Monster Master (Toru Tarakoto) is a former Fujiyama Industries research scientist based on a barren island in the Sea of Japan who sought to eliminate American influence by creating a destructive dragon robot. Bando Suboro is a villager of Jasmine Falls who trained former samurai and ninja (including Wolverine) in the way of peace. Inoshiro N. Kondo is the corrupt CEO of Ranma Inc. who sold his soul to the shinma demon Miyu in exchange for Element Z, a substance that enabled him to transmute his body into almost any substance. The Samurai Squadron was an elite 6-man division of the Imperial Japanese Army under the command of Sgt. Joe Morita during WWII.

Matsu'o Tsurayaba is the former crimelord responsible for the death of Wolverine's fiancée Mariko Yashida. Yukio is a former assassin for Clan Yashida who currently cares for Wolverine's adopted daughter Amiko Kobayashi. Ryoko Oshiba is an agent of the Japanese Department of Supernatural Sciences (JDSS) who assisted in Kitty Pryde's defeat of the Path of Destiny. Dr. Ishiro Yamane was the original curator of the Tokyo Giant Monster Museum & Expo Center who, prior to being killed by the Apocalypse Beast, secretly belonged to a cult worshipping the Beast.

SUPERHUMAN RESIDENTS: Deadpool (Wade Wilson) briefly resided in Japan while training as a sumo wrestler and working as a Yakuza assassin. Wolverine (James Howlett) spent many years training in Japan under Ogun. The mutants Storm (Ororo Munroe), Strong Guy (Guido Carosella), Callisto, and Masque resided in Japan while participating in the international mutant fighting facility known as the Arena. Elektra Natchios trained in Japan as both a member of the Chaste and the Hand, and Echo (Maya Lopez) was dispatched to Japan by the Avengers in the guise of "Ronin" to hamper the spread of organized crime.

DOMESTIC CRIME: The Yakuza and their affiliated groups (Aizukotetsu-kai, Blue Monkey Gang, Clan Dai-Kumo, Clan Orii, Clan Tatsu, Clan Yashida, Double Jade Clan, Dragon Clan, Ichiwa-kai, Inagawa-kai, Kanto-kai, Red Dragon Clan, Shitei-otaku, Sumiyoshi-kai, Tosei-kai, and Yamaguchi-gumi) are responsible for most of Japan's organized crime, drug trafficking, prostitution, and smuggling. The Path of Destiny, a cult formerly led by Ogun but currently led by Nao (who follows the deceased Ogun's journals), are also involved in many domestic crimes. Although the Japanese cell of the Brotherhood of Mutants was nearly wiped out by X-Statix, a more radical Dawn of the White Light mutant cult remains operational.

INTERNATIONAL CRIME: Japan has several ongoing territorial disputes with its neighbors. Although Mole Man is loosely recognized by the UN as ruler of the underground civilization of Subterranea, the sovereignty of Monster Island remains in dispute (the JDA maintains an outpost on the island to keep track of its mutate inhabitants). The Hand (Hiromotsu, Iron Monk, Izanama, Kirigi, Kuroyama, Pain, Shadow, Thought, others) and the Snakeroot (Bisento, Budo, Daito, Doka, Enteki, Feruze, Genkotsu, Osamo, Tekagi) are ancient clans of mystic ninja dedicated to serving the demonic Beast's dark agenda and wanted in several countries for various criminal activities. Various members of the Yakuza are also wanted for international drug trafficking and other transnational organized crime activities.

HISTORY: Billions of years ago, after many of the demonic Elder Gods were purged from Earth by the Demogorge, the pantheon of gods known as the Amatsu-kami originated in the otherdimensional realm known as Ama. Led by Izanagi, the progenitor and ruler of the pantheon, the Amatsu-kami traveled to Earth via the dimensional nexus known as Ama-No-Hashidate (the "Bridge of Heaven," which exists near Miyazu Bay in northern Kyoto Prefecture), and came to be worshipped by the native inhabitants of Japan as early as 10,000 BC during the Jamon period. Although the dimensional nexus between Ama and Earth was eventually severed, Izanagi's descendants still influenced the lives of the Japanese mortals. Other kami (divine spirits) also inhabited Earth during this period, including the Kinitsu-kami (guardian spirits and gods of the land), shinma (demons) who originated in Yomi (the Japanese underworld), and tengu (demon-like sprits with avian characteristics).

After the offshoot of humanity known as the Deviant race was forced underground by the Celestial Second Host approximately 20,000 years ago, they created the underground civilization of Subterranea, where they genetically engineered the Moloid race to act as their docile servants, as well as many monstrous mutates to participate in their conquests and sports. Through a series of caverns, Subterranea is linked to Monster Island, a land mass between the Sea of Japan and Sea of Okhotsk. When the Deviants abandoned their creations, many of the mutates began to roam free on Monster Island. In the mid-20th century, the Mole Man (Harvey Rupert Elder) washed ashore on Monster Island and located Subterranea, mastering the abandoned Deviant technology and becoming master of the mutates.

Thousands of years ago, the Spider-People (a race of humanoid arachnids descended from the spider-god Omm) built the Temple of the Spider in the subterranean caverns beneath the Hidaka Mountains (located in modern-day Hokkaidō Prefecture). During the Yayoi period (300 B.C. – 250 A.D.), many of Japan's Yamato tribes began organizing into larger political entities. It was during this period of political upheaval that guerrilla warfare tactics of subversive ninja clans began to emerge. The affiliated ninja clans known as the Hand and the Snakeroot Clan emerged sometime in the 10th century, worshiping the demon known as "the Beast" and learning to resurrect their fallen members as undead assassins. Soon after, mystic warriors formed the Chaste, a clan dedicated to preventing the spread of the Hand's influence. The power of the Imperial court gradually waned as the influence of the samurai (provincial military aristocracy) grew stronger; and, in 1185, the Minamoto family overthrew the government and established Japan's first shogunate military government, relegating the emperor to a figurehead.

By the mid-15th century, Japan descended into a century of civil war, with rival warlords battling for dominance. During this time, the immortal warrior Black Axe engaged in several of the battles and opposed the Hand. The demon blacksmith Muramasa forged the Black Blade with a portion of his own dark soul, causing all who possess it to be overcome

Art by Seth Fisher

bombing of Pearl Harbor, the US Marines deployed Captain Simon Savage and his Leatherneck Raiders to lead attacks against Japanese forces in the Pacific, bringing them into conflict with Colonel Sakata and the Samurai Squad. Japan also spent spies to infiltrate American society, but they were opposed on the American West Coast by the costumed Blue Blade.

Baron von Strucker contacted a secret society within the Japanese underworld (which included Hand members) and joined their ranks, convincing them to adopt the name "Hydra" for their organization. Although a Japanese national was selected as the first "Supreme Hydra," Baron von Strucker soon killed him and relocated Hydra's base of power to a remote island just north of Australia. In August 1945, the USA dropped atomic bombs on Hiroshima and Nagasaki, prompting Japan to surrender days later. Allied occupation forces led by the USA took control of Japan in September 1945. The emperor was relegated to a purely symbolic status and a true parliamentary government was established. In 1954, Japan entered a period where they sustained seemingly random attacks by the monstrous mutate inhabitants of Monster Island (known as "kaiju") for decades. The Japanese government responded with construction of the giant mechanical Otetsukun to serve as the country's defense against the increasingly frequent kaiju attacks. The government also began experimenting with megalosaurus DNA, which was found to be very versatile, while the Japanese Defense Agency spent billions on bio-research projects to help combat the kaiju (the only military research Japan was allowed to conduct following WWII). Approximately 13 years ago, with the debut of the Fantastic Four and their subsequent adventure on Monster Island, the kaiju attacks came to an end, prompting the Japanese people to hail the team as heroes who brought an end to the "Age of Monsters."

When the kaiju known as Godzilla resurfaced after years of inactivity, the 102-foot-tall Red Ronin robot was designed by Yuriko Takiguchi and Tamara Hashioka and constructed by Stark International, and a special SHIELD task force known as the "Godzilla Squad" was assembled to stop the monster. Shortly after, the terrorist Moses Magnum threatened to use his amplified powers to sink Japan if the prime minister did not recognize him as the nation's sole ruler; but he was defeated by Sunfire and the X-Men. Seeing the success of other national super-teams, the Japanese government formed a top-secret consortium of politicians and business entities known as the Giri to recruit and train potential superhuman operatives for Big Hero 6. The new team succeeded in its first mission against the Everwraith. Later, one faction of the Hand fell under the control of child assassin Junzo Muto, who planned a ritual that would cause the extradimensional realm of K'un-Lun to physically manifest in the place of Tokyo so that the Hand could conquer it and rule the world. Iron Fist (Danny Rand) inadvertently triggered the process, which caused K'un-Lun to start manifesting in the Earth dimension upon his arrival in Japan, but the process was reversed upon Iron Fist's death (although he was immediately resurrected via K'un-Lunian magic).

Many of Japan's Yakuza clans were briefly taken over by Mongolia's powerful Clan Kaishek crime family, but Clan Kaishek's dominance ended after several of its own members killed each other and the remaining family member was defeated by Wolverine, Silver Samurai, and Yukio. Later, the mutant Silver Samurai (Kenuichio Harada), a former Yakuza-affiliated crimelord who had since abandoned his criminal ways, had his memories regressed by Lady Deathstrike (Yuriko Oyama), causing him to again aspire to control the Japanese criminal underworld. After killing many rival Yakuza bosses, Silver Samurai, calling himself the "Silver Shogun," announced his plan to unite Tokyo's Yakuza gangs under his rule (the "Yashida-kai"), but his plans were thwarted by Sunfire and Rogue. The rehabilitated Silver Samurai was next briefly kidnapped by rogue SHIELD elements and incarcerated at the Raft super-prison in New York, but he escaped and returned to Japan, where he became the captain of the prime minister's personal security cadre.

with unquenchable bloodlust. One faction of the Hand, believing they could better serve the Beast, splintered into a separate cult known as the True Believers and relocated to Korea. Meanwhile, the Shoshei Order, led by a lineage of Miko priestesses of the Shinto religion, was formed to protect Japan from demons, curses, and other mystic threats. One such demon, Kao-Goto Suru (later known as the "Face Thief"), crossed the dimensional barrier between Yomi and Earth and wrecked havoc in Japan; he was eventually defeated by a group of samurai empowered by the Amatsu-kami, and these samurai subsequently founded the Masters of Silence to prevent any similar disturbances. Japan's civil wars were eventually brought to an end by three successive warlords: Oda Nobunaga, Hideyoshi, and Tokugawa Ieyasu.

The Hand saw resurgence in 1588, dedicating itself to purging Japan of all foreign influence, which prompted the newly formed Japanese government to investigate the clan's activities. In 1603, Tokugawa Ieyasu relocated Japan's capital to Edo (modern-day Tokyo) and forced the isolation of Japan from virtually all outside influence. Clan Ashura, a demon-worshipping group opposed to the Shoshei Order, convinced Hana, a disillusioned Shosei priestess, to join their cause and merge with the demon Ryuki in an attempt to open a gateway between Yomi and Earth. Hana was defeated when her sister Mana (who served as head Shoshei priestess) trapped her soul within a jeweled necklace (the Mark of Mana). In 1868, Japan's shogunate government ended with the accession of the Meiji Emperor. Shortly after, the underworld faction known as the "Path of Destiny" formed, dedicated to maintaining traditional Japanese values while incorporating Western philosophies to advance their position in the underworld. In the 1890s, as Japan began to industrialize and urbanize, modern-day Yakuza gangs began to emerge in Japan's cities, peddling violence for profit. Ancient familial clans, such as Clan Yashida, also began taking part in criminal enterprises associated with the Yakuza.

Near the turn of the 20th century, Japan became an imperialist power, defeating China in the Sino-Japanese War in 1895 and Russia in the Russo-Japanese War in 1905. With Japan's ultra-nationalists gaining political influence, plans were made to unite all of Asia under Japanese control, starting with the invasion and military takeover of eastern China in 1937. By 1940, Japan entered into the Tripartite Alliance with Italy and Nazi Germany. When the USA entered WWII following the Japanese

Monster Island
Soya Kaikyo (La Parouse Strait), Sea of Okhotsk, Northern Pacific Ocean

Coral	Caldera	Monster	Caldera	Monster	Inter-Governmental
Reefs	(612 Ft, msl, 1967)	Volcano	(978 Ft. msl,1948)	Monastery	Watch Station

Holy Crow Island

One Mile

Monster Lagoon

Temple of
Monsters

Mystic
Cave

Overview of Monster Island Anomaly and legendary
Temple of Monsters. Monster Island is located between
northern Japan and Kuril Islands (disputed between
Russia and Japan), occupied by Russia. Travel to this
island is banned to all U. S. citizens by The State
Department. The United Nations maintains an Inter-
Governmental Watch Station for cryptozoological
observations.
Image from the personal collection of Captain Benjamin Grimm, USAF, ret.

Japan's "Monster Island" should not be confused
with the "Isla De Los Monstruos (Monster Isle)"
of the Caribbean Sea

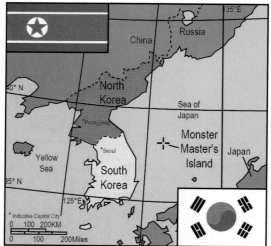

OFFICIAL NAME: (North) Democratic People's Republic of Korea (Choson Minjujuui Inmin Konghwaguk); (South) Republic of Korea (Daehan Minguk)

POPULATION: (North) 23,113,000 (South) 48,846,000

CAPITAL CITY: (North) Pyongyang (South) Seoul

PLACES OF INTEREST: (North) Baekdu Mountain (South) Gyeongju, Jeju Island, Kumgangsan, Temple of Cyttorak

GOVERNMENT: (North) Communist state one-man dictatorship (South) Republic

MAJOR LANGUAGES: Korean

MONETARY UNIT: (North) North Korean won (South) South Korean won

MAJOR RESOURCES: (North) rice, corn, potatoes, soybeans, cattle, pigs, pork, eggs, military products, machinery, electric power, chemicals, mining, coal, iron ore, limestone, magnesite, graphite, copper, zinc, lead, precious metals, metallurgy, textiles, merchant marine and food processing. (South) rice, root crops, barley, vegetables, fruit, cattle, pigs, poultry, milk, eggs, fish, electronics, telecommunications, automobile production, chemicals, shipbuilding, merchant marine and steel manufacturing.

NATIONAL DEFENSE: (North) The People's Army, comprising the Ground Force, Naval Force, Air Force and Civil Securities Force, numbering 1,210,000 active members. (South) Republic of Korea Army, Navy, Air Force and Marine Corps, numbering 680,000 active members.

INTERNATIONAL RELATIONS: (North) member of UNESCO and the United Nations. Has island sovereignty disputes with China, separated from South Korea by Demilitarized Zone. (South) member of the Association of Southeast Asian Nations, East Asia Summit, UNESCO, the United Nations and the World Trade Organization. Has island sovereignty dispute with Japan, separated from North Korea by Demilitarized Zone.

EXTRATERRESTRIAL RELATIONS: The Temple of Cyttorak has seen many manifestations of the extradimensional demon Cyttorak, including his demonic guardian Xorak.

NONHUMAN POPULATION: In the 16th century, Korea was terrorized by an immense dragon called the Wani.

DOMESTIC SUPERHUMANS: (South) The mutant Scrambler (Kim Il Sung) left Korea to become one of Mr. Sinister's Marauders. Another mutant, Chance, immigrated to the USA at a young age and became part of the Fallen Angels gang. The demon Cyttorak has had a variety of servants take up the mantle of the Juggernaut at his temple, including Jin Taiko, who was killed by his successor Cain Marko.

PROMINENT CITIZENS: (North) In 1954, Husu Ko was used as an agent of the military, but wound up killing his superiors after going insane. Sgt. Helen Kim once went on assignment to the USA, battling the Shockers created by the Brothers Grace. (South) Angela Yin immigrated to the USA at a young age, and became a reporter at the Daily Bugle.

SUPERHUMAN RESIDENTS: (South) When Cain Marko was first transformed into the Juggernaut at the Temple of Cyttorak, he remained in Korea at first, meting out Cyttorak's will.

DOMESTIC CRIME: (South) The demon Cyttorak has local followers in Seoul, the Chejo-Do clan. The True Believers are an offshoot of the Hand, and their ranks have included Dragonfly (Meiko Yin), Karsano, Madame Qwa, Yano, and Master Zei.

INTERNATIONAL CRIME: (North) North Korea's repeated attempts at developing nuclear weaponry have resulted in both Mystique and the Thunderbolts making raids upon their research into advanced weaponry, and an assault from the Japanese terrorist Samurai Steel (Yoshida Asano). (South) Ex-CIA Colonel Ross Whittaker was involved in the misappropriation of US defense money to South Korea, and was aided by others including Reverend Moon Teck-Yo in embezzling the funds under the front of Global Security, Inc.

HISTORY: Modern Korea was formed by the unification of ancient kingdoms around the 10th century AD. In 1905, the country was occupied by Japan. After Japan's defeat in World War II, the country was divided into North and South Korea, with the North occupied by the USSR and the South by the USA. In 1950, the North made an attempt to conquer the South, resulting in the Korean War, which lasted until 1953. Some of the many US soldiers who fought in the Korean War include Captain Simon Savage, Sgt. Nick Fury and his Howling Commandos, "Iron" Mike McGraw, "Combat Kelly," "Combat" Casey, "Battleship" Burke, "Rock" Murdock, "Battle" Brady and Kent Blake, as well as the 1950s versions of Captain America and Bucky (Jack Monroe). The US hero the Human Torch (Jim Hammond) once ventured into Korea when his sidekick Toro (Thomas Raymond) was briefly brainwashed by North Korea. North Korea has remained a communist state since then.

Art by Michael Ryan

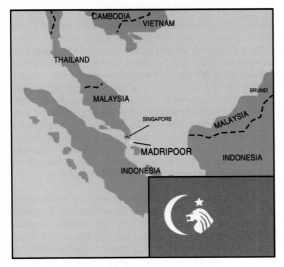

OFFICIAL NAME: Principality of Madripoor (Madripura)
POPULATION: 1,055,000 (estimated)
CAPITAL CITY: Madripoor
PLACES OF INTEREST: Buccaneer Bay, Madripoor Harbor, Central Highlands, Royal Palace & Museum, Hightown, Sovereign Hotel, Barker Plaza, Lowtown Central Bazaar, Madame Joy's, Foxy Den, Lotus Café, Hoggvelt Memorial Park; formerly Princess Bar/Seraph's
GOVERNMENT: Principality; former British colony
MAJOR LANGUAGES: English, Filipino, French
MONETARY UNIT: Madripoor dollar
MAJOR RESOURCES: Fishing, shipping, textiles, gambling, tourism, electronics; formerly slaves, ivory, rubber, teak
NATIONAL DEFENSE: None
INTERNATIONAL RELATIONS: Madripoor has no official relations with any other nations; however, due to the government's laissez-faire policy as well as its policy of not permitting other nations to extradite criminals from within its borders, Madripoor is an exotic diplomatic haven from which many international organizations conduct their business, be it legal or illegal. The international law enforcement agency SHIELD once had an office in Madripoor run by Agent Maria Hill.
EXTRATERRESTRIAL RELATIONS: The alien thief Jornik once crash-landed in Madripoor Harbor which caused the Urg egg he had stolen to hatch and the infant Urg to rampage through Lowtown where it was opposed by X-Factor before being teleported away by Lila Cheney. A K'lanti ship then arrived seeking the Harmonium that Lila had stolen from them and threatened to destroy Madripoor until it was returned to them. Madripoor was also once the site of an attempted invasion of Earth by the extradimensional warlord Khan that was thwarted by the X-Men.
NONHUMAN POPULATION: None known.
PROMINENT CITIZENS: In 1941, Seraph operated the island's most respected drinking establishment. Madripoor was ruled for many years by Prince Baran before his death, after which the criminal Viper laid claim to the throne until recently when she was deposed by crimelord Tyger Tiger (Jessan Hoan) with aid from Director of SHIELD Tony Stark. Lord Ranjamaryam and Johann served as Baran's chancellor and aide, respectively, before they were murdered. The island's police force has been led for many years by Chief Tai until his recent death. The man known only as O'Donnell purchased Seraph's and changed its name to the Princess Bar. Americans Jessica Drew and Lindsay McCabe once ran the private investigation firm Drew & McCabe Resolutions from an office in Lowtown. Archie Corrigan owned and operated the South Seas Skyways charter flight service until he was killed. Madame Joy runs the island's most reputed brothel. The super heroine Scorpion (Carmilla Black) was born in Lowtown as Thasanee Rappaccini before she was given away to the Prince Baran Hospice for Motherless Waifs to be adopted.

DOMESTIC SUPERHUMANS: The feral mutant Aardwolf; the super-powered mercenaries the Rising Sons (the shapeshifting Dragonwing, gravity-defying Spoilsport, tattooed magician The Sign, cyborg motorcyclist Jet-Black, Darkforce-sword-wielding Nightwind, and super-strong Tough Love).
SUPERHUMAN RESIDENTS: The mutant adventurer Wolverine resided in Madripoor for many years under the nom de guerre "Patch." For a time, the young mutant Karma (Xi'an Coy Manh) lived on the island with her uncle, crimelord General Nguyen Ngoc Coy. The interdimensional firm Landau, Luckman, & Lake maintained an office in Lowtown that was run by Mr. Chang until it was destroyed during a gang war. The island's criminal element has also employed superhuman enforcers in the past, such as Sapphire Styx, Razorfist, the Inquisitor, Bloodscream and Roughouse. The External Crule spent much time on Madripoor drinking and gambling. The super-powered Folding Circle resided in Lowtown for a time before becoming involved in Madripoor's gang wars. The metamorph Rose Wu retired from Landau, Luckman & Lake's Hong Kong branch and purchased the Princess Bar from O'Donnell. The genetically engineered warrior Shatterstar lived on Madripoor for months while participating in a gladiatorial arena located in a dimensional pocket beneath the Lotus Café.
DOMESTIC CRIME: Much of Madripoor's domestic crime was overseen by crimelord Roche until the arrival of rival crimelord Tyger Tiger (Jessan Hoan) who usurped control of Roche's empire with Wolverine's aid. Tiger later faced competition from a rival syndicate led by Coy who sought to resume the illicit drug and slave trades that Tyger Tiger had ended. Madripoor was also home to the Cult of the Black Blade before they were broken up by Wolverine and the Silver Samurai. A thieves' den exists in Lowtown, run by Ganif who takes in street children and trains them in exchange for shelter. The wharfside area was run by the enigmatic Mr. Morrow who once enlisted Wolverine's aid in opposing a challenge for control of the area by rival boss Piggot. Aardwolf once ran a criminal empire from his Hightown penthouse. Bao Tien and Noy were among the crimelords who sought to carve themselves a niche in Madripoor following Baran's death. The ninja Silence was one of seven assassins who sought the bounty placed on the head of the Punisher by mob leader Rosalie Carbone, but was ultimately killed by Microchip. Madripoor hosts an annual underground superhuman fighting tournament called the Bloodsport that attracts competitors from around the world. While ruling Princess, the Viper used profits generated by Madripoor businesses to fund her illegal Hydra operations.
INTERNATIONAL CRIME: In 1941, an alliance between the Japanese assassins known as the Hand and Nazi Germany's Baron Von Strucker was opposed by Wolverine, Captain America (Steve Rogers), and Ivan Petrovitch. In modern times, both the Hand and the terrorist organization Hydra have launched failed attempts to usurp control of Madripoor's throne. The Mutant Liberation Front once operated a base on the island that was dismantled by the combined forces of Cable, the New Mutants, Wolverine and Sunfire. The Adamantium-swathed criminal Cyber once attempted a criminal takeover of Madripoor but was defeated by Wolverine. The super-powered Crimson Pirates and the Goth once raided Hightown for slaves despite opposition from the X-Men. The 4T's gang operated part of their slave market in Madripoor.
FIRST APPEARANCE: New Mutants #32 (1985)
HISTORY: The Principality of Madripoor is a small island nation located south of Singapore in the vicinity of Kepuluan Riau and Kepulauan Lingga in the Indonesian archipelago. It was ruled for many years by Prince Baran, whose dynastic forebears were the leaders of the freebooters who conquered the island. Madripoor's heritage of piracy evolved into the present system of government whose laissez-faire policy allows for virtually any sort of business transaction provided that the ruling status quo is not threatened. As a result, Madripoor has become an exotic diplomatic haven for many international crimelords and organizations. These criminals help maintain the stability of the government through a sophisticated system of corruption that includes payoffs to the chancellor, who runs the day-to-day government operations, and, it is speculated, to the ruling prince as well.

The indigenous population is a polyglot of Chinese, Vietnamese, Thai, Filipino, British and other races, each seeking to preserve their own language and heritage while residing on the island. A tribe of nomadic natives also reside in the island's Central Highlands. While English and Filipino are the official languages of Madripoor, French is also commonly spoken, a reminder of the French colonial history in the area which included possession of Indochina (present day Vietnam, Cambodia, and Laos). Hinduism is the primary religion practiced in Madripoor, with its followers believing that, after death, the body must be returned to the Pancamahabhuta — the five sacred elements — before their soul can be released to meet the Supreme Being. Hence, elaborate funeral pyres are favored, especially for royalty. The religion also demands that bare legs be covered with sarongs within temple grounds.

Much of Madripoor's 377 square miles of land is covered in jungle, home to a species of spider monkey found nowhere else in the world that is revered in local superstitions and protected by local law, as well as other fauna including deer, wild dogs, boar and wolves. Little cleared land is able to be cultivated, thus Madripoor is dependent on imports for virtually everything. The island does lay claim to a thriving fishing trade, boosted by the residents of small neighboring islands such as Rumika, located just off Madripoor's southeast coast, which was home to a prosperous fishing village until its inhabitants were slain by mercenaries seeking the Master Form.

Because of its strategic location near one of the major trade routes, Madripoor's harbor and dock facilities are among the largest and most extensive in the world. In addition, the capital city has a large and modern international airport served by Sovereign Airways. In keeping with its history of piracy, there are numerous isolated landing strips, which are used for illegal operations ranging from slavery to drug running. The society and living conditions of Madripoor are an exotic paradox. The capital city lays claim to the most luxurious and expensive hotels in the world. At the same time, it possesses one of the most severe pockets of poverty on the planet. This economic polarization has effectively divided the capital city into two parts: Hightown — the high-tech haven of the very rich and powerful — and Lowtown — the medieval domain of the hopelessly poor.

For many years, Madripoor's criminal underworld was run by Roche until he was challenged by the upstart Tyger Tiger. With the aid of Wolverine, who had forged a reputation on the island as "Patch," Roche's forces were routed and Roche himself slain by Tyger. After petitioning Baran to be allowed to take control of Roche's empire, Tyger became the island's new crimelord and quickly ceased activities involving drugs and smuggling; however, this left a void that was soon filled by General Nguyen Ngoc Coy, which led to a gang war that was only resolved after both sides agreed to continue their operations without interfering in the other's. Tyger and Coy later faced opposition from Cyber who sought to usurp control of their criminal empires but was defeated by Wolverine. Soon after, the feral mutant Aardwolf sought to establish himself as a crimelord in Madripoor but faced opposition from the super-powered Folding Circle, until the situation was resolved by the heroic Night Thrasher.

Baran and Coy then conspired to eliminate the threat of Wolverine once and for all, hiring thugs to kill many of Wolverine's friends in Lowtown and pinning the deaths on him. With Tyger's aid, Wolverine discovered the truth and confronted the pair, whereupon Coy shot and killed Baran in an act of self-preservation but was himself shot by Tyger. Following Baran's death, the throne of Madripoor was left without an heir. Control of the nation was soon usurped by the criminal Viper after Wolverine was forced to marry her to fulfill an old debt. Viper had gambled that "Patch's" respectability in Madripoor would enable her to seize the throne. She also used him, along with his nemesis Sabretooth and his longtime friend and X-Men teammate Shadowcat, to foil an attempt by Hydra and the Hand to control the island. Subsequently, Viper was installed as the ruling prince of Madripoor, and Wolverine was declared an outlaw. Wolverine was subsequently invited back to Madripoor to participate in the Bloodsport. Later, Madripoor became the site of an attempted invasion of Earth by the extradimensional warlord Khan, which was ultimately repelled by the X-Men, much to Viper's chagrin.

Seeking to stop Viper's terrorist activities, Director of SHIELD Tony Stark clandestinely planned to have Viper overthrown. Meeting with crimelord Tyger Tiger, Stark assisted her in fomenting the populace to openly rebel against Viper, resulting in Tyger being crowned Princess in her stead.

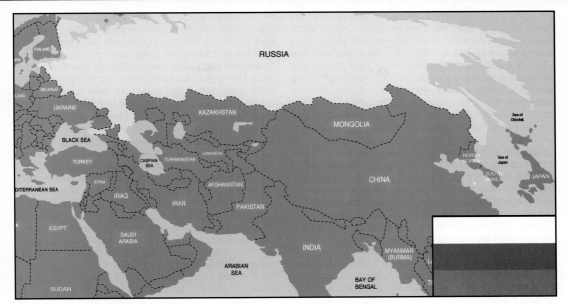

RUSSIA

OFFICIAL NAME: Russian Federation (Rossiyskaya Federatsiya)

POPULATION: 142,893,000

CAPITAL CITY: Moscow

PLACES OF INTEREST: Aquarium, Bitterfrost, Bolshoi Theatre, Fabrika, Khystym (the "Forbidden Zone"), Krasnaya Polyana, Kremlin, Polaria, Province 13, Rebirth Island, Red Square, Russian Museum, St. Isaac's Cathedral, St. Petersburg, Science City 53, Siberia, the Summer Palace, Volgograd

GOVERNMENT: Federation

MAJOR LANGUAGES: Russian

MONETARY UNIT: Russian ruble

MAJOR RESOURCES: Oil, natural gas, coal and timber. Massive expenditures in past development of robotics, cybernetics and genetic mutation for military use.

NATIONAL DEFENSE: The Armed Forces of the Russian Federation include the Air Force, Ground Forces, Navy, Rocket Forces, Space Troops and Airborne Troops. The Winter Guard are Russia's top superhuman team; their ranks include Fantasma, Powersurge, Sibercat (Illya Lavrov), the Steel Guardian, Vanguard and Vostok; previous state-sponsored teams included the People's Protectorate, the Supreme Soviets and the Soviet Super Soldiers.

INTERNATIONAL RELATIONS: Member of the Arctic Council, the Council of Europe, the East Asia Summit, UNESCO, the United Nations, the UN Security Council, and the World Trade Organization. Have island disputes with China and Japan, racial issues with Estonia and Latvia, fishing issues with Norway and border issues with the Ukraine and Kazakhstan; often at odds with Symkaria over Wild Pack mercenary operations.

EXTRATERRESTRIAL RELATIONS: In 1961, the Kigors brought the statue It to life, but were eventually driven out. Also in that year, Kusoom impersonated Premier Nikita Khruschev. Nezarr the Calculator of the Celestials visited Russia during the Fourth Host and prevented a nuclear attack from being launched against it. The Galadorian spaceknight Rom and his foes the Dire Wraiths were both active in Russia. During the "Maximum Security," Russia was invaded by the interstellar Starblasters mercenaries. The extradimensional being Tullamore Voge formerly operated a mutant slave trade in Moscow. The extradimensional New Son fought Gambit (Remy LeBeau) in Russia.

NONHUMAN POPULATION: The city of Polaria in the Ural Mountains of Siberia is inhabited by the Polar Eternals, a tribe of Eternals which includes Aginar, Ajak, Druig, Ikaris, the Interloper, Sigmar, Valkin and Zarin. The giant dragon Grogg formerly slept beneath the earth in

Russian territory until it was awakened by nuclear tests. Droog is a sentient dinosaur-like creature created by the Gremlin as his pet and friend. The Elements of Doom were originally developed by Dr. Vassily Khandruvitch in Russia. It the Living Colossus was a statue brought to life by the Kigors and later obtained by Robert O'Bryan in the USA. The Meatspore Stormtroopers were an army of cybernetic creatures designed in the 1950s and ultimately destroyed by X-Force.

DOMESTIC SUPERHUMANS: The Abomination (Emil Blonsky) is a former intelligence operative who became a gamma-powered creature while spying on the Hulk (Bruce Banner); he has since become a criminal in the USA. Black Brigade was an armored cyborg mercenary who served in Slorenia. The Black Widow and Red Guardian are a series of special intelligence operatives trained by the KGB's Red Room; the Black Widow Natasha Romanova is now a member of the Avengers while Yelena Belova is deceased; the Red Guardian Josef Petkus is now Steel Guardian, with predecessors including Alexi Shostakov and Krassno Granitsky. The Bogatyri were a team of criminals comprised of the stretching Dr. Volkh (Vladimir Orekhov), telepath Mikula Golubev, Zvezda Dennista (Marya Meshkov) and super-strong Svyatogor (Sasha Pokryshkin). Bora is a mutant criminal who relocated to the USA. The master spy Chameleon (Dmitri Kravinoff) and Kraven the Hunter (Sergei Kravinoff) are brothers who fought Spider-Man in the USA; Kraven's sons the Grim Hunter (Vladimir Kravinoff) and Alyosha Kravinoff followed in his footsteps. Mutant siblings Colossus (Piotr Rasputin) of the X-Men, Magik (Illyana Rasputin) of the New Mutants and Mikhail Rasputin have all been active in the USA. The Combine is a superhuman entity caused by the mutation of six terrorists of the Peace Corpse into a single individual. The Crimson Dynamo is a suit of battle armor originally conceived during the 1960s and perfected in recent years by Anton Vanko; Vanko wore the suit first, followed by intelligence agent Boris Turgenov; Vanko's aide Alex Nevsky, Yuri Petrovitch; Dmitri Bukharin while serving in the Soviet Super Soldiers (before joining the People's Protectorate as Airstrike); Valentin Shatalov of the GRU took the armor next and intended to lead his organization Remont 4 in reestablishing a communist government; Gennady Gavrilov discovered a second suit of armor built by Vanko, and has held on to it for personal heroics; other individuals have since appeared wearing Crimson Dynamo armor, evidently without Russia's approval. Dark Angel (Mia Lessing) was an intelligence agent who defected to the UK's MI-6. The Deadmaker (Gregori Anatolovich) was an assassin whose son later took up the identity. The Devastator armor built by the Gremlin has been assumed by Kirov Petrovna and Gregori Larionov, the latter serving in the People's Protectorate. Dr. Yes (Sergei Yesenofsky) was a criminal mastermind. In the 1950s, the electrical villain Electro and the Red Skull (Albert Malik) were among the USSR's costumed agents. Epilson Red and Omega Red (Arkady Russovitch) were a pair of mutant Super Soldiers designed by the military. The Exiles (or Siberforce) were a team of outcast mutants who protested their country's anti-mutant policies; their ranks included mesmerist Blind Faith (Alexi Garnoff); energy wielder Concussion; darkforce wielder Darkstar (Laynia Petrovna); super-durable Iron Curtain; precognitive Mentac; cat-like Sibercat (Illya Lavrov); telepath Stencil; shape-changing man-bear Ursa Major (Mikhail Ursus) and energy repeller Vanguard (Nikolai Krylenko). Fantasma is an illusion-caster. Firefox (Grigori Andreivitch) is a cybernetic assassin. The Gargoyle was an inventive genius; his son the Gremlin gave Russia the armored Soviet Super-Troopers. Geo was a cyborg ally of Cable (Nathan Summers). Kalashnikov was a mutate who fought Sabretooth (Victor Creed). In the 1960s, Katyusha was a Russian heroine who eventually defected to join the USA's First Line. The Metazoid was a mutate sent on an extraction mission to the USA, but died battling Captain Mar-Vell. Mindsinger (Gregor Buhkarov) is one of the Young Gods. Mongu (Boris Monguski) was a spy who disguised himself as an alien invader. Perun is one of the Russian gods, and has used Valeri Sovloyev as his human host while a member of the People's Protectorate. Professor Piotr Phobos raised and trained fellow mutants Darkstar, Ursa Major and Vanguard, but only to manipulate them for his own criminal plans. Powersurge (Illaion Ramskov) possesses radioactive powers. The Presence (Sergei Krylov) is the powerful father of Darkstar & Vanguard. The Purple Man (Zebediah Killgrave) is a former intelligence operative. The Rhino (Aleksei Sytsevich) has operated in the USA for most of his costumed career. Seraph was a telepath for intelligence. The mutant Sketch was once a slave to Ransome Sole. Slag was a wrestler in underground fight clubs. The twin Snow Leopards were agents of Yi Yang. The Soul Skinner was a dangerous mutant telepath. Starlight (Tania Belinsky) is a former Red Guardian and current lover of the Presence. Synthesizer (Zoya Vasilievna and Arkady Tegai) are a couple who can merge into a single, powerful entity. The Titanium Man (Boris Bullski) is one of the country's most powerful armored agents. The Underground Mutant Safe System attempted to defend the country's mutant population, but they were virtually all wiped out by Firefox. Unicorn (Milos Masaryk) received his power horn from Anton Vanko's work. Vindiktor was an armored intelligence agent who claimed to be Natasha Romanova's brother. Vostok (formerly Sputnik) is an android able to control other mechanical devices; he served in the People's Protectorate. Rawborgs and Warborgs are classes of cybernetic agents created from the remains of fallen soldiers.

PROMINENT CITIZENS: The Actor was a master of disguise in the employ of the military official "the Red Barbarian." Oksana Bolishinko was a ballet instructor to Natasha Romanova. Michael Corcoran was a US scientist who defected to Russia, only to be killed by the Black Widow. Val Dobrova and Maksim Golitsyn are Moscow detectives. Nadia Dornova was the wife of the Abomination. Zahvut Dragunov was a local vigilante until his death. Igor Drenkov was the spy who sabotaged the gamma bomb test that transformed Bruce Banner into the Hulk. Feliks Fershov is a scientist. Krushki was a member of the Red Skull (Johann Shmidt)'s Exiles. Valery Ivanov was an editor who was executed for speaking against the military. Elena Ivanova is the daughter of Epsilon Red. Vladimir Jakoff was a diplomat. Vassily Karpov was a World War II combatant and the initial handler of the Winter Soldier. Anton Kharkov is a politician; his wife is Idel, and his daughter is Sophia. Maria Komarovshky and Katya Kosinsky were friends of Natasha Romanova. Miklos Koslov helped drive Grogg from Russia. Colonel Kyril Kuslov was an officer in World War II who aided the Howling Commandos. Aleksander Lukin is CEO of the Kronas Corporation, and is secretly the host of the Red Skull's consciousness. Osaku was a member of the Hand's Snakeroot sect. Ivan Petrovitch is a former scientist who defected with Natasha Romanova. Boris

Petrovski was the sculptor who crafted It the Living Colossus in 1961. Nina Pushnikov aided the Red Ghost in one of his US plots. Constantin Racal designed the Warborgs. Grigori Rasputin was a trusted confidant of the Romanoff dynasty, and distant relative of Colossus. Nikolai and Alexandra Rasputin were the parents of Colossus; other distant relatives include Dimitriy, Klara, Konstantin, Vladimir and Yuri Rasputin. General Fyodor Shelkov is the military liaison to the Winter Guard. Josef Stalin was the country's notorious dictator from 1922-1953, and after death served the demon Satannish's Lethal Legion as Cold Steel. Gregori Suvarov is a political foe of Magneto (Erik Lehnsherr). Yuri Trifanov serves public relations for the Winter Guard. Anatoly Vonya helped train superhumans for the country. Colonel Alexei Vazhin is one of the country's top intelligence agents, and often dealt with international mutant affairs; his aide is Major Debra Levin. Other intelligence operatives include Yelena Brement, Yuri Brushov, Alexi Bruskin, the Executioner (Lupa Lupoff), Rosa Kleb, Anatoly Krylenko, Georgie Luchkov, Zhenya Penkovsky, Valentina Rychenko, Yuri Stalyenko

SUPERHUMAN RESIDENTS: Doppelganger was a German mutant who aided Russia for many decades in studying their own mutant population. The Mimic (Calvin Rankin) lived in Russia for a time. For many decades, the Winter Soldier (formerly Captain America's sidekick James "Bucky" Barnes) was used as an assassin by the KGB's Department X.

DOMESTIC CRIME: Local super-villains have included Black Death (Ivan Kivelki), a mutant based on Rebirth Island; the radioactive Meltdown; the Red Ghost and his Super-Apes (Peotor, Igor and Miklho); the mercenaries Hammer and Sickle, Cossack and the Russian; the assassins Confessor and Iron Maiden (Melina Vostokovna). The Peristrike Force (Psi-Wolf, Scattershot, Siberion, Volga Belle) are a team of superhuman terrorists. Known mobsters include Ivan "the Terrible" Pushkin, Gapon Dzhokhar, "the General," Valeri Kasatanov, thief Simyon Kurasov, Grigori Samsonov, Marcus Tsung, drug dealer Eddie Yarkov, Zoltaro and the 19th century crimelord Anatoly Fyskov (ancestor of Wilson Fisk) who moved to the USA.

INTERNATIONAL CRIME: Russia has been threatened by many powerful superhumans, including the mutants Black Box (Garabed Bashur), Cable, Magneto, the Neo and Wolverine (James Howlett). Terrorists such as AIM, the Brotherhood, Hydra, the Konsortium, the Mandarin, ULTIMATUM and the Viper have been active in Russia, along with counter-terrorist Solo (James Bourne) and mercenaries the Foreigner, Sabretooth and the Wild Pack.

HISTORY: Founded in the 12th century as the Principality of Muscovy, Russia grew to become the largest country on Earth. From 1917, the country was ruled by a communist regime, and absorbed surrounding territories into the USSR; a period of "Cold War" with the USA kept tensions heightened for decades, prompting vast expenditures on the military, and research into mutants, augmentation and armored battlesuits until the USSR split itself apart in 1991. Russia is still recovering from its transition out of communism.

Art by Joe Corroney

Polaria

Pechora Basin, near Kara City, Western Siberia, Russia

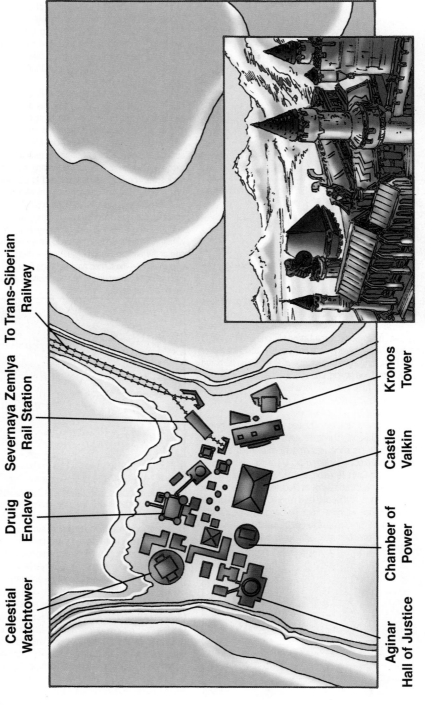

Celestial Watchtower

Druig Enclave

Severnaya Zemlya Rail Station

To Trans-Siberian Railway

Aginar Hall of Justice

Chamber of Power

Castle Valkin

Kronos Tower

Overview of The City of Polaria. Residence of the Polar Eternals.
*Image courtesy Everett K. Ross, Diplomat Plenipotentiary without Portfolio,
U.S. Dept. of State, retired and The Everett K. Ross Library*

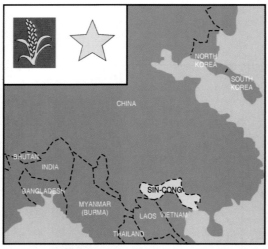

OFFICIAL NAME: Socialist Republic of Sin-Cong (Cong hoa Xa hoi Chu nghia Sin Cong)
POPULATION: 3,000,000
CAPITAL CITY: Thoat Nhin
PLACES OF INTEREST: The Imperial Palace
GOVERNMENT: Communist republic
MAJOR LANGUAGES: Sin-Congese, English, French, Chinese
MONETARY UNIT: Sing-Cong dollar
MAJOR RESOURCES: Oil, natural gas, coffee, rice, tea
NATIONAL DEFENSE: People's Armed Forces of Sin-Cong, includes Army, Navy and Air Force of 20,000 active members.
INTERNATIONAL RELATIONS: Member of the Association of Southeast Asian Nations , East Asian Summit, the United Nations and the World Trade Organization. Major military and political ally of China, poor relations with the USA, formerly a protectorate of France. The harbored terrorist Wong-Chu has made attacks upon Malaysia and Japan.
EXTRATERRESTRIAL RELATIONS: None known.
NONHUMAN POPULATION: None known.
DOMESTIC SUPERHUMANS: None known.
PROMINENT CITIZENS: Armand Duquesne was a prominent government official in Sin-Cong during its days as a protectorate of France, but would abuse his social standing by tormenting the Sin-Congese workers in his employ, including his butler Nguyen. Nguyen joined the forces of Wong-Chu's rebellion, and killed Armand at the first available opportunity. Armand's son Jacques Duquesne also served the rebellion as the Swordsman, and helped lead Wong-Chu's men in many encounters until the French withdrew from Sin-Cong. Wong-Chu was instrumental at inciting the Sin-Congese to rise up, pointing to China as an example to pattern themselves after. After leading the Sin-Congese

Art by Don Heck

to victory, Wong-Chu departed to serve the Mandarin, but later returned to use the country as his base of operations while committing acts of international terrorism.
SUPERHUMAN RESIDENTS: None known.
DOMESTIC CRIME: Minor source of drug trafficking, prostitution and slavery. A people's underground of Sin-Cong is believed to be in opposition to the Communist government.
INTERNATIONAL CRIME: Sin-Cong has attempted to embellish its own standing in the world by once tricking the Avengers into a fight with their Commissar robot, only to meet defeat. Iron Man (Anthony Stark) and the Sons of Yinsen have invaded the country in order to combat Wong-Chu.
FIRST APPEARANCE: Avengers #18 (1965)
HISTORY: Sin-Cong was founded as a French protectorate in the 1850s, and remained under French supervision until recent decades. The central figure in Sin-Cong's bid for independence was Wong-Chu, whose powerful rhetoric inspired locals to overthrow the French authorities. Wong-Chu's campaign received unexpected aid from Jacques Duquesne, son of the French government official Armand Duquesne. The Duquesnes were said to be descended from a World War I hero called the Crimson Cavalier who fought for France against Germany. Believing that the situation in Sin-Cong mirrored his supposed ancestor, Jacques designed the costumed identity of the Swordsman to lead Sin-Cong rebels into battle. After a year of fighting, the French finally withdrew from Sin-Cong. When Jacques learned that his father had been one of the earliest French casualties — despite Wong-Chu's promises of protection — he turned against Wong-Chu and left Sin-Cong, drifting into the life of a mercenary, and later serving as one of the Avengers at the time of his death.

Art by Dan Panosian

Wong-Chu helped install the new communist rule of Sin-Cong, and received major support from China. After Wong-Chu departed Sin-Cong to lead other rebels and terrorist factions, including servitude to the Mandarin, Chinese military adviser Major Hoy stepped in to manage Sin-Cong's government. Major Hoy employed a humanoid robot called the Commissar to serve as the country's new figurehead leader, taking advantage of the robot's superior physical capabilities to intimidate locals. Seeking an opportunity to humiliate the USA, Major Hoy sent a request for help from the Avengers, posing as a message from the Sin-Cong Underground. Captain America (Steve Rogers), Hawkeye (Clint Barton), Quicksilver (Pietro Maximoff) and the Scarlet Witch (Wanda Maximoff) responded to the summons at the Imperial Palace, and ultimately prevailed over the Commissar, destroying it, and exposed Major Hoy as a charlatan. Major Hoy returned to China in disgrace.

Wong-Chu eventually returned to Sin-Cong, establishing a fortress where he oversaw international acts of terrorism and ran prostitution and slavery rings, without censure from the government. Wong-Chu provoked his enemies Iron Man and the Sons of Yinsen into a confrontation and was briefly able to hold them prisoner, but they eventually overcame his forces and he was killed by one of his former slaves.

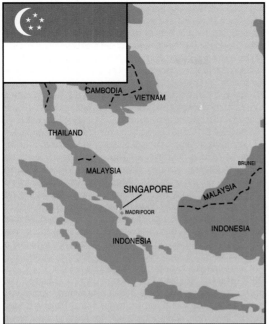

OFFICIAL NAME: Republic of Singapore (Xinjiapo Gonghuguo [Mandarin], Republik Singapura [Malay], Cinkappur Kudiyarasu [Tamil])

POPULATION: 4,492,000

CAPITAL CITY: Singapore

PLACES OF INTEREST: Chek Jawa wetlands, the Downtown Core, the Esplanade theatre, the Galleria, the Orchard Road, Raffles Place, the Singapore Botanical Gardens, Sri Mariamman Temple.

GOVERNMENT: Parliamentary republic

MAJOR LANGUAGES: Mandarin, English, Malay, Tamil

MONETARY UNIT: Singapore dollar

MAJOR RESOURCES: Fish, shipping, mineral fuels, consumer goods, chemicals, machinery, electronics

NATIONAL DEFENSE: Singapore Armed Forces, includes Army, Navy and Air Force; have an active force of 72,500 members. The Singapore Police Force has also seen action as an anti-terrorist force.

INTERNATIONAL RELATIONS: Member of the Association of Southeast Asian Nations, East Asia Summit, United Nations and Commonwealth of Nations. Have unresolved border issues with Indonesia and Malaysia. Formerly a participant in the X-Corporation, have good relations with the Avengers.

EXTRATERRESTRIAL RELATIONS: None known

NONHUMAN POPULATION: None known

DOMESTIC SUPERHUMANS: Singapore's mutant population was once banded together as the Mutant Underground of Singapore, fearful of anti-mutant sentiments in their country. Based in the Galleria and led by the Light (had the power to sense truth), known members included Crawler (could cling to surfaces), Slider (could control friction) and Leiko Tan (could sense other mutants). The Underground sought an alliance with Magneto when he was in their homeland, but many of them wound up being killed by an anti-mutant mob. Surviving members of the Underground were presumably all depowered on "M-Day."

PROMINENT CITIZENS: Tyger Tiger (Jessan Hoan), was once heir to the Hoan International Bank; when the bank went out of business, she relocated to Madripoor, where she became a crimelord. Philip Chan is a local newscaster.

SUPERHUMAN RESIDENTS: Lifeguard (Heather Cameron) and Thunderbird (Neal Shaara) of the X-Men both resided in Singapore while serving in the X-Corporation.

DOMESTIC CRIME: In 1940, the bandit leader Mungo held British consul Drew Murdock for ransom, but Murdock was rescued by the magician Dakor. In the 1950s, US citizen John Panyard dealt in illegal pearl trading. Contemporary mercenary leader Jackie Singapore manipulates his enemies by employing men and women whose aging has been retarded so that they appear to be children; he made several attempts at recruiting Cable (Nathan Summers) to his employ.

INTERNATIONAL CRIME: Singapore has been assaulted by several criminals, including the cybernetic Reavers, the Jemaah Islamiyah terrorists and the Si-Fan cartel. There is a large amount of illegal activities and trafficking that passes between Singapore and nearby Madripoor. The presence of the Mutant Underground of Singapore and X-Corporation has brought about acts of anti-mutant terrorism and state-sponsored persecution; even the X-Men were briefly held in Singaporean custody for having aided Magneto. Anton Kruch of the One World Church employed Lightmaster (Edward Lansky) to use the Facade Virus manufactured in Singapore's Sunic Pharmaceutical Corporation in an attempt to end bigotry by altering the skin color of every person on Earth, but Kruch was foiled by Cable. The mercenary Six Pack (G.W. Bridge, Cable, Domino, Grizzly (Theodore Wincester), Hammer (Eisenhower Canty), Garrison Kane) once fought criminals hired by their enemy Stryfe in Singapore. The Orchard Road was once the scene of a battle between Captain America (Steve Rogers), the Hulk (Bruce Banner) and MODOK (Damocles Rivas).

HISTORY: The island nation of Singapore was founded as a trading outpost by Great Britain in 1819 by Sir Thomas Stamford Raffles. During World War II the country was occupied by Japan, but returned to British control with Japan's surrender. After obtaining self-governance in 1959, the country was briefly merged in 1963 with Malaysia. Finally, the country became independent in 1965. Together, Singapore comprises 63 separate islands. The country has a powerful economy, and has attracted outside developers such as the Marrs Corporation and the Sunic Pharmaceutical Corporation.

Art by Greg Tocchini

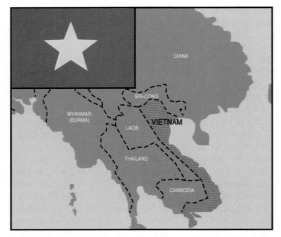

OFFICIAL NAME: Socialist Republic of Vietnam (Cong hoa Xa hoi Chu nghia Viet Nam)

POPULATION: 84,402,000

CAPITAL CITY: Hanoi

PLACES OF INTEREST: Agaphaur Temple, Da Nang, Flag Tower of Hanoi, Ha Long Bay, Hanoi Opera House, Hanoi Tower, Ho Chi Minh City, Ho Chi Minh Mausoleum, Hoan Kiem Lake, One Pillar Pagoda, Park of Reunification, Red River, Reunification Palace, Temple of Literature

GOVERNMENT: Communist state

MAJOR LANGUAGES: Vietnamese, English, French, Chinese, Khmer

MONETARY UNIT: Dong

MAJOR RESOURCES: Rice, coffee, rubber, cotton, tea, pepper, soybeans, cashews, sugar cane, peanuts, bananas, poultry, fish, seafood, food processing, garments, shoes, machinery, mining, coal, steel, cement, fertilizer, glass, tires, oil and paper.

NATIONAL DEFENSE: Vietnam People's Army, comprising 500,000 active members amongst the Ground Forces, Navy, Air Force and Coast Guard.

INTERNATIONAL RELATIONS: Member of the Association of Southeast Asian Nations, the East Asia Summit, UNESCO, the United Nations and World Trade Organization. Has border issues with Cambodia and Laos, refugee issues with China, and various island disputes with China, Malaysia, the Philippines and Taiwan.

EXTRATERRESTRIAL RELATIONS: Members of the Cotati race have dwelt near the Agaphaur Temple with the Priests of Pama. The mutant Vorm Star-Stalker once came to Agaphaur Temple to destroy the Priests of Pama. Vietnam was once briefly removed from existence by the time-travel custodian Immortus.

NONHUMAN POPULATION: The Priests of Pama are a sect descended from the extraterrestrial Kree who settled in the Agaphaur Temple near Ho Chi Minh City. Pacifists by nature, they raised the heroine Mantis.

DOMESTIC SUPERHUMANS: The mutant Arclight (Phillipa Sontag) left Vietnam to become one of Mr. Sinister's Marauders. The assassin Bengal lost his entire village during the Vietnam War, and has devoted his life to hunting the men responsible; he is currently serving as a member of the Initiative's Black Ops team. Local criminal Razorblade was an ally of the Titanic Three, and later served the Viper as one of her Fangs. The mutant Rolling Thunder formerly served the psychic Elias Bogan; her status following "M-Day" is not known. Karma (Xi'an Coy Manh), a mutant with the power to possess others, lives in the USA as a frequent aide to the Xavier Institute; her siblings Leong Coy and Nga Coy live with her; their brother Tran Coy Manh shared Karma's power, but used it for crime, finally dying at Karma's hands. The heroic Mantis of the Avengers lived in Vietnam until she went to the USA to join the Avengers. Brother Power (Achmed Korba) became a criminal in the USA, battling Spider-Man.

PROMINENT CITIZENS: During World War II, the pirate General Ten Per Cent made a name for himself by taxing all shipments of rubber through the Mekong. Amy Chen was once a prostitute in Vietnam, but became an assassin, eventually joining Symkaria's Wild Pack. Citizen Sha Shan left Vietnam for the USA, where she was romantically involved with Eugene "Flash" Thompson. The powerful sumo wrestler General Wo once fought Captain America (Steve Rogers) when he came to Vietnam to rescue a captured US pilot. The German Gustav Brandt fathered Mantis while he lived in Hanoi; he later became Libra of the Zodiac crime cartel. Businessman Gai No Don emigrated to the USA, becoming a board member of the Taylor Foundation. The disfigured scientist Half-Face was responsible for refitting the Titanium Man's armor.

SUPERHUMAN RESIDENTS: Russia's Crimson Dynamo (Alex Nevsky) and Titanium Man (Boris Bullski) were formerly teamed with China's Radioactive Man (Chen Lu) as the Titanic Three, and were stationed in Vietnam; during a battle with Iron Man, an experimental underground city the Vietnamese had been developing was destroyed, and the Titanic Three were arrested and exiled from Vietnam as a result. The Mandarin once had a fortress in Vietnam.

DOMESTIC CRIME: Vietnam is one of the countries comprising the so-called "Golden Triangle" of opium trade; the country also has a significant problem with drug addicts. Drug lord Nguyen Ngoc Coy has a made an international reputation for himself, often operating from Madripoor. One of the most infamous black marketeers in the country was Monsieur Khruul, now deceased. General Buktir Van Tranh went to Bolivia after the Vietnam War to become a drug lord, but later died at the hands of the Punisher (Frank Castle). The 4T's gang is part of an international slave market, with some of their members and trade taken from Vietnam.

INTERNATIONAL CRIME: The mutant criminal Sabretooth (Victor Creed) killed a number of prostitutes in Vietnam around 1968. Other criminals such as the Man-Beast, Scalphunter (John Grey Crow), and the Swordsman (Jacques Duquesne) have also operated in Vietnam. The superhumans Nuke (Frank Simpson) and Wolverine (James Howlett) both committed atrocities during the Vietnam War. The New York street gang Poison Memories is made up of young people of South Vietnamese ancestry.

HISTORY: Vietnam spent most of its early history under the rule of China, not obtaining independence until the 10th century. In the 19th century, the country was conquered by France, and was occupied by Japan during World War II; France was finally driven from Vietnam in 1954 by the forces of Ho Chi Minh, but the country became divided into a northern communist state and southern state backed by the USA. Despite a massive military campaign (the Vietnam War), the US was ultimately unable to support the south, and the country reunited in 1975 to a single communist state.

Art by Tom Mandrake

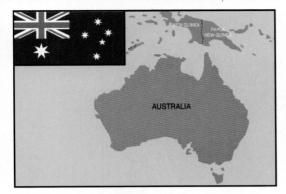

OFFICIAL NAME: Commonwealth of Australia
POPULATION: 20,264,000
CAPITAL CITY: Canberra
PLACES OF INTEREST: Ayers Rock (Uluru Northern Territory), "Anthill" (Northern Territory), Gibson Desert (Western Australia), Great Barrier Reef (Queensland), Surfers Paradise (Queensland), Temple of Watoomb (Daintree Rainforest, Queensland), Culgoora Radioheliograph (Narrabri, New South Wales), Mount Kosciusko (New South Wales), Harbor Bridge & Opera House (Sydney, New South Wales).
GOVERNMENT: Constitutional monarchy
MAJOR LANGUAGES: English
MONETARY UNIT: Australian dollar
MAJOR RESOURCES: Coal, gold, silver, meat, wool, bauxite, uranium, iron ore, wheat, natural gas, petroleum
NATIONAL DEFENSE: Australian Defence Force, including the Royal Australian Navy, the Australian Army and the Royal Australian Air Force.
INTERNATIONAL RELATIONS: The Australian government most recently hosted the 2007 Asia-Pacific Economic Cooperation (APEC) forum, holds membership in the Commonwealth of Nations, co-founded the ANZAC alliance, the United Nations, the South Pacific Commission, and the ANZUS treaty, and hosted a branch of the X-Corporation in Melbourne; the country has cooperated with SHIELD.
EXTRATERRESTRIAL RELATIONS: Sydney was once invaded by the alien Conquest who were repelled by the X-Men. The sentient alien spaceship Orphan crash-landed in the Queensland outback thousands of years ago. Australia was also among the nations invaded by the alien Phalanx who were defeated by the X-Men.
NONHUMAN POPULATION: The giant mutant-hunting robot Sentinels once operated out of an underground base dubbed the "Anthill" in the Northern Territory. The cyborg criminal Reavers once used an abandoned town in the Gibson Desert as their base before it was taken over by the X-Men.
DOMESTIC SUPERHUMANS: Superhuman Australians include the Aboriginal shamans Talisman, Gateway and Dreamguard (Willie Walkaway); mutant freedom fighter Jennifer Ransom who took up Australian citizenship after fleeing Genosha's mutant-oppressive government and worked for the Royal Flying Doctor Service; mutant brothers Key and Wall were depowered on "M-Day"; mutant detective Bishop, formerly of the X-Men; mutant siblings Lifeguard (Heather Cameron) and Slipstream (Davis Cameron); martial artist Red Lotus; Slayback (Gregory Terraerton), a mercenary from Melbourne who served in Department H's Weapon X Program; and Aboriginal mutant telepath Jack-in-the-Box who was pressed into service with the clandestine Weapon X organization.
PROMINENT CITIZENS: Australian World War II soldier Rolfe Harrison fought with the Howling Commandos and the Leatherneck Raiders against the Japanese during the war; General Thornton was a military leader during World War II until he was decapitated by Japanese agent the Head despite the best efforts of the Young Allies; Jaboa Murphy, an ancestor of the future Korvac who once housed his gene imprint; Sydney-based shark hunter Brent McCinley who was possessed by the Bane as

the Aboriginal shark god B'ngudja before being slain by Kate McClellan; wealthy Cootamundra land owner Jenks; former crimelord Miles "Viceroy" Warbeck; former restaurateur and local Triad leader Gow Yang Ju; Detective-Inspector Teri Baltimore of the Royal Sydney Constabulary who aided the X-Men in exposing a plot by Sebastian Shaw to usurp control of the Australian criminal underworld; and billionaire Sydney businessman Jarrah Brandis.
SUPERHUMAN RESIDENTS: The X-Men were based in an abandoned town in the Gibson Desert for several months; among their ranks at the time were Colossus (Peter Rasputin), Dazzler (Alison Blaire), Havok (Alex Summers), Longshot, Psylocke (Elizabeth Braddock), Rogue (Anna Marie), Storm (Ororo Monroe) and Wolverine (James Howlett), and allies Madelyne Pryor and Jubilee (Jubilation Lee). Super-strong Will Chance of the Clan Destine portrays super hero Cap'n Oz on television. American feline superhuman Tigra once lived with the Aboriginal people in Arnhem Land. An aspect of the Celestial Madonna Mantis once lived in Melbourne. The Hulk lived with an Aboriginal tribe in the Northern Territory during the "House of M" reality warp.
DOMESTIC CRIME: During World War II, after Herbert Cholmondeley narrowly lost a prime ministerial election he agreed to aid the Japanese war effort by collapsing the Australian economy with phony £10 notes in exchange for becoming PM after Japan conquered Australia; however, his plan was foiled by Captain Savage and his Leatherneck Raiders. U.S.-born Dirk Leyden operated as the electrically charged Megawatt before fleeing to Australia where he became the star of the "Bush Ranger" movies. Other Australian costumed criminals include the super-villains Boomerang (Fred Myers), Boomslang and the Kangaroo (Frank Oliver), mutant terrorist Pyro (St. John Allerdyce), former carnival hypnotist Randall Shire, super-strong Hydra agent Knockabout (Jarno Sprague) who infiltrated the SHIELD Super-Agents, and Outback of the Wanderers, among others; however, the scope of their operations has primarily been overseas.
INTERNATIONAL CRIME: During World War II, Namor the Sub-Mariner opposed an attempted Japanese invasion of Australia's northern coast with an Atlantean-designed submarine. He also prevented the Japanese from invading Australia via an undersea tunnel from Singapore. The Yellow Claw once had a base near King Hill in the Gibson Desert. The Cobalt Man (Ralph Roberts) once went on a rampage in Sydney, which was halted by the Hulk (Bruce Banner). The false mystic Kerwin Havelock once traveled through Australia. Plasma (Leila O'Toole) and the Cult of the Living Pharaoh formerly operated in Australia while they sought to manipulate Havok to their needs. Australia figured heavily in Dr. Demonicus' plot to raise the island of Demonica nearby, and he had his Pacific Overlords raid laboratories in Sydney. The Mandarin operated a facility in the Outback that was run by the super-powered New Zealander Tuatara, and also employed the German criminal Iron-Hand Hauptmann. International game warden Nicolette Giroux was transformed into the Exemplar Tempest after discovering the Temple of Watoomb in the Daintree Rainforest in Queensland. Long-standing Black King of the U.S. Hellfire Club, Sebastian Shaw, once maintained an office in Sydney. The Chinese Triad has a local chapter in Sydney's "Chinatown" district. The Indonesian terrorist group Jemaah Islamiyah recently attacked the Sydney Opera House but was thwarted by Iron Man and SHIELD.
HISTORY: Aboriginal settlers arrived on the continent from Southeast Asia about 40,000 years before the first Europeans began exploration in the 17th century. No formal territorial claims were made until 1770, when Captain James Cook took possession in the name of Great Britain. Six colonies were created in the late 18th and 19th centuries; they federated and became the Commonwealth of Australia in 1901. The new country took advantage of its natural resources to rapidly develop agricultural and manufacturing industries and to make a major contribution to the British effort in both world wars. In recent decades, Australia has transformed itself into an internationally competitive, advanced market economy.

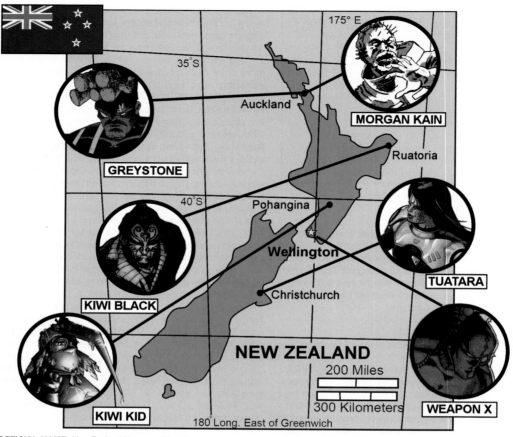

GREYSTONE

MORGAN KAIN

KIWI BLACK

TUATARA

KIWI KID

WEAPON X

35°S
Auckland
175° E
Ruatoria
40°S
Pohangina
Wellington
Christchurch

NEW ZEALAND
200 Miles
300 Kilometers
180° Long. East of Greenwich

OFFICIAL NAME: New Zealand (Aotearoa [Maori])
POPULATION: 4,165,600
CAPITAL CITY: Wellington
PLACES OF INTEREST: Thermal Reserves (Rotorua), Craters of the Moon (Lake Taupo), Sky Tower (Auckland), Mount Cook (Southern Alps, South Island), Mount Ruapehu (Tongariro National Park, North Island)
GOVERNMENT: Constitutional monarchy
MAJOR LANGUAGES: English, Maori, sign language
MONETARY UNIT: New Zealand dollar
MAJOR RESOURCES: Dairy products, meat, wool, fish
NATIONAL DEFENSE: New Zealand Armed Forces
INTERNATIONAL RELATIONS: New Zealand holds membership in the Commonwealth of Nations, the United Nations, and the Asia-Pacific Economic Cooperation (APEC) forum, amongst others. New Zealand co-founded both the ANZAC alliance and the ANZUS treaty, though the US suspended security obligations to New Zealand in 1986 after New Zealand declared itself a Nuclear Free Zone.
EXTRATERRESTRIAL RELATIONS: None known
NONHUMAN POPULATION: None known
DOMESTIC SUPERHUMANS: Maori mutant peace officer Devlin Greystone was briefly a member of American mutant team X-Factor prior to his apparent death in an aircraft explosion. Maori mutant teleporter Kiwi Black, one of the offspring of the demonic Azazel was depowered after "M-Day." "Big" John Anderson, the self-styled "Kiwi Kid," moved to New York in the hopes of becoming a super hero's sidekick, eventually realizing his dream coming to the aid of Spider-Man (Peter Parker) against Doctor Octopus (Otto Octavius). Morgan Kain was an operative of Dr. Demonicus (Douglas Birely) mutated to gain the power to become a giant, and served in the Pacific Overlords. The Canadian government's Department H's last known Weapon X test subject hailed from New Zealand, and fought Alpha Flight after escaping Department H. Maori

strongman Blok worked as a bodyguard for American mutant criminal Mister X, and fought Wolverine (James Howlett). Maori shape-shifter Tuatara (Araoha Tepania) administered the Mandarin's weapons design facility in outback Australia, battling Iron Man (Tony Stark) and the Black Widow (Natasha Romanova). Maori demigoddess Papahanau-Moku was once allied with the Sumerian god Marduk during his effort to use the soul-fuelled Genesis Well to reclaim his full godhood.
PROMINENT CITIZENS: Prime Minister Helen Clark
SUPERHUMAN RESIDENTS: None known
DOMESTIC CRIME: New Zealand has a minor drug abuse problem.
INTERNATIONAL CRIME: New Zealand was among the countries whose facilities were raided by Dr. Demonicus and his Pacific Overlords as they were preparing to launch their island nation of Demonica in the Pacific Ocean. Magneto (Erik Lehnsherr) once raided research facilities in New Zealand to supply him in his campaigns against humanity.
HISTORY: Eastern Polynesians first settled in New Zealand around 800-1300 AD, eventually developing into a distinct culture now known as Maori. In 1840, their chieftains signed the Treaty of Waitangi, which established British sovereignty over the nation while retaining their territorial rights. The British began the first organized colonial settlement in that same year; however, as settler numbers increased, conflicts over land led to a series of land wars between 1843 and 1872, which culminated in the imposition of British land law and severe Maori land loss. New Zealand was granted limited self-government in the 1850s, became an independent dominion in 1907, and eventually a fully independent nation in 1947 when the Statute of Westminster was ratified. Despite this, New Zealand still supported the British effort in both world wars, though their full participation in a number of defense alliances lapsed by the 1980s. In recent years, the New Zealand government has sought to address longstanding Maori grievances.

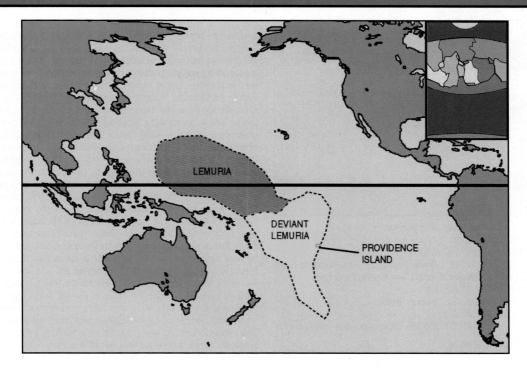

OFFICIAL NAME: Kingdom of Lemuria
POPULATION: 2,000
CAPITAL CITY: Lemuria
PLACES OF INTEREST: The Coliseum, Naga's palace
GOVERNMENT: Monarchistic Republic
MAJOR LANGUAGES: Lemurian, Atlantean
MONETARY UNIT: Unrevealed
MAJOR RESOURCES: Kelp, machinery, chemicals, oil.
NATIONAL DEFENSE: The Assassins Guild has been specially equipped for missions to the surface world. Lemuria formerly employed their most powerful men as Questers on an extended mission to locate the Serpent Crown for Naga.
INTERNATIONAL RELATIONS: On one occasion, Lemuria formed an alliance with its Deviant Lemuria counterpart. Lemuria has uneasy relations with Atlantis, and no formal relations to the surface world.
EXTRATERRESTRIAL RELATIONS: None known.
NONHUMAN POPULATION: Lemurians are an offshoot of humanity, part of the sub-species known as Homo mermani. Like their Atlantean cousins, Lemurians possess the ability to exist underwater indefinitely, using twin gills on their necks to extract oxygen from water. They are also able to withstand the tremendous pressures of the ocean's floor, can swim at a speed of 30 miles per hour, withstand near-freezing temperatures, and see with little or no light. Most Lemurians also have blue skin, but many have developed snake-like scales, some to the extent of their skin turning green. Lemurians have a lifespan of approximately 150 years. Some Lemurians possess telepathy. Lemurians have access to powerful undersea mutates such as the giant octopus Gargantos and the crab-like Krustatos.
DOMESTIC SUPERHUMANS: The human/Lemurian hybrid Llyron, son of Llyra, has abilities similar to the Sub-Mariner, and briefly ruled Atlantis; he is currently the leader of the terrorist At'la'tique.
PROMINENT CITIZENS: In the 15th century AD, Naga began his reign of Lemuria. Through the sacrifice of his aide Ontarr he obtained the Serpent Crown, granting him virtual immortality. A group known only as the "Ancients" and comprised of Aurwel, Bekkit, Jhandark and Pyscatos succeeded in stealing the Serpent Crown away from Lemuria and briefly maintained an outpost in Antarctica until their deaths. After Naga's death,

Karthon the Quester became king of Atlantis. Karthon's sister Llyna was killed by Naga while he was manipulating Prince Namor. One of the nation's greatest warriors is the Weapons-Man.
SUPERHUMAN RESIDENTS: The Interrogator, an agent of the Red Skull (Johann Shmidt) was stationed in Lemuria until his death battling Captain America (Steve Rogers). The Atlantean Hana served as the ambassador from Atlantis. The Atlanteans Namora and Namorita formerly lived in Lemuria.
DOMESTIC CRIME: Lemuria has tolerated the nearby presence of the Mer-Mutants, a band of misshapen humanoids. Since the fall of Naga, his descendant Nagala has been active in the At'la'tique. The ambitious half-human Llyra has made several bids for Lemuria's throne, even slaying Naga's son Prince Merro in one attempt.
INTERNATIONAL CRIME: Prince Byrrah of Atlantis has made treasonous pacts with Lemuria in the past.
FIRST APPEARANCE: Sub-Mariner #9 (1969)
HISTORY: Lemuria was originally one of the great continents of the ancient world, and was ruled over primarily by the Deviants and their human slaves. Only the state of Atlantis withstood conquest from Lemuria. However, in the event known as the Great Cataclysm, the continents of Lemuria and Atlantis were both submerged. The Deviants gradually retrofitted some of Lemuria's remains into a new kingdom for themselves, leaving behind many vacant cities at the bottom of the sea. Atlantis was inhabited by the species called Homo mermani, who took the Olympian god Neptune as their patron. However, some began to worship the elder god Set, and broke away from the Atlanteans, settling in unclaimed Lemurian ruins. In the 15th century AD, the Lemurian Naga claimed the Serpent Crown, the ancient source of Set's power on Earth. The crown's presence began to transform the Lemurians, granting some of them scales and/or green skin. The Serpent Crown was stolen from Naga by a group called the Ancients, who unfortunately also fell victim to Set's power and died. In recent years, the Serpent Crown was rediscovered and Naga dispatched his Questers to reclaim it. The Quester Karthon retrieved the crown from Prince Namor of Atlantis, but he ultimately turned against Naga, slew him, and was then proclaimed king himself.

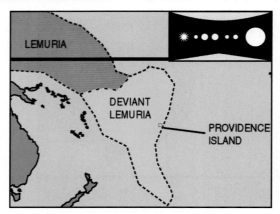

LEMURIA

DEVIANT LEMURIA

PROVIDENCE ISLAND

OFFICIAL NAME: Kingdom of Lemuria
POPULATION: 8,000
CAPITAL CITY: City of Toads
PLACES OF INTEREST: Arena of Combat, the Colosseum, the Flame Pits, Odds Inn, People's Assembly, Temple of the Priesthood
GOVERNMENT: Monarchistic
MAJOR LANGUAGES: Ophidian, English
MONETARY UNIT: Shear
MAJOR RESOURCES: Iron ore, uranium, precious metals, nuclear power
NATIONAL DEFENSE: The Deviant Armed Forces includes Ground Forces, Navy and Air Force featuring weapons and vehicles above Earth-norm.
INTERNATIONAL RELATIONS: Member of the United Nations. Deviant Lemuria has made occasional alliances with the other city of Lemuria and its people, and are on good relations with the Deviants of Lyonesse. Deviant Lemuria has a peace treaty with Atlantis and uneasy relations with China, the USA and Wakanda. Deviant Lemuria has been at war with other subterrestrial nations such as Netheria and the kingdoms of the Mole Man (Harvey Rupert Elder), the Lava Men and Tyrannus.
EXTRATERRESTRIAL RELATIONS: Lemuria has been visited repeatedly by the Celestials; on one visit, Eson the Searcher nearly destroyed the city by flooding while examining it.
NONHUMAN POPULATION: The Deviants are a subspecies of humanity which resulted from experiments conducted by the Celestials. The genetic code of the Deviant peoples is unstable, causing unstable mutations with each successive generation. Deviants typically possess strength and durability above those of humans, and may develop additional superhuman abilities. Deviants whose physical features most closely resemble humans are typically shunned in Lemuria, with the most human-like of them called "Rejects." On the other end of the spectrum, horribly mutated Deviants such as those possessing additional heads or appendages are considered "mutates," and are also undesirable. "Mutate" is also an appellation given to creatures designed by the Deviants via genetic engineering. Many of these mutates were originally purposed for use in military campaigns and hard labor. The Earth's mutate population is concentrated at Monster Island, a former Deviant outpost.
DOMESTIC SUPERHUMANS: Mutates created by the Deviants include the mind-controlling Bandrhude, the immense green Giganto, the amphibian creature Gigantus, the ape-like Gorgilla, the ant-like Grottu, the Lizard Men, the minotaur-like Megataur, the lava-dripping Molten Man-Thing, the rock-like Neolithic, the flesh-absorbing weapon called Spore, the three-headed winged creature Tricephalous and the gigantic World-Devouring Worm.
PROMINENT CITIZENS: Brother Kro is the current ruler of Lemuria, and has lived for thousands of years. Ghaur is the chief priest of the Deviant Priesthood, and has constantly manipulated the monarchy. Brother Brutus was briefly the ruler of Lemuria until it was discovered

that he was a mutate. Brother Visara was another ruler whose attempts to subvert the populace against leaders caused his own death. Brother Tode was reassembled at a molecular level, bringing an end to a long line of successive Deviant monarchs. His son Ranar attempted to claim the throne, but was put to death by the priesthood. King Phraug was the ruler of Lemuria around 18,000 BC when the original continent was sunk by the Celestials. Ahqlau and Lugner were spies used by Ghaur to monitor Kro in the past. Broop was court jester during the reign of Brother Tode. Cataphrax was a mutate warrior who was collected by the priesthood during "Purity Time." General Dasrax was a follower of Kro who was executed by Ghaur. Dragona and Erishkigal are winged sisters; Dragona is a protector of disadvantaged Deviants, while Erishkigal is a power-mad explorer. General Dulpus led an unauthorized invasion of China, using the mutate Glomm in his forces. Gelt and Morjak are a pair of agents stationed amongst humanity. Gort is a mutate who followed Brother Brutus. Ignatz is a miniature winged Deviant who served as the steed of Ant-Man (Scott Lang) for a time. Jorro was an ally of the being Terminus, and wore his armor in battle against the Avengers. The mutate Karkas and human-like Ransak the Reject were both gladiators, but were accepted into the Eternals society as friends. Karygmax and Nuncio Klarheit are members of the priesthood. Kra is a warlord in the military. Medula was the mother of Ransak the Reject. Metabo is a mutate designed to absorb the attacks of Eternals. Morga was the mother of Maelstrom. Ragar was Brother Tode's prime minister. Shelmar is a weapons officer in the military. Sluice was an administrator in Brother Tode's cabinet. Taras Vol was a scientist circa 18,000 BC. Tutinax is a powerful mutate, sometimes employed as a gladiator. Queen Vira was the wife of Brother Tode. Yrdisis is an artist in love with the Eternal Khoryphos, and with him has been smuggling Deviants from Lemuria into human society. Zakka was an inventor who could summon people from the past or future. Additional Deviants of Lemuria include Chudar, Coal, Darg, Fascit, Frathag, Haag, Spike and String.
SUPERHUMAN RESIDENTS: The Inhuman geneticist Phaeder lived near Lemuria for a time, and fathered Maelstrom with Morga; Maelstrom was briefly made a slave in Lemuria after Morga's death, but Phaeder rescued him. Khoryphos of the Eternals has lived in Lemuria since falling in love with Yrdisis, and assists her in smuggling Deviants from Lemuria who seek to integrate with human society.
DOMESTIC CRIME: High instances of murder. The office of every leader of the Deviants since the death of Brother Tode has been scandalized on various scores, including collaboration with Eternals (Kro), concealment of mutate status (Brutus) and deception of the public (Visara).
INTERNATIONAL CRIME: Lemurian territory has been repeatedly violated by the Avengers and Eternals. Human crafts that come within range of Lemuria are fired upon.
FIRST APPEARANCE: Eternals #1 (1976)
HISTORY: Lemuria is one of the oldest surviving civilizations of the ancient world. In the distant past, it was part of the continent Mu. By

Art by Jack Kirby

the time of 18,000 BC, Lemuria was a nation ruled by the Deviants, a subspecies of humanity that resulted from experiments conducted by the Celestials over a million years ago. With the exception of Atlantis, all known human civilizations of the time fell under the dominion of the Deviants, with outposts extending as far as that of Lemura in what is now known as the Savage Land. Worship of the Elder God Set (whose Serpent Men had lived in pre-Deviant conquered Lemuria) also flourished during this age. When the Second Host of the Celestials arrived in 18,000 BC, the Deviants made the mistake of attacking their creators; the Celestials retaliated by unleashing an assault that submerged all of Mu, including Lemuria. The Deviants suffered massive casualties in what became known as the Great Cataclysm, and their civilization has never fully rebounded from the event. Sunken Lemuria was eventually redeveloped into an underwater city, with other portions of their kingdom falling to the Homo Mermanus offshoot called Lemurians. Most of the Deviant kingdom retreated beneath the Earth's surface, carving out the immense subterrestrial world called Subterranea. Most of the access points to Lemuria are found within Subterranea, although there is also a passageway in the Orkney Islands. Using a quick transit system of rail cars, the Deviants are able to traverse from Lemuria to other points within Subterranea with ease. Most of the Deviants resources have been spent maintaining Lemuria's fragile environment. Attempts to create worker classes such as the Gortokians to assist in labor met with failure as their slaves rebelled against them, creating further setbacks and new enemies. The continued interference of the Eternals — another creation of the Celestials — has also held back Deviant progress.

Over time, a religion sprang up among the Deviants centered around a golden Celestial who had broken ranks with the others at the time of the Deviants and Eternals creation. The other Celestials rendered their comrade immobile and concealed him beneath San Francisco. It became known as the "Dreaming Celestial," and the Deviants believed that it had been personally responsible for their creation and punished for defending their existence. The priesthood that developed in this religion became so powerful that its priests were soon the true power behind the Deviant regime. The priesthood introduced the concept of "Purity Time," a time in which mutates would be rounded up and sent to the Flame Pits to be killed. However, the priesthood were actually placing the mutates into suspended animation so that they could raise an army to one day combat the Celestials. Until recent years, this secret was known only to the priesthood. When the Celestials came back to Earth with their Fourth Host, the Deviants attempted to manipulate humanity into attacking the Celestials for them, but the Eternals intervened yet again. When the Celestial Eson the Searcher came to examine Lemuria, its massive hand tore the city apart, forcing a mass evacuation into Subterranea. Although Lemuria was eventually rebuilt, it was yet another setback to the Deviant people. When Brother Tode led a bold attack into the Eternals home city of Olympia, he and his entire cabinet were molecularly rearranged into a block of solid matter, permanently depriving the Deviants of their leadership. The long-lived Warlord Kro ascended to leadership of his people, and, with minor interruptions, remains in that office, albeit under close scrutiny by the priesthood and their leader Ghaur. Kro has made attempts to integrate some Deviants into human culture using his Delta Network, a program established through the USA. Ghaur recently avoided a near-scandal when his daughter — a Reject — appeared in Wakanda, and was granted asylum by the Black Panther (T'Challa). Wakanda and Lemuria nearly went to war, but to avoid revealing the child's identity, Ghaur ultimately settled for placing the child in Atlantean custody. When Kang the Conqueror began an invasion of the Earth by offering a place in his empire to anyone who conquered territory in his name, the rogue general Dulpus led an invasion of China, which was halted by the Avengers. As a show of gratitude, Kro later aided the Avengers by bringing the US President to Lemuria for safekeeping while Kang invaded Washington DC.

Deviant Lemuria,
Near the Kermadec Trench, near the Southwest Pacific Basin

Note about graphic: Image content derived from Stark International High-Resolution P/S Wave Mohorovic Survey (1978), details interpolated. Specific legends from released interviews with Namor McKenzie, King Namor the First, by the U. S. State Department, 1968

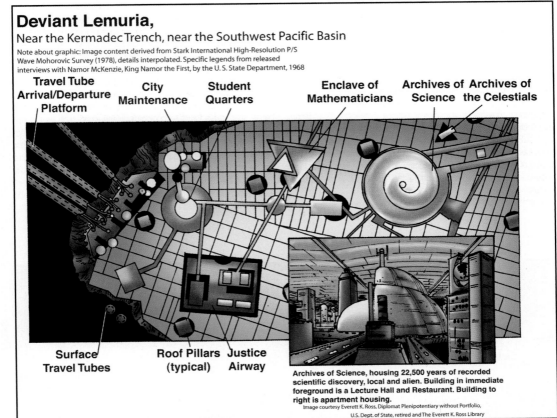

Travel Tube Arrival/Departure Platform

City Maintenance

Student Quarters

Enclave of Mathematicians

Archives of Science

Archives of the Celestials

Surface Travel Tubes

Roof Pillars (typical)

Justice Airway

Archives of Science, housing 22,500 years of recorded scientific discovery, local and alien. Building in immediate foreground is a Lecture Hall and Restaurant. Building to right is apartment housing.
Image courtesy Everett K. Ross, Diplomat Plenipotentiary without Portfolio, U.S. Dept. of State, retired and The Everett K. Ross Library

PROVIDENCE

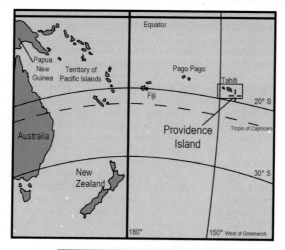

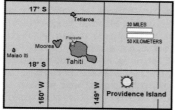

OFFICIAL NAME: None (Providence was not officially recognized as a sovereign nation)

POPULATION: None; formerly 200,000 (estimated)

CAPITAL CITY: Providence

PLACES OF INTEREST: Fountainhead Plaza, Tyler Dayspring Stadium

GOVERNMENT: Democracy

MAJOR LANGUAGES: English

MONETARY UNIT: None

MAJOR RESOURCES: Technology

NATIONAL DEFENSE: Providence Peacewatch Security Patrol

INTERNATIONAL RELATIONS: Providence had both trade and immigration agreements with nearby nations including China, Japan and Australia.

EXTRATERRESTRIAL RELATIONS: The cosmically empowered Zenn-Lavian Silver Surfer (Norrin Radd) once fought Cable in the vicinity of Providence. The Shi'ar Mummudrai Ev Teel Urizen once took possession of Cable in order to combat the sentient Shi'ar weapon the Hecatomb.

NONHUMAN POPULATION: None

PROMINENT CITIZENS: Journalist Irene Merryweather served as Providence's chief of staff. Former Interpol agent Johann Kriek was the island's head of security. Rabbi Rosen led the island's Jewish community.

DOMESTIC SUPERHUMANS: None

SUPERHUMAN RESIDENTS: Providence's creator, the future mutant soldier Cable, had a penthouse apartment on the island. The time-traveling former world conqueror Prester John was head of Providence's required multi-religious studies and was also a member of the Providence Peacewatch Security Patrol. Mutant information broker the Black Box (Garabed Bashur) joined Cable's cause as his chief information archiver. Super Soldier Captain America (Steven Rogers) briefly resided on Providence under the alias Roger Stevens while investigating Cable on behalf of SHIELD and joined the Public Works Division painting public murals. The mutant mercenary Domino also came to join Cable's cause shortly before the island's destruction. The Canadian mercenary Deadpool (Wade Wilson) was a repeated guest on Providence.

INTERNATIONAL CRIME: Haji Bin Barat, the world's most wanted terrorist, sought to martyr himself by destroying both Cable and Providence in an effort to launch a jihad against the western world; however, after being disarmed upon his arrival, Barat had no choice but to reside on the island and, exposed to its multi-cultural society, had begun to reconsider his terrorist ways.

DOMESTIC CRIME: Haji Bin Barat was murdered in his apartment by Deadpool. An explosion at the Waste Fusion Facility was caused by Deadpool in an act of sabotage.

FIRST APPEARANCE: Cable & Deadpool #6 (2004)

HISTORY: Created by the future mutant soldier Cable from pieces of his former space station Graymalkin, Providence was an artificial floating island situated 40 miles off the coast of Tahiti in the Pacific Ocean. Cable sought for the island to be the centerpiece of his effort to show mankind the potential of a unified future by uniting them against a common goal — himself. After his defeat by the Silver Surfer, Cable had his mercenary ally Deadpool lobotomize him to prevent his enhanced powers from killing him, but not before he saved Providence from falling by telekinetically lowering it into the ocean. Following Cable's sacrifice, Providence received 12,000 more immigration applications, and after his return following a period of recuperation Providence received over 2000 applications per day. Cable honored them all, hoping for Providence to become a global intellectual, philosophical and cultural hub. He also signed trade and immigration agreements with many nearby nations, began sharing his future technology with the world such as the self-subsisting solar-powered skimmer jets and fission waste processors, and negotiated a refugee relocation program with China. Providence was later devastated by a battle between the X-Men and the Hecatomb and began to sink. After ensuring the residents were safely evacuated to Australia, Cable activated the island's self-destruct to ensure his archival records and the island's technology would not fall into the wrong hands, and was seemingly killed in the explosion.

Art by Dave Ross

MARVEL ATLAS
BOOK II

80°

80° N

60°

60° N

40°

Tropic of Cancer

20° N

0°   120°   100°   80°

20° S

160° W

20° N

Hawaiian Island
Group

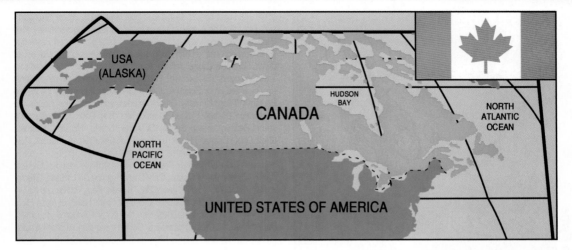

OFFICIAL NAME: Canada
POPULATION: 33,390,000
CAPITAL CITY: Ottawa (Ontario)
PLACES OF INTEREST: Provincial capitals: Edmonton (Alberta), Charlottetown (Prince Edward Island), Quebec City (Quebec), Toronto (Ontario), Victoria (British Columbia), Halifax (Nova Scotia), Fredericton (New Brunswick), St. John's (Newfoundland & Labrador), Regina (Saskatchewan), Winnipeg (Manitoba) and territorial capitals Iqaluit (Nunavut), Whitehorse (Yukon) and Yellowknife (Northwest Territories). Other locations: Calgary (Alberta), Vancouver (British Columbia), Hudson Bay, Alpha Flight Compound (Vancouver), Ararat Research Center, Department H HQ (Toronto), Hull House (Orloo, Ontario), Maison Alpha (Edmonton), Mansion Alpha (Tamarind Island, BC), Ice Box (NWT), Omega Flight HQ (Ottawa), Ravencrag Asylum (Montreal), Temple of Balthakk (Nunavut) and Parliament Hill (Ottawa).
GOVERNMENT: Constitutional monarchy that is also a parliamentary democracy and a federation
MAJOR LANGUAGES: English, French
MONETARY UNIT: Canadian dollar
MAJOR RESOURCES: Iron ore, copper, gold, lead, diamonds, silver, coal, petroleum, natural gas, timber, fish, wildlife, hydropower, nuclear power, chemicals.
NATIONAL DEFENSE: The Canadian Forces, including the Land Forces Command, Maritime Command, Air Command and Canada Command. Also served by the RCMP (national police), and intelligence agencies CISC, SIRC, CSE and CSIS; Omega Flight, Canada's national super-hero team serve under CSIS purview. Omega Flight's predecessor Alpha Flight (and associated teams Beta Flight and Gamma Flight) served under the authority of Department H; Department H's own forces were the Epsilons. Nova Scotia's Department K was part of the Weapon X Project, as well as enabling the black ops group Team X.
INTERNATIONAL RELATIONS: Canada is a member of Commonwealth of Nations, United Nations, World Trade Organization, UNESCO, North Atlantic Treaty Organization, North American Free Trade Agreement, Interpol and SHIELD. Canada has cooperated with the Avengers, Big Hero 6, China Force, People's Protectorate, X-Factor, the mercenary forces of Silver Sable and observed the Pan-European Conference on Superhuman Affairs. The USA is a major economic and military ally; the adoption of the Superhuman Registration Act (SHRA) has put pressure on Canada to enforce its borders. Canada has territorial claim disputes with Denmark. Wakanda caused an incident by gifting Anishinabe Island to the First Nations people. Latveria is on friendly terms with Canada.
EXTRATERRESTRIAL RELATIONS: Otherworldly visitors have included the Consortium, Dire Wraiths, Flb'Dbi, Klklk, Plodex (including Marrina of Alpha Flight and their ally Mar), and individuals such as Argon, Aron the Rogue Watcher, Beta Ray Bill, Collector, Rom, Super-Skrull (Kl'rt) and Terminus. Godly visitors have included, Loki, the Great Beasts (Kariooq, Kolomaq, Ranaq, Somon, Tanaraq, Tolomaq, Tundra) and their foes in the Inuit gods, which include Hodiak, Nelvanna and Turoq the Shaper. Extradimensional visitors have included the Beyonder, Cracass, Death Metal, Dreamqueen, Llan the Sorcerer and D'Von Kray. Department H created a Prometheus Pit that served as a portal to the Microverse.
NONHUMAN POPULATION: The Atlantean outpost of Sharka, home of barbarians such as Attuma is nearby Labrador. Yetrigar is an immense shaggy monster who was buried in Alberta until his discovery in recent years while battling Godzilla. The Deviants are known to have been active in Canada in the past. The Ska'r are an ancient race of demons who have been held in check by the Talisman. Delphine Courtney is a robot built by Roxxon Oil who served in Jerry Jaxon's Omega Flight. Psykos of the Eternals has been active in Toronto. Various Yeti-like creatures exist in the wilderness, including one whom Department H mistook for Sasquatch and recruited into Alpha Flight; the mystical Neuri are another race often taken for Yeti. The Wendigo is a mystical creature that has possessed several men, including Paul Cartier, George Baptiste, Francois Lartigue and Michael Fleet. The Jackal-Man, a New Man developed by Miles Warren, was sighted in Canada after escaping his creator. The Hunter in Darkness is one of many wolfen creatures who live in the northern wilderness. The Macro System are five transforming robots who serve the Canadian Forces.
DOMESTIC SUPERHUMANS: Heroes recruited into Department H's various "Flight" teams include Auric (Zhao Kwan), Aurora (Jeanne-Marie Beaubier), Box (Roger Bochs), Centennial (Rutherford Princeton), Diamond Lil (Lillian Crawley), Earthmover (Chuck Moss), Feedback (Louis Albert), Flashback (Gardner Monroe), Flex (Adrian Corbo), Flinch (Toby Wood), Ghost Girl (Lilli Stephens), Goblyn, Groundhog (Sean Benard), Guardian (James Hudson), Madison Jeffries, Major Mapleleaf (Edmond Sadler), Manbot (Bernie Lachenay), Manikin (William Knapp), Murmur (Arlette Truffaut), Nemesis (Amelia), Northstar (Jean-Paul Beaubier), Ouija (Bill Astin), Pathway (Laura Dean), Persuasion (Kara Killgrave), Puck (Eugene Judd), Puck (Zuzha Yu), Radius (Jared Corbo), St. Elmo, Sasquatch (Walter Langkowski), Shaman (Michael Twoyoungmen), Silver (Jimon Kwan), Smart Alec (Alexander Thorne), Snowbird (Narya), Stitch (Jodi Furman), Talisman (Elizabeth Twoyoungmen), Vindicator (Heather Hudson), Wild Child (Kyle Gibney), Witchfire (Ananym), Wolverine (James Howlett) and Yukon Jack (Yukotujakzurjimozoata). Department K's Weapon PRIME included the heroes Double Trouble, Killspree, Tigerstrike, and Yeti. Avro-X (Colin Richard) is an armored hero who serves in the Canadian Forces. Ajax, Deadpool (Wade Wilson), Garrison Kane, Mastodon, the Native, Sabretooth (Victor Creed), Silver Fox, Sluggo, Vole (Aldo Ferro), John Wraith and Wildcat are among the

PARLIAMENT HILL, OTTAWA

of Omega Flight operatives included Bile, Miss Mass, Sinew, Strongarm and Technoir. The Master once mutated humans into servants called "Remnant Men," but they were returned to normal by Talisman. Pestilence (F.R. Crozier) was a 19th century sailor whose touch could cause death. Scramble (Lionel Jeffries) was the criminal brother of Madison. The Derangers (Breakdown, Freakout, Janus) were mental patients experimented on by Scramble; they were used as lackeys by the insane Bedlam (William Nowlan). Other Canadian super-criminals include the Auctioneer, Caliber, Firebug, Lumbermen (Roy Cook, Chris Reichert, Jason Reichert, Kevin Smith), Sylvester "Snake" Marston, Outcasts (Cleft, Depth Charge, Flagstone), Pink Pearl (Pearl Gross), Ranark, Rok, Technomancer (Ted Larkin)

PROMINENT CITIZENS: Department H staff have included General Jeremy Clarke, Pierre Cloche, Gary Cody, Beatrice De La Salle, Director X, Myra Haddock, Horatio Huxley, Basil Kilgrew, Kerry Patrick and Ko Bin Su. CSIS agent Jeff Brown liaises to Omega Flight. Family of Alpha Flight members include Joanne Beaubier (Northstar's adopted daughter), Darby & Susan Dean (Pathway & Goblyn's parents), Richard Easton (Snowbird's father), Melanie Killgrave (Persuasion's mother), Veronica Langkowski (Sasquatch's ex-wife), Ramsey & Claire MacNeil (Vindicator's parents), Michael Sadler (Major Mapleleaf's brother), Thomas & Gladys Smallwood (Marrina's adopted parents), Daniel Smallwood (Marrina's brother), RCMP officer Douglas Thompson (Snowbird's husband) and Kathryn Twoyoungmen (Shaman's wife). Major Arthur Barrington was an official in Team X. Jerry Jaxon was an embittered foe of James Hudson who created the original Omega Flight to destroy Alpha Flight. Iceboy (Hamish Carlyle) joined SHIELD. Preston Dudley was an RCMP officer who aided Howard the Duck against Le Beaver. Raymond Belmonde was a friend to Northstar in his youth; his daughter Danielle betrayed him to Deadly Ernest. Anna Brooks was a Vancouver reporter who investigated a series of Wendigo murders. Sam Buchanan was an Interpol agent who joined the Darkhold Redeemers. Dwight Clive was a geneticist who created Alexis the Duck. Emily Doolin was the daughter of an RCMP officer, and hunted Wolverine, thinking he was her father's killer. Robby Kyle is an Olympic hockey player. Melissa Sparrow Bear is a Blackfoot who has opposed Roxxon Oil's activities. Jack Oonuk was a secret agent who aided the Punisher (Frank Castle). Jean-Pierre Rimbaud was a Montreal attorney. Calgarian Lucas Stang clashed with Ranaq in his youth; he was survived by his great-granddaughter Emily Stang. Jacqueline Starr is a reporter. General Brian Winslow served in the Canadian Forces. Joseph Legarde Stone served as spokesman for the First Nations when the Black Panther (T'Challa) offered Anishinabe Island to its original owners. Mary McKenna was a Drumheller paleontologist, and perished in an expedition to the Savage Land.

SUPERHUMAN RESIDENTS: UK citizen Windshear (Colin Ashworthe Hume) formerly served in Alpha Flight. The USAgent (John Walker) and Arachne (Julia Carpenter) moved to Canada to serve in Omega Flight; Guardian (Michael Pointer) was forced to kill most of Alpha Flight while possessed by the Collective, and now serves Omega Flight. Sunfire (Shiro Yoshida) spent time with Department H. Rictor (Julio Richter) and Grizzly (Theodore Wincester) formerly served in Weapon PRIME.

many superhumans used by the Weapon X project, initially headed by the Professor, Hines and Dr. Cornelius. Le Beaver (Pierre Dentifris) was an ultra-patriot who died battling Howard the Duck over Niagara Falls. Oxbow (Sam Matonabbe) was a member of the First Line. Birdy was a psychic who served Sabretooth. Two men called the Brass Bishop have been active in Canada; one was a mystic, the other led a criminal gang called the Chess Set. Chinook and Major Mapleleaf (Louis Sadler) were costumed heroes during World War II. The Living Totem (Whistle Pig) and Cold Winter are members of the Haida tribe whose mystical rivalry has extended over 150 years. Cyber (Silas Burr) served in the Devil's Brigade in World War II, and became an Adamantium-laced mercenary in modern times. Daydreamer (Catherine Moranis) was recruited into the Young Gods. Deadly Ernest (Ernest St. Ives) was a crimelord with a touch of death. Tyrell Farsa was a mercenary who once worked with the Taskmaster and Black Swan. Gilded Lily (Lillian von Loont) was Sasquatch's great-aunt, an alchemist and lover of Diablo. Graviton (Franklin Hall) gained his powers while working in Banff. Former wrestler Grizzly (Maxwell Markham) is a costumed criminal in the USA. Wyre was an assassin who worked for the Secret Empire, but later aided Alpha Flight. Mauvais was an 18th century sorcerer who has sought the power of the Wendigo in modern times and clashed with Wolverine. The half-Mohawk vigilante Night Raven was originally born in Alberta. Squid Boy (Sammy Pare) was a student at the Xavier Institute until his death at the hands of Black Tom Cassidy. Manimator (Laurent LeVessaur) could animate wax statutes. The Master of the World (Eshu) was joined with Plodex technology, and has since sought to conquer the Earth; his team

SARCEE RESERVATION, CALGARY

Art by Scott Kolins

Inferno (Samantha McGee) lived in Nunavut until gaining her powers. Hawkeye (Clint Barton) lived in a north for a time. Lynx is a feral woman who Wolverine sent to live in Alberta. Jade Dragon (Dei Guan) briefly held asylum in Canada. Jessica Jones fled to Canada at the start of the SHRA crisis. Nick Fury has at least one Canadian safehouse. The White Queen (Emma Frost) has a Canadian estate. Woodgod spent some time in Department H's custody for experimentation.

DOMESTIC CRIME: Canada is a producer of several drugs, many of which are smuggled into the USA. The separatist Front de liberation du Quebec (FLQ) were responsible for terrorist acts in the 1970s, and their example has inspired like-minded groups such as Cell Combattre (including Clementine D'Arbanville, Edoard Glissante, Northstar, Jacques Paradis). The Hardliners, including Reginald Tork were a band of mercenaries allied with politician Robert Hagen, and hunted superhumans for experimentation. In the 19th century, the Acrobat (Joe Clanton) was a lumberjack who turned criminal and fought the Rawhide Kid (Johnny Bart); Marcel Fournier was a fur trapper who joined the Two-Gun Kid (Matthew Hawk)'s Sunset Riders, but later betrayed him and was killed.

INTERNATIONAL CRIME: Criminal organizations including Fu Manchu's Celestial Order of the Si-Fan, Acolytes, AIM, Bogatyri, Brotherhood of Mutants, Collectors of Antiquities, Death's Head Guard, HELL, the Hellfire Club, Hydra, the Latverian Liberation Front, Peace Corpse, Roxxon Oil, Secret Empire and Zodiac have been active in Canada. Other criminals who have been active in Canada include Arcade, Asp (Cleo Nefertiti), Batroc, Brain Drain, Confessor, Daisy, Lyle Dekker, Dr. Octopus (Otto Octavius), Egghead (Elihas Starr) and his Emissaries of Evil, Future Man, Justin Hammer, Headlok (Murray

Singleton), Lady Deathstrike (Yuriko Oyama), the Leader (Samuel Sterns), Mad Dog (Robert Baxter), Mesmero, Mimic (Calvin Rankin), Mr. Hyde (Calvin Zabo), Nekra, Owl (Leland Owsley), Ronald Parvenue, the Purple Man (Zebediah Killgrave), Raptore, Red Skull (Johann Shmidt), Sauron (Karl Lykos), Scorpion (Mac Gargan), Scourge of the Underworld, Slag, Tentakill, Tiger Shark (Todd Arliss), Toad (Mortimer Toynbee) and Wrecking Crew.

HISTORY: The land of Canada was colonized by France in the 16th century, but England also laid claim to the territory, and after defeating the French in 1759 won the country in 1760. Shortly afterward, the country received an influx of British Loyalists fleeing from the newly formed United States of America. During the War of 1812, Canada fought back invading forces of the USA. In 1867, Canada was made a confederacy; following 1926, the governor-general's power over the Canadian government was greatly reduced, and although the country retains the UK's queen as their monarch, they are largely independent. Canada fought with the Allies during World War II, contributing greatly to the liberation of Holland; perhaps the best-known Canadian fighting force were the Devil's Brigade, whose ranks included James Howlett, later Wolverine. Quebec's quest for a separate identity — or outright separation — from Canada inspired the FLQ terrorists of the 1970s, and fractured attempts at forging a national identity. The Canadian government's premiere super-hero team was Alpha Flight up until their virtual destruction at the hands of the Collective; their replacements, Omega Flight were charged with the mission of defending the US-Canadian border from criminals fleeing the SHRA.

WINNIPEG

Art by John Byrne

Omega Flight Headquarters

Ottawa, Ontario Province, Canada

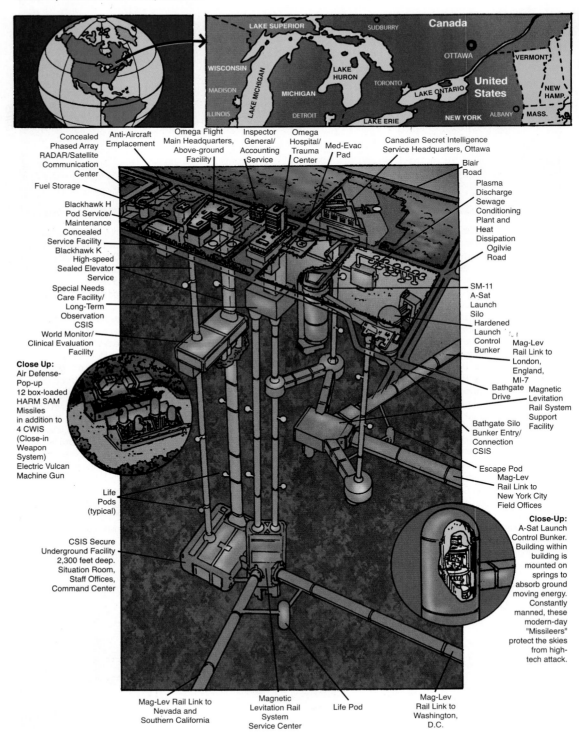

LAKE SUPERIOR · SUDBURY · Canada · OTTAWA · VERMONT · WISCONSIN · LAKE HURON · MADISON · MICHIGAN · TORONTO · LAKE ONTARIO · United States · NEW HAMP. · ILLINOIS · DETROIT · LAKE ERIE · NEW YORK · ALBANY · MASS.

Concealed Phased Array RADAR/Satellite Communication Center

Anti-Aircraft Emplacement

Omega Flight Main Headquarters, Above-ground Facility

Inspector General/ Accounting Service

Omega Hospital/ Trauma Center

Med-Evac Pad

Canadian Secret Intelligence Service Headquarters, Ottawa

Blair Road

Plasma Discharge Sewage Conditioning Plant and Heat Dissipation

Ogilvie Road

Fuel Storage

Blackhawk H Pod Service/ Maintenance Concealed Service Facility

Blackhawk K High-speed Sealed Elevator Service

Special Needs Care Facility/ Long-Term Observation CSIS

World Monitor/ Clinical Evaluation Facility

SM-11 A-Sat Launch Silo

Hardened Launch Control Bunker

Mag-Lev Rail Link to London, England, MI-7

Bathgate Magnetic Drive

Magnetic Levitation Rail System Support Facility

Bathgate Silo Bunker Entry/ Connection CSIS

Close Up:
Air Defense- Pop-up 12 box-loaded HARM SAM Missiles in addition to 4 CWIS (Close-in Weapon System) Electric Vulcan Machine Gun

Escape Pod Mag-Lev Rail Link to New York City Field Offices

Life Pods (typical)

CSIS Secure Underground Facility 2,300 feet deep. Situation Room, Staff Offices, Command Center

Close-Up:
A-Sat Launch Control Bunker. Building within building is mounted on springs to absorb ground moving energy. Constantly manned, these modern-day "Missileers" protect the skies from high-tech attack.

Mag-Lev Rail Link to Nevada and Southern California

Magnetic Levitation Rail System Service Center

Life Pod

Mag-Lev Rail Link to Washington, D.C.

OFFICIAL NAME: United Mexican States (Estados Unidas Mexicanos)

POPULATION: 108,701,000

CAPITAL CITY: Mexico City

PLACES OF INTEREST: Cancun, Guanajuato, Zucatecas, Aguacalientes, Campeche, Dolores Hidalgo (Guanajuato), Tlaxcala, San Miguel de Allende (Guanajuato), Veracruz, Valle de Bravo (Mexico City), Temple of Tirod, Isla Mujeres, Sea of Cortez, Temple of Huitzilopochtli, Castle Zemo (Malpaso)

GOVERNMENT: Federal republic

MAJOR LANGUAGES: Spanish, Mayan, Nahuatl

MONETARY UNIT: Mexican peso

MAJOR RESOURCES: Petroleum, natural gas, nuclear energy, mining, silver, copper, gold, lead, iron, steel, timber, motor vehicles, tourism.

NATIONAL DEFENSE: The Secretariat of National Defense, comprised of the Army, Mexican Air Force, Secretariat of the Navy and Mexican Navy.

INTERNATIONAL RELATIONS: Mexico is a member of the World Health Organization, World Trade Organization, UNESCO, the United Nations, SHIELD and the North American Free Trade Agreement. The country is on friendly terms with the Avengers. Mexico has significant border issues with the USA in the north and Guatemala in the south. China, Japan and the USA are its most important trade partners.

EXTRATERRESTRIAL RELATIONS: Rorgg, king of the "Spider Men" once invaded Mexico but was beaten by Tim Johnson. The Sandman was another alien invader, and was thwarted when it was exposed to water. The extradimensional Diablo invaded near Veracruz, but was driven away by monster hunter Ulysses Bloodstone. The fiery Vulcan Dragoom traveled through Mexico in its attempted conquest of Earth. The extradimensional Synraith was nearly summoned to Earth by accident through the magic of Gracie Destine. The Kree robot Sentry #459 and Ronan the Accuser once fought Captain Mar-Vell in Mexico City.

NONHUMAN POPULATION: Helmut Zemo formerly kept a number of bioplastoid creatures originally developed by Arnim Zola at his Castle Zemo. Some of the Eternals including Ajak, Valkin and Virako visited Mexico around 1000 AD. The creature Zzutak and an opposing monster were created by Frank Johnson using the mystic paints of Yucoya-Tzin. The Timespinner was a robot duplicate of Spider-Man (Peter Parker) made by the time-traveling Kang the Conqueror; it was based at the Temple of Tirod.

DOMESTIC SUPERHUMANS: In the distant past, Cuauhtli was a hero of the Aztec people; by the 19th century, his mantle had been past down to the sword-wielding masked hero el Aguila (Paco Montoya); Paco's successors kept the tradition alive, and some, including the modern-day el Aguila (Alejandro Montoya) of Spain have helped defend Mexico. Rictor (Julio Esteban Richter) was a mutant who joined the New Mutants and X-Force; after losing his powers on "M-Day," he joined X-Factor Investigations. The Cheetah (Esteban Carracus) gained powers from Sentry #459, but was eventually slain by the Scourge of the Underworld. Manuel Diego is a sorcerer and associate of Dr. Strange. Carlos and Eduardo Lobo were a pair of mutant werewolves who became crimelords in the USA; Eduardo was accidentally slain by his lover Gloria Grant. El Muerto (Juan-Carlos Estrada Sanchez) is a masked wrestler with mystical strength gained from the mysterious entity el Dorado. Noise (Julio Mendoza) was a mutant mercenary active in Costa Brava.

PROMINENT CITIZENS: In 1912, el Sombro (Juan Correo) was a masked hero believed by his foes to be a man returned from the dead; Juan's father the Wolf (Pedro Correo) had been a leader in Pancho Villa's revolution, and Juan turned on his father's enemies, including Dagger and el Toro; he eventually married Maria Duro, daughter of Governor Ramon Duro of Sonando. Enrique Montoya was the brother of the 19th century's el Aguila. Carlos Cortez was one of the Renegades, men believed to have turned coward at the battle of the Alamo. Rictor's

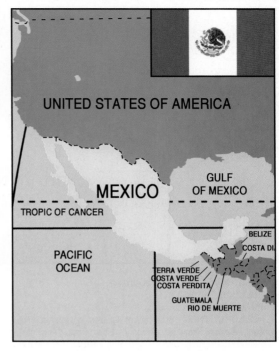

UNITED STATES OF AMERICA

MEXICO

GULF OF MEXICO

TROPIC OF CANCER

PACIFIC OCEAN

BELIZE
COSTA DI.
TERRA VERDE
COSTA VERDE
COSTA PERDITA
GUATEMALA
RIO DE MUERTE

family in Guadalajara includes his cousins Omar and Ramon and uncle Gonzalo. Tim Johnson was a teenager who defeated Rorgg. In the 19th century, a band of Aztecs including Xotoc, Itzamu and Konnu were found by the Rawhide Kid (Johnny Bart). Yucoya-Tzin adheres to the ways of the Aztec, and has sought repeatedly to bring his god Zzutak to life with mystic paints. Carlos Santos emigrated to the USA, where he joined the Legion of Living Lightning and died battling the Hulk; his son Miguel became the heroic Living Lightning.

SUPERHUMAN RESIDENTS: Baron (Helmut) Zemo formerly had a castle near Malpaso, and his wife Heike Zemo and ally Techno (Paul Ebersol) sometimes resided there as well. Gracie and Kay of the Destine family visited Mexico during the conquest by Cortés. The mystical Cult of the Harvester of Eyes was formerly based in a Mexican jungle.

DOMESTIC CRIME: There are numerous instances of prostitution and slave labor in Mexico. Several illegal drugs including heroin, cocaine and methamphetamine are produced in Mexico. Louis Alejandro Garabello Richter was a gun runner who perished in a clash with Stryfe; his son became the hero Rictor. Angelica Rojas was a slave runner who died in childbirth. Raoul Eschevarra was a local bandit whose mind was briefly imprinted upon Sentry #459.

INTERNATIONAL CRIME: The misunderstood US outlaws Rawhide Kid, Kid Colt (Blaine Colt), Phantom Rider (Carter Slade) and Black Rider (Matthew Masters) often entered Mexico in the 19th century to help combat dangerous criminals such as el Lopo, el Tyrano and el Ojo. The Mutant Liberation Front once had a base at Guadalajara. Apocalypse (En Sabah Nur) once threatened Mexico City with earthquakes. The Kingpin of Crime (Wilson Fisk) has been involved in the Mexican drug trade; in turn, this has drawn the attention of the Punisher (Frank Castle). AIM formerly had a facility in Black Mesa where they developed a cavourite crystal. Sabretooth (Victor Creed), Hydra, UNISYM and the Mys-Tech have also been active in Mexico.

HISTORY: In ancient times, Mexico was inhabited by the Olmec, Mayan, Toltec and Aztec civilizations. By 1521, Hernan Cortés had conquered the country for Spain, overthrowing the Aztec ruler Montezuma (although pockets of sovereign Aztec powers endured in secrecy until the late 19th century). Mexico was liberated from Spain from 1810 and established by 1824, but in 1848 the Mexican Wars with the USA cost Mexico nearly half of its territory to its northern rival.

UNITED STATES OF AMERICA

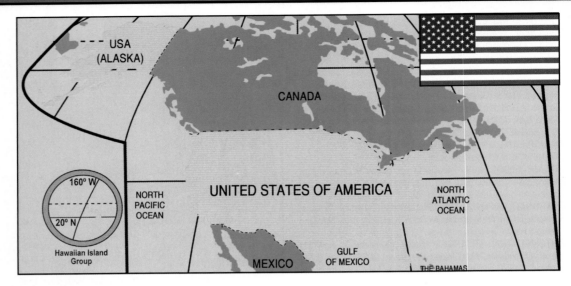

OFFICIAL NAME: United States of America

POPULATION: 301,140,000

CAPITAL CITY: Washington, DC

PLACES OF INTEREST: State capitals are: Montgomery (Alabama), Juneau (Alaska), Phoenix (Arizona), Little Rock (Arkansas), Sacramento (California), Denver (Colorado), Hartford (Connecticut), Dover (Delaware), Tallahassee (Florida), Atlanta (Georgia), Honolulu (Hawaii), Boise (Idaho), Springfield (Illinois), Indianapolis (Indiana), Des Moines (Iowa), Topeka (Kansas), Frankfort (Kentucky), Baton Rouge (Louisiana), Augusta (Maine), Annapolis (Maryland), Boston (Massachusetts), Lansing (Michigan), Saint Paul (Minnesota), Jackson (Mississippi), Jefferson City (Missouri), Helena (Montana), Lincoln (Nebraska), Carson City (Nevada), Concord (New Hampshire), Trenton (New Jersey), Santa Fe (New Mexico), Albany (New York), Raleigh (North Carolina), Bismarck (North Dakota), Columbus (Ohio), Oklahoma City (Oklahoma), Salem (Oregon), Harrisburg (Pennsylvania), Providence (Rhode Island), Columbia (South Carolina), Pierre (South Dakota), Nashville (Tennessee), Austin (Texas), Salt Lake City (Utah), Montpelier (Vermont), Richmond (Virginia), Olympia (Washington), Charleston (West Virginia), Madison (Wisconsin) and Cheyenne (Wyoming). Other significant places include the Abby (New York), Aerie (New Mexico), Area 102 (New Mexico), Asgard (Oklahoma), Avengers Compound (California), Avengers Mansion (Manhattan), Bar With No Name (various including Connecticut), Baxter Building (Manhattan), Camp Hammond (Stamford, Connecticut), Camp Verde (Arizona), Carmody Institute (Maine), Castle Doom (New York), Central City (California), Citrusville (Florida), the Colony (Arizona), Daily Bugle (Manhattan), Desert Base (New Mexico), Dorkham Asylum (Massachusetts), Empire State University (New York), Fire Lake (Massachusetts), Foxhole (Illinois), Gamma Base (New Mexico), Gammaworld (New Mexico), Haven (New York), Hellfire Club (Manhattan), the Hole (Colorado), Holy Ghost Church (Manhattan), the Hostel (California), Massachusetts Academy (Massachusetts), the Maze (Nevada), Middletown ("Gammatown," Arizona), the Mount (Arizona), Mount Charteris (Colorado), New Salem (Colorado), Nightwing Restorations (New York), Nüponder (Minnesota), Project: PEGASUS (New York), Ravencroft Sanitarium (New York), Richmond Riding Academy (New York), One Roxxon Plaza (Manhattan), Rosewell Sanitarium (Massachusetts), Ryker's Island (New York), Sanctum Sanctorum (Manhattan), Seagate (Georgia), Serpent Citadel (New York), Sink City (Illinois), Springdale (Connecticut), Stark Tower (Manhattan), Starkesboro (Massachusetts), Swamp City (Florida), Thunderbolts Mountain (Colorado), Timely Industries (Wisconsin), the Vault (Colorado), Whisper Hill (New York), Wondermont (Montana), X-Factor Investigations (Manhattan), Xavier Institute for Higher Learning (New York)

GOVERNMENT: Constitution-based federal republic

MAJOR LANGUAGES: English, Spanish, Hawaiian

MONETARY UNIT: US dollar

MAJOR RESOURCES: Mining, coal, copper, lead, phosphates, uranium, bauxite, gold, iron, mercury, nickel, potash, silver, tungsten, zinc, steel, timber, petroleum, natural gas, nuclear power, merchant marine, motor vehicles, food processing, consumer goods, aerospace, telecommunications, electronics, chemicals and superhumans.

NATIONAL DEFENSE: Army, Navy, Marine Corps, Air Force and Coast Guard. National security is also maintained by the National Guard, Office of Homeland Security, intelligence agencies CIA, FBI, NSA, DIA, INR, DEA, and superhuman agencies the Commission on Superhuman Activities (CSA), Office of National Emergency and 50-State Initiative. Current official superhuman defenses include Guardsmen and Sentinels; Anthony Stark has provided some military access to his Iron Man armor designs. Former national defenses include Freedom Force, Operation: Zero Tolerance, Weapon X and X-Factor.

INTERNATIONAL RELATIONS: The USA plays host to the international headquarters of the United Nations and SHIELD. It is also a member of the Arctic Council, Interpol, the North American Free Trade Agreement, North Atlantic Treaty Organization, the United Nations Security Council, UNESCO, the World Health Organization and the World Trade Organization. The locations of American Samoa, Baker Island, Guam, Howland Island, Jarvis Island, Johnston Atoll, Kingman Reef, Midway Islands, Navassa Island, Northern Mariana Islands, Palmyra Atoll, Puerto Rico, Virgin Islands and Wake Island are dependents. The US has been on amicable terms with virtually the entire western world, but in times past has been in conflict with Canada, Germany, Italy, Japan, North Korea and the UK. The country has forces deployed in Afghanistan and Iraq. The USA maintains a base at Guantanamo Bay, Cuba. There are recurring border issues with Mexico, territorial disputes with Haiti, controversial opposition to Wakandan sovereignty and even more controversial allegiances with Latveria. In the superhuman community, the US has received aid from Canada's Alpha Flight and Omega Flight, Symkaria's Wild Pack and Russia's Winter Guard.

EXTRATERRESTRIAL RELATIONS: Perhaps a hundred different races have visited the USA, some in peace, many with hostile intent. Races have included the Arcturans, Astrans, Autocrons, Badoon, Beyonders, Brood, Celestials, Contraxians, Dakkamites, Darbians, Dire Wraiths, Elan, Eternals of Titan, Fortisquians, Galadorians, Glx, Gramosians, Herms, Korbinites, Kree, Kronans, Krylorians, Kymellians, Laxidazians, Luphomoids, Makluans, Marvanites, Megans, Oobagonians, Phalanx, Plodex, Poppupians, Protars, Quists, Quons, Rigellians,

Roclites, R'zahnians, Sakaarians, Shi'ar, Sidri, Siris, Skrulls, Snarks, Solons, Spartoi, Stonians, Technarchy, Tribbitites, Troyjans, Tsiln, Ul'lula'ns, Vorms, Watchers, Xandarians, Xartans, Zen-Whoberis, Zenn-Lavians, Zhalla'kians, and Zundamites, as well as Ariel, Century, the Elders of the Universe, Galactus, Gosamyr, Halflife, Shaper of Worlds, Starblasters, Stranger, Terminus, Thor Girl and Ultimo. Some races have made long-term colonization, including the Kree and Skrulls of Raven's Perch. The city of Asgard has taken up residence above Oklahoma, and Thor helped found the Avengers. Many of the Olympian gods have lived and worked in the US, including Ares and Hercules of the Avengers. The Nexus of All Realities lies in a Florida swamp near Citrusville, and various extradimensional entities have traveled into the USA, including demons such as the N'Garai as well as Abraxas, Howard the Duck, Immortus, Jim Jaspers, Kang, Nightmare, Possessors, Mindless Ones, Ramades, Squadron Supreme and peoples of Counter-Earth, Dark Dimension, Dimension Z, Earth-A, Femizonia, Fifth Dimension, K'ai, Kosmos, Land Within, Machus, Microverse, Mindscape, Mojoverse, Negative Zone, Otherworld and Polemachus.

WHITE HOUSE

Art by Staz Johnson

NONHUMAN POPULATION: Numerous sub-species of humanity such as the Atlanteans, Deviants, Eternals and Inhumans have clashed with and lived among the peoples of the USA. The USA has the highest world population of robots, notably including Awesome Android, Bastion, Cerebro, Doomsday Man, Dragon Man, Jocasta, Machine Man (Aaron Stack), Quasimodo, Sentinels, Super-Adaptoid, Ultron and Vision, among many others.

DOMESTIC SUPERHUMANS: The USA leads the world with the highest number of costumed and super-powered humans. Within its 50-State Initiative is the black ops "Shadow Initiative," various cadets including Cloud 9, Debrii (Deborah Fields), Hardball (Roger Brokeridge), Komodo, Scarlet Spiders, Slapstick (Steve Harmon), Stature (Cassie Lang), Trauma (Terrence Ward) and Ultragirl (Susan Sheranan); and the assembled teams including Action Pack (Kentucky), Avengers (New York), Great Lakes Initiative (Wisconsin), Liberteens (Pennsylvania), Order (California), Rangers (Texas), Thunderbolts (Colorado). Other notable super-hero teams have included Agents of Atlas, All-Winners Squad, B-Sides, Champions, Crazy Eight, Darkhold Redeemers, Defenders, Earth Force, Fantastic Force, Fantastic Four, First Line, Force Works, Gamma Corps, Generation X, Heroes for Hire, Invaders, Jury, Kid Commandos, Legion of Night, Liberty Legion, Loners, New Mutants, New Warriors, Nextwave, Pantheon, Power Pack, Redeemers, Renegades, Runaways, Santerians, Secret Defenders, Skrull Kill Krew, Sons of the Tiger, Spider Society, Thunderiders, X-Factor Investigations, X-Force, X-Men, X-Statix and Young Avengers.

Some prominent US heroes include mutants (some now depowered): Angel (Warren Worthington III), Anole (Victor Borkowski), Beast (Henry McCoy), Blackwing (Barnell Bohusk), Blindfold (Ruth Aldine), Caliban, Cannonball (Sam Guthrie), Cyclops (Scott Summers), Cypher (Doug Ramsey), Dazzler (Alison Blaire), Firestar (Angelica Jones), Forge, Jean Grey, Havok (Alex Summers), Hellion (Julian Keller), Husk (Paige Guthrie), Justice (Vance Astrovik), Leech, Artie Maddicks, Mercury (Cessily Kincaid), Layla Miller, Danielle Moonstar, Multiple Man (Jaime Madrox), Night Thrasher (Donyell Taylor), Outlaw (Inez Temple), Polaris (Lorna Dane), Professor X (Charles Xavier), Razorback (Buford Hollis), Ricochet (Johnny Gallo), Rockslide (Santo Vaccarro), Rogue, Shadowcat (Katherine Pryde), Skids (Saly Blevins), Skin (Angelo Espinosa), Tabitha Smith, Squirrel Girl (Doreen Green), Stepford Cuckoos, Strong Guy (Guido Carosella), Synch (Everett Thomas), Tempest (Angel Salvadore), Thunderbird (John Proudstar), Toro

(Thomas Raymond), Warpath (James Proudstar), White Queen (Emma Frost) and Wondra (Jubilation Lee).

Gifted athletes and those with special devices include: Angel (Thomas Halloway), Annex (Alexander Ellis), Black Cat (Felicia Hardy), Black Marvel (Dan Lyons), Blizzard (Donald Gill), Bluebird (Sally Avril), Captain America (Steve Rogers & James Barnes), Challenger (William Waring), Constrictor (Frank Payne), Darkhawk (Chris Powell), Deathlok (Michael Collins), Dominic Fortune (Duvid Fortunov), Father Time (Larry Scott), Fin (Admiral Peter Noble), Fixer (Paul Ebersol), Foolkiller (Greg Salinger), Force (Clayton Wilson), Free Spirit (Cathy Webster), Freedom Ring (Curtis Doyle), Frog-Man (Eugene Patilio), Gauntlet (Joseph Green), High Tech (Curtis Carr), Iron Man (Anthony Stark), Misty Knight, MACH-4 (Abner Jenkins), Mockingbird (Barbara Morse), Night Thrasher (Dwayne Taylor), Nomad (Jack Monroe), Patriot (Jeff Mace), Prowler (Hobie Brown), Punisher (Frank Castle), Quasar (Wendell Vaughn), Ronin (Clint Barton), Rocket Racer (Robert Farrell), Jim Scully, Silver Scorpion (Elizabeth Barstow), Songbird (Melissa Gold), Star-Lord (Peter Quill), Steel Spider (Ollie Osnick), Stingray (Walter Newell), Sun Girl (Mary Mitchell), Turbo (Michiko Musashi), Two-Gun Kid (Matt Hawk), Vagabond (Priscilla Lyons), War Machine (James Rhodes), White Tiger (Kevin Cole), and Colleen Wing.

Those empowered by magic include: Black Crow (Jesse Black Crow), Blazing Skull (Mark Todd), Devil-Slayer (Eric Simon Payne), Dr. Druid (Anthony Druid), Dr. Strange (Stephen Strange), Gargoyle (Isaac Christians), Ghost Rider (Johnny Blaze & Daniel Ketch), Hellcat (Patsy Walker), Daimon Hellstrom, Satana Hellstrom, Iron Fist (Daniel Rand), Jennifer Kale, Hannibal King, Man-Thing (Ted Sallis), Ian McNee, Mechamage, Moon Knight (Marc Spector), Roger "Red" Norvell, Phantom Rider (Hamilton Slade), Red Wolf (Will Talltrees), Gabriel Rosetti, Sepulcre (Jillian Marie Woods), Ezekiel Sims, Spellbinder (Erica Fortune), Thunderstrike (Eric Masterson), Tigra (Greer Nelson), White Tiger (Hector Ayala & Angela Del Toro) and Zombie (Simon Garth).

US mutates include: American Eagle (Jason Strongbow), Ant-Man (Scott Lang & Eric O'Grady), Arachne (Julia Carpenter), Arana (Anya Corazon), Atlas (Erik Josten), Battlestar (Lemar Hoskins), Blue Shield (Joseph Cartelli), Amadeus Cho, Luke Cage, Captain Ultra (Griffin Gogol), Charcoal (Charlie Burlingame), Cloak (Tyrone Johnson), Comet Man (Stephan Beckley), Dagger (Tandy Bowen), Daredevil (Matt Murdock), Demolition-Man (Dennis Dunphy), Doc Samson (Leonard Samson), Drax (Arthur Douglas), Echo (Maya Lopez), Energizer (Katie Power), Falcon (Sam Wilson), Firebird (Bonita Juarez), Goliath (Bill Foster), Gravity (Greg Willis), Hulk (Bruce Banner), Human Torch (Johnny

Storm), Invisible Woman (Susan Richards), Jack Flag, Daisy Johnson, Jolt (Hallie Takahama), Jessica Jones, Lightspeed (Julie Power), Living Lightning (Miguel Santos), Mass Master (Jack Power), Mayhem (Brigid O'Reilly), Miss America (Madeline Frank), Mr. Fantastic (Reed Richards), Moondragon (Heather Douglas), Moonstone (Karla Sofen), Ms. Marvel (Carol Danvers & Sharon Ventura), Nighthawk (Kyle Richmond), Nova (Richard Rider), Paladin, Penance (Robbie Baldwin), Rage (Elvin Haliday), Monica Rambeau, Sentry (Robert Reynolds), She-Hulk (Jennifer Walters), Shroud (Maximilian Coleridge), Solo (James Bourne), Spider-Man (Peter Parker), Spider-Woman (Mattie Franklin), Terror (Laslo Pevely), Thin Man (Bruce Dickson), Thing (Ben Grimm), 3-D Man (Chuck & Hal Chandler), Toxin (Patrick Mulligan), Triathlon (Delroy Garrett), USAgent (John Walker), Volcana (Marsha Rosenberg), Wasp (Janet Van Dyne), Whizzer (Robert Frank), Will O' the Wisp (Jackson Arvad), Wonder Man (Simon Williams), Yellowjacket (Henry Pym & Rita DeMara) and Zero-G (Alex Power).

PROMINENT CITIZENS: In New York, Code: Blue provides significant police defense against superhuman threats; Damage Control helps clean up after superhuman battles. Staff of the Initiative include: Baron von Blitzschlag, Henry Peter Gyrich and Senator Marcus Woodman. The Daily Bugle's staff has included Lance Bannon, Betty Brant, Kathryn Cushing, Ken Ellis, Katherine Farrell, Sally Floyd, J. Jonah Jameson, Nick Katzenberg, Ned Leeds, Joy Mercado, Irene Merryweather, Glorianna O'Breen, Joe Robertson, Phil Sheldon, Leila Taylor, Ben Urich and Billy Walters. Famous battalions of World War II included the Deadly Dozen, Howling Commandos, Leatherneck Raiders, Maulers and Missouri Marauders. Other notable US citizens have included Marlene Alraune, Bambi Arbogast, Betty Banner, Becky Blake, Moira Brandon, G.W. Bridge, Laura Brown, Bethany Cabe, Vera Cantor, Sharon Carter, Peggy Carter, Millie Collins, Dr. Valerie Cooper, Senator Graydon Creed, Dr. Daniel Damian, Margo Damian, Jean DeWolff, Milla Donovan, Timothy "Dum-Dum" Dugan, Fred Duncan, Jane Foster, Nick Fury, Gloria Grant, Maya Hansen, Maria Hill, Harold "Happy" Hogan, Phineas T. Horton, Stevie Hunter, John Jameson, Rick Jones, Senator Robert Kelly, Sal Kennedy, Dr. Keith Kincaid, Rae LaCoste, Sidney Levine, Nathan Lubensky, Willie Lumpkin, Al Mackenzie, Louise Mason, Alicia Masters, Microchip (David Lieberman), Franklin "Foggy" Nelson, Kate Neville, Dakota North, Michael O'Brien, Robert O'Bryan, Harry & Liz Osborn, Norman Osborn, Karen Page, Ben & May Parker, Mary & Richard Parker, Alexander Goodwin Pierce, Virginia "Pepper" Potts, James & Margaret Power, Betty Prentiss, Clay Quartermain, Senator Robert Ralston, Lindy Reynolds, Franklin Richards, Nathaniel Richards, Valeria Richards, Dallas Riordan, Bernie Rosenthal, Everett K. Ross, General Thaddeus "Thunderbolt" Ross, Juston Seyfert, Raymond Sikorski, Jasper Sitwell, Candy Southern, George Stacy, Gwen Stacy, Sarah Stacy, Fabian Stankowicz, Howard & Maria Stark, Morgan Stark, Stunt-Master (George Smith), Colonel Glenn Talbot, Major William Talbot, Eugene "Flash" Thompson, Blake Tower, Bolivar Trask, Mary Jane Watson, Kate Waynesboro, Debra Whitman, Jim Wilson, Wyatt Wingfoot, Sara Wolfe and James Woo.

Heroes of the old west of the 19th century included Apache Kid (Dazii), Black Rider (Matthew Masters), Tex Dawson, Gunhawk, Gunsmoke Kid, Caleb Hammer, Sam Hawk, Hurricane (Harry Kane), Reno Jones, Kid Cassidy (Richard Cassidy), Kid Colt (Blaine Colt), Masked Raider (Jim Gardley), Outlaw Kid (Lance Temple), Phantom Rider (Carter & Lincoln Slade), Rawhide Kid (Johnny Bart), Red Wolf (Johnny Wakely), Ringo Kid and Matt Slade.

SUPERHUMAN RESIDENTS: The high population of super heroes and their teams have led many heroes from other lands to live in the US for brief or lengthy periods of time; virtually every foreign hero on Earth has spent some time in the US.

DOMESTIC CRIME: In the past, stability in the USA has been tried by zealous groups such as the Ku Klux Klan, Purity, Friends of Humanity, Humanity's Last Stand, Sons of the Serpent, Purifiers and X-Cell.

Significant crime cartels in the US include the Kingpin (Wilson Fisk)'s empire, Assassins Guild, Committee, Conspiracy, Corporation, Gnucci family, Hellfire Club, the Maggia, the Serpent Society, Thieves Guild, Upstarts and the Zodiac. Other criminal gangs include the Acolytes, Alliance of Evil, Ani-Men, Brotherhood of Mutants, Circus of Crime, Death-Throws, Deathweb, Desert Dwellers, Enforcers, Emissaries of Evil, Fallen Angels, Folding Circle, Frightful Four, Grapplers, Headmen, Lethal Legion, Marauders, Masters of Evil, Morlocks, Mutant Force, Night Shift, Organization, Pride, Psionex, Reavers, Resistants, Right, Riot Squad, Rocketeers, Salem's Seven, Serpent Squad, Sinister Six, Sinister Syndicate, Sisters of Sin, Squadron Sinister, Terrible Trio, U-Foes, U-Men, Watchdogs Wildboys and Wrecking Crew. Criminal-run businesses include Baintronics, Brand Corporation, Cybertek, Damocles Foundation, Ophrah Industries, Roxxon Oil and Shaw Industries.

Notable US criminals have included Absorbing Man (Carl "Crusher" Creel), Answer (Aaron Nicholson), Arcade, Armadillo (Antonio Rodriguez), Asbestos Lady (Victoria Murdock), Sunset Bain, Turk Barrett, Black Spectre (Carson Knowles), Black Talon (Samuel David Barone), Alexander Bont, Bullet, Bullseye, Callisto, Cardiac (Elias Wirtham), Carnage (Cletus Kasady), Chance (Nicholas Powell), Chemistro (Calvin Carr), Cobalt Man (Ralph Roberts), Controller (Basil Sandhurst), Copperhead (Lawrence Chesney), Copycat (Vanessa Carlysle), Corruptor (Jackson Day), Crimson Cowl (Justine Hammer), Crossbones (Brock Rumlow), Crossfire (William Cross), Crusader (Arthur Blackwood), Diamondhead (Arch Dyker), Dr. Bong (Lester Verde), Dr. Demonicus (Douglas Birely), Dr. Nemesis (Michael Stockton), Dr. Octopus (Otto Octavius), Damon Dran, Eel (Edward Lavell), Richard Fisk, Flying Tiger, Vincente Fortunato, Fox (Reynard Slinker), Ghost, Gibbon (Martin Blank), Gladiator (Melvin Potter), Glob (Joseph Timms), Goldbug (Matthew Gilden), Griffin (John Horton), Grim Reaper (Eric Williams), Justin Hammer, Hammerhead,

STARK TOWER

BAXTER BUILDING

Schultz), Sin-Eater (Stanley Carter), Slug (Ulysses X. Lugman), Slyde (Jalome Beacher), Alistaire Smythe, Speed Demon (James Sanders), Speedfreek (Joss Shappe), Spot (Jonathon Ohnn), Spymaster (Sinclair Abbott), Stained Glass Scarlet (Scarlet Fascinera), Stilt-Man (Wilbur Day), Tiberius Stone, Mendel Stromm, Sunturion (Arthur Dearborn), Taskmaster, Tiger Shark (Todd Arliss), Tinkerer (Phineas Mason), Titania (Mary MacPherran), Tombstone (Lonnie Lincoln), Trapster (Peter Petruski), Typhoid Mary, Underworld (Jackie Dio), Phil Urich, Vanisher, Venom (Eddie Brock & Mac Gargan), Vermin (Edward Whelan), Vulture (Adrian Toomes), Weasel, Whiplash (Mark Scarlotti), Whirlwind (David Cannon), White Rabbit (Lorina Dodson), Wizard (Bentley Wittman) and Zodiak (Norman Harrison).

INTERNATIONAL CRIME: The terrorist organizations AIM, al-Qaeda, FALN, Fenris, Force of Nature, Humans Off Planet, Hydra, Legion of Living Lightning, Mutant Liberation Front, New American Revolution, Secret Empire and ULTIMATUM have been active on US soil. Virtually every foreign superhuman criminal has been active in the US at one time, or has significant dealings with allies in the US.

HISTORY: Previously a British colony, men such as Captain America (Steven Rogers) and Ulysses Bloodstone helped fight the Revolutionary War (1775-1781), and the United States of America were established as an independent power in 1783. Relations with its North American neighbors were fractured in the 19th century, including battling Canada in the War of 1812, and the Mexican Wars, which stripped that nation of half its territory. The Civil War of 1862 finally brought an end to slavery in the country, at the cost of millions of lives. The US was a major factor in both World Wars, where it emerged as the world's greatest superpower. During its "cold war" with the USSR, the US attempted to fight communist powers in Korea and Vietnam. Since the 20th century, the USA has emerged as the world's richest source of superhumans, particularly costumed heroes. Although heroes were mostly welcomed and even government-sponsored for many years, the destruction of Stamford, Connecticut during a battle between the New Warriors and Nitro resulted in the adoption of the SHRA, and the forced conscription of all superhumans native to or residing in the USA into the 50-State Initiative.

Jonas Harrow, Hobgoblin (Roderick Kingsley & Jason Macendale), Cameron Hodge, Hood (Parker Robbins), Humbug (Buck Mitty), Hurricane (Albert Potter), Hyena (Henry Mortonson), Hydro-Man (Morris Bench), Isbisa (Simon Meke), Jack O' Lantern (Steven Levins), Jackal (Miles Warren), Jester (Jonathon Powers), Jigsaw, Jimmy-6 (Giacomo Fortunato), Joystick (Janice Yanizeski), Juggernaut (Cain Marko), Killer Shrike (Simon Maddicks), Leader (Samuel Sterns), Lightmaster (Edward Lansky), Living Laser (Arthur Parks), Lizard (Curtis Connors), Looter (Norton Fester), Machinesmith (Samuel Saxon), Mad-Dog (Robert Baxter), Mad Thinker, Madcap, Dr. Karl Malus, Man-Bull (William Taurens), Man Mountain Marko, Mandrill (Jerome Beechman), Marrow, Masked Marauder (Frank Farnum), Mauler (Brendan Doyle), Mentallo (Marvin Flumm), Mesmero, Mimic (Calvin Rankin), Mr. Fear (Lawrence Cranston), Mr. Hyde (Calvin Zabo), MODOK (George Tarleton), Molecule Man (Owen Reece), Molten Man (Mark Raxton), Morpheus (Robert Markham), Mysterio (Quentin Beck & Francis Klum), Nanny, Nekra, Nightshade (Tilda Johnson), Nitro (Robert Hunter), Orphan-Maker, Owl (Leland Owlsley), Power Broker (Curtiss Jackson), Puma (Thomas Firehart), Rampage (Stuart Clarke), Celia Ricadonna, Rose (Jacob Conover), Sandman (William Baker), Scarecrow (Ebenezer Laughton), Scourges of the Underworld, Nicholas Scratch, Shocker (Herman

XAVIER INSTITUTE

EMPIRE STATE UNIVERSITY

E.S.U.
EMPIRE STATE UNIVERSITY

CAMP HAMMOND
Stamford, Connecticut

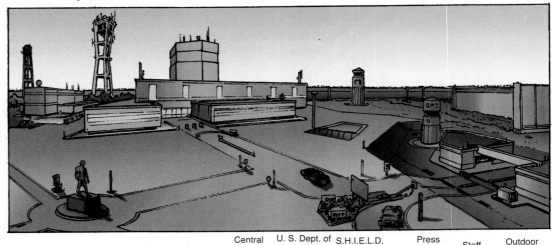

Comm and Security Towers (typical) · Brig and Interrogation Center · Central Command Complex · Mess Hall/ Kitchen · U. S. Dept. of Superhuman Armed Forces Field Office · S.H.I.E.L.D. Security/ Main Gate · S.H.I.E.L.D. Field Offices · Press Briefing Area · Parking · Staff Offices · Trainer Housing · Outdoor Training Area

Camp James Hammond, located on the "Gold Coast" of Connecticut's Fairfield County and within a short drive to the Lodge Turnpike (US I-95), is a relocation and training facility for the United States' Department of Superhuman Armed Forces.

Camp Hammond is the equivalent of an Ultra-Max Security Facility, but has elements of conventional military bases familiar to soldiers everywhere. Perimeter control is vigorous from both outside and in.

The camp's namesake, James Hammond, was the first android para-pyrotic, who devoted his life to integrating into human society. His legacy is the hope that special individuals everywhere can coexist with all of society in peace, harmony and security.

The camp training facilities are beyond cutting edge, with specially crafted training and educational devices and methods. Medical and psychological experts the world over have contributed to the design and execution of Camp Hammond. This will ensure the most successful group of soldiers and future leaders possible.

The Strategic Hazard Intervention and Espionage Logistics Directorate (S.H.I.E.L.D.) maintains a strong and protective presence on the base at all times.

--From the S.H.I.E.L.D. Press Relations Office, Office of the Director, 2007 "Get to Know Camp Hammond."

RINEHART RD · MACE RD · FRANK RD · FLETCHER RD · NASLAND RD · RINEHART RD

Outdoor Stadium · Firing Range · Event Parking · Parking · Gymnasium · "Deadline" High Security Perimeter · Security Towers (typical) · South Gate · Clinic/ Teaching Hospital/ ICU · Recruit/ Cadet Housing · Motor Pool · High-speed Security Repsonse Vehicle Exit (typical) · Trainer Offices · N-Portal Jump Station

GAMMA BASE
near BEATTY, NEVADA

Gamma Base, Nevada, is the repository of the quiescent Dr. Bruce Banner, better known as the Hulk, and others. It is located in a subterranean nuclear detonation cavity. There are numerous protective measures employed. All are Classified. There are various high security cells at the three mile deep main facility, informally called "Hulkbuster Base." The self-contained base uses a cold fusion energy system. The existance of extensive underground magnetic-levitation railways has never been confirmed. The three-mile deep base has several "fail-safe" measures in the event of catastrophe that are Classified.

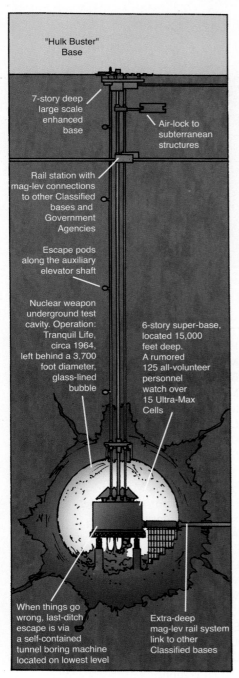

"Hulk Buster" Base

7-story deep large scale enhanced base

Air-lock to subterranean structures

Rail station with mag-lev connections to other Classified bases and Government Agencies

Escape pods along the auxiliary elevator shaft

Nuclear weapon underground test cavity. Operation: Tranquil Life, circa 1964, left behind a 3,700 foot diameter, glass-lined bubble

6-story super-base, located 15,000 feet deep. A rumored 125 all-volunteer personnel watch over 15 Ultra-Max Cells

When things go wrong, last-ditch escape is via a self-contained tunnel boring machine located on lowest level

Extra-deep mag-lev rail system link to other Classified bases

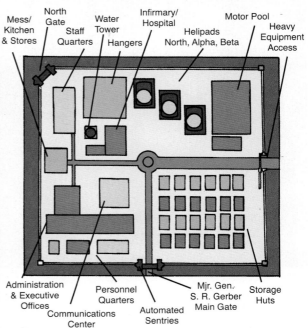

North Gate

Mess/ Kitchen & Stores

Staff Quarters

Water Tower

Hangers

Infirmary/ Hospital

Helipads North, Alpha, Beta

Motor Pool

Heavy Equipment Access

Administration & Executive Offices

Personnel Quarters

Communications Center

Automated Sentries

Mjr. Gen. S. R. Gerber Main Gate

Storage Huts

At three miles deep, the atmosphere, brought from the surface, is unbreathable. If the unimaginable occurs and escape is necessary, spacesuit style equpment is needed to survive outside the protected structure.
The Hulk is rumored to be in Ultra Cell #113. Nothing else is known for sure.

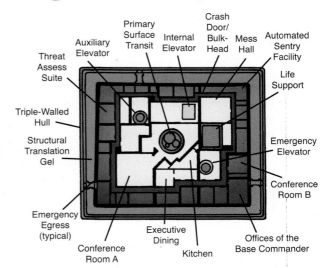

Crash Door/ Bulk-Head

Primary Surface Transit

Internal Elevator

Mess Hall

Automated Sentry Facility

Auxiliary Elevator

Threat Assess Suite

Life Support

Triple-Walled Hull

Structural Translation Gel

Emergency Elevator

Conference Room B

Emergency Egress (typical)

Conference Room A

Executive Dining

Kitchen

Offices of the Base Commander

Level One-- 15,650 feet below the surface. This is the only floor plan ever released by official sources. It hints at a major installation dedicated to securing any major threat. The "building within a building" structure is similar to the design of nuclear-hardened missile silos.

MANHATTAN

CENTRAL & SOUTH AMERICA

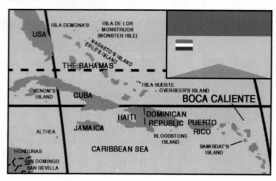

OFFICIAL NAME: The Independent Island of Boca Caliente (la Isla Independiente de Boca Caliente)

POPULATION: Current estimates unavailable.

CAPITAL CITY: Port-of-Boca

PLACES OF INTEREST: AIM Convention Center, AIM Administration Building, AIM Central Security Complex, AIM Command Center, Rojo Beach

GOVERNMENT: Autocracy

MAJOR LANGUAGES: Spanish, English

MONETARY UNIT: None (formerly Boca Caliente dollar)

MAJOR RESOURCES: Manufactured goods

NATIONAL DEFENSE: AIM maintained a large standing paramilitary force on Boca Caliente. Nonhuman defense included a fleet of Aquanoid androids, Adaptoid androids, and a highly advanced national missile defense system.

INTERNATIONAL RELATIONS: Boca Caliente held membership in the United Nations (UN).

EXTRATERRESTRIAL RELATIONS: None known.

NONHUMAN POPULATION: Under the leadership of Alessandro Brannex (the Super-Adaptoid), a majority of Boca Caliente's population was replaced with Adaptoid androids. AIM also created the Neo-Adaptoid (dubbed "Batch 13" by AIM scientists), but it developed premature awareness before its para-reality programming took hold, causing it to break free from its containment vessel and travel to New York City, where it reluctantly battled Captain America and Fantastic Force before being sucked through a portal to an uninhabited plane of reality.

DOMESTIC SUPERHUMANS: AIM transformed Hungarian Olinka Barankova into the cybernetic agent MODAM (Mental Organism Designed for Aggressive Maneuvers) on Boca Caliente in order to replace the deceased MODOK (Mental Organism Designed Only for Killing). AIM's "Project Resurrection" later restored MODOK (George Tarleton) to life via the Cosmic Cube.

PROMINENT CITIZENS: General Andres Pacheco led a successful military coup d'etat on Boca Caliente days prior to AIM's invasion of the island.

SUPERHUMAN RESIDENTS: None documented.

DOMESTIC CRIME: Under the leadership of AIM, domestic crime was virtually nonexistent on Boca Caliente.

INTERNATIONAL CRIME: Boca Caliente's AIM rulers were accused of state-sponsored terrorism and the subversion of foreign governments on several occasions; their own security was undermined when Hydra once invaded their facilities and stole their most advanced weaponry.

FIRST APPEARANCE: Iron Man #207 (1986)

HISTORY: The tiny island of Boca Caliente was first settled by the Ortoiroid people, who many believed migrated from South America's Orinoco River Valley in approximately 3500 BC. Christopher Columbus first visited the island in 1492, naming it "Boca Caliente" due to its sweltering heat and humidity. The islands remained a Spanish colony until 1898, when it gained independence following the Spanish-American War and was established as a republic. In the 20th century, the country became a popular US tourist destination.

In recent years, businessman Bernard "Bernie" Allen financed a revolution that enabled the forces of General Pacheco to overthrow the government of Boca Caliente; but when Pacheco refused to allow Allen's international organization to take over the country, Allen killed him. Meanwhile, AIM's Scientist Supreme Valdemar Tykkio set up the "Targo Corporation" as a legitimate business front and hired Iron Man (Tony Stark) to launch their satellite into space with the understanding that it was an orbiting observatory. In reality, the Targo Corp satellite contained the Orbiting Lens, which converted solar energy into a powerful electron beam capable of destroying entire cities from orbit. Tykkio immediately used the Orbiting Lens to destroy a military airfield on the outskirts of Port-of-Boca. The electron beam was then used to cut a destructive swath clean across the island-nation, killing everything in its path. A squadron of AIM aircraft was ordered to obliterate all buildings and kill those attempting to flee the island nation. Within hours, Boca Caliente's single airfield and the Presidential Palace were in ruins. AIM transport ships anchored in the bay emptied their cargo of manned tanks and war vehicles, which rumbled through Port-of-Boca's streets. Iron Man's immediate attempt to liberate the people of Boca Caliente failed. The UN soon recognized AIM as the sovereign rulers of Boca Caliente, affording them diplomatic immunity as heads of state. Unofficially renamed "AIM Island," Boca Caliente was used by AIM to stage many of their plans of world domination, but Tykkio was eventually killed and the organization soon found itself in a fiscal crisis due to overextending its operations.

Later, AIM's Super-Adaptoid android disguised itself as human "Alessandro Brannex," posed as AIM's newly appointed chairman of the board, and implemented a covert plan to gradually replace all of AIM's island-based agents with Adaptoid androids and replace the island itself with an illusion-generating AIM construct. Only a handful of indigenous humans were kept on the island in a small coastal village on Rojo Beach to serve as human shields in case of outside attack. Brannex oversaw the construction of an AIM Convention Center and hosted the First Annual AIM International Weapons Exposition, where he ingenuously announced that AIM's Executive Board determined that it no longer possessed the manpower or money to take over the world and thus abandoned its political agenda and demobilized AIM's entire paramilitary force. Instead, Brannex claimed that AIM only sought to become the premiere exotic arms and technology supplier to the world market. Diamondback (Rachel Leighton), Captain America (Steve Rogers) and Falcon (Sam Wilson) infiltrated Boca Caliente to attend the next AIM International Weapons Exposition, where Diamondback sought revenge upon the assassin Snapdragon (Sheoke Sanada) for nearly killing her. Snapdragon, now affiliated with the ultra-feminist Superia (Diedre Wentworth) and her Femizons, sought to assassinate Brannex and conquer Boca Caliente to further Superia's own plans of world domination. Superia's attempted assassination failed when Brannex was revealed as the Super-Adaptoid, and Diamondback drowned Snapdragon before being rescued from the island with Captain America, Falcon, and Shang-Chi by Nick Fury and SHIELD.

Leading an invasion force consisting of Falcon, Free Spirit (Cathy Webster), and Jack Flag, Captain America next returned to Boca Caliente to investigate SHIELD intelligence reports that AIM was attempting to recreate the reality-altering Cosmic Cube and intended to defeat the organization once and for all. The Avengers and Red Skull (Johann Shmidt) also traveled to the island to investigate the energy signatures emanating from the Cube, and Superia returned to Boca Caliente intending to steal the Cube's power for herself and exact revenge against AIM. Soon, the Cube's containment field breached, causing the artificial island that was once Boca Caliente to lose all power as a transdimensional rift opened in the sky. As the Avengers evacuated the island's remaining human population, a corrupted Adaptoid accompanying Captain America adapted into a containing wall and sealed the transdimensional rift, thus averting disaster.

OFFICIAL NAME: Republic of Cuba (Republica de Cuba)

POPULATION: 11,394,000

CAPITAL CITY: Havana

PLACES OF INTEREST: Bayamo, Santiago de Cuba, Camaguey, Baracoa, Trinidad Bayamo, Catedral de San Cristobal de la Habana (Havana), Castillo de San Pedro de la Roca (Santiago de Cuba), Valley de los Ingenios, Alejandrode Humboldt National Park, Old Havana, Cienfuegos Desembarco del Granma National Park, Camp Matanzas

GOVERNMENT: Communist state

MAJOR LANGUAGES: Spanish

MONETARY UNIT: Cuban peso

MAJOR RESOURCES: Cobalt, nickel, iron ore, chromium, copper, silica, steel, cement, timber, salt, sugar, tobacco, agriculture, petroleum, construction, pharmaceuticals, agricultural machinery, tourism.

NATIONAL DEFENSE: Revolutionary Armed Forces, including the Revolutionary Army, Revolutionary Navy, Revolutionary Air and Air Defense Force and the Youth Labor Army. Intelligence provided by the General Intelligence Directorate. Formerly held a stockpile of Sentinels for use against mutant populace.

INTERNATIONAL RELATIONS: Member of Interpol, the United Nations, UNESCO, the World Health Organization and the World Trade Organization. Cuba has important economic ties to Bermuda, Canada, China, Germany, Italy, the Netherlands and Spain. Venezuela is one of Cuba's strongest allies. Despite the end of the "Cold War," relations between the USA and Cuba remain uneasy; the US maintains an air force base at Guantanamo Bay, which includes a SHIELD facility.

EXTRATERRESTRIAL RELATIONS: None known.

NONHUMAN POPULATION: None known.

DOMESTIC SUPERHUMANS: The Crusher was once a noted Cuban scientist, but after obtaining superhuman strength attempted to bring down the USA's Stark Industries for the sake of his homeland, only to accidentally die while battling Iron Man (Tony Stark). Poison (Cecilia Cardinale) gained her powers while living as a refugee in the USA, and became a vigilante against drug suppliers in Florida. The heroine la Bandera was born in Cuba, but became the champion of Tierra Verde. The mutant Hope (Esperanza Ling) was orphaned by the Phalanx while in Switzerland and became an ally of Warlock. Evangelina Rivera was a mutant child whose psychic abilities were employed by the military to help operate the CPUs of their Sentinels; she was killed by her brother Lazaro to halt the Sentinels. Mutant Armena Ortega moved to the US, where she married Ismael Ortega.

PROMINENT CITIZENS: General Luis Diosvil was responsible for the country's Sentinel program in Bayamo. Arturo Guttierez and Luisa Prohias were among the forces sent to capture Ferdnand Hedayet. Umberto Safilios was a gunrunner who dealt with the USA in their plans to produce the super-gun SICCAEL, but he was killed by Nomad (Jack Monroe). Drug runner Rory Valdez dealt cocaine through Bolivia. Drug dealer Manuel Rivas was killed by the "Anti-Cap," an agent of the US Marines; his brother Damocles "the Saint" Rivas transferred his mind into the body of MODOK as part of a test to develop a new bio-weapon, but was eventually driven from MODOK's form.

SUPERHUMAN RESIDENTS: The Scarecrow (Ebenezer Laughton) once attempted to steal Stark Industries secrets and sell them to Cuba, but was thwarted by Iron Man (Tony Stark); he was briefly exiled from the USA and had to live in Cuba.

DOMESTIC CRIME: The group Humans for Genetic Equality, led by Lazaro Rivera have fought the government over anti-mutant policies, such as the choice to set up a Sentinel program.

INTERNATIONAL CRIME: Cuba is a destination point for prostitution and slave labor. Mercenaries active in Cuba have included the Black Widow (Yelena Belova). The Falcon (Sam Wilson) caused an international incident by breaking reporter Leila Taylor out of Guantanamo Bay. The terrorist forces of ULTIMATUM have made attempts at overthrowing the government. Many international criminals have been held at Guantanamo Bay, including Khalid el-Gamal of al-Qaeda, Ferdnand Hedayet and various agents of Hydra. The mutant Vanisher once operated a mutation drug trafficking regime out of Havana. Mystique (Raven Darkholme) and Shortpack once performed a black ops mission for Charles Xavier to help end Cuba's Sentinel program.

HISTORY: Cuba was occupied by the Spanish in the 16th century, but by the 19th century resistance had formed against them, leading to the Ten Years War of 1868-1878, and a revolt in 1895 that set off the Spanish-American War. Following this, the US occupied Cuba in 1902 as a military government, establishing a presence in Guantanamo Bay, which has endured to present times. Fidel Castro overthrew the government and installed a communist state in 1961, which has survived.

Art by Jorge Lucas

HAITI

OFFICIAL NAME: Republic of Haiti (Republique d'Haiti [French], Repiblik d'Ayiti [Creole])

POPULATION: 8,706,000

CAPITAL CITY: Port-au-Prince

PLACES OF INTEREST: Tortuga, Ile de la Gonave, Chaine de la Selle Mountains, Gulf of Gonave, Cap-Haitien Sans-Souci Palace, Devil's Grotto

GOVERNMENT: Republic

MAJOR LANGUAGES: French, Creole

MONETARY UNIT: Gourde

MAJOR RESOURCES: Bauxite, copper, gold, marble, cement, hydropower, agriculture, sugar, flour, textiles.

NATIONAL DEFENSE: The Haitian Armed Forces (including its army, navy and air force) have been demobilized, with the Haitian National Police taking over their duties; however, they are ill-equipped for the many violent outbreaks the country has endured.

INTERNATIONAL RELATIONS: Member of Interpol, the United Nations, UNESCO, the World Health Organization and the World Trade Organization. Haiti has important trading relations with China, the Netherlands and the USA. The United Nations has deployed peacekeeping forces in Haiti to help maintain civil order.

EXTRATERRESTRIAL RELATIONS: The mystic beings known as the Three Who Are All and their former allies Fire-Eyes and Dr. Glitternight once manifested at Devil's Grotto; Glitternight intended to take over the country, but was beaten by the Werewolf (Jack Russell).

NONHUMAN POPULATION: Haiti is home to many practitioners of voodoo; the undead creatures known as zombies (or zuvembies) have been raised on repeated occasions in Haiti, often by corrupt houngans.

DOMESTIC SUPERHUMANS: Brother Voodoo (Jericho Drumm) is the nation's best-known hero; originally, Jericho's brother Daniel wore the garb of Brother Voodoo as a houngan while Jericho studied psychiatry; after Daniel's death, Jericho learned voodoo from Papa Jambo, and took Daniel's spirit into himself, becoming Brother Voodoo. Calypso Ezili is a mamaloi who fell in love with Kraven the Hunter (Sergei Kravinoff) and used her abilities against his enemies before and after

Art by Johnny Craig

his death. Damballah (Josue Koulev) was a wicked houngan who slew Daniel Drumm, but then lost his life in a contest with Brother Voodoo. The Night Phantom (Travis Hoyt) was an embittered writer who gained superhuman strength from a radioactive pool and tried to halt Stark Industries' projects in Haiti, only to be beaten by Iron Man (Tony Stark).

PROMINENT CITIZENS: Bambu was the loyal servant of Brother Voodoo until his death at the hands of Marie Laveau, who used his life to revive that of the vampire Varnae. Papa Jambo taught Brother Voodoo his abilities before his death; he was later raised as a zombie, but Brother Voodoo helped restore him to rest. Brother Voodoo's only known living relative in Haiti is his aunt Matilda. Jeesala of the Thousand Years is a mamaloi who once advised Raymond Coker, a werewolf; another mamaloi is Mabambu. Jezabel Baka and her son Simi moved from Port-au-Prince to Manhattan, where they were menaced by the false houngan Brother Zed. Richard Ricard mutated Donna Garth into a spider-creature, which then killed her. Dr. Friday devised a serum, which could create false zombies ("zhambis") that he unleashed on New York, and was ultimately killed by his own ally el Brutale. The Grand Bois (Giscard Sepion) hoped to use his wangal to transform his armies into zombies, but was defeated by Brother Voodoo and Moon Knight (Marc Spector). Baron Samedi was an AIM agent who helped implement a plot to sap the will power of locals to make them virtual zombies; he was brought down by Brother Voodoo.

SUPERHUMAN RESIDENTS: The Zombie (Simon Garth) was sometimes active in Haiti while being drawn by the will of those who

Art by Johnny Craig

possessed the Amulet of Damballah. The sorcerer Cagliostro went through Haiti while questing for his rival Marie Laveau. Kraven the Hunter lived in Haiti during his romance with Calypso Ezili.

DOMESTIC CRIME: There have been many false and criminal practitioners of voodoo; in the 1950s, this included the Voodoo Master, a houngan who summoned his zombies through a mystical telephone, and Benzali, who would sell his abilities out to clients. Political instability in Haiti has led to various incidents of violence.

INTERNATIONAL CRIME: Haiti is a destination point in drug smuggling. The criminal empire of the Celestial Order of the Si-Fan and its leaders Fu Manchu and Fah Lo Suee once maintained a base in Haiti. AIM formerly had a base in Haiti while supporting Baron Samedi.

HISTORY: Haiti was colonized by France in the 17th century, and although the nation's tenure under the French was relatively brief, it permanently affected the country's culture from then on. Another vital part of Haitian culture is the religion voodoo, which came there from African slaves. Piracy was common in those times, and in that century the pirate leader Captain Tyger of Freres de la cote adventured with the brothers Laurent and Alexandre, who together became the first Brother Voodoo, a title inherited in modern times by Jericho and Daniel Drumm. Military coups and allegations of corrupt officials have soured the country in recent years, and led to many violent riots.

OFFICIAL NAME: Republic of Costa Salvador (República de Costa Salvador)
POPULATION: 5,948,000
CAPITAL CITY: San Jorge
PLACES OF INTEREST: San Jorge City Square (San Jorge)
GOVERNMENT: Democratic republic
MAJOR LANGUAGES: Spanish
MONETARY UNIT: Costa Salvadoran colon
MAJOR RESOURCES: Coffee, sugar, corn, rice, beans
NATIONAL DEFENSE: Costa Salvadoran Army, Costa Salvadoran Navy, Costa Salvadoran Air Force
INTERNATIONAL RELATIONS: Costa Salvador holds membership in the Association of Asian, Caribbean and Pacific Countries; Economic Community of Latin American Countries; International Criminal Court; Interpol; Latin American Economic System; Organization of American States; United Nations and UNESCO.
EXTRATERRESTRIAL RELATIONS: None known.
NONHUMAN POPULATION: None known.
DOMESTIC SUPERHUMANS: None known.
PROMINENT CITIZENS: None known.
SUPERHUMAN RESIDENTS: Maximus the Mad (Maximus Boltagaon) and his alliance of Inhuman criminals (Aireo, Falcona, Leonus, Nebula, Stallior & Timberius) briefly resided outside San Jorge while subjugating the Costa Salvadoran populace and plotting to enslave the entire human race.
DOMESTIC CRIME: The incidence of crime in Costa Salvador, including violent crimes such as armed robbery, shooting, stabbing, murder, and rape, has been on the rise (especially crimes directed against foreign tourists).
INTERNATIONAL CRIME: Costa Salvador is a transit country for narcotics, mainly cocaine and heroin.
FIRST APPEARANCE: Incredible Hulk #119 (1969)

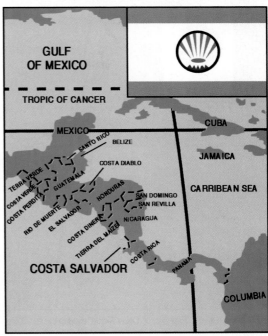

HISTORY: Costa Salvador was originally inhabited by the indigenous Pipil people as early as 2900 BC, who in turn were assimilated into Mayan culture by the 1st century AD. Although they were adept cotton farmers, some Pipil agricultural communities grew into large urban centers. Among these was the city of Bazuatán, which was constructed in a fertile farming valley and served as the center of Pipil commerce in the region. Spanish conquistadors first ventured to Costa Salvador from the Caribbean islands in the early 16th century, and Captain Vidal Vasquez finally succeeded in conquering the area in the name of the Spanish Crown in 1528, changing the name of Bazuatán to "San Jorge" in the process. Along with many other Central American nations, Costa Salvador declared independence from Spain in 1821 after many wealthy Costa Salvadoran merchants grew tired of Spain's interference with their business transactions. The newly independent Costa Salvador resisted incorporation into Mexico and Gran Columbia, and, unlike many of its immediate neighbors, did not suffer through many bloody revolutions during the late 19th and early 20th centuries. In fact, Costa Salvador's political stability prompted the United States government to enter into a mutual defense pact with the tiny nation in 1957, hoping that such a treaty would prevent the capitalist Costa Salvadoran government from being deposed by the communist revolutionaries that threatened neighboring nations.

In recent years, Costa Salvador became instrumental in one of Maximus the Mad's schemes to enslave mankind and rule the Earth. After making secret preparations for years, Maximus assembled a team of his fellow Inhumans who shared his megalomaniacal goals: Aireo, Falcona, Leonus, Nebula, Stallior, and Timberius. Together, these Inhuman criminals traveled to Costa Salvador where Maximus secretly constructed a statue-like robot in the capital city of San Jorge. Upon the robot's activation, it emitted beams of light energy, which controlled the minds of all it touched, with the light beams gradually expanding into the surrounding countryside. Maximus used this robot to enslave nearly

the entire populace of Costa Salvador, using his newfound slave labor to construct a stone fortress on a hill overlooking San Jorge Valley from which the Inhuman conquerors conducted their operations. With his conquest of Costa Salvador complete, Maximus planned to construct similar robots in cities across the world to allow him to enslave the entire human race and enable the Inhuman nation to inherit the planet under his command. Soon after, following a battle against Prince Namor of Atlantis, the Hulk (Bruce Banner) washed ashore in Costa Salvador. He immediately noticed the presence of the mind-control beam, but was able to resist its influence. Unable to destroy the robot in San Jorge's City Square, Hulk tracked down the Inhuman criminals to their nearby hilltop fortress and engaged them in battle.

Meanwhile, officials in the US Department of Defense noticed that all contact with Costa Salvador had suddenly ceased, including contact with the US Embassy in San Jorge. Under the terms of their mutual defense pact, the U.S. military sent a joint strike force into Costa Salvador led by General Thaddeus "Thunderbolt" Ross and Major Glenn Talbot of the US Air Force. The US strike force arrived in the skies over Costa Salvador during the Hulk's battle with the Maximus' Inhumans, and Maximus convinced the reluctant Hulk to join him in defending against the US military's attack. Hulk easily defeated the advancing US ground forces and deflected rockets with nauseating gas warheads, which temporarily incapacitated the remaining US ground forces. Maximus then ordered the Hulk to destroy the command plane from which General Ross and Major Talbot conducted operations; but when Hulk saw General Ross's stowaway daughter Betty Ross aboard the plane, he only damaged one of the wings so that the crew could parachute to safety. When Maximus tried to kill the survivors, Hulk turned against him and battled another of his robotic prototypes. During the course of the battle, the Hulk lifted Maximus' entire fortress and used it to crush his mind-control robots. With the US ground forces regaining consciousness, Maximus and his Inhuman allies retreated in an escape rocket that Maximus had hidden underground. With the threat of Maximus averted, order was restored to Costa Salvador as Hulk fled from the US military.

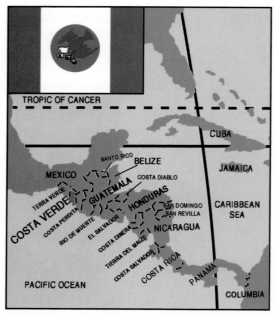

OFFICIAL NAME: Republic of Costa Verde (Republica de Costa Verde)

POPULATION: 2,800,000

CAPITAL CITY: Courantine

PLACES OF INTEREST: Kamekeri village, Presidential Palace (Courantine), Castillo de la Luz

GOVERNMENT: Republic

MAJOR LANGUAGES: Spanish, Portuguese, Quechua

MONETARY UNIT: Costa Verde peso

MAJOR RESOURCES: Mining, gold, silver, copper, tungsten, lead, zinc, timber, wildlife, fish.

NATIONAL DEFENSE: National Army of Costa Verde

INTERNATIONAL RELATIONS: Costa Verde participates in Interpol, the United Nations, UNESCO, the World Health Organization and the World Trade Organization. It has important economic ties to Costa Perdita, Nicaragua, Santo Rico, Venezuela and the USA, and has cooperated with the Avengers. Costa Verde formally objected to the USA's adoption of the Superhuman Registration Act when their hero Silverclaw was taken prisoner by US authorities.

EXTRATERRESTRIAL RELATIONS: The goddess Peliali lived in the mountains of Costa Verde for centuries and mothered Silverclaw; she died in recent years while resisting Kulan Gath. Thor of Asgard and Firelord (Pyreus Kril) of Xandar were both briefly dominated by Gypsy to serve the cause of el Lobo's revolution against President Elmirez. The extradimensional demons the N'Garai briefly manifested at Kamekari village when Kulan Gath summoned them.

NONHUMAN POPULATION: None known.

DOMESTIC SUPERHUMANS: Silverclaw (Maria de Guadalupe Santiago) is the shapeshifting daughter of the goddess Peliali and became a member of the Avengers.

PROMINENT CITIZENS: President Juan Elmirez is the leader of

Costa Verde. President Elmirez's guards include Fernando Pinto and Pedro Barbosa. General Andres Camarro is head of national defense. Jaime Santiago was the father of Silverclaw, and educated her in the traditions of the Kamekari people before his death. Maria Esmeralda Barranco was a classmate of Silverclaw. Rodrigo Valdez and Carlos Gormaz led a revolt, which was ended by the Avengers. El Lobo was a revolutionary leader who tried to overthrow Elmirez's government; his men included Manuel Hidalgo and Gypsy, who possessed a mystical jewel which controlled the minds of Firelord and Thor, but when the two regained their senses they captured el Lobo and all of his men, then turned them over to the army.

SUPERHUMAN RESIDENTS: The ancient sorcerer Kulan Gath transformed the Kamekari village into a replica of the Hyborian times he had once lived in, but was thwarted from spreading his spell by the Avengers and Peliali.

DOMESTIC CRIME: Costa Verde is a transit point for illegal narcotics trafficking. In the past, Costa Verde has seen violent upheaval during times of revolutionary uprisings.

INTERNATIONAL CRIME: The Living Laser (Arthur Parks) once supported the rebel forces of Rodrigo Valdez and Carlos Gormaz, briefly capturing Castillo de la Luz. Moses Magnum's army ("Magnum Shells") once hijacked a plane full of passengers in Costa Verde and used them as hostages in the US against the Avengers. The Taskmaster has used Costa Verde as a point to lie low while evading the authorities.

FIRST APPEARANCE: Avengers #35 (1966)

Art by Don Heck

HISTORY: Originally inhabited by Incan tribes, the Spanish conquistadors named the land Costa Verde ("green coast"). As the faiths of the peoples were converted to Christianity by missionaries, the volcano goddess Peliali of the Kamekari vowed to remain with her people, and retired to the mountains. Jaime Santiago found her in the mountains and fathered her daughter Maria, who grew into the heroine Silverclaw. Costa Verde endured significant hardships during at least two periods of revolution: one headed by Rodrigo Valdez, who employed the Living Laser to decimate the government's forces only to be beaten by the Avengers; the other by el Lobo who briefly controlled Thor and Firelord as minions. Now at peace, the nation was the launch pad for Kulan Gath's attempt at refashioning the world into a mirror of the Hyborian age he had originated from and sacrifice Peliali to his masters, the N'Garai; Silverclaw and the Avengers opposed Gath, and by inspiring the Kamekari to believe in Peliali they were able to save her from being sacrificed, leaving the N'Garai to claim Gath instead; Peliali died from injuries Gath had given her.

Art by George Pérez

OFFICIAL NAME: Republic of Santo Rico (Republica de Santo Rico)
POPULATION: 2,600,000
CAPITAL CITY: Libertad
PLACES OF INTEREST: Giant-Man & Wasp Monument (Libertad), Sinergy Technologies Complex, Pyramid of Kukulcan
GOVERNMENT: Democratic republic
MAJOR LANGUAGES: Spanish
MONETARY UNIT: Santo Rican colon
MAJOR RESOURCES: Mining, gold, silver, copper, tungsten, lead, zinc, timber, fish, machinery, electronics, aircraft.
NATIONAL DEFENSE: National Army of Santo Rico (infantry, air force & navy), Ministry of National Security (national police).
INTERNATIONAL RELATIONS: Santo Rico is a member of Interpol, the United Nations, UNESCO, the World Health Organization and the World Trade Organization. It has important trade relations with Costa Verde, Nicaragua, the USA and Venezuela. The country has cooperated with the Avengers and Worldwatch.
EXTRATERRESTRIAL RELATIONS: The Grandmaster once played an extradimensional game in which he hid an artifact from another universe within Santo Rico.
NONHUMAN POPULATION: None known.
DOMESTIC SUPERHUMANS: In the 1970s, Santo Rico was defended by the hero el Aguila, the latest of a line of heroes that had originated in Mexico with the Aztecs; he was a champion of the state's communist regime. In recent years, communist candidate el Toro became president by rigging the election; his deception was revealed by Giant-Man (Henry Pym) and the Wasp (Janet Van Dyne), and he was forced to flee to Hungary in shame. El Tigre (Juan Meroz) was a treasure hunter who received powers from the Sacred Pendant of Kukulcan and fought the X-Men; he later died while working in the Savage Land. Field Force were a sextet of operatives equipped with advanced armor by Sinergy Technologies.
PROMINENT CITIZENS: Luis Ramirez was one of the employees at the Sinergy Technologies Complex; after realizing the damage Sinergy was doing to the ecosystem, he contacted Worldwatch — and was executed by Sinergy. Ramon Dantas and Toloc were a pair of mercenaries who worked for el Tigre.

SUPERHUMAN RESIDENTS: None known.
DOMESTIC CRIME: Sinergy Technologies formerly manufactured powerpacks, which were supplied for use in weapons sold on the black market, but this business was halted after the Taylor Foundation bought out the company.
INTERNATIONAL CRIME: When Baron (Helmut) Zemo of the Thunderbolts used the bio-modem in order to control the minds of the world's armies, he used the Santo Rican forces to conquer their own capital for him.
FIRST APPEARANCE: Tales to Astonish #54 (1964)
HISTORY: Originally inhabited by the Mayan peoples, Santo Rico (sometimes called "San Rico") was founded as a Central American state by the Portuguese in the 17th century, and named for the riches found in its hills — particularly the wealth of gold. In recent years when el Toro rose to power as the country's communist president, Giant-Man and the Wasp were sent by the US government to determine if he had tampered with the elections. When the two heroes exposed el Toro's deception, he was run out of office, and the people raised a statue of Giant-Man and the Wasp beating el Toro in Libertad. Santo Rico was briefly conquered by el Tigre, who used the powers of the Sacred Pendant of Kukulcan to assume mystical powers of telepathy to control the people's minds, but he was defeated by the X-Men. When Sinergy Technologies brought its industry to Santo Rico it was welcomed at first, but they were soon scandalized by the deadly pollution it brought to the nation, and by the black market arms they helped manufacture; the intervention of the humanitarian Worldwatch and Night Thrasher (Dwayne Taylor) cleaned up Sinergy's operations.

Art by Jack Kirby

OFFICIAL NAME: Republic of Terra Verde (República de Terra Verde)
POPULATION: 5,364,000
CAPITAL CITY: Quetzalnango
PLACES OF INTEREST: Presidential Palace (Quetzalnango), Ruins of the Temple of Ixchel (Arozcapa)
GOVERNMENT: Constitutional democratic republic
MAJOR LANGUAGES: Spanish
MONETARY UNIT: Terra Verdean colón.
MAJOR RESOURCES: Coffee, sugarcane, petroleum, bananas, beans, cardamom
NATIONAL DEFENSE: Army, Navy, Air Force
INTERNATIONAL RELATIONS: Terra Verde holds membership in the United Nations, UNESCO, Organization of American States and the International Criminal Court.
EXTRATERRESTRIAL RELATIONS: None known.
NONHUMAN POPULATION: None known.
DOMESTIC SUPERHUMANS: None known.
PROMINENT CITIZENS: General Ernesto Robles was the former president of Terra Verde. General Luis Cruz was the former chief of the Secret Police under the Robles regime. General Carlos Castillo was the former chief of staff of the Air Force under the Robles regime.
SUPERHUMAN RESIDENTS: None documented.
DOMESTIC CRIME: Terra Verde is a major transit country for cocaine and heroin. As a result, money laundering related to drug trafficking and organized crime are prevalent, especially in the remote rural areas.
INTERNATIONAL CRIME: Several prominent members of the former Robles regime are currently wanted by international criminal tribunals for various violations, including torture, genocide, and crimes against humanity.
FIRST APPEARANCE: Fantastic Four #117 (1971)

HISTORY: The history of Terra Verde can be traced back to the arrival of the first human settlers, who migrated from the areas that constitute present-day Mexico and Guatemala approximately 10,000 years ago. The Maya civilization flourished in Terra Verde, with the skyfather Hunab Ku; the sun god Itzamna; the moon goddess Ixchel; and the death god Ahpuch serving as the primary deities worshipped by the indigenous population. Massive temples were constructed as shrines to the Mayan deities. Even as the great Mayan cities of the Petén Basin were gradually abandoned, the Mayan societies in the Terra Verdean lowlands continued to thrive until the arrival of Spanish conquistadors in 1525 AD.

Spanish Captain Manolo Eloganto brutally subjugated the native population and declared Terra Verde, named for its bountiful green valleys, a colony of Spain in 1531. Although Catholic missionaries attempted to convert the indigenous population, most maintained their unwavering belief in the traditional Mayan gods. In fact, many believed that Itzamna and Ixchul would return one day to liberate their worshipers from their European oppressors. Terra Verde was eventually liberated from Spanish domination by 1821, but not due to the intervention of the Mayan gods. Rather, dissatisfied landowners and merchants joined the rebellion against Spain, which was already initiated by neighboring colonies. After being briefly incorporated into the Mexican Empire, Terra Verde became a truly independent nation in 1823. The fledgling nation suffered through several minor revolutions in the late 19th century, but eventually established a stable constitutional republic by the early 20th century. Fifteen years ago, General Ernesto Robles of the Terra Verdean Army staged a bloodless coup d'état in order to remedy what he believed was an inefficient government. Installing himself as Terra Verde's president with absolute authority over both domestic and international policy, General Robles violently suppressed a series of revolts led by the impoverished, indigenous segments of the population. Many suspected rebels were imprisoned and tortured based solely on their ethnicity. By the second year of General Robles' regime, all resistance groups were thoroughly defeated. Worship of the Mayan gods was strictly prohibited under General Robles' rule.

More recently, the villainous alchemist Diablo (Esteban Corazon de Ablo) was sent to a post-apocalyptic future version of Earth by Dr. Doom (Victor von Doom), monarch of the Balkan nation of Latveria. After a period of being stranded in this alternate timeline, Diablo captured Crystal (Crystalia Amaquelin) and Lockjaw of the Inhumans, who had accidentally arrived in the same timeline after a misteleportation by Lockjaw, and concocted a potion to control their minds. Using Lockjaw's teleportation powers, Diablo brought Crystal to the nation of Terra Verde in the present day, where he used his mastery of alchemy to restore the crumbling Temple of Ixchel, a stone structure built centuries ago to honor the Mayan jaguar goddess. He then used the mind-controlled Crystal to trick Terra Verde's indigenous population into thinking she was Ixchel, who had returned to free her worshipers from the tyranny of General Robles as legends foretold. Although suspicious at first, the indigenous population was soon convinced that Crystal was their goddess and rallied behind her after witnessing her element-manipulating powers. Posing as Ixchel's priest, Diablo led a reinvigorated people's revolution against General Robles. However, Diablo secretly planned to conquer Terra Verde for himself, and then use the nation's rare chemicals to concoct stronger alchemist potions and use the nation's military to attack Latveria and gain vengeance upon Dr. Doom.

General Robles soon learned of the new revolutionary movement and sent the Terra Verdean Air Force to crush the rebels. However, the Human Torch (Johnny Storm) arrived in Terra Verde in search of the missing Crystal and defeated the Air Force's jets just as they were about to attack the rebel forces. Johnny reunited with Crystal, who rejected him because she still believed she was Ixchel. Meanwhile, Diablo used Lockjaw to teleport into the Presidential Palace in Quetzalnango and capture General Robles, returning with him to the Temple of Ixchel so he could force Robles to publicly announce his surrender. Before General Robles surrendered, Human Torch attacked Diablo, enabling Robles to escape in the confusion. Diablo attempted to retreat to his laboratory to renew his potions, but he was intercepted by the Fantastic Four, causing his mind-control spell over Crystal and Lockjaw to wear off. Diablo attempted to unleash a destructive potion as a last resort, but was assaulted by General Robles, causing the flask to drop and the Temple of Ixchel to explode with both men inside. With General Robles deposed and Diablo defeated, the people's revolution claimed victory and established a democratic republic in Terra Verde.

OFFICIAL NAME: Argentine Republic
POPULATION: 40,302,000
CAPITAL CITY: Buenos Aires
PLACES OF INTEREST: Cordoba, Purana River, Andes Mountains, Tierra del Fuego, Santa Cruz, Calchaqui Valleys
GOVERNMENT: Republic
MAJOR LANGUAGES: Spanish, English, Italian, German, French
MONETARY UNIT: Argentine peso
MAJOR RESOURCES: Lead, zinc, tin, copper, iron ore, steel, metallurgy, manganese, uranium, petroleum, nuclear power, food processing, motor vehicles, textiles, chemicals, printing
NATIONAL DEFENSE: Argentine Army, Navy of the Argentine Republic (including aviation and infantry divisions and the Argentine Air Force. Intelligence is headed by Sistema de Inteligencia Nacional.
INTERNATIONAL RELATIONS: Member of Interpol, Union of South American Nations, United Nations (and its Security Council), UNESCO, World Health Organization and World Trade Organization. Have had significant disputes with the UK over the Falkland Islands, and have claim disputes with the USA, Chile, Brazil and Uruguay. During World War II, the country was briefly invaded by Atlantis. The country has cooperated with SHIELD, the Avengers and Germany's Schutz-Heiligruppe. Argentina is a significant transit point for people coming and going to the remote Savage Land, and an underground passageway exists near Tierra del Fuego.
EXTRATERRESTRIAL RELATIONS: Part of the space station Graymalkin landed into Argentina when it fell from Earth's orbit. It was retrieved by Cable (Nathan Summers) for use in construction of Providence island. One of the portals of the Wellspring of All Things, a mystical font of metahuman energy existed in Argentina until it was sealed by the Grandmaster. Eric the Red (Davan Shakari) of the Shi'ar had an outpost in the Andes, which was raided by Captain Marvel (Genis-Vell) and Adam-X.
NONHUMAN POPULATION: Tunnels to Subterranea can be found in Cordoba, possibly leading to a portion of the Mole Man (Harvey Elder)'s kingdom. The passage to the Savage Land in Tierra del Fuego has led some dinosaurs into Argentinian territory, including the radioactive pterodactyls that empowered Sauron (Karl Lykos).
DOMESTIC SUPERHUMANS: Defensor (Gabriel Carlos Dantes Sepulveda) obtained a suit of Vibranium armor from Subterranea and was a local hero up until his murder at the hands of Zeitgeist (Larry Ekler). The mutant hero Saint Anna served in X-Force (the team that later became X-Statix) and died saving Paco Perez from forced experimentation by the US government. There is a long line of criminals who have born the guise of the Black Tarantula for over 600 years; the modern day Black Tarantula Carlos LaMuerto became an international crimelord, and made a bid for power in New York during one of the Kingpin (Wilson Fisk)'s absences.
PROMINENT CITIZENS: The Black Tarantula's chief aid is the diminutive Chesbro; his chief assassin was el Uno, who was slain by Delilah, enforcer of the Tarantula's rival the Rose (Jacob Conover).
SUPERHUMAN RESIDENTS: In the 19th century, Argentina was defended by its masked champion el Gaucho; in 1941, US exchange student Don Caldwell came to Buenos Aires and with the blessings of a local Don adopted el Gaucho's guise to combat local Nazi forces; Caldwell was also known as the American Avenger. Paco Perez of Bastrona came to live in Buenos Aires after X-Force saved him from experimentation

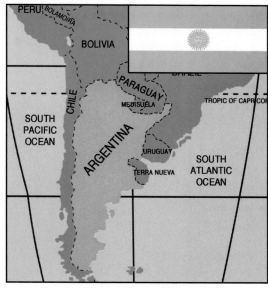

by the US government. Dr. Karl Lykos grew up in Tierra del Fuego, and became the creature Sauron after rescuing Tanya Anderssen from radioactive pterodactyls of the Savage Land.
DOMESTIC CRIME: Argentina has local drug abuse problems, and during the country's communist years the government faced opposition from the Argentine Anticommunist Alliance. The corporation Gentechnic attempted to harvest mutant tissue to cure diseases, but their operation was dismantled by X-Force.
INTERNATIONAL CRIME: Argentina is used as a transit and destination point for criminals dealing in money laundering, smuggling, arms dealing, narcotics, prostitution and slave labor. Mercenaries such as the Six Pack (G.W. Bridge, Cable, Domino, Grizzly (Theodore Wincester), Hammer (Eisenhower Canty), Garrison Kane) have been drawn to work in Argentina. The criminal Zeitgeist struck in Argentina, killing Defensor and later Blitzkrieger (Franz Mittelstaedt) of the Schutz-Heiligruppe when he came to investigate the crime. Criminals from the Savage Land such as the Savage Land Mutates have menaced Argentina while traveling through its borders. The Weathermen once bedeviled Buenos Aires with out-of-control weather, but their scheme was brought down by the Avengers.
HISTORY: Argentina was colonized in 1553 by Spanish forces expanding from Chile. Argentina gained independence by 1819, but struggled in later years with social and economic woes. The military government, which ruled from 1976-1982, led to the disastrous dispute with the UK over the Falkland Islands, causing open warfare between the nations and the eventual ousting of the government.

Art by Mike Allred

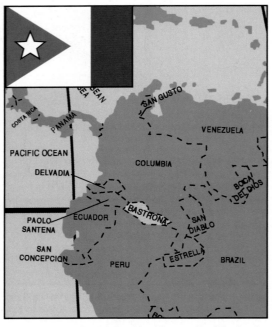

OFFICIAL NAME: People's Republic of Bastrona (República Popular Bastrona)
POPULATION: 11,119,000
CAPITAL CITY: Templana
PLACES OF INTEREST: The Capitolia (Templana)
GOVERNMENT: Communist state
MAJOR LANGUAGES: Spanish
MONETARY UNIT: Bastronan peso
MAJOR RESOURCES: Sugar, tobacco, citrus, coffee, petroleum
NATIONAL DEFENSE: Revolutionary Army, Revolutionary Navy, Revolutionary Air Defense Force, Young Workers' Battalion
INTERNATIONAL RELATIONS: Bastrona holds membership in the Non-Aligned Movement and United Nations (UN).
EXTRATERRESTRIAL RELATIONS: None known.
NONHUMAN POPULATION: None known.
DOMESTIC SUPERHUMANS: The mutant Paco Perez was born in Bastrona but has since relocated to Argentina.
PROMINENT CITIZENS: Information broker Diego Ardilles was killed during X-Force's rescue of Paco Perez.
SUPERHUMAN RESIDENTS: None known.
DOMESTIC CRIME: Violent crime rates in Bastrona have been on the upsurge in recent decades and are substantially higher in the nation's capital city of Templana. Although Bastrona is a signatory to the UN Universal Declaration of Human Rights, its communist government, which has been in power since the Bastronan Revolution of 1966, has been accused of numerous human rights violations, including political and religious persecution, torture, and execution without trial.
INTERNATIONAL CRIME: Forces of the Bastronan Army have clashed with those of the mutant heroes X-Force (later called X-Statix).
FIRST APPEARANCE: X-Force #117 (2001)

HISTORY: The area of land that constitutes modern-day Bastrona was first inhabited by indigenous Urarina hunters and gatherers who emigrated from the Chambira River Basin. The area was eventually conquered by and incorporated into the Incan Empire in the 16th century AD. Spanish conquistadors arrived in 1535 and, under the command of Captain Miguel Bastron, sought to conquer, colonize, and convert the indigenous population (although Catholicism was soon assimilated into the preexisting religious system of indigenous spirit worship), creating permanent settlements and renaming the land "Bastrona." Although

the indigenous population had always resisted Spanish rule, it was not until a nationalist uprising spearheaded by wealthy Spanish landowners that Bastronan independence from Spain was finally achieved. Joining other Spanish colonies in the region, Bastrona officially declared its independence in 1821 and promptly established a democratic republic.

With its breathtaking views of the Amazon rainforest, Bastrona attracted many foreign investors from capitalist nations who transformed portions of the nation into a booming tourist resort by the early 20th century, complete with hotels and casinos. However, many members of the indigenous population remained disfranchised and became disillusioned with Bastrona's succession of corrupt, pro-capitalist presidents. In 1966, before traveling to Bolivia, Marxist revolutionary Ernesto "Che" Guevara fomented a socialist revolutionary campaign in Bastrona that eventually forced leaders of the ruling political party to flee the country (in what was later termed the "Bastronan Revolution"). Under the new communist regime, all private businesses were nationalized and private property was expropriated. Relations with capitalist nations of the Western world rapidly deteriorated, with many nations imposing stringent trade sanctions against the Bastrona. Enemies of the new communist regime were summarily executed, prompting many Bastronans to flee the country.

The Perez family comprised three of the many Bastronans who sought to escape the dire conditions and economic hardships of their country. Unfortunately, the youngest member of the family, Paco Perez, a mutant whose DNA contained cures for nearly all known diseases, found himself orphaned after his parents were struck by a vehicle and killed shortly after crossing the Bastronan border. Paco Perez was seized by the Bastronan government and placed in a facility where state scientists could unlock the true potential of his mutant powers.

Art by Mike Allred

X-Force was instructed by their financiers to travel to Bastrona and bring Perez to the United States, where his mutant DNA could be converted into medicines and sold for inflated prices. X-Force teleported into Bastrona during what appeared to be a religious festival, but they soon discovered that their Bastronan contact, information broker Diego Ardilles, sold them out to the Bastronan military, who ambushed the team. In the ensuing battle, X-Force member Bloke (Mickey Tork) was killed by helicopter artillery fire. Deciding to spare Ardilles' life so he could lead them to Perez's hidden location, X-Force soon infiltrated the Bastronan government building where Perez was being held and attempted to secure the child. However, Perez's vital organs were connected to medical equipment designed to extract his mutant powers, and removing the tubes in the wrong order would have resulted in his death. As X-Force member Orphan (Guy Smith) attempted to free Perez, the rest of the team battled the Bastronan military forces storming the building. Perez was ultimately freed and X-Force teleported back to the United States, but not before team member Saint Anna and Ardilles were killed by gunfire during the battle. Against the wishes of his financiers, Orphan delivered Perez to Buenos Aires, Argentina, where Orphan thought he would lead a better life with the late Saint Anna's father.

OFFICIAL NAME: Republic of Bolivia (Republica de Bolivia)

POPULATION: 9,119,000

CAPITAL CITY: La Paz

PLACES OF INTEREST: Andes Mountains, Chacaltaya, Cochabamba, el Alto (la paz), el Dorado (aka "Forbidden Land"), Santa Cruz de la Sierra, Sucre, Temple of the Flame (el Dorado)

GOVERNMENT: Republic

MAJOR LANGUAGES: Spanish, Quechua, Aymara

MONETARY UNIT: Boliviano

MAJOR RESOURCES: Tin, zinc, tungsten, silver, iron, lead, gold, timber, natural gas, petroleum, hydropower, soybeans.

NATIONAL DEFENSE: Bolivian Armed Forces, including the Bolivian Army, Bolivian Navy and Bolivian Air Force.

INTERNATIONAL RELATIONS: Bolivia is a member of Interpol, United Nations, Union of South American Nations, UNESCO, World Health Organization and World Trade Organization. Bolivia is a major trading partner with Argentina, Brazil, Chile, Colombia, Japan and Peru. Bolivia has had boundary disputes with Chile, and went to war with Argentina and Chile in the 19th century.

EXTRATERRESTRIAL RELATIONS: The otherworldly Haag the hunter briefly captured mountain climbers from the Andes when he menaced the Earth.

NONHUMAN POPULATION: The site of el Dorado connects to the underground kingdoms of Subterranea, including stores of technology designed by the Deviants; Deviants were presumably active in the region in ages past. Helmut Zemo kept some of his experimental creations called Protoids within his fortress.

DOMESTIC SUPERHUMANS: None known.

PROMINENT CITIZENS: Oscar Ichazo was the founder of the Arica Institute and led his cult in the worship of a being called Toham Kum Rah in order to seek philosophical enlightenment. Dr. Franz Anton lived in Bolivia while undertaking a research project, and came upon el Dorado by accident. People of el Dorado included the high priest Tulak, the Keeper of the Flame and the regal Prince Rey, who were all slain when Tyrannus usurped the Flame of Life.

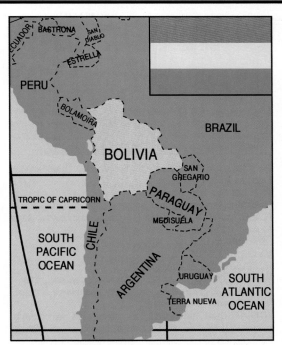

EL DORADO

SUPERHUMAN RESIDENTS: Baron (Heinrich) Zemo held a fortress in the Bolivian jungle for many decades, employing natives into forced slave labor; Zemo's fellow Masters of Evil Skurge the Executioner and Amora the Enchantress lived at the fortress during that time, and it was there that Simon Williams was transformed into Wonder Man, and Erik Josten into Power Man; after Heinrich's death, his son Helmut took over the fortress, and was sometimes assisted by his ally Techno (Paul Ebersol). The Canadian mercenary Deadpool (Wade Wilson) once took an assignment that pit him against the Bolivian army; after killing a general, Deadpool claimed his villa, referring to it as "Casa Deadpool." Deadpool used this structure as a base of operations for a time, and kept his precognitive friend/hostage Monty there. The superhuman geneticist Terrigene had a laboratory base in the Andes, and performed experiments on the Inhuman Sporr there. Tyrannus made el Dorado his base of operations during his manipulative scheme as part of "They Who

Wield Power," and attempted to draw the power of el Dorado's Flame of Life into himself, only to be consumed by its energies.

DOMESTIC CRIME: Bolivia is a major producer and abuser of cocaine, drawing many illegal druglords.

INTERNATIONAL CRIME: The Vietnamese General Buktir Van Tranh ran a cocaine operation from Bolivia until the vigilante Punisher (Frank Castle) uncovered his activities, slew Van Tranh and shut down his operations. Peru's Shining Path and Cuba's Rory Valdez have been involved in the Bolivian drug trade. The presence of the Zemo fortress has drawn vigilantes Citizen V (Dallas Riordan) and Scourge (Jack Monroe), as well as the Maggia's Cyclone (Pierre Fresson). The Roxxon Oil Corporation has a strong presence in Bolivia, overseen by their regional coordinator Curtis Henshaw and US Army ally Colonel Roland Gunderson; their Bolivian facilities were used to design the Repulsor armor and upgrade the abilities of the Scorpion (Mac Gargan). The Argentinian crimelord Black Tarantula (Carlos LaMuerto) was active in Bolivia, and assisted Roxxon with their local operations, but their hopes for a superhuman production plant were dashed when Dr. Marla Madison exposed the endeavor. The Acolytes, mutant followers of Magneto formerly stationed themselves in a citadel within the Andes; their presence also attracted the attention of the mutant-hating Humanity's Last Stand. The mutant assassin Sabretooth (Victor Creed) has been active in Bolivia, as were the mercenaries Swordsman (Jacques Duquesne); Saracen (Muzzafar Lambert); Janissary, an employee of Terrigene, as well as the thief Goldbug, who visited el Dorado.

HISTORY: In the 16th century, Incas from the land that would become Bolivia fled from the invading Spanish into the Andes Mountains, forming the colony of el Dorado, the fabled city of gold; connecting into abandoned subterranean passages built by the Deviants, and powered by the Deviants' Flame of Life, the el Doradians survived for centuries. The Spanish called the land "Lower Peru," until the people obtained independence in 1809, and established themselves as a republic in 1825, taking their new name from the leader Simon Bolivar. El Dorado's existence was discovered in recent years by the Avengers. The outsider Tyrannus eventually usurped el Dorado, and the city was destroyed when he tapped into the immense power of the Flame of Life. Surviving el Doradians fled into Subterranea; they later attempted the conquest of Moloids in the kingdom of Eurasia, but were driven off by the Sub-Mariner.

BOSQUEVERDE

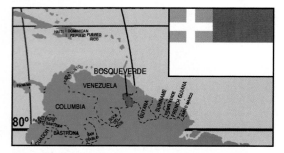

OFFICIAL NAME: Republic of Bosqueverde (República de Bosqueverde)
POPULATION: 35,201,000
CAPITAL CITY: Ciudad Leando
PLACES OF INTEREST: Presidential Palace (Ciudad Leando), Sierra Angeles
GOVERNMENT: Republic
MAJOR LANGUAGES: Spanish
MONETARY UNIT: Bosqueverde peso
MAJOR RESOURCES: Sunflowers, mangos, lemons, soybeans, grapes
NATIONAL DEFENSE: Bosqueverde Army, Bosqueverde Air Force, National Guard
INTERNATIONAL RELATIONS: Bosqueverde holds membership in Interpol, United Nations, UNESCO, Organization of American States, Rio Group, and the Latin American Economic System. The government has employed Symkaria's Wild Pack.
EXTRATERRESTRIAL RELATIONS: None known.
NONHUMAN POPULATION: None known.
DOMESTIC SUPERHUMANS: None known.
PROMINENT CITIZENS: Professor Hector Silva and Carmilla Dominguez serve as Bosqueverde's current president and vice president.
SUPERHUMAN RESIDENTS: None known.
DOMESTIC CRIME: Bosqueverde suffers from high rates of murder, rape, assault, and theft, particularly in the remote regions of the country controlled by local gangs of banditos.
INTERNATIONAL CRIME: Many participants in the Emmanuel Rodrigo Raposa regime have been charged with human rights violations and illegal efforts to suppress political opponents in coordination with foreign intelligence agencies.
FIRST APPEARANCE: Marc Spector: Moon Knight #15 (1990)

HISTORY: Bosqueverde's fertile river deltas were first inhabited by the Warao people centuries before the arrival of Spanish explorers in 1501. By 1528, Bosqueverde was colonized by Spain and the indigenous Warao tribesmen were either killed or forced to flee into the remote Sierra Angeles region when the Spaniards began constructing the settlement of Ciudad Leando along the Bosque River. Ciudad Leando became one of Spain's first permanent settlements in South America. Bosqueverde declared its independence from Spain in 1818 and, after only a few minor skirmishes with Spanish imperial forces achieved independence in 1820. A republic was established and a president was elected by 1822.

Approximately 12 years ago, General Hector Carranza of the Bosqeverdan National Guard seized power from Bosqueverde's democratically elected president in a military coup d'état. Although Carranza assumed dictatorial power to improve the government's efficiency and end legislative deadlock, his military junta became unpopular after Carranza and his top officials became heavily involved in organized crime and narcotics trafficking. Carranza was eventually removed from office in a bloodless coup led by a group of dissident military officers, students, and liberal professionals who sought to end Carranza's government-sponsored racketeering. Ricardo Dominguez was installed as Bosqueverde's new president, and General Carranza was forced to flee into the Sierra

Angeles, where he continued his involvement in narcotics trafficking. President Dominguez's democratically elected regime was only in its sixth month when a socialist uprising led by General Emmanuel Rodrigo Raposa of the Bosqueverdan Army began to gather strength among members of Bosqeverde's poorest social classes. Planning for his revolutionary movement (known collectively as the "Raposistas") to take the capital by force, General Raposa hired foreign mercenaries, such as American Marc Spector and Swede Broward "Bo" Ollsen, to assist in their assault on Ciudad Leando. Although they were ordered to capture President Dominguez alive, Spector shot and killed Dominguez after he reached for what Spector believed was a gun. With President Dominguez dead, General Raposa easily rose to power. César Bajete, a doctor of pathology and master of torture, served as General Raposa's right-hand man and was appointed to serve as general of the Secret Police, the position responsible for Raposa's infamous "death squads." However, supporters of the late President Dominguez refused to recognize General Raposa as Bosqueverde's legitimate leader and began to organize guerrilla attacks against Raposa's interests. Soon, Bosqueverde was plunged into another decade-long war, with the fear-stricken populace suffering from poverty, disease, and mutilation as a result of the fighting. After nearly 10 years of brutal, village-to-village combat, General Raposa's forces were finally defeated. Although Raposa himself escaped capture and fled the country, several of his highest-ranking allies, such as Bajete, were apprehended.

Months after Raposa's defeat, Professor Hector Silva, a former instructor at Ciudad Leando University and associate of President Dominguez who was instrumental in organizing the resistance movement that toppled Raposa's regime, became Bosqueverde's new democratically elected president, with the widow Carmilla Dominguez serving as his vice president. Although President Silva was reluctant to assume the presidency, the new Bosqueverdan government immediately set out to punish those affiliated with the Raposa regime for war crimes and human rights violations. The government contracted the service of Silver Sable's Wild Pack to bring Marc Spector to justice for his role in President Domniguez's assassination. The Wild Pack attempted to apprehend Spector in Manhattan, but Spector voluntarily surrendered himself and was delivered to Bosqueverdan authorities. Spector was transported to a Bosqueveran prison where he was incarcerated alongside others affiliated with the Raposa regime, including Bajete. A public tribunal before the People's Council of Justice was held in Bosqueverde's largest soccer stadium, with Vice President Domiguez serving as the prosecution's star witness. Spector and his fellow prisoners were charged with several counts of insurrection, torture, murder, kidnapping, treason, extortion, and assassination. Spector and his co-defendants were sentenced to the gallows to hang, but Bajete and his men escaped prison that night and set out to assassinate President Silva. As Moon Knight, Spector foiled the assassination attempt and convinced President Silva to pardon Marc Spector and overturn his death sentence in exchange for promising to deliver Raposa to justice. The next day, Bajete and his allies were hanged, but President Silva kept his promise to pardon Marc Spector; in turn, Spector found Raposa in Florida and turned him over to authorities. Months later, Hector Carranza was arrested by US Drug Enforcement Agency (DEA) authorities and incarcerated in a federal prison in Miami in connection with his continued narcotics-trafficking operations. However, using drug runners disguised as Florida National Guardsmen, Carranza escaped prison and fled on a cargo plane to Bosqueverde, where he turned himself into authorities to stand trial for racketeering. He was greeted in his homeland as a returning hero and "imprisoned" in a luxurious hacienda in the Sierre Angeles. The US vigilante known as the Punisher traveled to Bosqueverde to kill Carranza. Although Carranza hired Rabio Ramirez and his elite "Red Condor" unit of the Bosqueverdan Army to protect him for $3 million, the Punisher eliminated the Red Condors one by one before killing General Carranza with the Condor's own helicopter.

OFFICIAL NAME: Federative Republic of Brazil (República Federativa do Brasil)

POPULATION: 190,010,000

CAPITAL CITY: Brasília

PLACES OF INTEREST: Nova Roma (Amazon Rainforest), Temple of the Ancient Sun Demons (Amazon Rainforest), Iguaçu Falls (Paraná), Diamantina National Park (Bahia), Ipanema & Copacabana Beaches (Rio de Janeiro), Maracanã Stadium (Rio de Janeiro), Christ the Redeemer statue (Rio de Janeiro).

GOVERNMENT: Federal republic

MAJOR LANGUAGES: Portuguese, Spanish, English, French

MONETARY UNIT: Real

MAJOR RESOURCES: Bauxite, gold, iron ore, manganese, nickel, phosphates, platinum, tin, uranium, petroleum, hydropower, timber, textiles, steel, sugarcane, soybeans, coffee, beef.

NATIONAL DEFENSE: Brazilian Armed Forces (Forças Armadas Brasileiras), including the Brazilian Army, Brazilian Navy (Marinha do Brasil) and Marine Corps (Corpo de Fuzileiros Navais), and the Brazilian Air Force (Forca Aerea Brasileira).

INTERNATIONAL RELATIONS: Brazil's current foreign policy is based on the country's position as a regional power in Latin America, a leader among developing countries, and an emerging world power. Brazil is temporarily a member of the United Nations Security Council, and is a full member of such organizations as UNESCO and the Union Latina.

EXTRATERRESTRIAL RELATIONS: The alien Taboo crash-landed in an Amazonian swamp where it lay for ages before being discovered by adventure book writer Lewis Conrad who agreed to give it mankind's accumulated scientific knowledge; however, Taboo double-crossed the humans and sought to escape with the knowledge but was double-crossed in turn and blown up in Earth's atmosphere. The alien warrior Bombu arrived in the Amazon ages ago to prepare Earth for conquest; however, while posing as a native tribe's witch doctor, Bombu was knocked out by a bolt of lightning while demonstrating his powers to a pair of captured US businessmen. St. Cyrus Leviticus was a priest who had bonded with an alien symbiote that fed on the psionic turbulence of dying souls and sought to mass murder Carnaval revelers in Rio with an army of zombies before being slain by Wolverine.

NONHUMAN POPULATION: Bokk was a 30' tall gorilla who was worshipped as a god by a tribe of Chevante headhunters in the Brazilian rainforest and was later captured by explorers and taken to America where he was sold to a circus; however, he subsequently escaped and was opposed by Sun Girl who ultimately killed him with poisoned food. The villainous Piranha was originally a piranha fish from the Amazon inadvertently mutated by Dr. Lemuel Dorcas into a sentient aquanoid. The Damocles Foundation, comprised of members of the Deviant and Eternal races who sought to create and control the next species destined to rule the Earth, operated a clandestine base in Brazil.

DOMESTIC SUPERHUMANS: Roberto Da Costa was a talented soccer player for Rio's Vilár school before he was recruited into the American New Mutants team as Sunspot and later came to take over his father's role as head of Da Costa International before joining the Hellfire Club. Mutant heroine Magma (Amara Aquilla) hailed from Nova Roma before also joining the New Mutants. Dimbura was a native Amazonian sorcerer who trained young novice Owl. Captain Força was Brazil's national superhero until he was killed by Zeitgeist (Larry Ekler). Young Rio mutant Xande aspired to become an arena fighter. Mexer was a young mutant who was lobotomised by villainous mutant "healer" Kuhrra Daizonest.

PROMINENT CITIZENS: Brazilian President Luiz Inácio Lula da Silva; Emmanuel Da Costa was a wealthy businessman and member of the Hellfire Club prior to his death; renowned archaeologist Nina Da Costa once led an expedition to Nova Roma; Juliana Sandoval was Roberto Da Costa's girlfriend before she died saving him from Hellfire Club soldiers; Claudio Juarez was a Brazilian soccer star who aided the Protectors of the Forest against the Brazilian Logging Enterprises

firm run by wealthy businessman Antonio Matias then later became the armored environmentalist the Repulsor; Antonio Vargas once owned the Devil's Grill Tavern before becoming a detective in the Rio Police Department until he was killed by his vampiric ex-wife Ezra Asher; hunter Rodolfo Mico once led American archaeologist Professor Kenneth Robeson to the Temple of the Ancient Sun Demons deep in the Amazon jungle; Omar Barreños was a founder of Project: Earth.

SUPERHUMAN RESIDENTS: Mutant adventurer Wolverine (James Howlett) once lived for a year in Rio and worked as a bouncer at the Devil's Grill Tavern. Spanish mutant Empath (Manuel de la Rocha) once lived in Nova Roma for a time with Magma.

DOMESTIC CRIME: The unruly region at the convergence of the Argentina/Brazil/Paraguay borders is a locus of money laundering, smuggling, arms and illegal narcotics trafficking, and fundraising for extremist organizations. Illicit cannabis production occurs throughout the country, primarily in the Amazon region. Illicit narcotics proceeds earned in Brazil are often laundered through the financial system. Vampire hunter Frank Drake and Brother Voodoo once battled zuvembies in the Amazon basin. The armored Black Metal led a mercenary group who were once hired by Teng Yun-Suan to take over the neighboring country of Costa Brava but were defeated by the Agent (Rick Mason). Brazilian crimelord Kristina Ramos once sought to procure Stark Enterprises technology using super-powered agents Powderkeg and Moonstone (Karla Sofen) but was opposed by Captain Marvel (Monica Rambeau). The mercenary Motossera (Ripsaw) was once employed by the Brazilian Logging Enterprises firm to stop the Protectors of the Forest from interfering with logging endeavors. The assassin known only as Stiletto was one of seven who responded to a bounty placed on the head of the vigilante the Punisher (Frank Castle) by mob leader Rosalie Carbone only to be killed by the Punisher. The Hellfire Club has a chapter in Rio, which hosts the opulent Bacchus Feast year-end gala. Wolverine and Detective Vargas once investigated a series of murders in Rio revealed to have been perpetrated by Vargas's vampiric ex-wife Ezra Asher on behalf of St. Cyrus Leviticus. One of the Gladiator World Arena (GWA)'s underground mutant gladiator arenas was located in Rio, as was the illegal teenage mutant-fighting arena wherein reigning champion Juliana Jararaca slew challenger Thiago Piranha before being mind-wiped by Cable (Nathan Summers).

INTERNATIONAL CRIME: The Deviant Kro once allied with the Jivaro tribe's witch doctor Kepiquoatzi to spread a deadly body-wasting plague from the Amazon jungle, but they were opposed by the Eternal Makkari in his guise of Hurricane. Baron (Heinrich) Zemo once moved his base of operations to the Amazon jungle where he enslaved natives to construct a temple. Magneto once tracked Nazi war criminal Hans Richter to a Fourth Reich base in the Amazon jungle. Nazi criminal the Red Skull (Johann Shmidt) once based his New World Order organization in the Amazon rainforest where he dispatched the Juggernaut (Cain Marko) and a mind-controlled Hulk (Bruce Banner) to attack the Avengers. Superhuman vigilantes the Force of Nature, acting on behalf of Project: Earth, opposed contractors logging the rainforests. The terrorist mutant Brotherhood once operated a cell in Brazil.

HISTORY: Discovered by Portuguese navigator Pedro Álvares Cabral in 1500, Brazil endured three centuries under the rule of Portugal until finally becoming an independent nation in 1822 and a republic in 1889. By far the largest and most populous country in South America, Brazil overcame more than half a century of military intervention in the governance of the country when, in 1985, the military regime peacefully ceded power to civilian rulers. Exploiting vast natural resources and a large labor pool, it is today South America's leading economic power and a regional superpower, boasting the world's fifth-largest amount of territory and the world's 10th largest economy. In spite of important economic achievements, many social issues still hamper development.

The Amazon rainforest occupies 40 percent of Brazil's total area, and is thought to be the oldest tropical forest area in the world. The Amazon River basin is the largest in the world at approximately 4,195 miles long and is home to the notorious piranha and anaconda. The ancient mutant sorceress Selene founded the colony of Nova Roma in the Amazon rainforest. Patterned after ancient Rome, Selene populated the colony with kidnapped and mind-wiped people and their descendants. For centuries she sought to maintain the colony's isolation so as to retain control; however, after an encounter with the New Mutants in modern times, Selene was defeated. In recent times, Selene's spell began to fade, and so the mutant Empath used his powers to maintain the falsehood in order to remain living in the colony with his lover, the Nova Roman mutant Magma. After the truth was ultimately revealed, Empath and Magma remained to help the Nova Romans acclimate to 20th century life.

Brazilian culture is influenced by a wide variety of elements, primarily a potpourri of its Portuguese origins, African slavery years, and native South American influences. Brazil boasts the largest Roman Catholic population in the world, with the world famous Carnaval held annually to mark the beginning of Lent 40 days before Easter. The Rio Carnaval is the most famous, attracting tourists the world over including superhumans such as Domino, Puck (Eugene Judd), Mystique, and Wolverine. On the world sporting stage, Brazil excels in football (soccer) and motor racing.

NOVA ROMA

Art by Darick Robertson

OFFICIAL NAME: Republic of Delvadia (República de Delvadia [Spanish]; Delbadya Republika [Quechua])
POPULATION: 8,119,000
CAPITAL CITY: San Palo
PLACES OF INTEREST: Estatua del Condor, Andes Mountains outside San Palo
GOVERNMENT: Republic
MAJOR LANGUAGES: Spanish, Quechua
MONETARY UNIT: Delvadiano
NATURAL RESOURCES: Natural gas, soybeans and soy products, crude petroleum, zinc
NATIONAL DEFENSE: Delvadian Armed Forces: Delvadian Army, Delvadian Navy & Delvadian Air Force.
INTERNATIONAL RELATIONS: Delvadia holds membership in the United Nations (UN), UNESCO, Organization of the Petroleum Exporting Countries, and Organization of American States
EXTRATERRESTRIAL RELATIONS: None known.
NONHUMAN POPULATION: None known.
DOMESTIC SUPERHUMANS: The current Delvadian regime has employed two super-powered agents codenamed "Tarantula" in recent years: Anton Miguel Rodriguez and Luis Alvarez.
PROMINENT CITIZENS: The man known only as "el Tarantula" was an early costumed folk hero who battled on the side of the Delvadians during a war with Boca del Dios in the late 19th century, although he was presumed dead by the end of the conflict. In the early 20th century, a Delvadian father-son team assumed the heroic mantle of el Aguila ("the Eagle") following the death of the prior el Aguila, Spaniard Paco Montoya. In the 1930s, the son fought on the side of General Francisco Franco's Nationalist forces in the Spanish Civil War. "El Condor" was the nickname of a martyred Delvadian soldier who became a folk hero following his death 30 years ago. Government scientist Dr. Karl Mendoza, who served in the Red Skull's laboratories in his youth, transformed Luis Alvarez into the Tarantula, although Alvarez killed Mendoza soon after. Oscar Ortega served as Delvadian Ambassador to the US until he was assassinated by Deathstorm (Gabriel Grant). Professor Thomas Alvarez emigrated to the US, and was slain by the Tarantula for criticizing Delvadia. Enrico Elnardo is president of Delvadia.
SUPERHUMAN RESIDENTS: None known.
DOMESTIC CRIME: While nonviolent crimes such as theft have been prevalent for years, gangs of armed thieves are now common in the nation's largest cities, including the capital of San Palo. Delvadia's regime has been accused of genocide, torture and crimes against humanity, although these charges have yet to be substantiated.
INTERNATIONAL CRIME: The anti-terrorist Solo (James Bourne) and hero-killer Zeitgeist (Larry Ekler) were both active in Delvadia, and the terrorist organization ARES has been employed by the Delvadian government.
FIRST APPEARANCE: Daredevil #75 (1971)

HISTORY: Valdivian farmers first ventured inland to the area now known as Delvadia from the Santa Elena Peninsula in approximately 2000 BC. The land was conquered by the Incas around 1200. By 1533, Conquistador Francisco Pizarro defeated the Incan Empire and established Delvadia as a Spanish colony. In the early 19th century, Delvadia joined other colonies in their struggle for emancipation from Spanish colonial rule, eventually gaining independence from Spain in 1822 and briefly being incorporated into Simón Bolívar's Gran Colombia before truly becoming an independent nation following the Gran Colombia-Peru War in 1829. The newly formed Republic of Delvadia formed an alliance with the US government and elected a succession of conservative presidents. Nearly 40 years ago, Delvadia's Progressive Party led a liberal revolt that brought them to power, intending to improve public education and the railroad infrastructure. Soon after, the US provided clandestine military support to conservative-led forces rebelling against the Progressive Party's regime, with Captain Keith Bayard of the US Marines eventually leading the Delvadian rebels to victory. After the

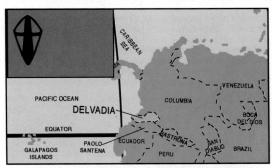

10-year civil war, a massive bronze statute was built on the mountain overlooking the capital city of San Palo depicting the man known only as "el Condor," a martyred soldier whose death rallied the Delvadian rebels to victory.

In recent years, another revolutionary assumed the name of el Condor, this time assisting the Chino Guardio socialist guerrillas opposing the US-backed capitalist government. This new el Condor capitalized on the superstitions of Delvadia's peasant population, who believed he was el Condor's ghost and followed him blindly. El Condor's revolutionaries abducted the US ambassador to Delvadia, prompting the US Senate to sponsor a fact-finding mission to Delvadia. Daredevil (Matt Murdock) investigated the kidnapping of Jerome Villiers, First Consul to the US Mission to Delvadia. The elderly Bayard reassembled his old brigade from the Delvadian Civil War, but Bayard and his men were defeated by the Chino Guardio. Daredevil battled el Condor on the mountain overlooking San Palo as lighting struck the el Condor statue, causing a landslide that buried the revolutionary. His body was never recovered, and his socialist movement soon crumbled. Another man later took up the identity of el Condor, but was slain by the hero-killer Zeitgeist.

A right-wing military junta toppled the government soon after, installing an oppressive conservative government. Anton Miguel Rodriguez was a freedom fighter in the rebel army of leftists that formed, but was expelled for being too bloodthirsty after murdering a guard without cause. Rodriguez switched sides and joined the Delvadian Army, and the government outfitted him as the Tarantula and sent him to kill his former comrades. However, Rodriguez was forced to flee the country after killing a government interrogator who would not use additional force against a prisoner. Rodriguez eventually arrived in New York City where he turned to a life of crime and was defeated by Spider-Man (Peter Parker) on several occasions. Tarantula became an agent of the Brand Corporation, and in an experiment to replicate Spider-Man's powers he became a monstrous spider-like monster and took his own life.

Upon Rodriguez's death, Captain Luis Alvarez of the Delvadian Army was chosen by the Delvadian government to inherit the Tarantula identity. His first mission was to eliminate all Delvadian political refugees seeking asylum in the US and kill Spider-Man, who the Delvadian government blamed for Rodriguez's death. With the help of rogue US State Department official Colonel Gulliver South, Tarantula teamed-up with Commission of Superhuman Activities agent Captain America (John Walker), but was defeated by Spider-Man. Alvarez was eventually captured and slain by members of the Jury. Later, ARES was employed by a faction of Delvadian revolutionaries to stop the passage of a UN resolution to launch "Operation: Omega Strike," a UN peacekeeping force which would prevent the revolutionaries from regaining control of Delvadia. ARES sent their agent Deathstorm to the Delvadian consulate in Manhattan to use force to persuade Ambassador Oscar Ortega to vote against the UN resolution, but Deathstorm killed the ambassador. ARES then infiltrated the UN, where they demanded that the Security Counsel dissolve the current Delvadian regime. However, the Security Counsel hostages were rescued by Spider-Man and Solo.

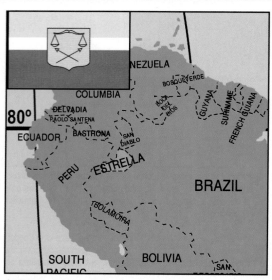

OFFICIAL NAME: Federative Republic of Estrella (Republica Federativa do Estrella)
POPULATION: 2,300,000
CAPITAL CITY: Terra Forte
PLACES OF INTEREST: Roxxon Dam
GOVERNMENT: Republic
MAJOR LANGUAGES: Portuguese, Spanish, Quechua, Aymara
MONETARY UNIT: Estrellan dollar
MAJOR RESOURCES: Mining, steel, copper, silver, gold, iron ore, coal, phosphate, potash, timber, petroleum, natural gas, hydropower, fish.
NATIONAL DEFENSE: Estrellan Armed Forces (including infantry, air force and navy).
INTERNATIONAL RELATIONS: Member of Interpol, Union of South American Nations, United Nations, UNESCO, World Health Organization and World Trade Organization. Estrella has important trade relations with Brazil, Peru, San Diablo and the USA.
EXTRATERRESTRIAL RELATIONS: None known.
NONHUMAN POPULATION: While Roxxon Oil was employed in the construction of Estrella's dam project, they dispatched numerous robot

Art by Jackson Guice

drones — "worker ants" — to facilitate work and defend the operation; they were deactivated by Deathlok (Michael Collins).
DOMESTIC SUPERHUMANS: None known.
PROMINENT CITIZENS: Joseph Verdugo was a leader of the resistance against Roxxon's dam project, and received aid from Deathlok in halting the dam. Joseph's young daughter Emilia also traveled with the resistance.
SUPERHUMAN RESIDENTS: None known.
DOMESTIC CRIME: The Estrellan government's attempt to have Roxxon Oil construct a dam within the Amazon rainforest threatened to destroy countless villages of the local natives; this inspired an armed uprising against the Estrellan military.
INTERNATIONAL CRIME: Roxxon Oil originally employed Deathlok as an operative to demolish the local resistance so that the dam project could proceed; he eventually turned against them and aided the resistance instead.
FIRST APPEARANCE: Deathlok #1 (1990)

Art by Jackson Guice

HISTORY: Estrella lies within the Amazon River basin, and contains part of the immense Amazon rainforests. Unfortunately, the marshy land has rendered construction projects difficult, and the Estrellan government despaired over their attempts to fully industrialize the country. The Roxxon Oil Corporation was brought in to construct a damn that would divert the rivers and eventually lead to more dry land to be built upon. Unfortunately, diverting the river would also destroy the homes of numerous villages, and the villagers rose up into a resistance to combat the military and attempt to destroy the dam. Although the resistance fought spiritedly, the dam project continued; unfortunately for Roxxon, the cost of completing the dam skyrocketed with each incident by the resistance. Roxxon turned to its division Cybertek to release their cybernetic warrior Deathlok against the resistance and wipe them out. However, Deathlok's computer brain was rewritten by the organic brain of Michael Collins, a programmer whose mind had been utilized for storage; Collins prevented himself from killing Emilia Verdugo, and after obtaining full control of Deathlok he returned to Estrella and led Joseph Verdugo's resistance into battle with Roxxon and the military, ultimately crushing their forces and deactivating the "worker ants" that had been placed on guard. The failure of the dam project was an embarrassment to Roxxon, and brought the Estrellan government to its knees.

OFFICIAL NAME: Republic of Medisuela (República de Medisuela)
POPULATION: 4,275,000
CAPITAL CITY: Medisuela City
PLACES OF INTEREST: Presidential Palace (Mediseula City)
GOVERNMENT: Republic
MAJOR LANGUAGES: Spanish
MONETARY UNIT: Medisuelan peso
MAJOR RESOURCES: Cotton, sugarcane, coca, marijuana, soybeans, corn, wheat, tobacco, cassava
NATIONAL DEFENSE: National Defense Force (includes Army, Air Force, and National Guard).
INTERNATIONAL RELATIONS: Medisuela holds membership in the United Nations, UNESCO, Organization of American States, and Mercosur.
EXTRATERRESTRIAL RELATIONS: None known.
NONHUMAN POPULATION: None known.
DOMESTIC SUPERHUMANS: None known.
PROMINENT CITIZENS: General Miguel Alfredo Navatilas was a Medisuelan leader notorious for human rights abuses and narcotics trafficking. Colonel Antonio Veneno was a member of the Medisuelan National Defense Force under the Navatilas regime, and once succeeded in capturing Captain America (Steve Rogers).
SUPERHUMAN RESIDENTS: None known.
DOMESTIC CRIME: Corruption is widespread and Medisuela is a haven for smuggling, money laundering, and organized crime. Armed robberies, carjacking, and burglaries are common in both urban and rural areas. Pickpocketing and mugging are prevalent in the cities, particularly in downtown Medisuela City. High-ranking officials of the former Navatilas regime have been charged with murder, torture, rape, and other crimes against humanity.
INTERNATIONAL CRIME: In recent decades, Medisuela has become increasingly involved in illegal narcotics production and trafficking, attracting the attention of the Punisher (Frank Castle). The nation also has several ongoing border disputes with Paraguay, and has claimed sovereignty over the Argentina's Misiones Province in the past.
FIRST APPEARANCE: Punisher/Captain America: Blood & Glory #1 (1992)

HISTORY: The Guaraní people were the first known inhabitants of the land that constitutes modern-day Medisuela. Although originally nomadic, they eventually established agricultural communities along the Paraná River. Spanish Conquistador Ramiro Montoya discovered the area in 1521 AD on an expedition into the South American interior. Medisuela City was founded in 1534, which became the center of a Spanish colonial province. A nationalist movement swept through the colony in the early 19th century, and a revolutionary army of Medisuelan separatists ousted the local Spanish authorities from power in 1809. The Republic of Medisuela was established approximately two years after, in 1811.

More recently, right-wing General Miguel Navatilas of the Medisuelan National Defense Force rose to power in a military coup backed by the United States. However, he soon fell out of favor with the US due to his reputed links to narcotics trafficking, strong-arm tactics, human rights abuses, and electoral fraud. Unknown to Navatilas and most US government officials, US Attorney General Roger Mollech and his aide, Angela Stone, who had formed a secret alliance with the Medisuelan dictator, devised an elaborate plan to double-cross Navatilas and take over the nation for themselves. Mollech sold the illegal drugs seized by the US Department of Justice on American streets to create a surplus of untraceable capital revenue, and then used those funds to commission the creation of sabotaged weapons that he secretly sold to the Navatilas regime. Not realizing that Mollech was setting him up with malfunctioning weapons, Navatilas received these illegal arms shipments believing that he was intended to use them to overthrow the governments of neighboring countries, which Mollech deemed unsympathetic to US

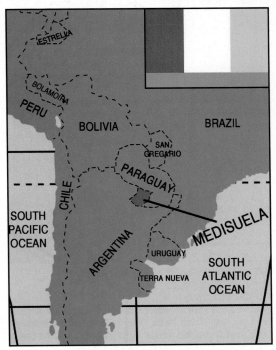

interests, a plan which was dubbed "Project: Democracy." Allied with Attorney General Mollech was a team of rogue US Defense Intelligence Agency (DIA) and Air Force servicemen: Colonel Max Kalee, Lieutenant Peter Malev, Sergeant Cain Kyffin, Sergeant Kane Kyffin, and Sergeant Lykaios Theopolous.

Eventually, the Punisher, who had been investigating Mollech's drug sales, and Captain America, who had been investigating the illegal arms sales to the Navatilas regime, reluctantly joined forces and journeyed to Medisuela to uncover the conspiracy's mastermind. Attorney General Mollech then orchestrated events so that Captain America was presumed dead, which allowed Mollech to publicly accuse General Navatilas of ordering Captain America's assassination and use his death as grounds for the invasion of and installation of US puppet regime in Medisuela. However, the US president and Congress thwarted Mollech's attempts to have the US immediately declare a full-scale war against Medisuela. Undeterred, Mollech arranged for his allies within the US military to covertly infiltrate Medisuela in uniform and begin an assault on the country, which he believed would force the US government to either admit to rogue elements within the military or commit to a full-scale US invasion. However, Mollech's plans went awry when Captain America and the Punisher traveled to Medisuela City and defeated Mollech's invading allies, but not before Mollech's men succeeded in assassinating General Navatilas. The super-powered private investigator known as Terror, who was previously hired by General Navatilas to keep tabs on Captain America and the Punisher upon their arrival in Medisuela, used the deceased general's body parts to discover the extent of the conspiracy to overthrow the Medisuelan government. Learning of Mollech's involvement from Terror, Captain America and the Punisher traveled to Dallas, Texas where the attorney general was attempting to flee the country, and brought him to justice. Mollech was soon indicted and incarcerated for his treasonous crimes in office.

PERU

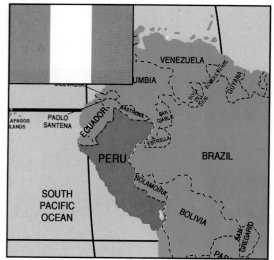

OFFICIAL NAME: Republic of Peru (Republica del Peru)

POPULATION: 28,675,000

CAPITAL CITY: Lima

PLACES OF INTEREST: Andes Mountains, Amazon River, Amazon Rainforest, Lake Titicaca, Nazca, Casa de Pizarro (Lima), Cathedral of Lima, Jorge Chavez International Airport (Callao), City of the Space Gods, Temple of Farallah, Temple of the Great Weaver

GOVERNMENT: Constitutional republic

MAJOR LANGUAGES: Spanish, Quechua, Aymara

MONETARY UNIT: Nuevo sol

MAJOR RESOURCES: Mining, steel, copper, silver, gold, iron ore, coal, phosphate, potash, timber, petroleum, natural gas, hydropower, fish, textiles, clothing, food processing.

NATIONAL DEFENSE: Peruvian Army, Peruvian Navy (includes aviation, infantry and coast guard) and Peruvian Air Force.

INTERNATIONAL RELATIONS: Member of Interpol, Union of South American Nations, United Nations (and its Security Council), SHIELD, UNESCO, World Health Organization and World Trade Organization. Peru has had border troubles with Chile, Ecuador and Bolivia, but has important trade relations with Argentina, Brazil, Canada, China, Colombia, Ecuador, Estrella, Japan, Switzerland, the USA and Venezuela.

EXTRATERRESTRIAL RELATIONS: The enigmatic Celestials visited Peru on at least two occasions; during the "Third Host," approximately 1000 years ago, the City of the Space Gods was built as a tribute to them in the Andes Mountains. When the "Fourth Host" came in recent years, the Celestials used the City as their base of operations during their judgment of Earth. The Celestials' presence has drawn the gods of Asgard, Olympus and Nirvana to the City of the Space Gods. The extradimensional sorcerer Tiboro had Peruvian followers in the distant past. The mystical Yazdi Gem was sighted in ancient Peru. The demonic entity Farallah left its icon the Fearsome Fist of Farallah within a temple in the Andes where it was eventually found by Count Andreas Zorba, transforming him into Carnivore of the Exemplars. The extradimensional Gatherers were once based out of a citadel in the Andes where they kept Ute the Watcher as a prisoner. The Kree rebels who formed the Lunatic Legion once launched an attack on the Avengers in the Andes.

NONHUMAN POPULATION: Many of the Eternals and Deviants have been drawn to Peru due to the activities of the Celestials. Ajak and a crew of fellow Eternals spent a thousand years in suspended animation within the City of the Space Gods to await the coming of the Fourth Host. The Deviant el Toro Rojo is bound to the autistic Peruvian boy Tupac Amaru through a bull totem, and can take Tupac's place on Earth. The Deviant Dromedan was entombed within Peru for centuries by the Eternals to prevent him from using his mind-control powers on humans. During one escape, Dromedan enslaved some of the Peruvians, and unleashed creatures such as Thunder and the World-Devouring Worm upon them. The mystical creature the Gatekeeper was summoned to do battle with Ezekiel Sims and Spider-Man (Peter Parker).

DOMESTIC SUPERHUMANS: Arachne (Sylvie Yacqua) obtained spider-powers from a project of the Commission on Superhuman Activities and used her abilities for criminal gains as part of the Deathweb. The mystical tribes known as the Spider Clan (including their priestess Taran) and the Snake Clan (led by Fair de Lain) dwell near the Nazca River. M'Gumbu is a witch doctor with mystical talents who lives in the Amazon jungle. Miguel Legar helped to empower Ezekiel Sims, and later served as mentor to Araña as part of the Spider Society, ultimately perishing in battle with their mortal foes the Sisterhood of the Wasp.

PROMINENT CITIZENS: Dr. Daniel Damian, a US archaeologist spent many years studying the City of the Space Gods. Finance minister Victor Nazario and his daughter Freda were among the Shining Path's victims; Dani Simpson reported on their deaths.

SUPERHUMAN RESIDENTS: Ezekiel Sims obtained his spider-like powers through ceremonies performed by Miguel Legar. Mimic (Calvin Rankin) was held prisoner in for a time by the Prime Sentinels. The criminal Hijacker (Howard Mitchell) obtained his special knock-out gas from time spent living in Peru.

DOMESTIC CRIME: The Communist Party of Peru — better known as the Shining Path — have been involved in countless guerrilla and drug-related acts; the leader Ernesto Sanz preached a policy inclusive to mutants, using their abilities to bolster the Shining Path's power; they have employed mercenaries such as Saracen (Muzzafar Lambert); other members of the Shining Path have included Angel Esteban. The Leopard Cult are a tribe in the Amazon jungles who were taken over by Fu Manchu, leader of the Celestial Order of the Si-Fan; the principal warrior of the Leopard Cult, Maru, was granted immunity to pain through enhancement Fu Manchu granted him.

INTERNATIONAL CRIME: Peru is a source of illegal drug production, with significant amounts smuggled through the Colombian border; this has drawn the attention of the vigilante Punisher (Frank Castle). The Shining Path have also been fought by Cable (Nathan Summers). Jason Beere planted a powerful neutron bomb in Peru, but it was retrieved by Captain America (Steve Rogers). The mutant criminal Sabretooth (Victor Creed) and the mercenary Scorpio (Mikel Fury) have been active in Peru. When Fu Manchu was active in Peru, he drew in associates such as Fah Lo Suee and Maximillian Zaran. The presence of the Temple of Farallah drew in the covetous Collectors of Antiquities. A rogue team of Prime Sentinels from Operation: Zero Tolerance operated out of a base in the Peruvian jungles until they were drawn out by Excalibur.

HISTORY: In ancient times, Peru was occupied by the Incan peoples; around 1000, they were visited by the Celestials, and honored them by constructing the City of the Space Gods in the Andes. In the 16th century Peru was conquered by Spain, who made the city Lima the capital of their South American empire. Peru declared independence in 1821, drove the Spanish out in 1824, and fought Spain again in 1866. During the 20th century, the country was kept in turmoil by a succession of military coups.

CITY OF THE SPACE GODS

VROOMMM

Art by Jack Kirby

OFFICIAL NAME: Federal Republic of San Diablo (Republica Federativa do San Diablo)
POPULATION: 1,700,000
CAPITAL CITY: Diablo Sorrindo
PLACES OF INTEREST: Mount Diablo, the Executioner's villa
GOVERNMENT: Federal republic
MAJOR LANGUAGES: Spanish
MONETARY UNIT: Diablo peso
MAJOR RESOURCES: Gold, iron ore, steel, nickel, platinum, tin, uranium, petroleum, timber, agriculture, textiles, footwear, cement, aircraft, motor vehicles, machinery, chemicals.
NATIONAL DEFENSE: San Diablo Armed Forces, including infantry and air force.
INTERNATIONAL RELATIONS: Member of Interpol, Union of South American Nations, United Nations, UNESCO, World Health Organization and World Trade Organization. San Diablo has significant trade relations with Brazil, Ecuador and Estrella.
EXTRATERRESTRIAL RELATIONS: The Asgardian god Thor once visited San Diablo and fought the Executioner.
NONHUMAN POPULATION: None known.
DOMESTIC SUPERHUMANS: Zona Rosa was a local heroine who was killed by Zeitgeist (Larry Ekler).

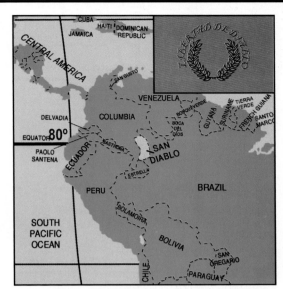

Art by Jack Kirby

PROMINENT CITIZENS: The Executioner was a prominent leader of the communist faction who sought to rule San Diablo; when he abandoned his own men in fear of Thor, he was killed by them. Machete (Ferdinand Lopez) left San Diablo to seek work as a mercenary in order to help fund the revolutionary cause; he joined Batroc's Brigade, and was ultimately slain by Zeitgeist; his brother Alfonso assumed his identity in the Batroc's Brigade, but was himself slain by STAR agent Kali Vries; their brother Mariano was the current Machete, and like his brothers served in Batroc's Brigade.
SUPERHUMAN RESIDENTS: None known.

DOMESTIC CRIME: San Diablo has frequently been in a state of civil unrest, with various armed uprisings against the government.
INTERNATIONAL CRIME: The vigilante Zeitgeist assassinated local hero Zona Rosa and criminal Machete (Ferdinand).
FIRST APPEARANCE: Journey into Mystery #84 (1962)
HISTORY: San Diablo was colonized by the Spanish during the 17th century, and named after a local legend, which maintained that a benevolent spirit watched over the people. After gaining its independence in the 19th century, San Diablo began to demonstrate real power of its own, but economic hardships in the 20th century led to civil unrest. In recent years, a power struggle emerged between the forces trying to maintain a democratic order and those who wished to topple the government and install a communist republic; the chief leader of the communist faction was known as the Executioner, so called for his propensity to dispose of those who displeased him. Medical staff from the USA who came to volunteer in San Diablo included Dr. Roger Graham, Dr. Donald Blake and nurse Jane Foster. Dr. Blake assumed his other guise as the mighty Thor to combat the Executioner, and used his hammer to set off Mount Diablo, frightening him. When the Executioner tried to flee the scene with his money, his own men turned on him for his cowardice and murdered him. Although this incident weakened the communist's resolve, rebel factions continue to operate such as that which Ferdinand Lopez belonged to. Lopez became the sword-wielding Machete to earn money to help finance the revolution, only to be killed by the vigilante Zeitgeist. Ferdinand was soon followed by his brother, Alfonso. It is not known whether Mariano also seeks to finance the revolutionary cause.

Art by Jack Kirby

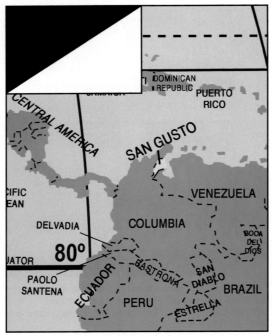

OFFICIAL NAME: Republic of San Gusto (República de San Gusto)
POPULATION: 3, 256,000
CAPITAL: La Ciudad de los Bolívar
PLACES OF INTEREST: Pico Del Caballero; Hate-Monger's underground base
GOVERNMENT: Federal republic
MAJOR LANGUAGES: Spanish, Italian, Wayúu
MONETARY UNIT: San Gusto Peso
MAJOR RESOURCES: Natural gas, petroleum. Fishing, formerly a large component of the economy, has declined as pollution in Lake Maracaibo has increased.
NATIONAL DEFENSE: San Gusto's national armed forces, the Fuerza Armada Nacional, are broken into three services, the 11,000 strong Army (Fuerzas Terrestres), a small Navy (Fuerzas Navales) and even smaller Air Force (Fuerzas Aviacion)
INTERNATIONAL RELATIONS: San Gusto works hard to maintain good relations with its immediate neighbors, Venezuela and Colombia, though there are outstanding disputes with the former over fishing rights in Lake Maracaibo, and with the latter over repeated Colombian-organized illegal narcotics and paramilitary territorial crossings. Because of its comparatively large gas and oil reserves, San Gusto's political stability is of disproportionate interest to the USA, who fear that problems there may have a ripple effect across the entire region; as a result the USA has invested billions in foreign aid in the hopes of ensuring the country remains democratic, and a smaller, but still significant amount, in secretly financing local groups deemed sympathetic to US interests. San Gusto is a member of the United Nations, UNESCO, World Health Organization, Union of South American Nations, and Union Latina.
EXTRATERRESTRIAL RELATIONS: None known.
NONHUMAN POPULATION: San Gusto's jungles are home to tribes of Vasitri, a kind of South American Sasquatch.
DOMESTIC SUPERHUMANS: The heroine Ojo Macabra (Candelaria Vélez), able to petrify

at a glance, was one of San Gusto's few super heroes, until she was slain by the American hero-killer Zeitgeist.
PROMINENT CITIZENS: Former rebel leader el Lobo (Ricardo Arroyo-López) fled San Gusto at the end of the civil war, to become a low rent slumlord in New York.
SUPERHUMAN RESIDENTS: None known.
DOMESTIC CRIME: San Gusto is a relatively prosperous nation, and enjoys a low crime rate.
INTERNATIONAL CRIME: Several years ago the Hate-Monger (Adolf Hitler) constructed an underground base in San Gusto, and used the country as a testing ground for his new Hate-Ray, sparking off a short lived civil war that threatened to cause the government to collapse. Having proved his weapon's viability, the Hate-Monger also planned to use the country as the staging point to fire his Hate-Ray at the moon, intending to bounce the beam off the lunar surface and back to encompass the entire Earth. His plans were disrupted by the American Fantastic Four and the CIA agent Nick Fury, and with the destruction of the Hate-Ray, San Gusto's internal dissent soon dissipated. Both before and after this incident, the American CIA have maintained a close interest in the country, viewing its stability as vital to the region, and covertly backing pro-American interests, their actions sometimes straying into illegality. San Gusto's shared border with Colombia sometimes often sees the country used as a trans-shipment point for illegal narcotics. The hero-killer Zeitgeist (Larry Ekler) assassinated local heroine Ojo Macabra.
FIRST APPEARANCE: Fantastic Four #21 (1963)
HISTORY: Archaeological finds place human inhabitants in the region now occupied by San Gusto at least as far back as 15,000 years ago. Located at the uppermost end of the Andes, and next to Lake Maracaibo, San Gusto was on the edge of the Chibcha Empire, inhabited by a mix of tribes, including Caribs and Wayúu. European colonization began around 1524 with Spanish explorers establishing permanent settlements in the region, soon coming into conflict with the indigenous population, though it was the spread of European diseases that did most damage to the natives. By 1570 San Gusto had been established as a gateway to the South American continent, an important component of the Spanish Empire, and in 1717 it was absorbed into the newly established Viceroyalty of New Granada (Virreinato de la Nueva Granada). Desire for independence from Spain grew in San Gusto as it did across most of the region, and in the early 1820s, Simón Bolívar, dubbed el Libertador ("the Liberator"), led a successful campaign that established the republic Gran Colombia, incorporating the areas which broke off when Gran Colombia collapsed in 1830 to form the independent nations of Colombia, Venezuela, San Gusto, Ecuador and Panama. The country struggled with democracy, and for most of the 19th and early 20th centuries it swung back and forth between elected governments, which usually collapsed and were deposed for corruption, and relatively benign military dictatorships. In the late 1940s the USA became more involved in the region, pumping billions of dollars into San Gusto over the next few decades to encourage the growth of democracy. A little over a decade ago the Hate-Monger temporarily disrupted years of work by triggering a civil war using his Hate-Ray, but the device was destroyed by the Fantastic Four, and the conflict soon ended.

DURING THE HATE-MONGER'S CIVIL WAR

Art by Jack Kirby

OFFICIAL NAME: Republic of Santo Marco (República de Santo Marco)

POPULATION: 198,000

CAPITAL CITY: Santo Marco

PLACES OF INTEREST: Presidential Palace, Navidad Square, Montalva Hills

GOVERNMENT: Dictatorship; formerly democratic republic

MAJOR LANGUAGES: English, Spanish, Portuguese, French

MONETARY UNIT: Santo Marco Peso

MAJOR RESOURCES: Coffee, cocoa, timber, tourism

NATIONAL DEFENSE: Santo Marco Armed Forces, including the Santo Marco Army and Navy.

INTERNATIONAL RELATIONS: Santo Marco is a member of organizations including UNESCO, United Nations and the Union Latina.

EXTRATERRESTRIAL RELATIONS: None known

NONHUMAN POPULATION: None known

DOMESTIC SUPERHUMANS: None known

PROMINENT CITIZENS: Head of the Santo Marco Armed Forces General Luis Augustine currently rules the country as a dictatorship; Carlos Zapatero leads the Popular Front of Santo Marco, which was formed in opposition to Augustine's rule; Felix Navidad was the nation's elected president until his government was overthrown by Magneto; General Alejandro Montalva once led Santo Marco into achieving independence.

SUPERHUMAN RESIDENTS: Magneto and his Brotherhood of Evil Mutants — including Mastermind (Jason Wyngarde), Quicksilver (Pietro Maximoff), Scarlet Witch (Wanda Maximoff) & Toad (Mortimer Toynbee) — briefly resided in the country after usurping control of the government.

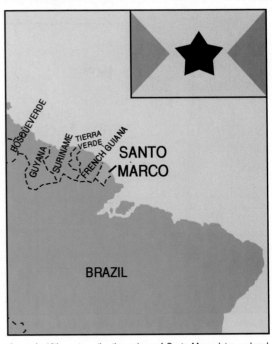

Art by Jack Kirby

PRESIDENTIAL PALACE

FLAG UNDER MAGNETO'S RULE

DOMESTIC CRIME: Illegal narcotics trafficking are a frequent problem due to the country's close proximity to the Amazon rainforest.

INTERNATIONAL CRIME: Mercenaries Jim Rhodes and Parnell Jacobs once ran guns for the then-dictator of Santo Marco. Magneto and his Brotherhood of Evil Mutants once attacked Santo Marco by first shelling the hills behind the capital from a stolen naval craft, then creating an illusory army to overthrow the government. Santo Marco is a growing transshipment point for illegal South American narcotics destined for Europe and the USA.

FIRST APPEARANCE: X-Men #4 (1964)

HISTORY: Founded during Spanish colonization of South America in the early 16th century, the tiny colony of Santo Marco later endured Portuguese, Dutch and French domination until finally achieving independence in the early 19th century when General Alejandro Montalva assumed power. After suffering for decades under his cruel dictatorship, the people of Santo Marco rebelled and overthrew Montalva's corrupt regime. Felix Navidad was elected president and ruled peacefully for many years until his government was overthrown by mutant terrorist Magneto and his Brotherhood of Evil Mutants. Opposed by his nemeses the X-Men, Magneto was forced to flee, but not before activating a nuclear bomb in an attempt to destroy the entire country. Santo Marco was saved by Brotherhood member Quicksilver, who disagreed with Magneto's hatred of humans. After Magneto's departure, commander of the Santo Marco Armed Forces General Luis Augustine assumed control, plunging the nation into another dictatorship. In protest, the Popular Front for Santo Marco was formed by outspoken activist Carlos Zapatero to alert the world to Santo Marco's plight. The Popular Front continues to harbor a grudge against the Brotherhood for enabling Augustine's rise to power.

NAVIDAD SQUARE

Art by Lewis LaRosa

TIERRA VERDE

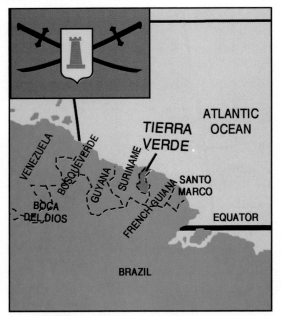

OFFICIAL NAME: Republic of Tierra Verde (República de Tierra Verde)
POPULATION: 719,000
CAPITAL CITY: Puerto Verde
PLACES OF INTEREST: El Jardín Del Rey Mountains, Tierra Verde Medical Center (Puerto Verde)
GOVERNMENT: Totalitarian republic
MAJOR LANGUAGES: English, Spanish
MONETARY UNIT: Lempira
MAJOR RESOURCES: Timber, bananas, coffee, shrimp, coal, copper; formerly cocaine
NATIONAL DEFENSE: Tierra Verde Armed Forces, including army and air force.
INTERNATIONAL RELATIONS: Member of UNESCO, United Nations, World Health Organization, & World Trade Organization. Tierra Verde's government was once backed by the United States, despite the country's global reputation as a banana republic run by a drug czar.
EXTRATERRESTRIAL RELATIONS: None known
NONHUMAN POPULATION: The remains of the ancient Deviant weapon Spore once existed in the soil of the el Jardín Del Rey mountainside.

PUERTO VERDE

Art by John Byrne

DOMESTIC SUPERHUMANS: Sister Salvation was a nun with mutant healing powers before she burned them out destroying Spore. In the 1980s, the regime was supported by the masked hero el Aguila.
PROMINENT CITIZENS: Enríque Rosales is the currently elected president. Felix Guillermo Caridad ruled the country until his death at the hands of the Spore. His son Palo served in the Tierra Verde Army.
SUPERHUMAN RESIDENTS: Former Nazi war criminal Geist once acted as Caridad's special advisor in his quest to create a superhuman agent.
DOMESTIC CRIME: Illicit cocaine production once occurred throughout the country, fostered by Caridad's corrupt government.
INTERNATIONAL CRIME: Cuban mutant adventurer la Bandera opposed Caridad's corrupt regime after his drug trafficking ruined her family by inspiring the local populace to revolt. To oppose her, Geist hired the mercenary Tiger Shark (Todd Arliss), who was defeated by Wolverine (James Howlett).
FIRST APPEARANCE: Wolverine #18 (1989)
HISTORY: Once part of Spain's vast empire in the New World, Tierra Verde ("green earth") declared its independence in the early 19th Century. Years of civil unrest all but decimated the country until President Felix Caridad assumed power through a combination of military

EL JARDIN DEL RAY MOUNTAINS

Art by John Byrne

success, anti-communist politics, and a personal fortune gained from the illegal trafficking of cocaine. In an attempt to distance his country from its drug-plagued reputation, Caridad enacted a series of sweeping reforms, including construction of the region's premier medical facility in his nation's capital. In recent times, Caridad sought for his country to have a super-powered symbol akin to the USA's Captain America. To that end he recruited the services of the cybernetic former Nazi Geist, who learned that the cocaine harvested from the el Jardín Del Rey jungle mountainside contained special properties that incited violence in its users. Using this, Geist sought to turn the mercenary Roughhouse into Caridad's superhuman symbol, but was opposed by mutant adventurer Wolverine. Geist was also tasked with opposing an attempted rebellion against Caridad's regime being fostered by Cuban mutant heroine la Bandera, employing the super-powered mercenary Tiger Shark to dispose of her. However, Tiger Shark was defeated by Wolverine, who then teamed with la Bandera in opposition to Caridad. Ultimately, it was revealed that the cocaine had been tainted centuries ago by the remains of the ancient Deviant weapon Spore. Upon imbibing a massive dose of the cocaine in order to empower himself, Caridad allowed Spore to reform, killing him. Spore was ultimately destroyed by Caridad's wife Sister Salvation with her mutant healing power. La Bandera's revolution ultimately succeeded, and after order was restored democratic elections were held with Enríque Rosales voted in as president.

OFFICIAL NAME: Bolivarian Republic of Venezuela (Republica Bolivariana de Venezuela)

POPULATION: 26,023,000

CAPITAL CITY: Caracas

PLACES OF INTEREST: Los Teques, Maracaibo, Valencia, Canaima National Park, Orinoco River, Palacio de Miraflores (Caracas), Parque Central Towers (Caracas)

GOVERNMENT: Federal republic

MAJOR LANGUAGES: Spanish

MONETARY UNIT: Bolivar

MAJOR RESOURCES: Petroleum, natural gas, iron ore, steel, gold, bauxite, hydropower, diamonds, construction materials, food processing, textiles, motor vehicles.

NATIONAL DEFENSE: National Armed Forces, including Ground Forces, Naval Forces (includes marines & coast guard), Air Force and Armed Forces of Cooperation (national guard).

INTERNATIONAL RELATIONS: Venezuela is a member of Interpol, Latin Union, Organization of Petroleum Exporting Countries, Union of South American Nations, United Nations, World Health Organization and World Trade Organization. Venezuela has important trade relations with Bermuda, Brazil, China, Colombia, Costa Verde, Mexico, Panama and Santo Rico. Venezuela has claim disputes with Guyana. Venezuela has had several disputes with the USA over allegations of covert actions, but it remains a major trading partner. The nation has cooperated with SHIELD authorities.

EXTRATERRESTRIAL RELATIONS: The malevolent extra-dimensional creature Synraith was summoned to Venezuela in ancient times by the sacrifice of a million victims.

NONHUMAN POPULATION: The Carnal Serpent was an ancient creature of great power that lived in the jungles and consumed the god Priapus.

DOMESTIC SUPERHUMANS: Sofia Mantega was born and raised in Caracas; after the death of her mother, she went to live with her American father in the USA, eventually becoming a student at the Xavier Institute with the codename Wind Dancer, and leading the New Mutants squad at the school; after losing her powers on "M-Day" she became a member of the New Warriors.

PROMINENT CITIZENS: Hugo Chavez, who led a failed coup in 1992, was elected president in 1999; his attempts to spread socialism have been controversial, and placed the nation at odds with the USA. Miranda Mantega was the mother of Sofia, and was killed during a riot in Caracas; Miranda was survived by her brother Paolo. Joy Adams worked as a guide.

SUPERHUMAN RESIDENTS: Nearby Zenith Island was home to an experimental hivemind society developed by Dr. Mark Cushing, but it had to be dismantled when MODOK and AIM sought to usurp the technology. "The Rev" (Samuel Smith) operated his Church of the Saved in Venezuela as a cover for his drug smuggling operations.

DOMESTIC CRIME: Venezuela has difficulties with forced slave labor

operations.

INTERNATIONAL CRIME: The drug trade and violence of neighboring Colombia have often spilt across Venezuela's border, attracting criminals such as Jigsaw (Billy Russo), and the vigilante Punisher (Frank Castle). The god Priapus' quest for the Carnal Serpent also entangled the mercenary Terror, Silver Sable of Symkaria's Wild Pack and the heroic Luke Cage. When the terrorist Mutant Liberation Front were being led by Stryfe, they maintained a safe house in Caracas. Venezuela was threatened by a chronal bomb designed by time traveler Arthur Zarrko, but it was defused by Spider-Man (Peter Parker) and the Human Torch (Johnny Storm).

HISTORY: Despite spirited resistance from the locals, Venezuela was colonized by Spain in the 16th century, naming it "Little Venice;" from 1819-1831 it was part of Gran Colombia. Attempts to claim independence continued into the 19th century, until the Spanish were finally driven out in 1830. Venezuela became an affluent nation in the 20th century due to its wealth of oil, but a collapse in prices eventually brought the economy down. The resulting instability led to armed coups, eventually placing former combatant Hugo Chavez as president.

Art by Keron Grant

AFRICA &
THE MIDDLE EAST

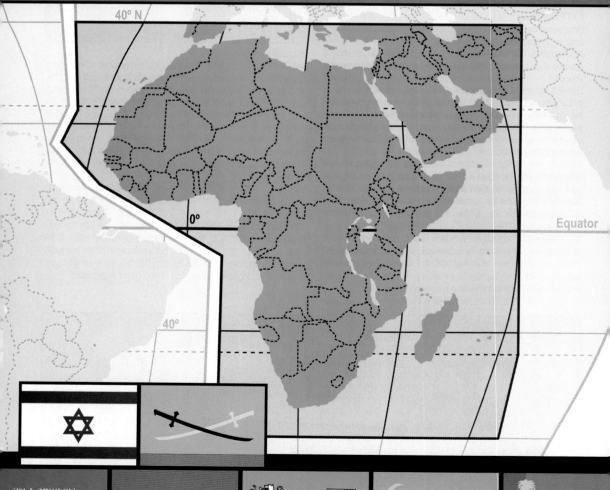

40° N

0°

Equator

40°

OFFICIAL NAME: People's Democratic Republic of Algeria (Al Jumhuriyah al Jaza'iriyah ad Dimuqratiyah ash Sha'biyah)

POPULATION: 33,333,000

CAPITAL CITY: Algiers

PLACES OF INTEREST: Ahaggar Mountains, Oran, Constantine, Tipaza, the Casbah (Algiers), M'Zab Valley, Djemila, Timgad, Al Qal'a of Beni Hammad, Tassili n'Ajjer

GOVERNMENT: Republic

MAJOR LANGUAGES: Arabic, French

MONETARY UNIT: Algerian dinar

MAJOR RESOURCES: Petroleum, natural gas, petrochemicals, iron ore, phosphates, uranium, lead, zinc, mining, agriculture, food processing.

NATIONAL DEFENSE: The National Popular Army, the Algerian National Navy, Air Force and Territorial Air Defense Force. Intelligence is provided by Department du Renseignement et de la Securite.

INTERNATIONAL RELATIONS: Member of African Union, Interpol, Organization of the Petroleum Exporting Countries, United Nations, UNESCO, World Health Organization and World Trade Organization. Algeria has had disputes with Libya in the past, and has ongoing disputes with Morocco. Algeria's important trade partners include China, France, Germany, Italy, Spain, Turkey and the USA. Symkaria's Wild Pack has been active in Algeria.

EXTRATERRESTRIAL RELATIONS: None known.

NONHUMAN POPULATION: None known.

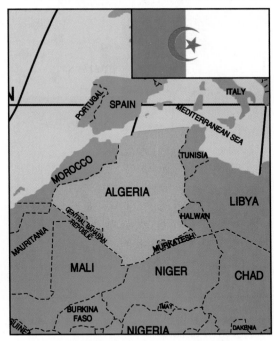

Art by Larry Lieber

DOMESTIC SUPERHUMANS: The mutant siblings Emplate (Marius St. Croix), M (Monet St. Croix) and Claudette & Nicole St. Croix were born in Algiers, but grew up in Monaco; Emplate became a criminal, feeding off the genetic material of other mutants to sustain himself, while M was a student of the Xavier Institute and eventually joined X-Factor Investigations; Claudette & Nicole merged into one to impersonate Monet for a time.

PROMINENT CITIZENS: Louis Cartier St. Croix is an ambassador to the US, father of Emplate, M, Claudette & Nicole, and a member of the mutant-sympathizing Mutant Underground. The Finisher (Karl Fiers) was an employee of the Red Skull (Albert Malik), and was responsible for engineering the death of Richard & Mary Parker; he died while battling Spider-Man. Sandor was a strongman who served Malik. Charlie Shaddock was another of Malik's men, and later confronted the android replicas Harry Osborn had made of the Parkers, mistaking them for the real people.

SUPERHUMAN RESIDENTS: The Red Skull (Albert Malik) who had served Russia in the 1950s later moved to Algeria to continue his criminal operations; when FBI agents Richard & Mary Parker came to investigate his actions, he arranged their deaths; the Parkers' son Peter later avenged them as Spider-Man; when he threatened the world with a nuclear device, the Red Skull was finally removed from Algeria by the forces of Silver Sable, which included Hawkeye (Clint Barton),

le Peregrine (Alain Racine) of France and Sandman (William Baker); the Red Skull later died at the hands of a Scourge of the Underworld during a prison break.

DOMESTIC CRIME: Algeria has had issues with prostitution and forced slave labor, and the Algerian government has been violently opposed by the Armed Islamic Group.

INTERNATIONAL CRIME: The terrorist al-Qaeda have been active in Algeria. Donald Pierce of the Hellfire Club kept a base in Algeria. Brock Rumlow was active in Algeria as one of the Red Skull (Malik)'s mercenaries, but later transferred his loyalties to the original Red Skull (Johann Shmidt) as Crossbones.

HISTORY: The lands of Algeria were occupied by the Roman Empire in 146 BC, and in 637 by the Arabs; France conquered the nation in the 1830s; the Front de Liberation Nationale was eventually organized to help drive the French out, and independence was achieved in 1962. Since then, the country has struggled with the application of democracy to its people.

Art by Larry Lieber

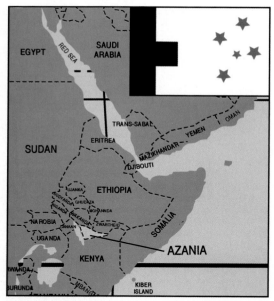

OFFICIAL NAME: Republic of Azania
POPULATION: 11,594,000
CAPITAL CITY: Fischerstadt
PLACES OF INTEREST: Supremacists' special weapons facility, Azanian volcanic missile base.
GOVERNMENT: Military dictatorship
MAJOR LANGUAGES: English, Swahili, German
MONETARY UNIT: Azanian schilling
MAJOR RESOURCES: Mineral wealth, notably gold, platinum, uranium. Azania used to be one of the world's major diamond providers, but excessive mining saw the supply drastically drop in the last decade.
NATIONAL DEFENSE: Azania maintains a well-equipped military, with the Army often being used for "peacekeeping" duties against the disenfranchised black population during the apartheid era. They have a sizable Air Force, but being mostly landlocked have no Navy. Azania revealed itself to be a nuclear and paranormal power during the Black Panther uprisings, having developed both missiles and superhuman agents.
INTERNATIONAL RELATIONS: Azania is a member of the United Nations (UN). It formerly had good relations with nearby Rudyarda. However it was on tense grounds with several other countries, notably neighboring Wakanda, which disapproved of Azania's apartheid system; for much of the apartheid era, Azania maintained a façade of diplomacy with their powerful neighbor, but during the Panther uprising, Azania wrongly suspected Wakandan involvement, and violated Wakandan borders with its Supremacists, before attempting a nuclear launch on them; both were thwarted. With the current unrest and ongoing power struggle, all past international relationships are void, at least until a clear ruling group takes power.
EXTRATERRESTRIAL RELATIONS: None known.
NONHUMAN POPULATION: The Panther God (Bast) has manifested within Azania at least once, to empower Sekhem Naville.
DOMESTIC SUPERHUMANS: Sekhem Naville was a self-proclaimed holy man empowered by the Panther God, who targeted the ruling white minority as Panther. The Supremacists, who served and were mostly empowered by the apartheid-era government, included the super-strong White Avenger (Dieter Steinhauer), living flamethrower Commander Blaze (Konrad Fassbinder), force-field generating Barricade (Alistair Koch), the armored flier Harrier (Johannes Haff), and energy-draining Hungyr (Frank Baer); White Avenger and Barricade were accidentally drained of their powers by Hungyr during the Wakandan incursion. Blaze, Hungyr and a new Harrier (Katrina von Gerber) allied with the

racist Purity Front during the subsequent civil war.
PROMINENT CITIZENS: General Pieter Magnus Moorbecx was the commander in charge of both Azania's nuclear and superhuman programs, ordering the Supremacists to attack Wakanda and slay the Black Panther (T'Challa), and planning the subsequent nuclear strike on Azania's neighbor. Reverend Niklas Treurnicht was an influential member of the Azanian church who preached that apartheid was dictated by God in the Bible and that it maintained the separate races' cultural identities. Governor Jonas Fugard was a government minister who argued for the end of apartheid. Both were slain by Panther. Civil servant Ralph van Slambrouck reluctantly signed an eviction notice to destroy a number of shanty towns, after it was made clear by his superiors that if he refused he would be fired and another would do the deed; he, his wife Mary, and young daughter Jan, were all brutally savaged by Panther, narrowly surviving. During the civil war General Hendrik Oostkamp seized power at the head of a biracial junta, maintaining control by persecuting all colors equally; his unexpected death plunged Azania back into civil war.
SUPERHUMAN RESIDENTS: After initially entering Azania pursuing the Zambian criminal Impala, Zimbabwean hero Voortrekker (Rutger van Bokhoven) was enticed to join the Supremacists for a time.
DOMESTIC CRIME: During the apartheid era there was a minimal crime rate, as criminals were often rounded up without trial, tortured until they confessed, and then imprisoned or executed. During Azania's civil war the country spent a period of near-complete lawlessness, until Oostkamp instigated draconian martial law measures. Though a nominal peace is now under way, the rule of law is patchy at best.
INTERNATIONAL CRIME: During the civil war Azania became home for a variety of international terrorist and criminal groups from places such as Liberia, Sierra Leone and the Ivory Coast.
FIRST APPEARANCE: Black Panther #1 (1988)
HISTORY: Azanian history goes back millennia, when human hunter-gatherers colonized the region. Around 2000 years ago the Bantu people immigrated in, and between the 14th and 15th century Azania was a minor province of the Empire of Kitara. The German explorer Gustav Adolf Fischer discovered the Azanian valleys in 1884, beginning a period of European colonization. Though initial settlers were German, in 1896 Kaiser Wilhelm II signed a treaty giving Azania to the British Empire in return for them ceding rights in other parts of Africa. However, during World War I, Azania revolted against British rule in support of Germany; though British forces eventually regained control, after the war Azania was granted dominion status, effectively gaining self rule, and in 1957 Azania left the Empire, declaring itself a republic. The ruling white minority instigated an apartheid system, copying South Africa far to the south. They designated black "homelands" on unusable land, uprooting whole communities, and maintained power through fear and oppression. Unrest grew as the international community isolated Azania, and Wakanda's Black Panther applied economic pressure and covert aid hoping to achieve change peacefully. However rebellion erupted when Sekhem Naville began slaughtering government officials; the Azanian government initially believed the rebellion had been incited by Wakanda, but upon discovering this was not the case, the realization that the disenfranchised black community could arise without external aid brought home how precarious white rule had become, and the government promised to dismantle apartheid and instigate reforms. The hard-line Purity Front refused to accept this, dragging the country into civil war, which ended only after General Oostkamp's biracial military junta seized power; little more than criminals themselves, they persecuted all Azanian citizens equally. Oostkamp's unexpected demise triggered all factions to begin fighting again; Black Panther and the US hero Night Thrasher (Dwayne Taylor) assisted one another in evacuating their respective countries' ambassadors. Wakandan pressure at the UN saw an international peacekeeping force sent in to stabilize things until free elections could be held; despite the fragile peace being briefly broken when various factions vied for control of a piece of the powerful mutant Doop's brain, Azania seems to slowly be returning to normality, the southern veldts even becoming something of a tourist attraction.

OFFICIAL NAME: People's Republic of Burunda (República Popular da Burunda [Portuguese], Repubilka ya Bantu ya Bulunda [Domi])
POPULATION: 20,000,000
CAPITAL CITY: Freedomtown
PLACES OF INTEREST: Presidential Palace (Freedomtown), Arbiza Plain, Northern Frontier; Bari Marsh
GOVERNMENT: Totalitarian republic
MAJOR LANGUAGES: Portuguese, Domi, English
MONETARY UNIT: Burundan kulanza
MAJOR RESOURCES: Coffee, tin, hemp, coal (formerly poppy and coca)
NATIONAL DEFENSE: Burunda People's Defense Force: Army, Air Defense Command (includes Air Wing), Popular Defense Forces
INTERNATIONAL RELATIONS: Burunda holds membership in United Nations, UNESCO, International Criminal Court (ICC), and Interpol.
EXTRATERRESTRIAL RELATIONS: None known.
NONHUMAN POPULATION: None known.
DOMESTIC SUPERHUMANS: None known.
PROMINENT CITIZENS: Former General-President Raoul Armand Bushman (presumed deceased); General Jonathan B'kosa (deceased)
SUPERHUMAN RESIDENTS: None known.
DOMESTIC CRIME: Poachers on the Arbiza Plain on Burunda's Northern Frontier harvest the horns of the black rhinoceros, which are used by Freedomtown's Chinese population for medicinal purposes. Reported instances of murder, rape, robbery, and aggravated assault skyrocketed under the Bushman regime; however, these numbers have decreased significantly since Bushman's ouster from office.
INTERNATIONAL CRIME: Under the Bushman regime, Burunda engaged in the exportation of heroin and cocaine for sale on the world black market.
FIRST APPEARANCE: Marc Spector: Moon Knight #2 (1989)

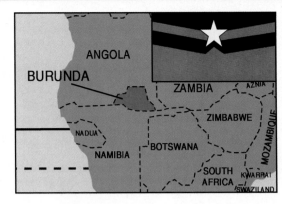

HISTORY: The area of modern-day Burunda was inhabited since prehistoric times by Bushmen hunters and gatherers. By the 6th century AD, the first Domi tribes arrived in Burunda, using their advanced iron-working technology and traditional swordsmanship skills to easily dominate the Bushmen. Later, in the 9th century AD, Nubian settlers from northern Sudan settled in the area, bringing with them their worship of the gods of Egypt. Burunda was first discovered by Europeans in 1452, when Portuguese explorer Rugato Munoz traveled inland from the coast of Angola. Burunda was officially named a Portuguese colony in 1584. Chinese indentured laborers were brought to Burunda by the Portuguese in the 19th century to work on coffee plantations and in the coal mines. By the mid-20th century, a fervent Burundan nationalist movement demanded independence from Portugal. The Portuguese ignored these demands for separatism, which provoked an armed conflict known as the War for Freedom, only ending after Portugal finally acquiesced and granted Burunda independence in 1971. In honor of this event, the Burundans renamed their capital city "Freedomtown." A parliamentary republic was established soon after.

In recent years, former mercenary Raoul Armand Bushman, a member of Burunda's Domi ethnic majority, became a notorious mercenary feared for his sadistic and bloodthirsty tactics. After years traveling the world as a freelance soldier of fortune, Bushman returned to Burunda and eventually became a general in the nation's army. Portraying himself as a benevolent "champion of the Third World" and "man of the people," Bushman led a military coup d'état that toppled the Burundan government. Appointing himself as "General-President for eternity," Bushman eliminated the intricate government bureaucracy and made himself Burunda's sole ruler, claiming that doing so would allow him to deal with the problems plaguing his nation more efficiently. Only members of Bushman's Domi ethnic group were now entitled to participate in government. Under Bushman's regime, Burunda was transformed into a socialist state and drastic policy changes were soon implemented: privately owned businesses (such

as Freedomtown's Hilton Hotel) were seized by the government and nationalized; public curfews were imposed; unauthorized photographs were strictly prohibited; military spending increased tenfold; and the borders with the neighboring nations of Angola and Namibia were closed. From his base of operations within Freedomtown's Presidential Palace, Bushman also caused Burunda's diplomatic relations with many first-world nations to sour, claiming that the USA was an imperialist society. However, conditions only worsened under Bushman's regime, as its people became more impoverished and mortality rates began to skyrocket as Bushman used the nation's income to purchase lavish personal affects. Those who spoke out against Bushman faced exile or death, such as General Jonathan B'kosa of the Air Defense Command, who fled to Paris, France.

To seek revenge upon his old enemy Marc Spector (Moon Knight), Bushman traveled to the Burandan consulate in Manhattan and orchestrated the kidnapping of Marlene Alraune, Spector's girlfriend, demanding that Spector pay a ransom of $10 million to secure her release. Moon Knight infiltrated the consulate in an attempt to rescue Alraune, but discovered that Bushman had already fled with her to Burunda. Moon Knight journeyed to Burunda and entered the country in the guise of British photojournalist Ian Waller. Arriving in Freedomtown, he infiltrated the Presidential Palace and rescued Marlene after defeating Bushman in hand-to-hand combat. Soon after, Bushman began making preparations to enter into the international drug trade to increase his personal fortune. He ordered the Army to level entire villages in order to make room for fields to plant coca plants and poppies that could be processed into cocaine and heroin. A rival drug cartel, which possessed a monopoly on the illicit drug trade in Central Africa, learned of this and conspired to end Bushman's illegal narcotics-trafficking operations before they began. The rival cartel covertly organized a revolution to overthrow Bushman's regime, secretly returning General B'kosa to Burunda so that he could assemble an army of disenfranchised citizens. The cartel also recruited freelance mercenary Arsenal, who in turn recruited Moon Knight to lead B'kosa's rebellion against Bushman. After learning the nature of Arsenal's criminal employers, Moon Knight ended his alliance with the mercenary and traveled to Burunda himself to meet with General B'kosa. With Moon Knight's guidance, B'kosa's forces torched Bushman's poppy fields and began marching toward Freedomtown. However, Bushman's soldiers soon found the rebel base camp and killed General B'kosa. With B'kosa dead, the rebels amassed outside Freedomtown joined forces with Arsenal, who led the attack on the Presidential Palace while other groups of rebels seized the airport and public radio station. With most of Bushman's soldiers deployed in the field to locate Moon Knight, the Presidential Palace was easily captured. After Bushman was defeated by Moon Knight at Burunda's southern border, his own soldiers turned on him. Bushman was taken into custody and a new president was immediately installed by the rebels. Much later, Bushman met his seeming demise in a subsequent battle with Moon Knight in Manhattan.

CANAAN

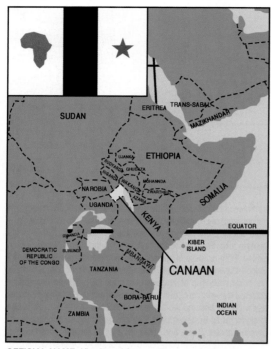

OFFICIAL NAME: Kingdom of Canaan (Royaume du Canan)
POPULATION: 4,763,000
CAPITAL CITY: Canaan
PLACES OF INTEREST: Presidential Palace, Canaan
GOVERNMENT: Totalitarian republic (former monarchy)
MAJOR LANGUAGES: English, French
MONETARY UNIT: CFA Franc
MAJOR RESOURCES: Uranium, cotton, peanuts, cattle, sheep, goats, camels, textiles
NATIONAL DEFENSE: Canaan Military Force
INTERNATIONAL RELATIONS: Canaan maintains peaceful relations with neighboring nations, particularly Wakanda, and is a member of the African Union, United Nations, UNESCO, World Health Organization, World Trade Organization, and participated in the Pan-African Congress on the Treatment of Superhumans.
EXTRATERRESTRIAL RELATIONS: None known
NONHUMAN POPULATION: None known
DOMESTIC SUPERHUMANS: King Baru ruled Canaan until he was overthrown by Moses Magnum and fled to Wakanda where he was later captured by alchemist Diablo and transformed into a creature of living Vibranium.
PROMINENT CITIZENS: General Umbaja leads the Canaan Military Force.
SUPERHUMAN RESIDENTS: Ethiopian technosmith Moses Magnum usurped control of Canaan from King Baru. Among his super-powered naturalized agents were the sentient database Phreak and mercenary weapons master Killjoy.

DOMESTIC CRIME: None known
INTERNATIONAL CRIME: Under Magnum's rule, Canaan once undertook a failed invasion of Wakanda.
FIRST APPEARANCE: Deathlok #23 (1993)

HISTORY: Formed by an alliance of neighboring African tribes, the Kingdom of Canaan was one of several victims of the European penetration of Africa in the late 19th century when France usurped control of the country. Ultimately regaining independence in the mid-20th century when King Baru claimed the throne, Canaan enjoyed years of peace until Baru was overthrown by super-powered technosmith Moses Magnum who sought for Canaan to become a homeland for disenfranchised African-Americans. To that end, he began a naturalization process for all African-Americans that immigrated to Canaan, and broadened the nation's industrial base with money from a multibillion dollar defense contract secured by his Magnum Munitions company. To ensure Canaan's economic independence, Magnum sought to secure the Vibranium resources of neighboring Wakanda,

KING BARU

Art by Walter McDaniel

and so dispatched his agent Phreak to steal Wakanda's military secrets. However, Phreak was defeated by the cyborg Deathlok, whose aid Wakanda's King T'Challa had enlisted. Next, Magnum dispatched mercenary weapons master Killjoy to assassinate T'Challa, but Killjoy was also defeated by Deathlok. Magnum then sought to take Wakanda by force, invading the country with his military forces; however, thanks to Deathlok's aid, the Wakandan Army prevailed. Baru sought to reclaim his throne but was rejected by his people and fled to Wakanda. There, he was captured by the alchemist Diablo and transformed into a creature of living Vibranium to become part of Diablo's Masters of Alchemy; however, Baru's spirit rebelled and he turned on Diablo, defeating the remaining alchemical creatures. As Vibranium, Baru vowed to use his newfound abilities for the good of his people and Canaan as a whole. However, Moses Magnum remains Canaan's ruler.

PRESIDENTIAL PALACE

Art by Walter McDaniel

OFFICIAL NAME: Democratic Republic of the Congo (Republique Democratique du Congo)
POPULATION: 65,751,000
CAPITAL CITY: Kinshasa
PLACES OF INTEREST: Nyiragongo, Bukava, Goma, University of Kinshasa, Kisangani, Lubumbashi, Matadi, Dahomey Reserve, New Crete, Temple of Lost Souls
GOVERNMENT: Republic
MAJOR LANGUAGES: French, Lingala, Kingwana, Kikongo, Tshiluba
MONETARY UNIT: Congolese franc
MAJOR RESOURCES: Mining, cobalt, copper, diamonds, gold, silver, zinc, manganese, tin, uranium, coal, timber, cement, petroleum, hydropower, agriculture, consumer products, commercial ship repair, textiles, footwear, processed food, cigarettes.
NATIONAL DEFENSE: The Armed Forces of the Democratic Republic of the Congo, with divisions of the Army, Navy, and Congolese Air Force.
INTERNATIONAL RELATIONS: Member of African Union, Interpol, United Nations (UN), SHIELD, UNESCO, World Health Organization and World Trade Organization. Former colonizer Belgium remains an important economic and military ally. The Congo also has important trade relations with Chile, China, Finland, France, Kenya, South Africa, the USA, Wakanda and Zambia. The Congo has been in conflict with Angola, Uganda and Rwanda.
EXTRATERRESTRIAL RELATIONS: None known.
NONHUMAN POPULATION: Dinosaurs, which were evidently bred by Deviant scientists, have been sighted within the Congo's jungles, including "Mokele Mbembe."
DOMESTIC SUPERHUMANS: None known.
PROMINENT CITIZENS: Ka-Zar (David Rand) was born in South Africa, but was stranded in the Congo as a child in 1921; he became a defender of the natives and wildlife he grew up with, and even battled invading Nazis during World War II. Trojak "the Tigerman" was a white man raised by natives who defended the jungles from outsiders in the 1940s, including invading Nazis. The heroic hunter Cliff Mason operated in the Congo in the 1950s, aided by his native guide Kai-Su. Jann of the Jungle (Jane Hastings) operated out of the Congo in the 1950s, battling poachers and defending innocents, often aided by her photographer friend Pat Mahoney. Shanna O'Hara grew up in the Congo with her parents Gerald & Patricia; when Gerald accidentally killed Patricia, mistaking her for a wild leopard, Shanna earned a lifelong hatred of guns, and grew up to become a powerful defender of animal rights known as Shanna the She-Devil, operating from the Dahomey Reserve but eventually living in the Savage Land. Patrick McShane was game

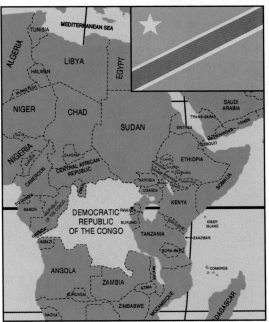

Art by Roger Cruz

warden of the Dahomey Reserve until his death at the hands of Nekra. King Phobotauros (General Elam) was once the high priest of New Crete; Erakes led a resistance against Phobotauros, aided by Shanna. Jakunga Singh was a local SHIELD representative who occasionally recruited Shanna for SHIELD missions. Jean N'Dosa, Victor Obiang and Jacques Tsolo are pygmies who assisted an expedition searching for Mokele Mbembe, led by Lt. Bokenga and Corporal Ebambe of the Armed Forces. Eric Heller was a reporter assigned by the government to investigate Sir Guy Cross-Wallace's activities, only to be killed.
SUPERHUMAN RESIDENTS: The Gorilla-Man (Ken Hale), lived in the jungles of the Congo for several decades until recent years, when he returned to the USA to join SHIELD. Kraven the Hunter (Sergei Kravinoff) lived and hunted in the Congo for a time. The adventurer Venus who believed herself to be an Olympian god dwelt in the Congo for a time.
DOMESTIC CRIME: Out-of-control militia forces have led to violence, and the necessity of UN peacekeeping forces. Sir Guy Cross-Wallace of the UK lived out of a citadel in the jungles, and ran a diamond smuggling ring that was ultimately broken up by Shanna.
INTERNATIONAL CRIME: The Congo is site of drug production and animal poaching, which has attracted the attention of vigilantes such as the Punisher (Frank Castle). In the 1930s, the illegal emerald smuggler Paul de Kraft operated in the Congo and clashed with Ka-Zar. "Ivory" Dan Drake was a poacher whose operation was broken up by Shanna. The Yellow Claw, Blind Al, Deadpool (Wade Wilson), Gene Dogs, Mandrill (Jerome Beechman), Nekra Sinclair and the vampire group called the Nosferatu have all been active in the Congo. The mercenary Air Force (Cardinal, Killer Shrike, Sparrow, Tanager) and New Warriors helped aid Rwandan refugees at the Congo's border, clashing with the Soldiers of Misfortune. The superhuman Advisor was active in the Congo, using his manipulative abilities to help generate more violence.
HISTORY: The Congo's primary inhabitants for ages were the Bantu peoples, although the small colony of New Crete was founded by wandering Cretans; it was not discovered until recent years. The Congo's territory was claimed by Belgium in 1908 for its economic potential. The country obtained independence in 1960, and in 1970 changed its name to Zaire in the hopes of creating a new national identity based on its people's history. However, the Alliance of Democratic Forces for the Liberation of Congo staged in a coup in 1997 and changed the country's name to the Democratic Republic of the Congo.

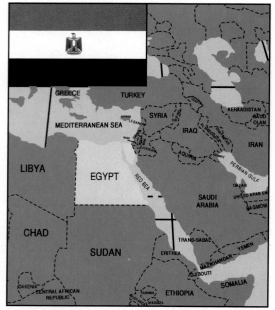

OFFICIAL NAME: Arab Republic of Egypt (Jumhuriyat Misr al-Arabiyah)

POPULATION: 80,335,000

CAPITAL CITY: Cairo

PLACES OF INTEREST: Alexandria, Cairo University, Nile River, Aswan, Suez Canal, Bibliotheca Alexandria, the Great Sphinx, the Valley of the Kings, the Pyramids of Giza, the Giza Necropolis, the Red Sea, the Museum of Egyptian Antiquities, Thebes, Luxor Temple, Karnak Temple, the Sahara Desert

GOVERNMENT: Republic

MAJOR LANGUAGES: Arabic, English, French

MONETARY UNIT: Egyptian pound

MAJOR RESOURCES: Petroleum, natural gas, nuclear energy, iron ore, lead, cement, asbestos, talc, agriculture, tourism.

NATIONAL DEFENSE: Army, Navy, Air Force and Air Defense Command. Intelligence provided by Mabahith Amin al-Dawla al-'Ulya.

INTERNATIONAL RELATIONS: Member of African Union, Interpol, United Nations, UNESCO, World Health Organization and World Trade Organization. Egypt has had significant disputes with Israel. Egypt has important trade relations with China, France, Germany, Italy, Saudi Arabia, Spain, Syria, the UK and the USA, and cooperates with SHIELD authorities.

EXTRATERRESTRIAL RELATIONS: In ancient times Egypt was visited by the Horusians who masqueraded as gods; the Sphinx, which by some accounts is a Horusian vessel, by other accounts the inanimate robot Shagg; one of the Time-Keepers; the Caretakers of Arcturus; the immense "mummies" Mummex (Raaka) of Andromida and Gomdulla; Kaaris'a of the Dire Wraiths; and the jackal-like Neron-Alak. In modern times, otherworldly visitors have included the Elementals (Hellfire, Hydron, Magnum, Zephyr), Deathbird of the Shi'ar, the Skrulls, and Warlock and Magus of the Technarchy. The authentic gods of Egypt have been active in times both ancient and recent.

NONHUMAN POPULATION: The robot Alkhema formerly held the base Robotopia in Al-Luxor. The demonic creatures Gog and Magog were awakened in recent times from an archaeological site, but fought off by the Arabian Knight (Abdul Qamar). One of the immense ancient creatures known as the Roc was found in Egypt in the 1960s.

DOMESTIC SUPERHUMANS: Superhumans of ancient Egypt included: Ashake, a sorceress and ancestor of Storm; Heka-Nut, a sorcerer who fought Ashake; Apocalypse (En Sabah Nur), the immortal mutant; Ozymandias, a former king turned to stone and made to serve Apocalypse; the Sphinx (Anath-Na-Mut), a mutant who gained immortality through the Ka Stone and shared his power with Meryet Karim; Khafre, a pharaoh who transferred his soul into a statue; the Living Mummy (N'Kantu), a former Swarili chieftain cursed with immortality; Garrett, a sorcerer around 3500 BC who helped create the Ruby Scarab; Akhenaten (Amenhotep IV), a pharaoh who gained cosmic power and returned in modern days to threaten the Earth, only to be slain by Thanos the Titan; Zota, a sorcerer who was bested by a time-traveling Dr. Strange on two occasions; Nephrus, a mystic who cheated death by possessing the forms of others; Rakses, a necromancer; and Shadowcaster, a mystic. In World War II, the Scarlet Scarab (Abdul Faoul) was the leader of the Sons of the Scarab, and with the Ruby Scarab led attacks against British and Nazi forces; his son Mehemet Faoul is the modern day Scarlet Scarab. The Priests of Khonshu were a trio of elderly men who delivered messages from the god Khonshu to Moon Knight. Rama Kaliph was a sorcerer and ally of Dr. Strange until his death at the hands of Silver Dagger; his pupil was Abu Ben Hakim. Amun is an assassin who worked in the US for the Sisterhood of the Wasp. Storm (Ororo Munroe) grew up in Egypt, and was orphaned there when her parents were killed; she later joined the X-Men. The Asp (Cleo Nefertiti) joined the Serpent Society. The Living Monolith (Ahmet Abdol) was a mutant criminal who originally operated as the Living Pharaoh.

PROMINENT CITIZENS: Baal and his followers the Sandstormers raised En Sabah Nur in his youth. Pharaoh Tut-kin-Tut was evidently the time traveler Ashley Hunt, who lost his memory upon arriving in the past. Aram-Set was pharaoh around 1050 BC, and was advised by Nephrus. Fan-Le-Tamen was an ancient princess whose soul was later claimed by the Yellow Claw. Hatsushep possessed the Amulet of Pazuzu in ancient times. The Mad Pharaoh (Hatap) was a rival of Cleopatra, and died battling a time-traveling Iron Man (Tony Stark). Dr. Alexei Skarab is an anthropologist who befriended the Living Mummy. Hassan Kareem was an archaeologist who sacrificed his life to awaken Gog & Magog, hoping they would destroy Israel. Abdul Kazir was a terrorist who fought against SHIELD. Dr. Scarabeus was a criminal geneticist who fought the Hulk. Anubis (Ahmad Azis) was a madman garbed in homage to the jackal god, and was bested by Moon Knight. Jellim Yussaf was a plunderer of historic sites who was halted by Moon Knight. The Asp (Richard Harper) was a thief, but became an ally of the Living Mummy. Achmed el-Gibar was a member of the Thieves Guild in Cairo, and served as mentor to Ororo Munroe; his other thieves included Hakiim, Nari, Jamil and Karima.

SUPERHUMAN RESIDENTS: The time-traveling Rama-Tut formed a kingdom in ancient Egypt, and ruled as a pharaoh in two separate reigns between resuming his identity as Kang the Conqueror; he fathered his son Ramades around 3000 BC, and Ramades also grew to become a time-traveling menace. Immortals including Black Axe, the Forever Man (Morgan MacNeil Hardy), Centurious and Candra were active in Egypt at points in their lives. The hero Moon Knight (Marc Spector) began his affiliation with Khonshu in Egypt, and has occasionally returned to combat criminals.

DOMESTIC CRIME: Egypt has difficulties with drug trafficking.

INTERNATIONAL CRIME: Egypt is a source of prostitution and money laundering. The Celestial Order of the Si-Fan often operated in Egypt, including the forces of the Cult of Kali. The malevolent Shadow King was active in Egypt while in his Amahl Farouk host body. Raoul Bushman, the Mutant Liberation Front, New World Order, the Sept and the Dark Riders were also active in Egypt.

HISTORY: Egypt is one of the oldest nations on Earth; the country was ruled by pharaohs as far back as 3400 BC, and its famous rulers included Alexander the Great (332 BC) and Cleopatra (31 BC). Egypt became the Byzantium Empire in 340, but was later conquered by Arabia, resulting in its transformation to an Islamic state. England made Egypt a protectorate from 1882-1922, interested primarily controlling the Suez Canal, a vital trading hub. During the 1960s and '70s Egypt had open hostilities with Israel, including 1967's "Six-Day War" but has since made a treaty and attempted to help Israel and Palestine make peace.

OFFICIAL NAME: Republic of Genosha
POPULATION: Indeterminate; formerly 16,521,063
CAPITAL CITY: Hammer Bay
PLACES OF INTEREST: Carrion Cove, Ridgeback Mountains, Prenova Province, Crescent Bay Beach, Krölik Foothills, Fenyick Caves, Enmann Beach; formerly Magda Square
GOVERNMENT: None; former dictatorship, technocracy, democracy
MAJOR LANGUAGES: English
MONETARY UNIT: None; formerly Genoshan Magister
MAJOR RESOURCES: Iron ore; formerly Mutates, steel, kinizasa
NATIONAL DEFENSE: None; formerly Genoshan Unified Military Patrol, Acolytes, Magistrates
INTERNATIONAL RELATIONS: Despite having invested billions in the US, Genosha was subjected to international sanctions after capturing members of the X-Men, X-Factor and the New Mutants. These sanctions continued after Magneto was ceded sovereignty of the country; however, after much rebuilding and reparation, Genosha sought the sanctions be lifted and that they be granted access to international monetary assistance to which end the United Nations (UN) appointed Magneto's daughter the Scarlet Witch to act as an independent observer.
EXTRATERRESTRIAL RELATIONS: None known
NONHUMAN POPULATION: None known.
PROMINENT CITIZENS: Madame Reneau was president during the time of Genosha's exploitation of mutates. David Moreau served the government as Genengineer, responsible for the mutate-bonding process. Jennifer Ransome's father was a government minister who was stripped of his post after it was revealed he had falsified the results of her genetic test. Moreau's son Phillip came to oppose the oppressive regime, fleeing to political asylum in the US before returning to join Ransome as governor. Tam Anderson served as chief magistrate until her death while opposing Crucible. Sasha Ryan was the government's last appointed Genengineer tasked with reversing the mutate process; however, she secretly conspired with the Isolationist (Joseph Huber) to rid Genosha of mutants entirely. Jared Barthmounte was minister of public health during the nation's Legacy Virus crisis. World-renowned biogeneticist Renée Majcomb helped found the Genoshan Bipartisan Rebel Battalion. Mutant sociopolitical expert Dr. Alda Huxley served as Genosha's ambassador to the UN during Magneto's rule. Delphi ran a curio shop in Hammer Bay that sold memory boxes psychically imprinted with actual memories. Mayor Böerke was mayor of Carrion Cove before its destruction by Magneto.
DOMESTIC SUPERHUMANS: The Genoshan Press Gang (Hawkshaw, Pipeline, Punchout, Wipeout, Gunshot) were mutants in the employ of the Genoshan government. Shola Inkosi was a Genoshan student who was smuggled to safety in the US before he was depowered on "M-Day." Wicked, Freakshow, Hack, Hub, Purge, Broadband and Book were among the Genoshan mutants who survived the Sentinel attack only to be depowered on "M-Day." Numerous mutates included #1 (Edgerton), #18, #21, #29, #31, #41, #46, #49, #51, #55, #56, #71, #85, #101, #109, #110, #146, #163, #178, #201, #229, #238, #243, #248, #270, #283 (Jomo Kimane), #312, #315, #337, #360, #370, #376, #407, #416 (Piecemeal), #523, #530, #628, #633, #650, #665 (Thomas Moreau/Zealot, who led a rebellion against Magneto's rule), #682, #722, #767, #806, #831, #888, #918, #937, #965, #1021, #1351, #1585, #3801, #6171, #6711, #7781, #8765, #9212, #9817 (Jennifer Ransome, who fled her country's oppressive regime and resided in Australia for a time before being granted political asylum in the US and ultimately returning to become governor), #24601, Abyss (Nils Styger), the X-Patriots (Prodigal, Lukas, Pirouette, Taylor/Mutate #687), the Unforgiven (Skelter, Syth, & others), Farisa Mansour, Harry Soong, those recruited into the Acolytes by Exodus (3:16, Brother Three, Brother Seven, Burst, & numerous others), and those who fled Magneto's rule to a refugee camp in Tanzania.
SUPERHUMAN RESIDENTS: The alternate reality Sugar Man aided Moreau in creating the mutate-bonding process. The technomorphic Cameron Hodge aided the oppressive regime in its effort to bring the

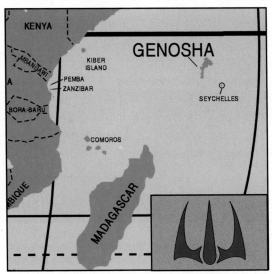

X-Men and their allies to task for their "interference" in Genoshan politics until his defeat by the X-Men. Former X-Man Havok (Alex Summers) briefly served as a Magistrate while amnesiac. The mutant terrorist Magneto was ceded control of the country by the United Nations, and he formed a cabinet that included Ransome, Phillip Moreau, Pipeline, Huxley, Cortez, Amelia Voght, and Magneto's mutant children Quicksilver and Polaris. Several of Magneto's Acolytes subsequently served in the Genoshan Unified Military Patrol. Former Acolyte Joanna Cargill served as Genoshan ambassador to the United Nations. Emma Frost became a schoolteacher prior to the country's decimation by Sentinels. Ellie Phimister (Negasonic Teenage Warhead) was one of her students who died during the attack. After the country's decimation, the X-Men's founder Professor Charles Xavier sought to rebuild the shattered nation alongside Magneto and others.
DOMESTIC CRIME: For years Genosha was plagued by infighting between various factions. The Genoshan Resistance was formed to oppose the oppressive former regime. The Bipartisan Rebel Battalion consisted of humans and mutates who banded together in an effort to stop the Genoshan civil war. After Magneto was given rule over Genosha, he was forced to deal with a mutate uprising led by Zealot, an attempt by the Magistrates to reclaim power, a resistance cell operating out of Carrion Cove, and the Homo Sapiens Liberation Army.
INTERNATIONAL CRIME: The X-Men, X-Factor and the New Mutants once invaded the country to rescue their imprisoned teammates and helped overthrow the ruling regime. Magneto's Acolytes then attacked Hammer Bay in retribution for the government's past actions. Former Acolyte Fabian Cortez incited a mutate rebellion, which resulted in the assassination of the entire Genoshan government. The criminal Enclave once used Genosha as a terrorist base before their defeat by the Fantastic Four. X-Force once aided Pete Wisdom in recovering an experimental CPU from Genosha and, after encountering Magneto, sabotaged the country's electricity grid to force Magneto into confronting the Magistrates instead of them. The Carrion Cove rebellion forces were given supplies by multinational corporation Roxxon and were granted aid by the UN in the form of the Avengers to prevent Magneto from accessing a device in Carrion Cove that could restore him to full power. Genosha was later decimated by Sentinels controlled by Cassandra Nova. During rebuilding attempts, Genosha became the target of many seeking to plunder what remained, including former Magistrates, Stripmine and his band of scavengers, and the Sugar Man.
FIRST APPEARANCE: Uncanny X-Men #235 (1988)
HISTORY: Originally a haven for pirates, and rumored to be the destination of one of Sinbad's legendary voyages, Genosha was settled during the great ages of exploration. The deep-water harbor of Hammer

HAMMER BAY

later forcibly recruited into aiding the Genoshan government by giving it a technological edge to hasten the civil war's end, but he was soon rescued by his teammates and together they foiled a plot by the Enclave to take advantage of the country's crisis for their own ends.

Following Magneto's threatening the world with an electromagnetic pulse, Dr. Huxley convinced the United Nations to cede sovereignty of Genosha to him in exchange for a permanent cessation of hostilities. Upon hearing of Magneto's imminent arrival on the island, many humans fled rather than live under his rule.

Bay formed the foundation of the fledgling nation's commerce with trade becoming the major source of wealth until the discovery of iron ore and other precious metals in the Ridgeback Mountains, which led to a flourishing steel industry. Genosha became known as "a green and pleasant land" for its high standard of living, an excellent economy led by advanced technology companies who later diversified into computer sciences and space technology, freedom from the political and racial turmoil that characterized neighboring nations, and a self-sufficient agricultural industry. However, this apparent utopia was anything but, as Genosha's entire sociopolitical economic infrastructure was built on the backs of its mutant population. Genoshan citizens were required to undergo genetic testing upon turning 13 years old, and those who tested positive with the mutant gene were forced to undergo a process created by the reality-displaced Sugar Man, based on the work of the evil geneticist Mr. Sinister, and implemented by David Moreau, the original Genegineer, which physically altered and psychokinetically conditioned them, stripping them of their free will and tailoring them to perform a specific task. Locked inside skin-bonded suits and rendered sterile, mutates were easily identified by a unique number and were considered state property. Citizenship in Genosha was permanent, with the government refusing to recognize any attempts at emigration. Any citizens that did leave the country were tracked down and forcibly returned by a special police force called the Magistrates and their mutant specialist taskforce, the Press Gang. Ultimately, the Genoshan government crossed paths with the mutant heroes the X-Men, resulting in the defeat of the mutant-oppressive regime. The military quickly assumed temporary control of the government pending lawful elections, which resulted in a new pro-mutant government operating under sanctions imposed by the United Nations.

Soon after, the return of Magneto panicked the human Genoshans who feared this would incite their former slaves to rebel. A decision was made to eradicate the mutates, but they fought back and the country descended into civil war. Magneto's former Acolyte Fabian Cortez attempted to take advantage of the situation and proclaimed himself leader of the rebellion. Following the assassination of the entire Genoshan government, Cortez declared himself president; however, his rule was brief as he was soon seemingly slain by Magneto's self-proclaimed successor Exodus, and the civil war was soon after quelled through the efforts of the X-Men and the Avengers. A new bipartisan government was formed by former mutate Jennifer Ransome and her lover Phillip Moreau. Mutate rights were soon restored; however, they refused to work without pay and as such the Genoshan economy collapsed, plunging the nation into another civil war. Ultimately, the two sides were forced to work together alongside the mutant soldier Cable and his mercenary mutant ally Domino to prevent the Sugar Man destroying the country with a thermo-nuclear device. Reed Richards of the Fantastic Four was

Quickly assembling a new cabinet, Magneto swiftly dealt with the threat posed by a fanatical band of mutates led by the Zealot. He also demanded that the United Nations honor his sovereignty, destroying their spy satellites and reconnaissance planes as a warning, and followed that up by announcing that he intended to close Genosha's borders completely. Magneto began a rebuilding process, facing a range of problems including an imminent famine, the Legacy Virus, and a new resistance movement operating out of the small fishing port of Carrion Cove, which he soon crushed after regaining his full powers. After the release of a cure for the Legacy Virus, Magneto found himself with a veritable army of mutates and mutant immigrants with which to wage war on mankind; however, his plans were thwarted by the X-Men.

Later, Xavier's genetic twin Cassandra Nova unleashed giant Sentinel robots on Genosha, decimating the island and its population. The island was placed under global interdict, with a security cordon set up to prevent anyone from leaving. Seeking to atone for the sins of his twin, Xavier left the X-Men to assist the survivors in rebuilding the nation, despite electronic devices no longer working on the island. Joined by Magneto, Xavier gathered a small band of heroes to aid in the reconstruction and oppose such threats as Unus and his gang, former Magistrates, Stripmine's scavengers, and the returned Sugar Man, as well as aiding neighboring nation Zanzibar against the Weaponeers. After a reality warp created by Magneto's daughter, the Scarlet Witch, Xavier was missing and Magneto and his fellow Genoshan mutants were depowered. After being repowered by Quicksilver's use of the Inhuman's Terrigen Mists, the majority of mutants left the island, leaving Magneto alone. He was later repowered by the Collective, but was subsequently seemingly killed in an explosion after a battle with the Avengers, leaving Genosha's reconstruction unfinished.

MAGDA SQUARE

OFFICIAL NAME: Kingdom of Halwan (al-Mamlaka al-Halwan)
POPULATION: 4,329,000
CAPITAL CITY: Kamilabad
PLACES OF INTEREST: The Castle of the Lion Throne, a Moorish castle outside Kamilabad; the ancient mountain fortress of Jera'ad Al-Din.
GOVERNMENT: Absolute monarchy
MAJOR LANGUAGES: Arabic
MONETARY UNIT: Halwan dinar
MAJOR RESOURCES: Extensive deposits of petroleum, gold, iron, uranium, heavy metals.
NATIONAL DEFENSE: Halwan maintains a large, well equipped army and air force.
INTERNATIONAL RELATIONS: Halwan is a member of the United Nations, UNESCO, Arab League, and Organization of the Islamic Conference. The USA, Russia and several western countries have trade and mining agreements with Halwan. There is a long history of hostility between Halwan and neighboring Murtakesh.
EXTRATERRESTRIAL RELATIONS: None known.
NONHUMAN POPULATION: None known.
DOMESTIC SUPERHUMANS: The immensely powerful sorcerer Master Khan was allegedly a Halwani scholar who centuries ago refused to use his powers in the service of the Halwani king, and saw his daughter tortured to death as a result.
PROMINENT CITIZENS: King Kadar ruled Halwan in the early 1980s; his heir presumptive Princess Zafina had American hero Mr. Justice (Tim Carney) tortured. The current monarch is King Haladj, with his daughter Princess Azir first in line. For over 1000 years the Lion Throne has been served by one family of royal bodyguards; Jameel Bey protected Princess Zafina, while Khumbala Bey guards Azir. Khumbala briefly fell under Master Khan's influence, but has since regained his royal appointment. Another generational family is the Scimitars, trained from childhood to master bladed weapons. The Scimitar of Zafina's day slew Blackjack of the First Line, but was slain in turn by Positron; the current Scimitar fell into Master Khan's service, and has since dishonored his family by becoming a mercenary. Other notable Halwani include Dr. Khadijah, cousin to Zafina, who studied in the US as a physician, and later defected to the US, and Alpar, Halwan's US ambassador. Among Master Khan's Halwani servants were Hassan, Rakim, Ortega, Domeq, and Major Gamal Hasson of the Halwani Revolutionary Army. Rahbin and Ariel were two youths who aided Iron Fist (Daniel Rand), hoping he could avert war with Murtakesh.
SUPERHUMAN RESIDENTS: Angar the Screamer (David Angar) resided in Halwan while serving Master Khan. Russian agents Boris and Ninotchka resided in Halwan while Russia was wooing the king for mining rights.
DOMESTIC CRIME: Petty crimes, such as pick-pocketing and mugging, are common in Halwan, but overall crime is low due to the draconian punishments meted out on those who are caught.
INTERNATIONAL CRIME: Halwan's mineral wealth has generated multiple precious metal smuggling operations. The Black Tiger (Brillalae), leader of the Murtakesh rebellion, has extended her freedom fighting operations to oppose the Halwani government as well as her own.
FIRST APPEARANCE: (Mentioned) Marvel Premiere #24 (1975); (seen) Iron Fist #2 (1975)
HISTORY: Phoenician explorers established the first permanent settlements in the Halwani region around 700 BC. Around 750 AD Islamic Moors immigrated into the region, their religion soon spreading to become dominant. In 879, King Ahirom of the Lion Throne founded the

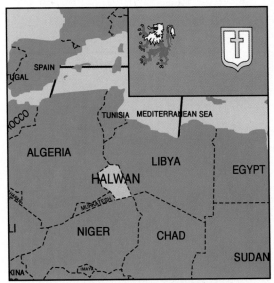

Kingdom of Halwan; his unbroken line continues to rule to the modern day, meeting foreign incursions and internal dissent equally harshly. For hundreds of years Halwan has been at odds with neighboring Murtakesh, and the two countries have often been at the brink of war. In the early 1980s, believing the US was aiding Halwani republican movements, the Halwan government took US diplomats hostage; American hero Mr. Justice flew to the region to rescue the prisoners, but was captured himself. In response to the crisis the US launched two rescue missions, sending a CIA team commanded by Nick Fury to free the diplomats, and the First Line to retrieve Mr. Justice, but both failed their respective tasks; instead Mr. Justice convinced Princess Khadijah, the king's niece, to help him escape, rescue the diplomats, and then defect with him, a major embarrassment to Halwan. Relations with the USA gradually improved with time, but internal dissent grew to the Lion Throne's rule as they struck deals with foreign powers to strip mine the country's wealth, dispossessing entire towns to do so while the wealth generated bolstered the royal treasury rather than alleviating the masses' poverty. Recently Master Khan sought revenge on Halwan for wrongs done centuries past, but was thwarted by the American hero Iron Fist; Princess Azir cultivated a friendship with him, and then had the Halwani press carry stories of the Lion Throne's alliances with US superhumans to keep the unhappy populace in line. In spite of this, resistance continued to grow, with Halwani ex-pats bombing Halwani embassies and overseas diplomats; then Murtakesh freedom fighters led by the Black Tiger expanded their operations to fight for Halwan's oppressed people. Suspicious that the Murtakesh government might be supporting the attacks, Halwan pursued the previous Black Tiger, Abe Brown, before learning that his former associate Brillalae now led the movement, and that she opposed the Murtakesh government too. Her example has inspired a redoubled Halwani resistance, which has dubbed itself the Black Tigers. While they present little real threat to the Lion Throne as yet, with backing from Brillalae's movement, and no attempt to lessen the average Halwani's intense poverty, the problem continues to grow, and may yet bring about an end to one of the world's oldest surviving dynasties.

Art by John Byrne

IMAYA

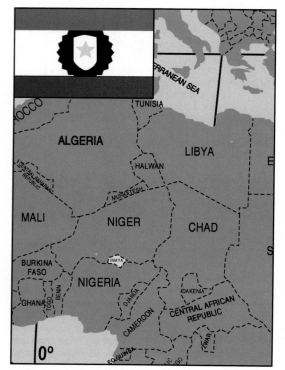

OFFICIAL NAME: Republic of Imaya
POPULATION: 1,900,000
CAPITAL CITY: Imaya City
PLACES OF INTEREST: Executive Palace
GOVERNMENT: Republic
MAJOR LANGUAGES: French, English, Hausa
MONETARY UNIT: CFA franc
MAJOR RESOURCES: Uranium, coal, iron ore, steel, tin petroleum, natural gas, agriculture, textiles, food products, cement.
NATIONAL DEFENSE: Imayan Armed Forces, including infantry and air force.
INTERNATIONAL RELATIONS: Imaya is a member of the African Union, Interpol, United Nations (UN), UNESCO, World Health Organization and World Trade Organization, and has cooperated with SHIELD forces. Sandwiched between Niger and Nigeria, Imaya has had difficulties with cross-border conflicts entering its territory.
EXTRATERRESTRIAL RELATIONS: None known.
NONHUMAN POPULATION: None known.

DOMESTIC SUPERHUMANS: None known.
PROMINENT CITIZENS: President Letumba was deposed and beheaded by General Eda Arul, a former prison guard who was aided by the Advisor in his rise to power; Arul was ultimately executed by War Machine (James Rhodes). President Cimbuka was a former resistance leader who helped overthrow Arul and assumed the presidency after Arul's defeat, vowing to clean up the country's reputation and better the standard of living for his people. Vincent Cetewayo was a political activist who left Imaya to become a world-renowned lecturer and humanitarian; shortly after founding the benevolent Worldwatch organization and publishing a book of memoirs, Cetewayo was captured and brought to Imaya where he was imprisoned for criticizing Arul in his book; Cetewayo was rescued from his cell by Cable (Nathan Summers), but was ultimately slain by the Advisor, who believed that if Cetewayo lived, he could have brought peace to the world.
SUPERHUMAN RESIDENTS: The enigmatic being known only as the Advisor formerly served as chancellor under the rule of President Eda Arul, and was interested mainly in increasing local hostilities.
DOMESTIC CRIME: Imaya has difficulty with local narcotics trafficking and forced slave labor operations.
INTERNATIONAL CRIME: The capture of Vincent Cetewayo set off an international incident, which led to condemnation from the UN; the vigilantes Cable, Deathlok (Michael Collins) and War Machine each entered Imaya to facilitate Cetewayo's rescue, and War Machine remained to help overthrow Arul and install Cimbuka as president.
FIRST APPEARANCE: War Machine #1 (1994)
HISTORY: The nation of Imaya underwent a brutal series of political transitions that nearly brought the country to its knees. The plight of Imaya was highlighted by former citizen and founder of Worldwatch Vincent Cetewayo, whose book A Destiny to Create outlined his hopes of global peace. General Eda Arul was infuriated by the book, and arranged to have Cetewayo captured while he was in mid-flight over Africa, forcing the plane to land in Imaya. Cetewayo's kidnapping created a difficult international incident, and with the UN unable to take immediate action, the three vigilantes Cable, Deathlok and War Machine took matters into their own hands to bring Cetewayo to safety. Their involvement in turn brought in the forces of SHIELD, who were bound to defend General Arul's presidency. Cable set Cetewayo free, and Deathlok escorted citizens needing medical attention away from the combat zone, while War Machine led the rebel forces of Cimbuka against Arul. Cimbuka claimed the title of president from Arul, and acting SHIELD representative Major Bathsheva Joseph refused to interfere. Arul drew a gun on her, and was shot dead by War Machine. While this was occurring, the Advisor found Cetewayo and killed him so that he could not oppose his campaign of evil. War Machine took Cetewayo's place as leader of Worldwatch, vowing to become as good a man as Cetewayo had been.

OFFICIAL NAME: Republic of Kenya (Jamhuri y Kenya)
POPULATION: 36,914,000
CAPITAL CITY: Nairobi
PLACES OF INTEREST: Mombasa, Turkana, the Great Mosque of Gedi, Lake Victoria, the Great Rift Valley, Mount Kenya, Eldoret, Lodwar, Mandera, Kisumu, Nakuru, Temple of Ikonn, University of Nairobi
GOVERNMENT: Republic
MAJOR LANGUAGES: English, Kiswahili
MONETARY UNIT: Kenyan shilling
MAJOR RESOURCES: Limestone, gemstones, zinc, aluminum, steel, lead, cement, salt, flour, agriculture, consumer goods, textiles, plastics, furniture, batteries, soap, cigarettes, clothing, horticulture, tourism, commercial ship repair.
NATIONAL DEFENSE: The Kenyan Army, Kenyan Navy and Kenyan Air Force.
INTERNATIONAL RELATIONS: Member of African Union, Commonwealth of Nations, Interpol, United Nations, UNESCO, World Health Organization and World Trade Organization. Kenya has important trade relations with China, India, Japan, Saudi Arabia, South Africa, the UK and the USA. Kenya assists in peacekeeping duties for Somalia. Kenya has cooperated with the X-Men and O*N*E.
EXTRATERRESTRIAL RELATIONS: The demon Ikonn placed its Ivory Idol within a temple in Kenya, where it transformed Olisa Kabaki into Bedlam.
NONHUMAN POPULATION: The immense ant Grottu, a mutate bred by the Deviants, once assaulted Mombasa where it was slain by monster hunter Ulysses Bloodstone.
DOMESTIC SUPERHUMANS: The mutant Kidogo (Lazaro Kotikash) was formerly a student in the USA's Xavier Institute, serving in the school's Alpha Squadron. The weather-manipulating mutant Deluge fought the X-Men in Kenya, and was ultimately destroyed trying to absorb the power of Cyclops (Scott Summers). Bedlam (Olisa Kabaki) was one of the Exemplars. Ainet was a mystic priestess who befriended Storm during her time in Kenya. Samuel Mbende was one of Operation: Zero Tolerance's Prime Sentinels.
PROMINENT CITIZENS: M'Kumba was one of Storm's friends when she lived in Kenya. N'Dare Munroe was the mother of Storm, and

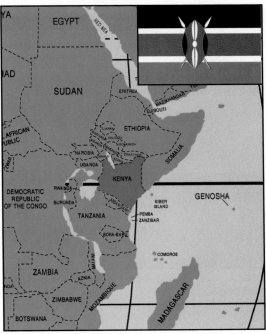

married US citizen David Munroe; they both died in Egypt during a bombing raid.
SUPERHUMAN RESIDENTS: Kraven the Hunter (Sergei Kravinoff) once lived and hunted near Nairobi. Ken Hale was transformed into the Gorilla-Man after hunting and killing a legendary ape in the Kenyan jungles, transferring the creature's curse to himself; he later moved to the Congo. Storm (Ororo Munroe) lived in Kenya for a time when she believed that her mutant powers had made her a goddess. Some of the Obeahmen mystics reside in Kenya.
DOMESTIC CRIME: Factions within the Kenyan government who disapproved of Storm's marriage to the Black Panther (T'Challa) employed the Man-Ape (M'Baku) to sabotage the wedding day, but he failed them. Kenya has difficulties with prostitution, forced slave labor and drug production. With the scarcity in worldwide numbers in mutants post "M-Day" a trade in mutants sprang up, spearheaded by Colonel Shetani, but he was brought down by the X-Men. Kenya also has issues with poachers, such as the ivory hunter Jan Van Ocken; Shanna the She-Devil has helped combat poaching.
INTERNATIONAL CRIME: The terrorist forces of al-Qaeda have been active in Kenya. A Maasai princess' life was once threatened by the cosmic-powered Leonard Tippit, but she was defended by the Avengers. Andreas "the Bull" de Ruyter once clashed with Ororo Munroe and Prince T'Challa in Kenya back when the duo were teenagers. The malevolent psychic entity known as the Shadow King has been active in Kenya, masquerading as one of the Ananasi gods. Fenris (Andrea and Andreas von Strucker) made an attempt on Storm's life while she was in the Serengeti.
HISTORY: Originally populated by the Bantu peoples, the Portuguese colonized Kenya in the 15th century. Over the centuries, the country was also run by Oman (1699) and England (1888). A secret society called the Mau Mau led uprisings against the British in the 1950s, and the country became independent in 1963. Since then, the government has faced running accusations of corruption.

Art by Robert Q. Sale

MBANGAWI

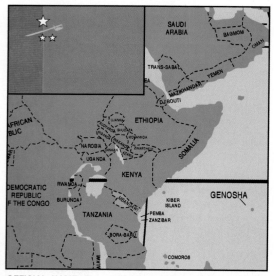

OFFICIAL NAME: Blessed Kingdom of Mbangawi (Baraka Ufalme Cha Mbangawi)
POPULATION: 6,523,000
CAPITAL CITY: Uzuri
PLACES OF INTEREST: Emperor's Compound (Uzuri)
GOVERNMENT: Absolute monarchy
MAJOR LANGUAGES: Swahili, English
MONETARY UNIT: Mbangawi shilling
MAJOR RESOURCES: Gold, hydroelectric power
NATIONAL DEFENSE: Ujeshi la Mbangawi (the Fighting Service of Mbangawi), consisting of an Army, Air Force and small Navy.
INTERNATIONAL RELATIONS: Mbangawi maintains steadfastly amicable relations with its larger neighbors Kenya and Tanzania, with President N'Dingi a close friend of Zanzibar's president Jono Baraka. Though it rarely has direct relations, Mbangawi has openly condemned the racist policies pursued by both Azania and Rudyarda to the north. It is member of the United Nations, UNESCO, SADC (Southern African Development Committee), AU (African Union), and British Commonwealth, and was an active participant in the recent Pan-African Congress on the Treatment of Superhumans.
EXTRATERRESTRIAL RELATIONS: The time/space-spanning mercenaries called the Technet once invaded Mbangawi to steal Jamie Braddock from Dr. Crocodile.
NONHUMAN POPULATION: The Maasai sky god Engai, who may be another name for the creator god Mulungu, has occasionally manifested himself in Mbangawi.
DOMESTIC SUPERHUMANS: Mbangawi's most famous superhuman is its ruler, the cyborg Joshua N'Dingi, affectionately dubbed Dr. Crocodile by his people because of his scarred appearance. His close advisor is Kura, the "Witch Woman," a tribal mystic of surprising power. Howitzer (Shaka) of STORM's Gene Dogs, was born in Mbangawi, but now mostly resides in the United Kingdom.
PROMINENT CITIZENS: The late Samuel N'Dingi, leader of the dominant Gawan tribe, led Mbangawi to independence in 1961, garnering himself the nickname "Maliki Uhuru" (King Liberty). His family has reigned over Mbangawi to the present day as absolute monarchs, but ruling (mostly) through popular acclaim of their people.

SUPERHUMAN RESIDENTS: None known.
DOMESTIC CRIME: Up until the rule of Jonas N'Dingi, Mbangawi suffered from chronic low level governmental corruption; since coming to power, Jonas' son Joshua has made a point of rooting out such corruption using his Witch Woman's powers to see into men's minds. He has also clamped down on the formerly grievous problems of muggings, burglary and armed robbery, and Mbangawi now enjoys one of the lowest crime rates in Africa.
INTERNATIONAL CRIME: Mbangawi's veldt suffers from ruthless poacher gangs who target the native wildlife, though such incursions have become much rarer under President N'Dingi's rule. Not limiting his desire for justice to crimes which had directly affected Mbangawi, Dr. Crocodile had his soldiers abduct Jamie Braddock, a British drug-runner and slaver who had raided aid convoys in other parts of Africa, bringing him to Mbangawi to administer justice and mystical rehabilitation. Doc Croc also lured Jamie's brother Brian (Captain Britain) to Mbangawi, wrongly believing him involved with Jamie's crimes; upon learning otherwise, Joshua let Brian go. Hired by the UK-based crimelord Sat-Yr9, the extradimensional parahuman mercenaries, the Technet, invaded Mbangawi to rescue Jamie, inadvertently taking Joshua with them when they teleported back to the UK.
FIRST APPEARANCE: Captain Britain #9 (1985)
HISTORY: At least as far back as 10,000 years ago Mbangawi was the home of Khoisan-speaking hunter-gatherer tribes; around 5,000 years ago Cushitic-speakers migrated into the region, gradually assimilating the existing population, and introducing a more agricultural society. Further immigrations brought fresh concepts, and with the establishing of trade with Arabia and Persia, coastal cities arose, including Uzuri, where gold and ivory was exported, and which would eventually become the Mbangawi capital. However in the 16th century, the Portuguese conquered the region, beginning a lengthy period of European rule; Germany took the region from Portugal late in the 19th century, only to lose it to the United Kingdom following World War I. In 1961 Mbangawi gained independence, with the dominant Gawan tribe's chieftain Samuel N'Dingi becoming the king, taking the Emperor's Compound (formerly the Kaiser's Compound) as his new palace. Though the N'Dingi family ruled as fairly and equitably as they could, and largely with popular support, the country suffered from tribal rivalries, and corrupt government officials working secretly in conjunction with foreign companies to exploit Mbangawi's natural resources purely for their own gain. Returning from overseas upon his father's death, Joshua N'Dingi took immediate steps to end these problems; against advice from his own tribe's elders, he took on the rival J'Dare tribe's "witch woman" Kura as his confidante and advisor, using her powers to root out governmental corruption. She later proved her loyalty when he was kidnapped by the Technet and transformed by reality-warper Jamie Braddock, rescuing him and returning him to his normal form. Though his people consider him more a god than a king, uncomfortable with this idolatry, Joshua prefers to use the title of president; he continues to protect his country, while working alongside like-minded African leaders, such as Wakanda's King T'Challa, for the advancement of the continent as a whole.

Art by Alan Davis

OFFICIAL NAME: State of Narobia (Dawlat al Narobia)
POPULATION: 1,500,000
CAPITAL CITY: Narobia City
PLACES OF INTEREST: Imperial Palace
GOVERNMENT: Absolute monarchy
MAJOR LANGUAGES: English, Swahili, Arabic
MONETARY UNIT: Narobian shilling
MAJOR RESOURCES: Petroleum, natural gas, salt, zinc, diamonds, coal, lead, iron ore, steel, aluminum, wildlife, agriculture, consumer goods.
NATIONAL DEFENSE: Narobian Armed Forces, including infantry and air force. Princess Zanda has a personal entourage of heavily armed mercenaries.
INTERNATIONAL RELATIONS: Member of African Union, Interpol, Organization of Petroleum Exporting Countries, Pan-African Congress on the Treatment of Superhumans, United Nations, UNESCO, World Health Organization and World Trade Organization. Narobia is an ally of Afrikaa, Canaan, France, Mbangawi and Saudi Arabia and an uneasy ally of Wakanda.
EXTRATERRESTRIAL RELATIONS: None known.
NONHUMAN POPULATION: Princess Zanda has various creatures of unknown origin among her collection at the Imperial Palace
DOMESTIC SUPERHUMANS: None known.
PROMINENT CITIZENS: Princess Zanda is the ruler of Narobia, and is known internationally as a thief; she is wanted in fifteen countries. Zanda ascended to the throne upon the death of her father, Emir Zander.
SUPERHUMAN RESIDENTS: None known.
DOMESTIC CRIME: Princess Zanda's administration has been accused of decadence and corruption, with little impact on her continued criminal activities.
INTERNATIONAL CRIME: Princess Zanda's associates in the Council of Antiquarians including Mr. Abner Little, Silas Mourner, Colonel Nigel Pigman and Count Andreas Zorba have each spent time in Narobia as Zanda's guests and rivals.
FIRST APPEARANCE: Black Panther #4 (1977)
HISTORY: Narobia is one of the wealthiest nations of Africa, containing valuable deposits of diamonds and oil. Emir Zander built the secretive emirate nation into a powerful industrial locale. After his death, Princess Zanda continued her father's work, but has been continually distracted by her passion for collecting. A member of the Council of Antiquarians (the Collectors), Zanda's international treasure hunts have made her an enemy of many foreign powers, casting a poor reflection upon

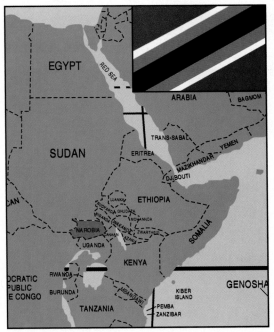

Narobia. During her quest for the lost treasure of King Solomon — in particular a pair of brass frogs that could function as a time machine — Zanda crossed swords with Wakanda's Black Panther (T'Challa). Joining forces, they found the Tomb of King Solomon in the Sahara, but they accidentally destroyed it through misuse of the brass frogs. Afterward, the Council of Antiquarians forced T'Challa to aid them in the hunt for the fountain of youth, purported to be possessed by a hidden city of samurai in Asia. To ensure his compliance, Princess Zanda targeted Wakanda with her nation's missiles. T'Challa returned with the water they requested, and while they fought for its possession he tricked Zanda's men into destroying their missiles. Princess Zanda continued to hunt treasures such as the quest for the Blinding Brazier of Balthakk in Nunavut, and recovering one of the brass frogs when it summoned Kiber the Cruel from the past. When T'Challa announced he would be marrying Storm (Ororo Munroe) of the X-Men, Zanda was infuriated, determined that she would make him her king. She clashed with Storm in New York, and was easily beaten. After Storm & T'Challa's wedding, Zanda met them again when she represented Narobia at the Pan-African Congress of the Treatment of Superhumans, in which the assembled nations attempted to draft a reaction to the USA's adoption of the Superhuman Registration Act, but they were unable to reach an agreement.

Art by Jack Kirby

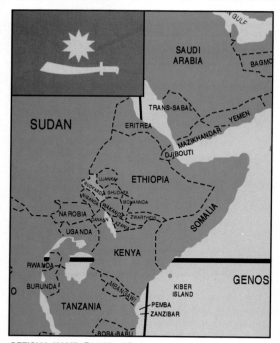

OFFICIAL NAME: Republic of Rudyarda
POPULATION: 1,650,000
CAPITAL CITY: Viceroy
PLACES OF INTEREST: Viceroy Academy, Viceroy Prison
GOVERNMENT: Republic
MAJOR LANGUAGES: English, Afrikaans
MONETARY UNIT: Rudyarda shilling
MAJOR RESOURCES: Iron ore, steel, gold, coal, uranium, diamonds, mining, timber, machinery, metallurgy, aircraft.
NATIONAL DEFENSE: Armed Forces of Rudyarda, including infantry and air force.

Art by John Buscema

INTERNATIONAL RELATIONS: Rudyarda is a member of the United Nations, UNESCO, and World Health Organization. Rudyarda has a close alliance with Azania, a consulate in Manhattan, New York City, New York, and were formerly an economic and political ally of Genosha. On poor terms with Wakanda, Rudyarda caused a diplomatic incident by briefly jailing Prince T'Challa (the Black Panther).
EXTRATERRESTRIAL RELATIONS: None known.
NONHUMAN POPULATION: None known.
DOMESTIC SUPERHUMANS: Rock Python (M'Gula) is a black citizen with superhuman durability; after amassing a criminal record in Rudyarda, he turned mercenary and went to the USA to join the Serpent Society.

PROMINENT CITIZENS: Ronald Pershing is the ambassador for Rudyarda in the USA, and a political opponent of the Black Panther. Nathan Kumalo was a black citizen who entered Wakanda with Jeth Robards to steal the Vibrotron, but Robards double-crossed him, leaving him in Rudyarda. Jeth Robards arranged to sell the Vibrotron to Ulysses Klaw, but when the Human Torch (Johnny Storm), Thing (Ben Grimm) and Black Panther became involved he panicked, and Klaw killed him.
SUPERHUMAN RESIDENTS: None known.
DOMESTIC CRIME: Significant strife between the black and white classes has led to many violent reprisals on both sides.
INTERNATIONAL CRIME: Ulysses Klaw came to Rudyarda to broker a deal for Wakanda's Vibrotron with Jeth Robards; he wound up killing Robards, and was himself beaten by the Thing, Human Torch and Black Panther, then placed in federal custody; Klaw was abused in prison, and thereafter vowed that he would one day have revenge on Rudyarda.
FIRST APPEARANCE: Fantastic Four #119 (1972)

Art by John Buscema

HISTORY: Rudyarda was founded by voortrekkers (roaming Boers) who had left South Africa in the early 20th century, frustrated by the 2nd Boer War. Rudyarda was named in honor of British author Rudyard Kipling, whose 1899 poem "The White Man's Burden" was seen by many as championing the superiority of imperialism. In recent times, Ulysses Klaw arranged for Nathan Kumalo and Jeth Robards to steal into Wakanda and take the Vibrotron, a device designed to collect the energy absorbed by Vibranium. The Black Panther came to Rudyarda to retrieve it, but was arrested and jailed for not carrying identification papers. The Human Torch and Thing staged a prison break, and they were able to halt Klaw and turned him over to the authorities. Klaw was indignant toward Rudyarda over how the prison system treated him, and he later impersonated ambassador Ronald Pershing in a plot to trick T'Challa into surrendering the throne of Wakanda, hoping to seize Wakanda and take it into war with Rudyarda, but the Panther saw through his disguise and ended the scheme.

OFFICIAL NAME: Republic of South Africa
POPULATION: 43,997,000
CAPITAL CITY: Pretoria
PLACES OF INTEREST: Bloemfontein, Cape Town, Johannesburg, Stellenbosch, Sutherland, Carlton Center (Johannesburg), Castle of Good Hope (Cape Town), Dagbreek (Stellenbosch), Southern African Large Telescope (Sutherland), Union Buildings (Pretoria)
GOVERNMENT: Republic
MAJOR LANGUAGES: IsiZulu, IsiXhosa, Afrikaans, Sepedi, English, Setswana, Sesotho, Xitsonga
MONETARY UNIT: Rand
MAJOR RESOURCES: Mining, gold, chromium, coal, iron ore, steel, manganese, nickel, platinum, vanadium, tin, uranium, diamonds, salt, chemicals, phosphates, natural gas, motor vehicles, machinery, textiles, fertilizer, commercial ship repair.
NATIONAL DEFENSE: South African National Defense Force, including the South African Army, South African Navy, South African Air Force, Joint Operations Command, Joint Support Command and Military Intelligence.
INTERNATIONAL RELATIONS: Member of the African Union, Commonwealth of Nations, Interpol, United Nations, UNESCO, World Health Organization and World Trade Organization. China, Germany, Japan, the Netherlands, Saudi Arabia, the UK and the USA are major economic allies. Refugees from Burundi, the Democratic Republic of the Congo, Somalia and Zimbabwe have complicated the nation's borders. Relations with Wakanda were strained by the imprisonment of Ramonda, stepmother of the Black Panther (Prince T'Challa).
EXTRATERRESTRIAL RELATIONS: The immense alien robot Ultimo was once sent by its master the Mandarin to South Africa.
NONHUMAN POPULATION: None known.
DOMESTIC SUPERHUMANS: Maggott (Japheth) was a mutant hero with "slugs" named Eany and Meany who could devour matter to provide him with sustenance; Maggott joined the X-Men, but was eventually slain by Mr. Sinister (Nathaniel Essex). Target was a member of Elektra's Ryu clan who perished battling the Hand's Snakeroot clan.
PROMINENT CITIZENS: Archbishop Desmond Tutu, the first black minister of South Africa was instrumental in the fight to abolish apartheid. Nelson Mandela was the first president to be voted in after the abolishment of apartheid; he was a friend to the Wakandan royal family. David Rand was born in Johannesburg to his parents John and Constance, but it was in the Congo after his parents' death that Rand became the hero Ka-Zar. Waku was a warrior chieftain of the Bantu in the early 20th century. Dr. Harrison Taylor developed a mutant strain of smallpox with an eye to creating a biological weapon, but he was slain by the Host. Anton Pretorius was magistrate of communications, and kept Ramonda his prisoner for years over an infatuation with her; he employed local mercenaries (Elmer "Sex N Violence" Gore, Miyo Moshigo & Strike) and military (Percy Boraine, Doeke Riebeeck & Eugene van der Merwe) against the Black Panther when he came for Ramonda. Ramonda, spent years as a prisoner of Pretorius before finally being released by her stepson, the Black Panther. Patrick Slade was a white merchant in Pretoria who alerted the Black Panther to Ramonda's imprisonment, but was eventually slain by Elmer Gore; he was survived by his wife Sarah. The Black Panther was also aided by Zanti Chikane, a gold miner and husband of Miriam. Nkosi was a black radical who fought the Black Panther during his quest for his mother; Nkosi's riot accidentally led to the death of Theodore Olebogeng, survived by his brother Walter. Andreas "the Bull" de Ruyter was a member of state security who clashed with Ororo Munroe and Prince T'Challa years before either

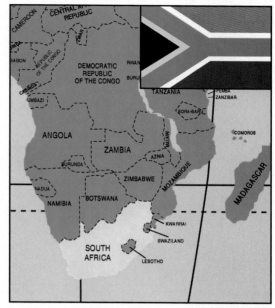

became costumed heroes; he harbored a vendetta against the two for decades. Commander Jacob van Vroot was a financier and rival of US mogul Gregory Gideon.
SUPERHUMAN RESIDENTS: None known.
DOMESTIC CRIME: South Africa has significant production and transportation of illegal drugs. There are also difficulties with forced slave labor operations.
INTERNATIONAL CRIME: Magneto attempted to recruit Maggott to his side when he was twelve, but the boy rebuffed him. The Living Laser (Arthur Parks) was sent to steal diamonds for the Mandarin's hate-ray plot and was supplied with the robot Ultimo to assist him, but they were defeated by the Avengers. Gerald O'Hara, father of Shanna the She-Devil was slain in South Africa by Nekra Sinclair. The mutant disease-carrier the Host came to Johannesburg to "liberate" the mutant smallpox developed by Dr. Harrison Taylor, but was bested by Mystique (Raven Darkholme) and Shortpack, who had come to destroy it. The superhuman Advisor was active in Johannesburg, using his manipulative abilities to help generate violence.
HISTORY: Originally populated by the Bantu peoples, South Africa was colonized by the Dutch in the 16th century; Dutch pioneers who flocked to the country became known as "Boers." South Africa became prized by other nations for its rich resources, leading the Dutch and British to conflict there in the Boer Wars, ultimately ending the 19th century with the nation under British rule. Unfortunately, the country developed a deep racial divide, as black residents were denied equal citizenship. Full voting rights were finally established in 1994, and the country has since tried to heal its fragmented past.

Art by Michael Ryan

poachers on the Katavi Plain Game Reserve, then was later slain while helping Shanna oppose Cross-Wallace's efforts to rule Africa with ancient magic.

SUPERHUMAN RESIDENTS: None known

DOMESTIC CRIME: Tanzania has a growing role in the transshipment of Southwest and Southeast Asian heroin and South American cocaine destined for South African, European, and US markets. Money laundering is also a frequent problem.

INTERNATIONAL CRIME: The Hellfire Club's White Queen Courtney Ross once sought to destabilize Zanzibar's economy by employing the mercenary Viper, the terrorist Weaponeers and their super-powered agent Scimitar; however, they were defeated by Askari with assistance from Angel, Husk (Paige Guthrie), and reinforcements from nearby Genosha. Terrorist groups active in Tanzania include the Fist of the People, the Revolutionary Army and the Tiger's Tooth.

HISTORY: Shortly after achieving independence from Britain in the early 1960s, Tanganyika and Zanzibar merged to form the nation of Tanzania in 1964, though Zanzibar still maintains a degree of autonomy. Today, Tanzania is one of the poorest countries in the world with the economy depending heavily on agriculture, accounting for almost half of the country's GDP, providing 85% of exports, and employing 80% of the work force. Tanzania is home to some of the oldest human settlements unearthed by archaeologists, including fossils of early humans found in Olduvai Gorge, and also contains many large and ecologically significant wildlife parks. Recently, the Zanzibar government brokered a deal with Courtney Ross, head of Fraser's Bank of London, for long-term development grants and loans.

OFFICIAL NAME: United Republic of Tanzania (Jamhuri ya Muungano wa Tanzania)

POPULATION: 39,384,000

CAPITAL CITY: Dar es Salaam (traditional), Dodoma (political)

PLACES OF INTEREST: Zanzibar (autonomous state); Mount Kilimanjaro; Lake Victoria; Ngorongoro Crater; Katavi Plain Game Reserve; Olduvai Gorge; Serengeti National Park; Bora-Buru

GOVERNMENT: Republic

MAJOR LANGUAGES: Kiswahili (Swahili), English, Arabic

MONETARY UNIT: Tanzanian shilling

MAJOR RESOURCES: Hydropower, tin, phosphates, iron ore, coal, diamonds, gemstones, gold, natural gas, nickel, coffee, tea, cotton, pyrethrum, tobacco

NATIONAL DEFENSE: Tanzanian People's Defense Force (Jeshi la Wananchi la Tanzania)

INTERNATIONAL RELATIONS: Tanzania is a member of Interpol, UNESCO, United Nations (and temporarily in its Security Council), World Health Organization and World Trade Organization. Tanzania once declared war on neighboring Uganda after they invaded and sought to annex the northern Tanzanian province of Kagera. In recent times, Tanzania is host to more than a half-million refugees from strife-torn neighboring nations, more than any other African country; mutants fleeing Genosha would often seek refuge in Tanzania. Disputes with Malawi over the boundary in Lake Nyasa (Lake Malawi) and the meandering Songwe River remain dormant. Zanzibar is home to the inaugural office of the Mutantes Sans Frontières global mutant outreach organization established by Warren Worthington III (Angel of the X-Men).

EXTRATERRESTRIAL RELATIONS: The Vegan Colossus once scouted the Bora-Buru region but was driven away by Giant-Man (Henry Pym)

NONHUMAN POPULATION: None known

DOMESTIC SUPERHUMANS: President of Zanzibar Jono Baraka is also the retired super hero Askari ("The Spear").

PROMINENT CITIZENS: Tanzanian President is Jakaya Mrisho Kikwete; Zanzibar Vice President Umbaja is also general of the Zanzibar Armed Forces and has a daughter, Taniqa; British diamond smuggler Sir Guy Cross-Wallace once lived in a villa in Tanzania; Gamekeeper Jeremy Mchele was once aided by Shanna the She-Devil in opposing

ASKARI

Art by Aaron Lopresti

OFFICIAL NAME: Kingdom of Wakanda
POPULATION: 6,000,000
CAPITAL CITY: Central Wakanda
PLACES OF INTEREST: Black Warrior Creek, Central Wakanda Palace, Chams of the Chilling Mist, Crystal Forest, Domain of the White Gorillas, Jabari village, Mount Kanda, Mount Wakanda, N'Jadaka village, Panther Island, Paradise Forest, Pirahna Cove, Primitive Peaks, Resurrection Altar, River of Grace & Wisdom, Serpent Valley, T'Chaka Path, Techno-Jungle, Torment Forest, Tranquility Temple, Twisted Visions Lake, Vibranium Mound, Warrior Falls, Woods of Solitude
GOVERNMENT: Absolute monarchy
MAJOR LANGUAGES: Wakandan, Yoruba, Hausa
MONETARY UNIT: Wakandan dollar
MAJOR RESOURCES: Vibranium, uranium, coal, diamonds, aeronautics, aircraft manufacture
NATIONAL DEFENSE: The Wakandan Army is the country's main ground forces, while the Wakandan Navy oversees naval operations. The Wakandan Air Guard is the nation's air force, which includes pilots wearing powerful suits of combat armor. Specialized forces include the Panther Guard (aka "Panther Posse"). The Hatut Zeraze ("Dogs of War") was formerly the nation's secret police; although officially disbanded, they continue to operate in what they believe is their homeland's best interests. The Dora Milaje are the king's personal bodyguards.
INTERNATIONAL RELATIONS: Member of African Union, Pan-African Congress on the Treatment of Superhumans, UNESCO, United Nations and World Health Organization. Wakanda has provided significant technological support to the Avengers, Fantastic Four, SHIELD and X-Men. Although Wakanda has never officially gone to war, its relationship with Atlantis, Azania, Canaan, Canada, Deviant Lemuria, Genosha, Ghudaza, Kenya, Latveria, Mohannda, Narobia, Niganda, Rudyarda and the USA is often tense. Wakanda's closest allies include Attilan, Dakenia, France, the Savage Land and South Africa; their former neighbor Kwarrai was absorbed into the country.
EXTRATERRESTRIAL RELATIONS: The legendary Vibranium Mound is believed to be of extraterrestrial origin. The Asgardian Frost Giant Ymir was once summoned to Wakanda by the Sons of Satannish. Uatu the Watcher attended the wedding of the Black Panther and Storm. The Panther God of the Wakandans is believed to be the god Bast, once worshiped by the Egyptians. The K'un-Lun native Black Dragon (Chiantang) clashed with Wakanda, and was taken into custody.
NONHUMAN POPULATION: Dinosaurs that were the result of Deviant experiments have appeared in Serpent Valley. THROBs are a limited series of robots built partially from Vibranium who serve in national defense. The Prowlers are immense panther-shaped robots that serve as one of the nation's last lines of defense.
DOMESTIC SUPERHUMANS: The Black Panther (T'Challa) is the nation's sovereign, and has served overseas in the Avengers; previous Black Panthers include Bashenga (founder of the Black Panther Cult), Azzari the Wise, Chanda and T'Chaka, T'Challa's father. Gentle (Nezhno Abidemi) is a mutant, and became a student of the Xavier Institute. Icon (Dr. A'kurru U'mbaya) was in opposition to T'Challa's rule. Ivory (K'Maria) joined SHIELD's Super-Agents but was killed by her teammates when they turned out to be double agents for Hydra. General Jakarra was a member of the extended royal family who was mutated from Vibranium exposure into a monstrous creature. Solomon Prey was altered by surgical experiments to obtain bat-like wings, and clashed with the Black Panther; Prey's lackeys were called Lightning Lancers. The Vibravore was a creature composed of victims from a Vibranium experiment, fused into a powerful entity. Vibraxas (N'Kano) gained powers from Vibranium, which he used in Fantastic Force.
PROMINENT CITIZENS: A'Kane was the mother of Vibraxas. B'Tumba aided AIM in an illegal Vibranium mining operation. The Death Tiger was a costumed ally of the Jabari tribe. Young Kantu's parents Karota & M'Jumbak were killed by Erik Killmonger, and he helped the Black Panther defeat Killmonger. Kazibe and Tayete are a pair of local criminals who have served masters including Erik Killmonger. Derek Khanata is a

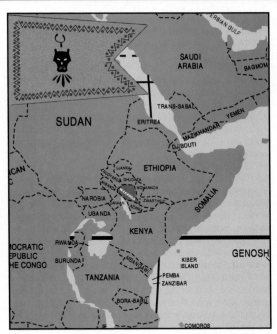

former member of the Hatut Zeraze and current agent of SHIELD. Kono is the son of W'Kabi and became a priest. Kunta & Ogun work security in Wakanda's New York consulate. Monica Lynne lived in Wakanda for years while engaged to T'Challa. M'Chata, N'Taka & Naraba are members of the Jabari who allied with the Man-Ape. M'Daka formerly served in the Avengers support crew. M'Koni is T'Challa's cousin and married Wheeler of the Air Guard; Wheeler was ultimately slain by Malice. "Mama" is a physical trainer. Mendinano is a medicine man who oversees care of the heart-shaped herb. Mubaru once attempted an illegal Vibranium mining operation. N'Baza was a medicine man, and uncle to T'Challa. N'Dede is the country's ambassador to Azania. N'Gami serves as a member of SHIELD. N'Gamo is of the Jabari tribe and often aids the Man-Ape in his goals. N'Gassi is one of T'Challa's advisors. N'Kano is the stepfather of Vibraxas. Okoye is one of the Dora Milaje. Omoro runs the Wakandan consulate in New York. Queen Divine Justice is a Dora Milaje from the Jabari tribe who was raised in the USA. Ramonda is the stepmother of T'Challa. S'Yan is T'Challa's uncle. Shuri is T'Challa's sister. T'Shan is the ambassador to the USA, but has been possessed by the nation's enemy Cannibal. Taku is the head of communications. Tanzika was a servant of T'Challa who murdered Zatama on behalf of Killmonger. W'Kabi is the head of national security. White Wolf (Hunter) was the adopted son of T'Chaka, and is head of the Hatut Zeraze. Zatama was a councilman who was murdered by Tanzika. In the 1950s, Zawadi was an adventurer who joined the Monster Hunters. Zuri is a bodyguard to T'Challa. Minor members of the royal family include Ishanta, Dr. Joshua Itobo, Khanta and Zuni, also known as the "Black Musketeers." Other known Wakandans include Moise Bomvana, Chandra, Damola, G'Mal, Jarak, Jarkanga, Jiomo, Jiru, K'Bali, Kaleb, Dr. Kaza, Kimbay, Kradada, M'Bambway, M'Bata, M'Butu, M'Gari, M'Halak, M'Kambi, M'Naka, M'Tume, M'Zaki, Malaika, N'Banu, N'Basa, N'Debele, N'Dele, N'Gama, N'Yaga, R'Shumba, Rakeisha, T'Arrance, T'Kora, T'Swana, Dr. Tambak, Toyosi, Umu, W'Tabe, W'Tambi, Wali, Wazira and Zambada.
SUPERHUMAN RESIDENTS: Storm (Ororo Munroe) of the X-Men is King T'Challa's queen. Venomm is a snake tamer who was once an agent of Killmonger, but now defends Wakanda; he is one of the few white men in the country.
DOMESTIC CRIME: Achebe has made several attempts to snare the throne of Wakanda. Erik Killmonger (N'Jadaka) has lead the undead hordes of the Death Regiment against T'Challa, and employed superhuman agents including Baron Macabre, King Cadaver, Lord

Karnaj, Madame Slay, Malice, Salamander K'Ruel and Sombre. Malice (Nakia) is a rogue member of the Dora Milaje. The Man-Ape (M'Baku) is of the Jabari tribe and the Cult of White Gorilla, rivals to the Cult of the Panther.

INTERNATIONAL CRIME: Ulysses Klaw has made repeated invasions of Wakanda, both solo and with personal armies. AIM, Diablo, the High Evolutionary (Herbert Wyndham), Moses Magnum, Nazi Germany and Roxxon Oil are among those who have tried to harvest the country's Vibranium supply. Kiber the Cruel was stationed on Kiber Island nearby Wakanda and captured Wakandans in his attempts to cure his condition. Nightshade (Tilda Johnson) was briefly tolerated when her scientific expertise was needed.

FIRST APPEARANCE: Fantastic Four #52 (1966)

HISTORY: Ages ago, a meteor crashed into Wakanda, leaving behind an immense deposit of the rare ore called Vibranium. Gradually, the Wakandans learned to employ the metal in their spearheads; the Vibranium also proved to have mutagenic properties that transformed some into monsters. The Cult of the Panther sprang up, and the one who bears the title of Black Panther has almost always served as chieftain; the Wakandans have followed the line of Black Panthers back to the first, Bashenga, and the tradition continues in the modern day with Prince T'Challa. Each Black Panther partakes of a heart-shaped herb found at Mount Kanda, which grants them low-level superhuman abilities, and a mystical connection to the Panther God. Surrounded by mountains, Wakanda's borders have been carefully controlled over the last 200 years, with all attempts at invasion repelled. Until recent years, the Wakandans were so secretive that most people on Earth were unaware of the country's existence. Word of the Vibranium's presence drew outside nations during World War II, and King T'Chaka made a deal with Captain America (Steve Rogers) to provide him with Vibranium, subsequently used in the construction of the Captain's shield. T'Chaka made a fatal mistake by later allying himself with Ulysses Klaw;

Art by Jack Kirby

Klaw killed T'Chaka and enslaved the Wakandans while pillaging the Vibranium, but young Prince T'Challa drove Klaw out. T'Challa became the Black Panther upon reaching adulthood, and has carefully brought the nation more fully into the outside world, but the country's intentions are often misunderstood and feared by outsiders. The Wakanda Design Group is the nation's most important technological firm for contact with the outside world. Wakanda's parliament is comprised of 18 different tribes, and for many years T'Challa employed the tradition of the Dora Milaje, taking women from each tribe as prospective brides in order to maintain peace. T'Challa ultimately chose the outsider Ororo Munroe to be his queen. Wakanda is possibly home to the world's most powerful armed forces, and steps have been taken to conceal their true military might for fear of backlash from other nations.

Art by Scot Eaton

KINGDOM OF WAKANDA
Equatorial East Africa

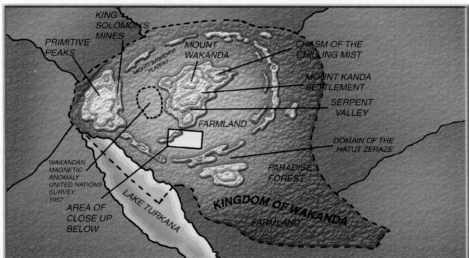

PRIMITIVE PEAKS

KING SOLOMON'S MINES

MIGHTY BASHENGA PLATEAU

MOUNT WAKANDA

CHASM OF THE CHILLING MIST

MOUNT KANDA SETTLEMENT

SERPENT VALLEY

FARMLAND

DOMAIN OF THE HATUT ZERAZE

PARADISE FOREST

WAKANDAN MAGNETIC ANOMALY UNITED NATIONS SURVEY, 1957

AREA OF CLOSE UP BELOW

LAKE TURKANA

KINGDOM OF WAKANDA

FARMLAND

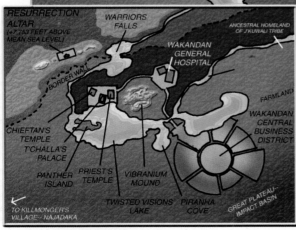

RESURRECTION ALTAR
(+7,753 FEET ABOVE MEAN SEA LEVEL)

WARRIORS FALLS

ANCESTRAL HOMELAND OF J'KUWALI TRIBE

WAKANDAN GENERAL HOSPITAL

BORDER WALL

FARMLAND

WAKANDAN CENTRAL BUSINESS DISTRICT

CHIEFTAN'S TEMPLE

T'CHALLA'S PALACE

PANTHER ISLAND

PRIEST'S TEMPLE

VIBRANIUM MOUND

TWISTED VISIONS LAKE

PIRANHA COVE

GREAT PLATEAU-IMPACT BASIN

TO KILLMONGER'S VILLAGE-- NAJADAKA

CENTRAL WAKANDA

T'CHALLA PARK, *DOWNTOWN WAKANDA*

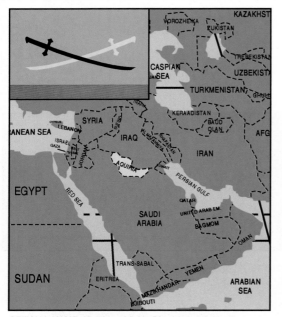

escaping conquest by the Ottoman Turks in 1560, the modern Kingdom of Aqiria was established in 1756 when Sheikh Muhammed al-Kafir established the House of Kafir to promote a more purified and simple version of Islam. In the mid-20th century, Aqiria became a close ally of the United States in its battle against Soviet expansion in the region. Vast reserves of oil were discovered in May 1940, making Aqiria one of the wealthiest nations in the world today.

In recent years, Sheikh Farouk al-Fasaud, believed by many to be one of the wealthiest men in the world, became Aqiria's minister of oil. For years, al-Fasaud was the most influential person involved in OPEC, although only high-ranking members of certain governments were aware of the true extent of al-Fasaud's influence. That changed when investigative journalist Gregory Dunbar of the CBS News Cairo Bureau launched an investigation into al-Fasaud's activities, exposing many illicit and unscrupulous transactions. Dunbar's reports led to several full-scale media exposés concerning Fasaud's lifestyle and ill-gotten gains, causing the sheikh to lose considerable influence in the world community. Blaming Dunbar for his downfall, Fasaud attempted to kill the reporter with a dagger while he was working at an Aqirian satellite uplink studio, but Dunbar dodged the attack and Fasaud's dagger instead pierced a nearby television camera. The electrical current coursed through Fasaud's body and transformed him into a being of electromagnetic energy.

Although Aqiria's King Kahil al-Kafir publicly claimed that he had discharged al-Fasaud from his post as Aqirian minister of oil (and alleged that al-Fasaud continued to harass his government as a result), the two secretly remained allies (a fact also known by certain high-raking members of the US government). At that time, the US government was not permitted to send space shuttles into flight after several disastrous missions conducted by the National Aeronautics and Space Administration (NASA); so the US government entered into an agreement with King al-Kafir to secretly launch shuttle flights from Aqiria in order to transport US military satellite equipment into space.

Meanwhile, Gregory Dunbar transferred to CBS News' New York Bureau following Fasaud's failed attack, but Fasaud followed Dunbar and made another attempt on his life at CBS News Headquarters. The Fantastic Four prevented Fasaud from killing Dunbar, and the Thing (Ben Grimm) and Ms. Marvel (Sharon Ventura) journeyed to Aqiria in pursuit of Fasaud where they were greeted by King al-Kafir and US Ambassador to Aqiria Windsor Raynes. While searching for Fasaud, the Thing and Ms. Marvel discovered the secret Aqirian government compound from which the US was launching space shuttles, but they were ambushed and incapacitated by al-Fasaud immediately after. Although King al-Kafir and Ambassador Raynes agreed that the Thing and Ms. Marvel should be killed to prevent information about the secret shuttle program from leaking, the heroes escaped into space aboard the shuttle. They were pursued by Fasaud, who uploaded himself into a US military satellite, but the Thing destroyed the satellite, forcing Fasaud to transmit himself into the shuttle. The Thing then short-circuited all of the shuttle's electrical systems, thus short-circuiting Fasaud as well.

However, Fasaud survived the altercation and resurfaced later as an operative of the terrorist organization known as Radically Advanced Ideas in Destruction (RAID). He compromised British security systems to enable several other RAID operatives and their weapons to enter Britain undetected. However, he was soon discovered in the MI5 computer network by a telepath and trapped inside a Faraday cage designed to block out external electrical fields, after which he agreed to cooperate with British authorities. It is unknown if al-Fasaud remains affiliated with the current Aqirian regime.

OFFICIAL NAME: Kingdom of Aqiria (Mamlakat al-'Aqiriyya)
POPULATION: 7,493,000
CAPITAL CITY: Burbok
PLACES OF INTEREST: al-Kafir Palace (Burbok), al-Fasaud Palace (Hamraa); Aqiria International Airport (Burbok)
GOVERNMENT: Absolute monarchy
MAJOR LANGUAGES: Arabic
MONETARY UNIT: Aqirian dinar
MAJOR RESOURCES: Crude oil production, petroleum refining, basic petrochemicals, wheat, barley
NATIONAL DEFENSE: Land Forces (Army), Air Force, Air Defense Force, National Guard, Ministry of Interior Forces (paramilitary), Royal Guard
INTERNATIONAL RELATIONS: Member of Arab League, International Atomic Energy Agency, Islamic Development Bank, Interpol, Organization of Petroleum Exporting Countries (OPEC), United Nations and World Health Organization.
EXTRATERRESTRIAL RELATIONS: None known.
NONHUMAN POPULATION: None known.
DOMESTIC SUPERHUMANS: Fasaud (Sheikh Farouk al-Fasaud) is Aqiria's former minister of oil who now exists as a being of electromagnetic energy.
PROMINENT CITIZENS: King Kahil al-Kafir
SUPERHUMAN RESIDENTS: None documented.
DOMESTIC CRIME: Street crime is generally not a problem in Aqiria. However, private Aqirian citizens who perceive that a foreigner is not observing conservative standards of conduct may harass and/or assault that person.
INTERNATIONAL CRIME: Large sections of the boundary with Saudi Arabia are not defined and remain disputed. Critics claim Aqiria is a state sponsor of terrorism (specifically, that it deploys the superhuman Fasaud abroad to clandestinely influence events in its favor), but Aqiria currently denies any connection to Fasaud.
FIRST APPEARANCE: Fantastic Four #309 (1987)

HISTORY: The first inhabitants of Aqiria were Nabataean traders who made use of the nation's many desert oases on their treks between the Persian Gulf and Red Sea. The Roman Emperor Trajan (Marcus Ulpius Nerva Traianus) conquered Aqiria in approximately 110 AD and incorporated it into the Roman Empire. In the 7th century, Aqiria was conquered by the Arabs during the Byzantine-Arab Wars. Narrowly

OFFICIAL NAME: Republic of Iraq (Al Jumhuriyah al Iraqiyah)
POPULATION: 27,499,000
CAPITAL CITY: Baghdad
PLACES OF INTEREST: Basra, the Ishtar Gate, Imam Husayn Shrine, Saq Al Masgoof, Ctesiphon, Baghdad Tower, Temple of Ishtar; in ancient times, Babylon, the Hanging Gardens of Babylon, the Tower of Babel, and Uruk.
GOVERNMENT: Parliamentary democracy
MAJOR LANGUAGES: Arabic, Kurdish, Assyrian, Armenian
MONETARY UNIT: New Iraqi dinar
MAJOR RESOURCES: Petroleum, natural gas, phosphates, sulfur, chemicals, fertilizer, agriculture, textiles, leather, construction materials, food processing.
NATIONAL DEFENSE: The Iraqi Armed Forces (includes Iraqi Army, Iraqi Navy, Iraqi Air Force), and the National Police. Formerly defended by Desert Sword, the national superhuman team, which consisted of Aminedi, the Arabian Knight (Abdul Qamar), Black Raazer (Razer), Sirocco and Veil.
INTERNATIONAL RELATIONS: Member of Interpol, the Organization of the Petroleum Exporting Countries, the United Nations, UNESCO and the World Health Organization. Receives significant military support from Poland, SHIELD, the UK and the USA, including US superhuman support from the Avengers, Force (Clay Wilson), Weapon X and the Gauntlet (Joseph Green); Symkaria's mercenary Wild Pack, led by Silver Sable, have undertaken missions on Iraqi soil. Major trade partner of Canada, Jordan, Spain, Syria, Turkey and the USA.
EXTRATERRESTRIAL RELATIONS: The Kronans scouted Iraq in ancient times, but were repelled from Earth by Gilgamesh and the time-traveling Captain America (Steve Rogers). The extradimensional being New Son once fought Gambit (Remy LeBeau) in Iraq.
NONHUMAN POPULATION: Iraq is the apparent site of the ancient kingdom of Uruk, which was ruled over by Gilgamesh (aka the Forgotten One of the Eternals). The Eternals Sersi and Utnapishtim lived in the nearby area at the time, as did the beast-man Enkidu, Gilgamesh's closest friend. The god Marduk lived in Iraq in ancient times, later adopting the mortal guise of Zoltan Nestor.
DOMESTIC SUPERHUMANS: Vitriol (Leyla) was a Kurdish woman whose family died during "Desert Storm;" empowered by an acidic symbiote, she provided acid-based weapons to Kurdish dissidents and clashed with Iron Man (Tony Stark). Blind Ali (Ali Al-Zubaidi) was a blind mutant with superhuman senses who joined Euro-Trash and died battling X-Statix. One-time sorcerer supreme Salome was originally active in ancient Assyria and in recent times organized the Shrieking Rain Jihad.
PROMINENT CITIZENS: Former dictator Saddam Abed Dassam collaborated with Hydra forces in his search for the Scorpio Key, but was ultimately slain by Elektra; Dassam's vice president was Yassin Damadan; his prime minister was Tariq Aziz; Dassam's media consultant was Azil Muhammad. Hashid Vrackne is an Iraqi reporter.
SUPERHUMAN RESIDENTS: None known.
DOMESTIC CRIME: Terrorist Faysal Al-Tariq journeyed to the USA to target Centerville for an attack, but was defeated by Captain America (Steve Rogers).
INTERNATIONAL CRIME: The instability within Iraq has attracted terrorist forces including al-Qaeda, Ansar al-Islam, Hydra, Scimitar and the Shrieking Rain Jihad, as well as the Advisor, a superhuman manipulator.

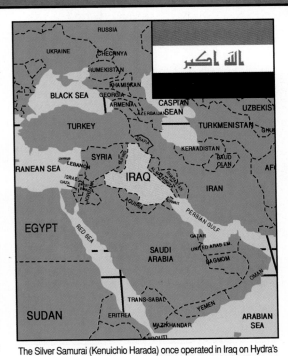

The Silver Samurai (Kenuichio Harada) once operated in Iraq on Hydra's behalf. The Fixer (Paul Ebersol) performed acts of subterfuge in Iraq, and Cybertek attempted to sell their Cyberwarriors to the Iraqi military. Other criminals who have operated in Iraq include Elektra and the Russian.

HISTORY: Known in ancient times as Mesopotamia, the ancient peoples of Iraq included the Akkadians, Sumerians, Babylonians and Assyrians. It was in the land of Iraq that the Hammurabi code upon which most fundamentals of modern law were written; Iraq was also the home of Abraham, father of the Jewish faith, and Gilgamesh, king of ancient Uruk. Iraq was conquered by Alexander the Great (323 BC), the Parthians (138 BC-637), and was brought to ruin by Mongol raids in the 13th and 14th centuries. The Ottoman Turks ran Iraq from 1534 until World War I, when England made it a British mandate; Iraq finally claimed independence in 1932. In the 20th century, Iraq was an ally of both sides during the "cold war," supporting the USA and USSR simultaneously; Iraq's invasion of Kuwait in 1990 led to 1991's Persian Gulf War, which drove them out, and at the same time incited uprisings amongst the Kurdish and Shia peoples. In 2003, the USA invaded Iraq believing it was in possession of "weapons of mass destruction;" still occupied by the US and its allies, Iraq remains in transition.

Art by Stefano Caselli

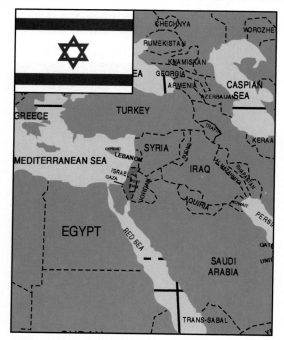

OFFICIAL NAME: State of Israel (Medinat Yisra'el)

POPULATION: 6,426,000

CAPITAL CITY: Jerusalem

PLACES OF INTEREST: Beersheba, Bethlehem, Galilee, Haifa, Rehovot, Nazareth, Tel Aviv, Mossad headquarters (Tel Aviv), Negev Desert, Jordan River, Sea of Galilee, the Dead Sea, Knessef (Jerusalem), Weizmann Institute of Science (Rehovot), Dome of the Rock

GOVERNMENT: Parliamentary democracy

MAJOR LANGUAGES: Hebrew, Arabic, English

MONETARY UNIT: New Israeli shekel

MAJOR RESOURCES: Timber, potash, copper, clay, cement, chemicals, natural gas, nuclear energy, phosphates, agriculture, tobacco, construction, plastics, textiles, footwear, fiber optics, aviation technology, communications technology, computer technology, medical electronics.

NATIONAL DEFENSE: Israel Defense Forces, Israel Naval Forces and Israel Air Force. Intelligence provided by the Military Intelligence Directorate and Mossad.

INTERNATIONAL RELATIONS: Member of Interpol, the United Nations (UN), UNESCO, the World Health Organization and the World Trade Organization. Major economic ally of Belgium, China, Germany, Switzerland and the USA. In 1967, Israel fought "The Six-Day War" with Egypt, Jordan and Syria. The country's primary superhuman agent Sabra (Ruth Bat-Seraph) has been loaned to the UK and USA in times of crisis; in turn, the X-Men and X-Factor have cooperated with the Israeli government.

EXTRATERRESTRIAL RELATIONS: The godly Nauda of the Silver Hand sent a construct to Jerusalem to absorb power from the people's emotions, but the construct was destroyed by the Young Gods. The Silver Surfer (Norrin Radd) once passed through Israel's borders. Lilandra Neramani and other members of the Shi'ar came to Israel to assist the X-Men in halting Legion (David Haller). Uatu and other Watchers visited Israel at the same time to observe Legion's actions.

NONHUMAN POPULATION: None known.

DOMESTIC SUPERHUMANS: The Arabian Knight (Navid Hashim) is a Palestinian who left Israel to enter the service of the Saudi Arabian government. Brightsword (Carter Dyam) is a former member of the Israel Defense Forces, and lost his father in the Six-Day War; he was selected to become one of the Young Gods, examples of the best of humanity, and was presented to the enigmatic Celestials, causing them to judge

in favor of humanity's continued existence. Mutant hero Sabra is the country's premiere super hero and an agent of Mossad, motivated to combat terror after the tragic death of her son Jacob. Windstorm was another superhuman agent who gained her powers from Sabra, but became an anarchist and had to be defeated by Sabra. Messiah (David Kessler) possessed magical powers that he believed were angelic in nature, but upon learning he was powered by demons and working their will, he killed himself to stop them. Gretta Rabin is the young daughter of a member of legislature, and possesses powerful psychic abilities; she is possibly destined to enable the rise to power of a future dictator. Legion was the son of Charles Xavier, and like his father was a powerful mutant telepath; Legion absorbed the psyches of others into his mind, developing new powers for each of his multiple personalities.

PROMINENT CITIZENS: Mossad agent Rachel Goldberg participated in a mission to the USA to determine if Mendell Stromm was supplying robots to Palestinian terrorists. Benjamin Abramov was a government agent who alerted Moon Knight (Marc Spector) to the danger posed by Nimrod Strange's Slayers Elite, immediately before being assassinated by Strange's agent Master Sniper; Abramov was survived by his wife Anna. Jordana Altman, an agent of Mossad is another ally of Moon Knight. Wild Rose (Rose Kugel) is an elite Mossad agent who has fought terrorists worldwide, often as an ally of the Punisher (Frank Castle). Racha Meyer was a member of the Defense Forces who encountered the Living Mummy (N'Kantu). Hayyan Zarour was a prominent Palestinian leader who was briefly held hostage by Dr. Octopus (Otto Octavius) while touring the USA. Major Bathsheva Joseph was an agent of SHIELD and later Worldwatch, but died as the result of a time travel adventure with War Machine (James Rhodes). Max Meer was the son of US ambassadors based in Jerusalem, and was mistaken by Achilles for a prophesied future dictator; the true threat was Gretta Rabin. Daniel Shomron operated a psychiatric hospital near Haifa, and was tragically slain by terrorists. Gabrielle Haller was one of Shomron's patients, and became the mother of Legion, Charles Xavier's son; she later became an ambassador to the USA, advisor to the UN Security Council, and advocate for Magneto.

SUPERHUMAN RESIDENTS: The mutants Magneto and Charles Xavier lived in Israel for a time prior to either one becoming rallying figures for mutantkind; they assisted Daniel Shomron in his therapy work. Magneto's clone Joseph stayed at Beersheba while questing to learn his true identity.

DOMESTIC CRIME: Have difficulties with drug trafficking.

INTERNATIONAL CRIME: The terrorists of al-Qaeda and Hydra (including their agent Catalyst) and Nimrod Strange's Slayers Elite (Jou-Jouka, Kareesh-Bek, Sumaro) have been active in Israel; the Palestine Liberation Organization were formerly designated terrorists. The Hulk (Bruce Banner) fought with the military during a journey through Tel Aviv; later, Achilles of the Pantheon attempted to murder Max Meer in Jerusalem, bringing the Hulk to Israel once again. The mutant criminals Avalanche (Dominikos Petrakis), Mystique (Raven Darkholme) and Sabretooth (Victor Creed) as well as the Neo-Nazi Baron von Blimp and Operation: Zero Tolerance's Prime Sentinels have been active in Israel.

HISTORY: In ancient times, the land of Israel was the promised land of the Jewish peoples. However, from 70-1948 the country was known as Palestine, and run in succession by Romans, Byzantines, Arabs, Christian crusaders and Ottoman Turks. Jews began to immigrate to Palestine in 1882; immigrants increased in numbers during World War II due to the massacres in Nazi- and USSR-occupied territories, and the state of Israel was finally established in 1948. Israel has been in conflict with virtually all of its neighbors at one time or another, although the United Nations (and USA in particular) have come to its aid. Israel made itself one of the premier nations in the hunt for Nazi war criminals, and continues to press searches for men such as Baron Wolfgang von Strucker. Strife between the Israeli and Palestinian groups has led to many violent military reprisals, terrorist bombings, local and international interventions.

OFFICIAL NAME: Arab Republic of Mazikhandar (Gumhuriyyat Mazikhandar al-'Arabiyyah)

POPULATION: 2,105,000

CAPITAL CITY: Yaridh

PLACES OF INTEREST: Capitol Building (Yaridh)

GOVERNMENT: Republic (currently a Protectorate of the Kingdom of Atlantis)

MAJOR LANGUAGES: Arabic (official), English and Atlantean widely spoken

MONETARY UNIT: Mazikhandarian rial

MAJOR RESOURCES: Petroleum, petrochemicals, fish, fruits, grain

NATIONAL DEFENSE: Land Forces, Mazikhandarian Navy, Mazikhandarian Air Force, Mazikhandarian Liberty Legion (National Guard).

INTERNATIONAL RELATIONS: Mazikhandar holds membership in the Arab Fund for Economic and Social Development, Arab League, Interpol, OPEC, United Nations (UN) and UNESCO.

EXTRATERRESTRIAL RELATIONS: None known.

NONHUMAN POPULATION: As a Protectorate of the Kingdom of Atlantis, Mazikhandar currently has a large population of Atlantean diplomats and warriors living within its borders.

DOMESTIC SUPERHUMANS: None known.

PROMINENT CITIZENS: Former President Hamzah Hasaan; Colonel Mutasim Zai'id of the Mazikhandarian Liberty Legion; General Dauod Rafiq of the Land Forces

SUPERHUMAN RESIDENTS: None known.

DOMESTIC CRIME: Armed carjacking was once a problem in Mazikhandar, but occurrences of such crimes have declined since the Axis Mundi invasion.

INTERNATIONAL CRIME: Under the Axis Mundi puppet regime, human rights violations (including torture and execution without trial) were widespread in Mazikhandar. As a Protectorate of the Kingdom of Atlantis, these violations have significantly subsided.

FIRST APPEARANCE: Avengers #83 (2004)

HISTORY: The first inhabitants of the modern-day nation of Mazikhandar were Minaean spice traders who traveled eastward in search of new routes for their frankincense and myrrh in approximately the 7th century BC. Islam was introduced to Mazikhandar in the 7th century AD, after which it was ruled as part of Arab-Islamic caliphates, with Mazikhandar becoming a province in the Islamic empire. In approximately 1520 AD, the Mazikhandarian governor surrendered to the Ottoman Empire, and Turkish armies subsequently overran the country. The Ottomans did not withdraw until 1917, and the fledgling Kingdom of Mazikhandar was soon overthrown by revolutionary forces, leading to the creation of the Arab Republic of Mazikhandar in 1921. Crude oil fields were discovered in 1938, transforming Mazikhandar into a prosperous nation.

Recently, when the Axis Mundi (a global terrorist network dedicated to reestablishing the Third Reich and funded by Baron Wolfgang von Strucker) formed, they planned to strategically eliminate key world leaders and replace them with bioengineered replicas. Mazikhandarian President Hamzah Hasaan was the first such political figure to be assassinated and replaced with a replica controlled by the Axis Mundi. Upon its secretive installation, Hasaan's replica began influencing Mazikhandarian foreign and domestic policy to coincide with Axis Mundi's plans of world domination. Mazikhandar soon declared war on the neighboring countries of Oman and Yemen. Meanwhile, Axis Mundi member the Red Skull (Johann Shmidt) posed as US Secretary of Defense Dell Rusk and established a clandestine shadow cabinet within the American government to form a new strike force of super-powered American operatives known as the Invaders, who were intended to unwittingly further Axis Mundi's plans abroad. However, after the Red Skull was publicly exposed, the Invaders fell under the leadership of the Thin Man (Bruce Dickson), who convinced the United States and British governments to allow the Invaders to remain together to combat Axis

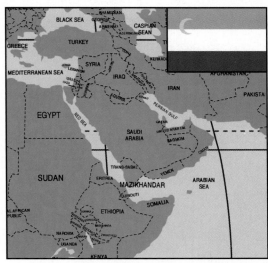

Mundi's operations. After sharing intelligence concerning Axis Mundi's worldwide activities, the governments of the US and UK sanctioned a joint invasion of Mazikhandar to overthrow Axis Mundi's puppet regime.

Meanwhile, in order to control the flow of oil to the United States, the Mazikhandarian government deployed its Navy to sink OPEC tankers in international waters. However, Mazikhandar eventually expanded its attacks and began sinking tankers in Atlantean waters, resulting in massive oil spills that caused significant Atlantean casualties. Prince Namor of Atlantis immediately retaliated against Mazikhandarian naval fleets in the Persian Gulf. Invaders operative USAgent soon convinced Atlantis to assist the joint US/UK operation to overthrow the Axis Mundi puppet regime in Mazikhandar. Plans were made to install the pro-Western General Dauod Rafiq of the Mazikhandarian Land Forces as the nation's new leader, with the Invaders agreeing to help overthrow the current regime in exchange for obtaining the synthetic Hasaan replica alive.

Backed by a massive Atlantean invasion force, the Invaders and their international coalition infiltrated the Mazikhandarian border and soon arrived at the capital city of Yaridh. Meanwhile, the Avengers, who were unaware of the extent of the Axis Mundi infiltration and believed the Invaders were still carrying out orders from the Red Skull, arrived in Mazikhandar to confront the Invaders. After the Invaders seized the Axis Mundi replica, General Rafiq was introduced as Mazikhandar's new president-elect and then promptly shot the Hasaan replica. This angered the Invaders, who had hoped to obtain the replica alive for further study. Prince Namor promptly declared Mazikhandar a Protectorate of the Kingdom of Atlantis and appointed his counselor Sulumor as Atlantean Advisor to Mazikhandar. The Invaders established a temporary headquarters and remained in Mazikhandar to help the coalition of American, Atlantean, and British forces defend against Axis Mundi's terrorist army, which began swarming across the nation through sub-dimensional space and staging daily attacks. Thin Man soon convinced the V-Battalion to join the operation in Mazikhandar, and the Invaders captured Axis Mundi operative Jonas Wilhelm Eckhardt, who used his necromancy skills to create new foot soldiers for the Axis Mundi. However, Wolverine (James Howlett), who served as a brainwashed assassin at the time, was sent by von Strucker's Hydra terrorist organization to assassinate Eckhardt so that he could not divulge Axis Mundi's secrets to the enemy. Although Wolverine was prevented from assassinating Eckhardt by the Invaders, he was able to kill Sulumor. Under the terms of their treaty with Mazikhandar, Atlantis has vowed to maintain their forces in the nation until the threat of Axis Mundi has completely subsided.

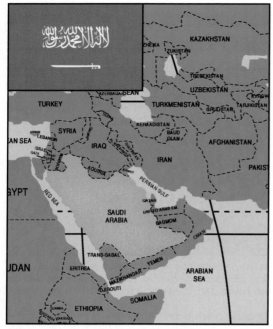

OFFICIAL NAME: Kingdom of Saudi Arabia (Al Mamlakah al Arabiyah as Suudiyah)

POPULATION: 27,601,000

CAPITAL CITY: Riyadh

PLACES OF INTEREST: Aqabah, Jeddah, Al-Balad (Jeddah), Al Faisaliyah Center (Riyadh), Berri Oil Fields, Q'Raq Oil Field, Deera Square (Riyadh), Red Sea, SHIELD Training Facility, Uqair

GOVERNMENT: Absolute monarchy

MAJOR LANGUAGES: Arabic

MONETARY UNIT: Saudi riyal

MAJOR RESOURCES: Petroleum, natural gas, petrochemicals, industrial gases, ammonia, iron ore, gold, copper, cement, plastics, fertilizer, agriculture, commercial ship repair, construction.

NATIONAL DEFENSE: Land Forces, Navy, Air Force, Air Defense Force and National Guard. Intelligence provided by Ministry of Interior Forces.

INTERNATIONAL RELATIONS: Member of Interpol, SHIELD, the Organization of the Petroleum Exporting Countries, the United Nations, UNESCO, the World Health Organization and the World Trade Organization. Major economic ally of China, Germany, Italy, Japan, Narobia, Singapore, South Korea, Taiwan and the USA. Saudi Arabia clashed with Iraq during the Persian Gulf War. The country's primary superhuman agent, the Arabian Knight (Navid Hashim) has been loaned to the UK in times of crisis.

EXTRATERRESTRIAL RELATIONS: The Silver Surfer (Norrin Radd) once traveled through Saudi Arabia's borders.

NONHUMAN POPULATION: The Demon of the Dunes was a malevolent entity that clashed with the Arabian Knight (Abdul Qamar).

DOMESTIC SUPERHUMANS: Originating in the 8th century, Abdul Alhazred is one of history's greatest sorcerers and was the author of the Necronomicon, one of the most powerful tomes on magic. Saudi Arabia's most famous hero is the mystical champion known as the Arabian Knight, a line of warriors, which dates back to the 13th century, each one armed with a mystical scimitar and flying carpet; in recent years, the Bedouin chieftain Abdul Qamar became the Arabian Knight to combat the demons Gog and Magog in Egypt, and went on to serve his country — as well as spying on Iraq's Desert Sword; when Qamar was killed by the powers of the mutant Humus Sapien, Navid Hashim (an Arab, originally from Israel) became the next Arabian Knight, and entered into the service of the Saudi government. Francesca Grace, a native of Jeddah and head of the Mys-Tech's Omni Corporation became possessed by the demonic Bane, but later gained control and joined the heroic Knights of Pendragon.

PROMINENT CITIZENS: The deceased Arabian Knight (Qamar) is survived by his family, including his wives Maya, Rana and Almira and his sons Faisal and Hassim. Abdul bin Tariq is an agent of the Ministry of Interior Forces and participated in a mission to the USA to determine if Mendell Stromm was behind a robot attack on a Saudi mosque.

SUPERHUMAN RESIDENTS: The mystical Order of Tyrana has been active in Saudi Arabia, seeking to aid a democratic revolution. The malevolent psychic being called the Shadow King was active in Saudi Arabia during the time when it used the Egyptian man Amahl Farouk as its host. The American Sandstorm has the ability to manipulate particles of sand; an embittered anti-Saudi, he was fought off by the Arabian Knight (Qamar).

DOMESTIC CRIME: Criminal sheik Abdul Hurani masterminded a number of robberies in Saudi Arabia, but was constantly thwarted by the Arabian Knight (Qamar); he enlisted the American Water Wizard (Peter Van Zante) to assist him in overthrowing the monarchy, but their alliance was brought down by the Arabian Knight and Ghost Rider (Johnny Blaze).

INTERNATIONAL CRIME: Have difficulties with forced labor operations. Numerous terrorists have been active in Saudi Arabia, including Osama bin Laden, the Jackal, Saracen (Muzzafar Lambert), the Irish Republican Army, Hezbollah, Shining Path, AIM, Tamil Militia, Khmer Rouge, Palestine Liberation Organization, Sendero Luminoso, World Revolutionary Party and Humans Off Planet; many such organizations gathered in Rub-Al-Khali at the site of the First World International Terrorism Convention, drawing the attention of the vigilante the Punisher (Frank Castle) and Israel's Mossad agent Wild Rose (Rose Kugel). The Berri Oil Fields were once menaced by an out-of-control Iron Man drone, but the drone was destroyed through the efforts of the Fantastic Four and Iron Man (Tony Stark).

HISTORY: The land of Saudi Arabia — home of the prophet of Islam Muhammad (570 AD) — was made into a powerful kingdom beginning in 1744 through Muhammad bin Saud, establishing a monarchy that has endured to the present. During the Persian Gulf War, Saudi Arabia accepted refugees from Kuwait into their borders. The stationing of US soldiers within Saudi territory has resulted in numerous terrorist attacks.

Art by Lewis LaRosa

OFFICIAL NAME: Republic of Trans-Sabal (Jomhuru-ye Sabal as-Trans); formerly Kingdom of Trans-Sabal (al-Mamlaka al-Sabal as-Trans)
POPULATION: 1,563,000
CAPITAL CITY: Jaffan
PLACES OF INTEREST: Farnoq Dahn's fortress (Jaffan)
GOVERNMENT: Republic; formerly absolute monarchy
MAJOR LANGUAGES: Arabic, Persian
MONETARY UNIT: Sabalian rial
MAJOR RESOURCES: Petroleum; despite its small size, Trans-Sabal sits upon one of the largest oil deposits in the Middle East.
NATIONAL DEFENSE: The 50,000-man-strong Sabalian Army, Navy and Air Force were previously supplemented by US allies, who provided them with advanced SHIELD technology, including Mandroid armor. Despite UN bans and weapons inspections, during Farnoq Dahn's reign Trans-Sabal was secretly working on becoming a nuclear power, and developing long range missile capability.
INTERNATIONAL RELATIONS: Sitting on valuable oil deposits, Trans-Sabal's immediate neighbors have repeatedly suggested they might send in "peacekeeping forces" to "ensure the stability of the region." Seeking to ensure US oil supplies, the US turned a blind eye to Sawalha Dahn's human rights violations, and the CIA supplied him with advanced SHIELD technology and trainers for the Sabalian army; after Dahn's demise, the CIA switched their backing to pro-US General Halladah. Other countries similarly backed the People's Armed Forces Front (PAFF), which is currently winning the civil war. Trans-Sabal is a member of the United Nations (UN), who embargoed the country's attempts to develop nuclear weapon capabilities.
EXTRATERRESTRIAL RELATIONS: None known.
NONHUMAN POPULATION: None known.
DOMESTIC SUPERHUMANS: None known.
PROMINENT CITIZENS: Sawalha Dahn seized power a little over a decade ago, through a combination of force of arms and exploiting the Sabalian's religious beliefs, declaring himself Farnoq, the chosen of God; as a result, many Sabalians obeyed him unquestioningly. After Sawalha's death, his cousin Jalfaha Dahn declared himself Farnoq, claiming the title was hereditary. His claim was disputed by General Alim Halladah, who had the armed forces' backing; he promised to maintain amicable relations with the USA (and provide cheap oil), ensuring CIA backing, but was eventually slain by Araq Mezdabah. Shurk was a rebel whose parents had died under Dahn's regime; Shurk joined the Pantheon-assisted rebellion, but was killed during the fighting. Jolel and Sandah were brother and sister who lived in Jaffan; Jolel was a Farnoq zealot, taking X-Factor's Wolfsbane (Rahne Sinclair) prisoner believing she was helping the rebels. Sandah stopped Jolel from killing Wolfsbane, but was slain by her irate brother; an enraged Wolfsbane killed Jolel in turn. Tomas DeFalcone was a presidential candidate assassinated by the Foreigner.
SUPERHUMAN RESIDENTS: Pantheon agent the Arabian Knight (Abdul Qamar) spent some time working undercover in Trans-Sabal.
DOMESTIC CRIME: Petty crime was virtually nonexistent during Farnoq Dahn's reign, thanks to a ruthless secret police; as many as 70,000 people may have died during his rule, mostly political prisoners. Violence against women, considered subservient to men, remained prevalent. During the rebellion looting, murders (not related to the conflict), rape and theft became daily occurrences across Trans-Sabal.
INTERNATIONAL CRIME: Breaking numerous UN embargoes, the CIA has supplied pro-US forces in Trans-Sabal with advanced weapons; the Pantheon similarly supplied rebels during the Dahn era, while other countries have done so post-Dahn. The Pantheon, including US citizens the Hulk (Bruce Banner) and Rick Jones also invaded Trans-Sabal to lend personal assistance, with Rick eventually killing Dahn. Terrorist training camps for Muslim extremist groups sprang up after Dahn's demise. During the civil war, the Force of Nature (Aqueduct, Firebrand, Skybreaker, Terraformer) illegally entered Trans-Sabal to stop oil fires on behalf of the activist group Project: Earth; alongside USA's New

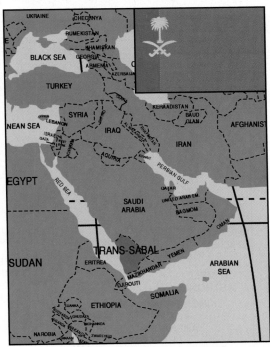

Warriors, they assisted the rebels against Halladah's army, unaware that rebel leader Araq Mezdabdah worked for an Eastern country with its own designs on Trans-Sabal. Some Trans-Sabal revolutionaries sold captured Mandroids to Ivan Tsibliyev, agent of the Genoshan Expatriate.
FIRST APPEARANCE: Incredible Hulk #390 (1992)
HISTORY: From the 10th through 14th centuries Sabalia was ruled by the Farnoq, a series of religious leaders who claimed to be God's chosen. As an era of poets and prophets, where tiny Sabalia resisted all invaders and held disproportionate power in the Middle East, modern Sabalians tend to idealize that period. Following the Farnoq era, the al-Rashid family ascended to power, but during the 18th century the region fell under British rule. Britain granted Trans-Sabal independence in 1930 only to invade it during World War II to ensure the country's oil supplies remained in Allied hands; the occupation ended in 1947 with the al-Rashid monarchy restored. In 1967 a military coup backed by the USSR ousted the al-Rashids; over the next few decades Trans-Sabal became a republic, its stability constantly threatened by rival foreign powers backing differing government factions, and its oil wealth rarely reaching the common people, causing growing unrest. Just over a decade ago Sawalha Dahn harnessed this disquiet to lead a popular revolution and declare himself Farnoq. Though many Sabalians accepted his divine authority, Dahn proved an egotistical tyrant; his secret police rounded up anyone who openly spoke out against him, and his military ruthlessly crushed any more overt rebellion. In recent years the Pantheon organization lent assistance to the rebels; Dahn in turn negotiated with the CIA to provide oil to the US in return for military technology. As the situation escalated both the Pantheon (led by the Hulk) and X-Factor (called in by the CIA) entered Trans-Sabal to support the opposing factions. However Dahn took X-Factor's leader Havok (Alex Summers) prisoner, seeking to harness his mutant powers to give Trans-Sabal nuclear missile capability; the Hulk and X-Factor freed him and captured Dahn, who was slain by the Hulk's ally Rick Jones. Civil war erupted, as the American-backed army vied with Dahn's cousin and foreign-backed rebels for control of the country. The New Warriors and Force of Nature assisted the rebels in gaining the upper hand, but Trans-Sabal remains unstable.

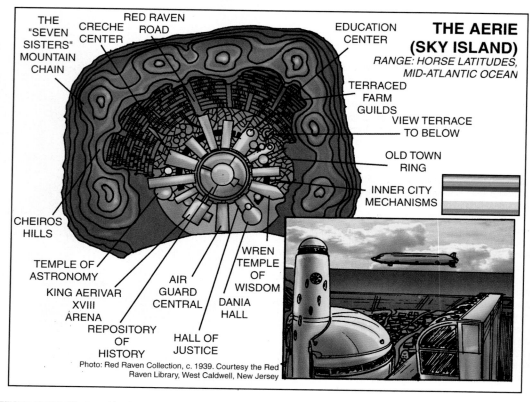

THE "SEVEN SISTERS" MOUNTAIN CHAIN

CRECHE CENTER

RED RAVEN ROAD

EDUCATION CENTER

THE AERIE (SKY ISLAND)
RANGE: HORSE LATITUDES, MID-ATLANTIC OCEAN

TERRACED FARM GUILDS

VIEW TERRACE TO BELOW

OLD TOWN RING

INNER CITY MECHANISMS

CHEIROS HILLS

TEMPLE OF ASTRONOMY

KING AERIVAR XVIII ARENA

REPOSITORY OF HISTORY

AIR GUARD CENTRAL

HALL OF JUSTICE

DANIA HALL

WREN TEMPLE OF WISDOM

Photo: Red Raven Collection, c. 1939. Courtesy the Red Raven Library, West Caldwell, New Jersey

OFFICIAL NAME: City-state of the Aerie
POPULATION: 50,000
CAPITAL CITY: Aerie
PLACES OF INTEREST: Hall of Science, Learning Center, Royal Palace, Tomb of Kylus
GOVERNMENT: Monarchy
MAJOR LANGUAGES: English, Tilan
MONETARY UNIT: None known
MAJOR RESOURCES: Robotics, machinery
NATIONAL DEFENSE: Air Guard (national police)
INTERNATIONAL RELATIONS: The Aerie has refused all invitations from the international community, preferring to remain independent; their one ally is the city of Sunev. The Avians have negotiated their air zone treaties through the US law firm Goodman, Lieber, Kurtzberg & Holliway. No formal relations with the Inhumans are known to exist.
EXTRATERRESTRIAL RELATIONS: The Bloodravens once summoned the extradimensional Wayfinder to the Aerie in the hopes that it would destroy their enemies. While the Aerie was under the rule of the Order, it was visited by the Silver Surfer (Norrin Radd), Captain Marvel (Genis-Vell), Yandroth, and the Masters of Mental Arts of Yann.
NONHUMAN POPULATION: The Avians comprise the majority of the Aerie's population; descended from a tribe of the Inhumans, they each possess a pair of bird-like wings that enable them to fly. Avian science has produced at least two copies of the Bi-Beast, a two-headed android who stores the entire civilization's knowledge and culture and was originally programmed to help defend the Aerie. An android of Red Raven was employed in order to deceive the outside world into believing the Aerie was destroyed.
DOMESTIC SUPERHUMANS: Red Raven is the leader and champion of the Avians. His daughter Dania, half-Avian has also taken the name and costume of Red Raven. Known Avians have included their first king Kylus, the peaceful Cheiros, King Aerivar XVIII, Brother Wren of the priesthood and Kestrus of the Air Guard.

PROMINENT CITIZENS: No normal human residents known.
SUPERHUMAN RESIDENTS: None known.
DOMESTIC CRIME: The Aerie has a recurring problem in the Bloodravens, a doomsday cult who hate surface people; in recent years the Bloodravens summoned the Wayfinder to the Aerie and fought on its side against Red Raven and the Defenders, but they were all defeated. The Condor left the Aerie and became a criminal in the outside world, besmirching the Avians' reputation.
INTERNATIONAL CRIME: The Aerie has seldom been visited by outsiders; the city has faced temporary conquest and plundering at the hands of Diablo, MODOK (George Tarleton), forces of AIM and the Order (Dr. Strange, Hulk, Namor and the Silver Surfer).
FIRST APPEARANCE: Red Raven Comics #1 (1940)
HISTORY: The Avian people were originally part of the Inhuman race. Around 1000 BC, the numbers of winged Inhumans had increased so that their leader Kylus demanded a separate home they could live in. Attilan's King Nestor agreed, and the Aerie was raised above Attilan with anti-gravity technology, tethered so that it would hover above the city. However, relations between the Avians and Inhumans deteriorated. When the bat-winged Cheiros advocated peace, Kylus had him and all other whose wings were not white-feathered put to death. King Nestor cut the Aerie loose from its tether, casting them out. Over time the Avians used the anti-gravity technology to increase the city's size. In the 1920s, a commercial plane crashed on the Aerie, and a surviving child was adopted by King Aerivar XVIII and reared into the 1940s hero Red Raven. When the Bloodravens sought to lead the Avians into war, Red Raven had all of the city's warriors placed into suspended animation and guarded by an android of himself. In recent years, the android accidentally destroyed itself in despair when it thought that the Avians were all dead. The alchemy of Diablo later revived the Avians, and they restored the Aerie to its prime. The Avians still have little love for surface-dwellers, and prefer isolation.

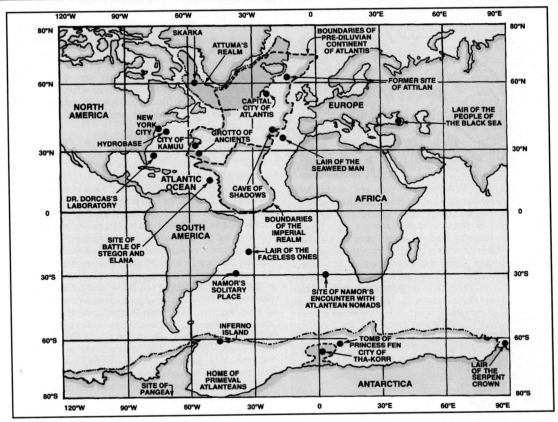

Map labels (clockwise/by region):

120°W 90°W 60°W 30°W 0 30°E 60°E 90°E

80°N

SKARKA

ATTUMA'S REALM

BOUNDARIES OF PRE-DILUVIAN CONTINENT OF ATLANTIS

FORMER SITE OF ATTILAN

60°N

CAPITAL CITY OF ATLANTIS

EUROPE

LAIR OF THE PEOPLE OF THE BLACK SEA

NORTH AMERICA

NEW YORK CITY

CITY OF KAMUU

HYDROBASE

GROTTO OF ANCIENTS

30°N

ATLANTIC OCEAN

CAVE OF SHADOWS

LAIR OF THE SEAWEED MAN

AFRICA

DR. DORCAS'S LABORATORY

0

SOUTH AMERICA

BOUNDARIES OF THE IMPERIAL REALM

SITE OF BATTLE OF STEGOR AND ELANA

LAIR OF THE FACELESS ONES

30°S

NAMOR'S SOLITARY PLACE

SITE OF NAMOR'S ENCOUNTER WITH ATLANTEAN NOMADS

INFERNO ISLAND

60°S

TOMB OF PRINCESS FEN CITY OF THA-KORR

LAIR OF THE SERPENT CROWN

HOME OF PRIMEVAL ATLANTEANS

ANTARCTICA

SITE OF PANGEA

80°S

OFFICIAL NAME: Empire of Atlantis

POPULATION: 9,000

CAPITAL CITY: Thakorr City

PLACES OF INTEREST: Cave of Shadows, Grotto of Ancients, Tomb of Lady Dorma, Tomb of Princess Fen

GOVERNMENT: Monarchistic republic

MAJOR LANGUAGES: Atlantean

MONETARY UNIT: Unrevealed

MAJOR RESOURCES: Kelp, machinery, chemicals, oil

NATIONAL DEFENSE: The Armed Forces of Atlantis maintain civil order; the Atlantean armory includes various vessels with dual functions for service underwater and in aerial combat; many of the underwater models can be modified to appear as a marine creature. Defense of the capital is maintained by the Atlantean Royal Guard.

INTERNATIONAL RELATIONS: Atlantis utilizes the United Nations for most diplomatic contact with the surface world. Atlantis has an uneasy relationship with other underwater civilizations, including Mu, Neptunia, the land of the Seal People, the People of the Black Sea and both civilizations of Lemuria. Atlantis once helped construct the underwater Hydropolis base to assist relations with surface people. Attilan and Latveria have been occasional allies. Invasions of the USA, Argentina and Canada have failed; an invasion and occupation of Mazikhandar succeeded. The Avengers and Fantastic Four have usually been welcomed guests of Atlantis.

EXTRATERRESTRIAL RELATIONS: Members of the Banari brotherhood came to Atlantis to seek aid against their people's extinction, but fearful Atlantean guards slew them; Tamara Rahn of the Banari sisterhood subsequently came to live in Atlantis, and became a close ally to Namor; some of the servant creatures of the Banari called the Haab were also brought to Atlantis by the Banari, but were eventually slain. Virago of the extradimensional Zephyrland has warred with Atlantis.

NONHUMAN POPULATION: Atlanteans are an offshoot of humanity, part of the subspecies known as Homo mermani. They possess the ability to exist underwater indefinitely, using twin gills on their necks to extract oxygen from water. They are also able to withstand the tremendous pressures of the ocean's floor, can swim at a speed of 30 miles per hour, withstand near-freezing temperatures, and see with little or no light. Pure-blood Atlanteans have blue skin; most have a lifespan of approximately 150 years. Atlanteans also have access to powerful undersea mutates such as the Behemoth, Megasaur and the whale-like Giganto and its offspring; such creatures can be made to follow orders with the Horn of Proteus. Atlantean science has developed a handful of robots, notably including the Retrievers of Atlantis (Aeristron, Capiotron, Ducotron, Electron, Scyphozotron, Thermatron).

DOMESTIC SUPERHUMANS: Deathcharge is a mercenary who obtained energy-channeling abilities from an accident. Mako was a warrior woman genetically engineered in the 1960s by Vyrra to help defend Atlantis in Namor's absence; she died aiding Earth's heroes against a Skrull invasion. Namor the Sub-Mariner has most often been king in recent years, and has been a member of the Avengers and the Defenders. Namora was Namor's cousin, and adventured with him in the 1940s and '50s; in recent years, she has been one of the Agents of Atlas. Namora's daughter Namorita was a member of the New Warriors, and was slain while battling Nitro. Orka was a citizen of Sharka who often aided Attuma. Proteus was a shapeshifter who aided Jacqueline Trufaut against Namor. Surf (Eel, Sharkskin, Undertow) were a trio of young Atlanteans who obtained powers through nearby atomic tests. Tareva is a sorcerer. Tyrak is one of Attuma's barbarians, and gained additional strength from experiments. The Hydro-Men (Henry Croft, Joseph Jennings, Betty Prentiss and others), victims of mutation at the hands of Dr. Hydro lived in Atlantis until their condition was cured.

PROMINENT CITIZENS: Andromeda is the daughter of Attuma, and was a member of the Defenders. Lord Arno is one of Attuma's chief

Art by Jack Kirby

commanders. Attuma is a barbarian from Sharka who has ruled Atlantis in the past; his ancestor was Attumacht. Brodar, Burka, General Epititus, Gort, Grokko, Kor-Konn, Lorvex, Mako, Saru-San, Serestus, Worta and Wurta were all followers of Attuma. Byrrah is a cousin to Namor and has often sought the throne for himself. Dorma was the lover of Namor, and died at the hands of Llyra. Namor's mother Princess Fen, grandfather Emperor Thakorr and Namora's husband Talan were all killed in Destiny's assault on Atlantis. Hana is the nation's ambassador to Lemuria. Ikthon was one of Atlantis' greatest scientists. Kamuu founded the ruins of ancient Atlantis, and took Zartra as his bride. Warlord Keerg

Art by Cliff Richards

once seized power during one of Namor's absences. Warlord Krang has often competed with Namor. Remora was a scavenger who befriended Tiger Shark. Sibyl was a young woman who was transformed into a Homo mermani to save her life, and became a priestess. Sulumor aided the invasion and occupation of Mazikhandar, and was killed by Wolverine (James Howlett). The U-Man (Meranno) served the Nazi cause in World War II, and later switched loyalties to Attuma. Lord Vashti is Namor's vizier, and a close friend. Vyrra was a geneticist who perfected cloning Atlanteans. Namor's son Kamar was a leader of sleeper agents who clashed with US authorities; other sleepers included Arath, Janus and Krakos. Other known Atlanteans include General Argos, Arkus, Ashur, Askid, Prince Balaal, Banara, Beemer, Bobo, Cirin, Corak, Coral, Numara D'athahr, Daka, Colonel Dakkor, Lord Dara, Elanna, Fara, Gorgul, Ambassador Govan, Jakka, Kalen, Karal, Kavor, High Priest Kormok, Queen Korra, Korro, Kyral, Maddox, Morel, Nautak, Nereus, Orelem, Orrek, King Ossem, Politus, Raman, Ramin, Rennar, Ronga, Ruthar, Lord Seth, Shalak, Shem, Stegor, Tanas, Warlord Thakos, King Thallo, Timoran, Tornaga, Volpan, Xiomara, Zantor, Zarina, Zoga and Zoran.

SUPERHUMAN RESIDENTS: While Attuma ruled Atlantis, he welcomed Nagala, the Piranha, Sea Urchin (Jeremy Swimming Bear) and Tiger Shark (Todd Arliss) in Atlantis as part of his Deep Six.

DOMESTIC CRIME: The terrorist organization At'la'tique (Bloodtide, Dragonrider, Llyron, Manowar, Nagala, Sea Leopard, Shakkoth) has made strikes against both the surface world and Atlantis, with some Atlantean sympathizers amidst their ranks. In the past, some subversive elements in Atlantean society worshiped Set the Elder God; most of these people left to found Lemuria. The School (Crab, Minnow, Mussels, Seahorse, Seaweed, Squid) were a gang of rough Atlantean teenagers. In the distant past, the clone Delta Nine caused an uprising, leading to

the outlawing of cloning.

INTERNATIONAL CRIME: The super-criminal Nitro (Robert Hunter) was made a captive of Atlantis for murdering Namorita. Invaders from the surface have included AIM, Dr. Lemuel Dorcas, Magneto, Morgan Le Fay and Nazi Germany. Lemurians including Llyra have had designs on Atlantis' throne, and the princess Rathia once influenced Namor into warring against the surface. Suma-Ket has led armies of undead Atlanteans (the Unforgiven Dead), seductive Nereids and the carnivorous Faceless Ones against Atlantis, first around 5800 BC, and again in modern times.

FIRST APPEARANCE: (Partial) Motion Pictures Funnies Weekly #1 (1939); (full) Marvel Comics #1 (1939)

HISTORY: The undersea civilization of Atlantis was once a great continent in the distant past, but was sunk around 10,000 BC during the Great Cataclsym. The Homo mermani, a water-breathing race of unknown origin colonized the ruins around 6000 BC under the rule of Kamuu and Zartra, who each bore the names of the last rulers of the surface's Atlantis. The Olympian god Neptune became the patron of the Atlanteans and defended them against Set the Elder God. Atlantis has often been based in the Antarctic (a city named for Emperor Thakorr), but have also been based in the North Atlantic; other Atlantean colonies over the years have included Deluvia (now abandoned), Maritanis (destroyed in atomic tests), New Pangea and Sharka (near Labrador, Canada). Namor the Sub-Mariner has helped guide Atlantis since the 20th century as it has faced many catastrophes. In recent years, Atlantean sleeper agents who had been kept in reserve for decades were called into action by the death of Namorita at the hands of Nitro. The actions of the sleeper agents reflected upon Atlantis, and the surface world became adamant that Atlantis allow itself to placed under constant surveillance. Namor faked the deaths of his people by causing Nitro to detonate his powers within Atlantis. The now-outcast Atlanteans have been offered refuge in Latveria by Dr. Doom.

Art by Jack Kirby

ATLANTIS
UNDERSEA KINGDOM
CURRENTLY LOCATED -9,000 FT BELOW SEA LEVEL,
NEAR EASTERN EXTENT OF CHARLIE-GIBBS FRACTURE ZONE

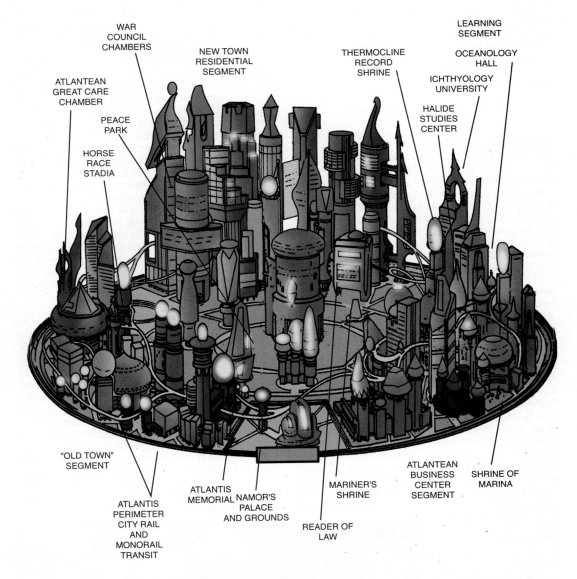

WAR
COUNCIL
CHAMBERS

NEW TOWN
RESIDENTIAL
SEGMENT

THERMOCLINE
RECORD
SHRINE

LEARNING
SEGMENT

OCEANOLOGY
HALL

ATLANTEAN
GREAT CARE
CHAMBER

ICHTHYOLOGY
UNIVERSITY

HALIDE
STUDIES
CENTER

PEACE
PARK

HORSE
RACE
STADIA

"OLD TOWN"
SEGMENT

ATLANTIS
PERIMETER
CITY RAIL
AND
MONORAIL
TRANSIT

ATLANTIS
MEMORIAL

NAMOR'S
PALACE
AND GROUNDS

MARINER'S
SHRINE

ATLANTEAN
BUSINESS
CENTER
SEGMENT

SHRINE OF
MARINA

READER OF
LAW

--Image synthesized from side-scan sonar data collected by the National Oceanographic Atmospheric
Administration, The Environmental Protection Agency, Woods Hole Oceanographic Institute and details
obtained from "The Real Prince Namor" by Sue Richards, People Magazine, 1981

SAVAGE LAND

OFFICIAL NAME: Savage Land
POPULATION: Undetermined
CAPITAL CITY: None
PLACES OF INTEREST: Pangea, Aerie Shalan (Pangea), Athmeth (Pangea), Dis (Pangea), Gondora, Haven, Lemura (Pangea), New Britannia, Palandor, Parni, Sylanda, Tandarr-Kaa, Tordon-Na, Vala-Kuri, Zarhan (Lemura), Black Cave, the Dinosaur Graveyard, Eternity Mountains, Fintal Bay, Forbidden Swamp, Gondor River, Gorhan Sea (Pangea), the Great Rift, Haunted Swamp, Lost Lake, Mount Flavius (Pangea), Mountain of Darkness, the Mystic Mists, River of the Afterlife (Tordon-Na), Skull Island, Tabarr River, Valley of Flame, City of the Sun God, Dream Temple of Kandu Ra (Sylanda), Fort Rex, Gwunda village, Hall of the Dead (Tordon-Na), the High Evolutionary's citadel, Ka-Zar's Summer Palace, Magneto's citadel, UN/SHIELD Command Center.
GOVERNMENT: Tribal council with limited monarchy
MAJOR LANGUAGES: English, Gorankian, Bhadwuan
MONETARY UNIT: None
MAJOR RESOURCES: Petroleum, natural gas, uranium, Vibranium (anti-metal), thermal reserves, wildlife, fish
NATIONAL DEFENSE: None; peace enforced by local militias.
INTERNATIONAL RELATIONS: The United Nations respects the sovereignty of the Savage Land, and seeks to prevent the plundering of its resources. Canada, Chile, Russia and the USA have performed expeditions to the Savage Land under Ka-Zar's permit. SHIELD has maintained bases within and nearby the Savage Land to help police the area. The activist group Gaea is among those who have campaigned for the Savage Land to remain autonomous from the outside world. The Avengers, Fantastic Four and X-Men have often defended the Savage Land from external menaces.
EXTRATERRESTRIAL RELATIONS: 250 million years ago, the Nuwali were contracted by the Beyonders to create a nature preserve on Earth; their environmental generators were responsible for the creation of the Savage Land. Gog, an immense member of the Tsiln race arrived on Earth in the Savage Land, and was cared for by Kraven the Hunter (Sergei Kravinoff). The lovers Damon and Lelania came to the Savage Land around 3000 BC, and spent most of the intervening years in suspended animation before finally returning to the stars in recent years. The warrior Grond slumbered in the Savage Land for ages, outliving his own people and finally met his doom in battle with Ka-Zar. The Sagittarians sent their robot Umbu the Unliving to the Savage Land to assist the Galaxy Master in destroying the Earth; Umbu was worshiped by the Swamp Men, but ultimately destroyed by the Hulk (Bruce Banner). Beings of the Sheenarian and Quarlian races briefly invaded the Savage Land when their home dimensions intersected with the Savage Land's environment. The extradimensional woman M'Rin saved many of the Fall People from Jorro by bringing them to her dimension aboard her flying creature C'Jime. Part of Pangea was briefly conquered by Tantalus, a Deviant from the planet Armechadon. The Super-Skrull (K'lrt) helped with an illegal refinery project in the Savage Land. The extradimensional Hauk'ka (Kaidan, Masado, Raina, Vikram), a race of humanoids evolved from dinosaurs colonized part of the Savage Land after vacating their home reality. Devil Dinosaur and Moon Boy have often made the Savage Land their home since becoming stranded from their home reality of Earth-78411.

NONHUMAN POPULATION: The Savage Land plays host to numerous species of animals thought extinct by the outside world; the best-known such creature is Zabu, the saber-toothed tiger (smilodon) who befriended Ka-Zar. Others include the allosaurus, apatosaurus, archaeoptrex, coelophysis, eohippus, mastodon, plesiosaur, pterosaurs, smilodectes, spinosaurus, stegosaurus, trachodon, triceratops, tsintaosaurus, tylosaurus, tyrannosaur, velociraptor, wooly mammoth and wooly rhino. Experiments by the ancient Atlanteans also created species including griffins and unicorns. The immense reptile Kandu Ra was worshiped and offered sacrifices by a cult until it was slain by Ka-Zar. The bird-like Chtylok the Che'k'n Kau is worshiped by the Fall People tribe.

There are many nonhuman races in the Savage Land, including the winged Aerians (Buth, Chan, Dephine, K'lm Fhet, Garvan, Khup, Sep, Tal, Tilbrok, Lord Yl'Dom Typ, Ver-Jeel, Wend); the gold-skinned Golden People (Nuba, Sagyr [chieftain]); muscular Gorankians (Etuban); winged reptilian Klantorrs; reptilian Lizard Men; neanderthal Man-Apes (Maa-Gor [chieftain], Michael, Zodan); grotesquely mutated Neo-Men; winged Ngu'ghari (Avia, Nhu'abdar); pterodactyl-like Pterons (Khalf, Phangor); reptilian Reptile Men (Quor [chieftain]); neanderthal Swamp Men (Savage Land Mutates, Sivtar); the ape-tailed Tree People (Jeerka, Jolis, Kalpa, Leila, Mele, Nulu, Rhaza); amphibious Tubanti; and the muscular Uruburans. The Saurians (C'Rel, Jimi, Khadar, M'Kai, Madri, S'Gur, Viri), mutated humanoid lizards, colonized the Savage Land in recent times. The High Technician mutated dinosaurs into Dino-Men, including Bront and Styro; their fates are not known. Dherk is an android constructed from technology of the ancient Atlanteans and possessing most of the remnants of Atlantean knowledge in his systems.
DOMESTIC SUPERHUMANS: The notorious Savage Land Mutates are comprised mainly of Swamp Men who were mutated by the genetic accelerator technology of Magneto; their ranks include Amphibius, Barbarus, Brainchild, Gaza, Equilibrius, Leash, Lorelei, Lupa, Lupo, Piper, Vertigo, Whiteout and Worm. The trio of mutates dubbed Avian, Crag and Primate briefly teamed with Vindicator (Heather Hudson) as "Alpha Prime." The sorceress Iranda used magic to turn men into Lizard Men. The being Garokk the Petrified Man is worshiped by the Sun People, and has often claimed humans (including Kirk Marston) to serve as its host.
PROMINENT CITIZENS: The many human-like tribes of the Savage Land include: Bhadwuans (Zira); the cat worshiping Cat-People; the Durammi; Fall People (Barok, Emueli, Fahe, Gronk, Khonsah, Klara, Kronak, Lodah, Mathalai, Mela, Nereel, Norak, Peter, Sarak, Selma, Seesha, Shakani, Sher-La, Tatia, Tinta, Tongah [chieftain], W'Kandro, Yadai), who traditionally wear their hair in a mohawk fashion and are close friends of Ka-Zar; Gondorans (Montgomery Ford, Frita, Gorno, Kamil, Mando, Ro, Sandratha, Tul, Yiri); Hill-Forest People (Nouka); the Jeriens; the Kanto; the Karem (Beel, Schoed, Smoot); Lemurans (General Kamin, Queen Leanne, Ular); the Locot; the N'Gala; the Nowek (Leesha); Palandorians (Jurrlor, Omell, Sann); River-Forest People (Sira); the Sun People (Zaladane), who worship Garrok; Sylandans (Cletus, Ghort); the T'okchi; Tandarr-Kaans (Sar Derkin, Dram, Ghakar, Kuurak Ghodar, Bar Horkus, Kem Horkus, Jira); Tordon-Naans (Durnon, Illyana, Sanda, Sylitha); the Tribe of Fire (Chakel, Erista, Falke, Gahck, Glumph, Kaffkal); and the striped Zebra People (Charn, Karanda, Maza, Sharka, Sheesa, Zaurai).

MAGNETO'S CITADEL

generators to preserve the environment, and the heat of the local volcanoes helped maintain warmth. Over millions of years, the Nuwali collected examples from the Triassic to Pleistocene eras, but eventually the Beyonders lost interest in the Savage Land, and the Nuwali abandoned the project. Eventually, humans from the civilization of Atlantis discovered the Savage Land and marveled at the wildlife preserved there. Their scientists expanded the generators of the Savage Land into a joined colony called Pangea, and performed genetic experiments on humans to create human/animal hybrids; the Atlanteans hoped that Pangea would serve as an amusement park for travelers. However, around 18,000 BC Atlantis was destroyed in the Great Cataclysm, and Pangea was cut off from the outside world; the upheaval caused by the Cataclysm destroyed the beginnings of civilization in the Savage Land, and most of the peoples descended into savagery.

Over the centuries, some of the tribes were able to reclaim some traces of civilization, notably the Fall People and many of the Pangean races. Deities worshiped in the Savage Land included Garokk, worshiped by the Sun People and the extraterrestrial robot Umbu the Unliving, worshiped by the Swamp Men. During World War II, the crews of two British and German submarines became stranded in the Savage Land, and made it their new home. The two groups continued to wage war with each other for decades, unaware that the war was over, and spread their ideologies to their descendants. They also helped teach modern languages to the local tribes, and English became a common tongue for some peoples.

Roughly 20 years ago, Robert Plunder came to the Savage Land in search of the rare metal Vibranium, and found a version that became known as "anti-metal" because of its impurity, producing waves that destroy other metals. Robert locked the anti-metal away and designed a pendant to serve as a key; he gave one half of the pendant to each of his sons, Kevin and Parnival. When Robert's life was placed in jeopardy by criminals who wanted the anti-metal for themselves he placed Parnival in the custody of his butler Willis, and brought Kevin with him to the Savage Land to hide. Unfortunately, Robert was slain by Maa-Gor the Man-Ape; Kevin was saved by the arrival of the smilodon he named Zabu, and the two formed a close bond. Kevin grew to maturity and became famed in the Savage Land as Ka-Zar, respected by most tribes with the authority of a monarch. In recent years, the Savage Land's existence became known to the outside world and Ka-Zar briefly returned home, but ultimately chose to remain in the Savage Land. Word of the Savage Land's valuable resources quickly brought scores of thieves and hunters, making Ka-Zar's work more important than ever.

The Deviant Jorro, working on behalf of the extraterrestrial Terminus wore a version of Terminus' armor in an assault on the Savage Land, and destroyed the Nuwali technology, slaughtering most of the inhabitants. Ka-Zar and his family were among the handful of survivors; many of the Fall People tribe were preserved by the extradimensional benefactor M'Rin. The High Evolutionary finally sought to restore the Savage Land, and was able to infuse Garokk with the land itself, renewing the lost environment, creatures and tribes. The United Tribes were established to help govern the people from then on.

Other known residents of various tribes include Benaza, Delage, Vaninor Dharan, Dharu, Gregor, Jagatar, Keeto, Linak, Lowani, Miesho, Myrain, Rhyla, Sakaa, Tomas and Xantia. Immigrants from the outside world include: Ka-Zar, his wife Shanna O'Hara and their son Adam Plunder; Bernard Kloss, a paleontologist; reporter Tandy Snow; Heinrich Draco, his son Gerhad Draco and other men descended from a Nazi outpost; Edward Culhaney, an Irishmen who fled to the Savage Land to escape the outside world; and Clete Brandon, an ex-soldier who became stranded in the Savage Land and over time descended into savagery.

SUPERHUMAN RESIDENTS: Magneto has kept several bases in the Savage Land, including the citadel at which he created the Savage Land Mutates. The High Evolutionary (Herbert Wyndham) set up a base during his revitalization of the Savage Land, and has maintained an irregular presence in the territory since; his apprentice the High Technician served the interests of AIM. The sorcerer Khor captured men from the outside world in the 1940s to use as slaves but was halted by the Vision (Aarkus). Stegron (Vincent Stegron) transformed himself into a stegosaurus-like being and has often lived in the Savage Land since then. Sauron (Karl Lykos) has considered the Savage Land his true home since his transformation into a pterodactyl-like being. The demonic sorcerer Belasco has held court at Mount Flavius in Pangea, and repeatedly sought to force Ka-Zar and Shanna into aiding him in his quest for power.

DOMESTIC CRIME: Outbursts of violence within and without local tribes are frequent.

INTERNATIONAL CRIME: The Savage Land's rich resources have attracted raiders such as Count Nefaria, Mr. Sinister (Nathaniel Essex), the Plunderer (Parnival Plunder), Klaw (Ulysses Klaw), Ward Strongbow, Volcanus, AIM, Pluto Fuel, Rand-Meachum Inc., Roxxon Oil and SHIELD. The wildlife of the Savage Land have faced illegal hunting by Kraven and Maximillian Zaran, and drawn mercenaries including Arcade, el Tigre (Juan Meroz), the White Rabbit (Lorena Dodson), the Warlord (Huang Zhu) and the combatants brought to a fighting tournament, including Dragonfly (Andre LeRoux), Len Arkwright and the Lawnmower. The geneticists of HELL developed their creature Prime Evil in a Savage Land facility. Jorro the Deviant once devastated the Savage Land while wearing the armor of Terminus.

FIRST APPEARANCE: (Unnamed) Marvel Mystery Comics#22 (1941); (named) X-Men #10 (1964)

HISTORY: The Savage Land is an artificial environment preserving a tropical climate, hidden within a ring of volcanoes in Antarctica. In the distant past the otherdimensional beings called the Beyonders contracted the Nuwali to fashion a game preserve on Earth and gather into it examples of the flora and fauna of the time. The Nuwali designed

THE SAVAGE LAND, PANGEA
BASE OF THE PALMER PENINSULA, ANTARCTICA

SOUTH ATLANTIC OCEAN

PALMER PENINSULA (ANTARCTIC ARCHIPELAGO)

WEDDELL SEA

TIERRA del FUEGO ARGENTINA SOUTH AMERICA

MARGUERITE BAY

DRAKE PASSAGE/ CAPE HORN

SAVAGE LAND (PANGEA)

ALEXANDER ISLAND

ANTARCTIC CIRCLE

THE SAVAGE LAND PREHISTORIC REFUGE
(AFTER NATIONAL GEOGRAPHIC/SHACKLETON EXPEDITION, 1909/ GOODMAN, 1938)

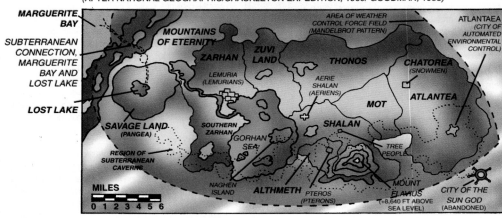

MARGUERITE BAY

SUBTERRANEAN CONNECTION, MARGUERITE BAY AND LOST LAKE

LOST LAKE

MOUNTAINS OF ETERNITY

ZARHAN

LEMURIA (LEMURIANS)

ZUVI LAND

THONOS

AREA OF WEATHER CONTROL FORCE FIELD (MANDELBROT PATTERN)

ATLANTAEA (CITY OF AUTOMATED ENVIRONMENTAL CONTROL)

CHATOREA (SNOWMEN)

AERIE SHALAN (AERIENS)

ATLANTEA

MOT

SAVAGE LAND (PANGEA)

SOUTHERN ZARHAN

GORHAN SEA

SHALAN

TREE PEOPLE

REGION OF SUBTERRANEAN CAVERING

NAGHEN ISLAND

ALTHMETH

PTEROS (PTERONS)

MOUNT ELAWUS (+8,640 FT ABOVE SEA LEVEL)

CITY OF THE SUN GOD (ABANDONED)

MILES
0 1 2 3 4 5 6

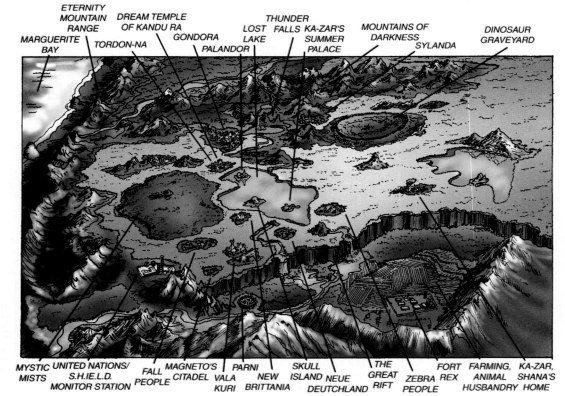

ETERNITY MOUNTAIN RANGE

DREAM TEMPLE OF KANDU RA

THUNDER FALLS

KA-ZAR'S SUMMER PALACE

MOUNTAINS OF DARKNESS

DINOSAUR GRAVEYARD

MARGUERITE BAY

TORDON-NA

GONDORA PALANDOR

LOST LAKE

SYLANDA

MYSTIC MISTS

UNITED NATIONS/ S.H.I.E.L.D. MONITOR STATION

FALL PEOPLE

MAGNETO'S CITADEL

VALA KURI

PARNI

NEW BRITTANIA

SKULL ISLAND

NEUE DEUTCHLAND

THE GREAT RIFT

ZEBRA PEOPLE

FORT REX

FARMING, ANIMAL HUSBANDRY

KA-ZAR, SHANA'S HOME

APPENDIX: SUBTERRANEA

Subterranea is the informal designation for the many networks of underground caves and tunnels that exist miles beneath the Earth's surface. Most of the tunnels of Subterranea were originally carved by the Deviants, a subspecies of humanity who ruled over most of the surface world until their kingdom of Lemuria was sunk beneath the ocean in the Great Cataclysm. The Deviants employed powerful mutates called Rockgnashers to build Subterranea, and engineered species such as the Gortokians to serve them. Eventually, most of the Deviants were driven from Subterranea, leaving behind much of their technology such as Rail-Jet crafts, which joined outposts together. Those who followed the Deviants have made use of Subterranea for themselves, notably the Mole Man. Although the Deviants have made attempts to reconquer their lost territory, the various Subterranean kingdoms remain independent. Some points in Subterranea feature spatial distortions that allow Subterraneans to travel vast distances within minutes. The tunnels of Subterranea extend to remote places such as Monster Island and the Savage Land.

Known peoples and places of Subterranea include:

Abysmia, a civilization led in the 1940s by the heroic Rockman. USA Comics #1 (1941)

Eurasia, an underground city inhabited by the former residents of el Dorado, Bolivia who mastered Deviant technology. Namor the Sub-Mariner Annual #1 (1991)

Gortokians were bred as slaves by the Deviants, but rebelled against their masters thousands of years ago. The Gortokians thrived until recent years when evidently all but Grotesk was slain in an atomic test. X-Men #41 (1968)

Lava Men were Gortokians who worshiped the demon Cha'sa'dra, and were transformed into inhuman lava-like creatures by him. Usually ruled by King Basallo or witch doctor Jinku, and once by Grotesk of the Gortokians. Journey into Mystery #97 (1963)

Lizard Men were Deviant-bred creatures who developed their own underground civilization, but were known to hold loyalties to the Deviants as late as the 1950s. Journey into Mystery #64 (1961)

Lyonesse, inhabited by Deviants who originated on the planet Armechadon; led by Lord Tantalus, they sought the eventual conquest of Earth. Thunderstrike #6 (1994)

The Mole Man discovered Subterranea from Monster Island; blinded in the Valley of Diamonds, he employed former Deviant slaves dubbed "Moloids" in his service, along with vast numbers of Deviant mutates and abandoned technology. He has also welcomed fellow misfits from the surface, including the mutates who make up his Outcasts. Fantastic Four #1 (1961)

Netheria was a former part of Atlantis, and its people have virtual immortality while they live within its borders; their queen Kala fell in love with the Mole Man. Tales of Suspense #43 (1963)

The Skull-Men, an intelligent race of skeletal beings who lived beneath China in the 1940s and transformed Mark Todd into the Blazing Skull. Mystic Comics #5 (1941)

Tyrannus was once Roman emperor Romulus Augustulus who was banished to Subterranea by the wizard Merlin. Kept young by the Fountain of Youth and served by former Deviant slaves dubbed "Tyrannoids," Tyrannus has made and broken various alliances with Kala and the Mole Man. Incredible Hulk #5 (1963)

There are also various collections of sewer-dwelling humans, notably in New York where the mutant outcasts of the Morlocks inhabited the Alley, the Night People inhabited sunken Zerotown, the death-worshiping Ungrateful Dead, the Abomination's followers the Forgotten, the King of the Sewers and the Underground defended by the Peacekeeper. Also significant are the San Francisco Underground, a clan of homeless people who were defended by Venom, the Children of the Night of Montreal, Canada who were made to obey the criminal Rok, and the Hyde Park Underworld, a tribe of mutants similar to the Morlocks who lived below London, England.

APPENDIX: OTHER NATIONS

Alberia Europe Tales of Suspense #69 (1965)
Al-Mazahmiya Middle East Deadpool #26 (1999)
Althea Island Caribbean island Darkhawk #14 (1992)
Aznia Africa X-Factor #89 (1993)
Bagmom Middle East Howard the Duck Annual #1 (1977)
Bartovia Europe Solo Avengers #7 (1988)
Baud Olan Middle East Captain America & the Falcon #13 (2005)
Bloodstone Island Caribbean island Rampaging Hulk #2 (1977)
Boca Del Dios South America Venom: Sinner Takes All #1 (1995)
Bolamoira South America Spider-Man: Web of Doom #1 (1994)
Bora-Buru Africa Tales to Astonish #58 (1964)
Celsia Europe Morbius #26 (1994)
Central Saharan Republic Africa Uncanny X-Men #444 (2004)
Costa Brava South American microstate The Agent (1989)
Costa Diablo Central America Iron Man #148 (1981)
Costa Dinora Central America Marvel Comics Presents #5 (1988)
Costa Perdita Central America Warlock #1 (2004)
Dakenia Africa Black Panther #57 (2003)
Demonica Pacific island Avengers West Coast #74 (1991)
Dhakran Middle Eastern microstate Power Man & Iron Fist #103 (1984)
Djanda Africa Elektra #25 (2003)
Draburg Europe Incredible Hulk #386 (1991)
Eden Island Caribbean island Super Spider-Man & Captain Britain #239 (1977)
Europa Europe X-Statix #13 (2003)
Femizonia Atlantic island Captain America #390 (1991)
Ghudaza Africa Black Panther #3 (1999)
Ghulistan Middle East Avengers Spotlight #39 (1990)
Grand Nixon Island Pacific island Punisher #3 (2001)
Hidden Isle Mediterranean island Fantastic Four #9 (1962)
Hydra Island Pacific island Strange Tales #156 (1967)
Inferno Island Atlantic island Tales to Astonish #91 (1967)
Isla Suerte Caribbean island Iron Man #4 (1998)
Kaiwann Chinese coast Marvel Two-in-One #25 (1977)
Kamuni Atoll Pacific island Battletide #1 (1992)
Kanem Middle Eastern microstate Wonder Man #26 (1993)
Keraadistan Middle East Captain America & the Falcon #13 (2005)
Khamiskan Europe Captain America #42 (2001)
Khotain Middle Eastern microstate Power Man & Iron Fist #103 (1984)
Kiber Island African coast Black Panther #11 (1978)
Kirikhstan Eastern European microstate Iron Man #29 (2008)
Koma Koi Pacific island Marvel Comics Presents #132 (1993)
Ksavia Europe Untold Tales of Spider-Man #13 (1996)
Lakini Pacific island Iron Man #31 (1970)
Lichtenbad Europe Daredevil #9 (1965)
Maura Pacific island Avengers #179 (1979)
Mohannda Africa Black Axe #5 (1993)
Murkatesh Africa Power Man & Iron Fist #82 (1982)
Nadua Africa Night Thrasher #9 (1994)
Niganda Africa Black Panther #3 (2005)
Paolo Santera South America Black Panther #41 (2002)
Paradise Island Atlantic island New Mutants #58 (1987)
Puerto Dulcer European island Punisher War Journal #27 (1991)
Puerto Salvaje Florida keys island Punisher: Kingdom Gone (1990)
Rhapastan Middle East Black Widow #1 (1999)
Rio De Muerte Central America Captain America #206 (1977)
Rumika Pacific island Wolverine #27 (1990)
Ruritania Europe Uncanny X-Men #204 (1986)
St. Cyril Caribbean island Marvel Fanfare #26 (1986)
San Concepcion South America Elektra: Assassin #1 (1986)
San Domingo Central America Punisher: Bloodlines (1991)
San Gregario South America Venom: Sign of the Boss #1 (1997)
San Migeule South American microstate Hulk Comic #3 (1979)
San Pablo Caribbean island Sub-Mariner #34 (1973)
San Revilla Central America War Machine #15 (1995)
Slovinia Europe Skrull Kill Krew #2 (1995)
Sufind Middle East Spectacular Spider-Man #257 (1998)
Temasika Pacific island Marvel Comics Presents #162 (1994)
Terra Neuva South America Power Man & Iron Fist #70 (1981)
Tierra Del Maiz South America Alpha Flight #102 (1991)
Timbetpal Asian microstate Iron Man #31 (2000)
Trafia Middle East Punisher #47 (1991)
Trebekistan Europe Avengers '99 Annual (1999)

Trepica Pacific island *Marvel Comics Presents #85 (1991)*

Triji Pacific island *Punisher War Journal #20 (1990)*

Ujanka Africa *Black Panther #3 (1999)*

Umbazi Africa *Captain Britain #39 (1977)*

Volcan Domuyo South America *Black Panther #9 (1999)*

Yashonka Asia *Tales of Suspense #86 (1967)*

Zenith Island Caribbean island *Iron Man/Captain America 1998 Annual (1998)*

Zukistan Middle East *Punisher #47 (1991)*

Zwartheid Africa *Wolverine #41 (2006)*

APPENDIX: EARTH'S SATELLITES

ACTIVE SATELLITES

Devastator's Satellite Broadcasts microwave energy to Devastator's armor. *Incredible Hulk #186 (1975)*

Eve NASA space station. *Marvel Preview #4 (1976)*

High Evolutionary's Space Station Used in plot to remove mutant powers. *Uncanny X-Men 1999 Annual (1999)*

Hydra Satellite Sought by Sinister Six to commandeer its weapon cache. *Spider-Man #22 (1992)*

Magneto Protocols Series of over two dozen satellites equipped by Forge with electromagnetic generators to bar Magneto from entering Earth's atmosphere; later usurped by Thunderbolts. *X-Men #25 (1993)*

Mandarin's Killer Satellite Orbital weapon used by Mandarin against Iron Man (Tony Stark). *Tales of Suspense #61 (1965)*

Mys-Tech's Satellite Used to incite violence on Earth. *Dark Angel #7 (1993)*

Omnivac Sentient station commanded by Leader, programming disabled by Jackdaw. *Incredible Hulk #157*

Samarobryn Built by Hate-Monger (Adolf Hitler clone), later used by Egghead and Weathermen, now utilized for scientific research. *Nick Fury, Agent of SHIELD #10 (1969)*

Simulacra NASA station commandeered by Brood. *X-Men/Fantastic Four #1 (2005)*

Solar Mirror Used by GRAMPA to destroy vampires on Earth. *Amazing Fantasy #15 (2006)*

Space Station 8 NASA station, post of Gazer. *X-Men #169 (2005)*

Starcore Station Current Starcore research base headed by Dr. Peter Corbeau. *X-Men Unlimited #13 (1996)*

Stark Satellite One Research facility built by Stark Enterprises, abandoned after virus released aboard by AIM. *Iron Man #207 (1986)*

INACTIVE SATELLITES

AIM Space Platform Commanded by MODOK, destroyed by Avengers. *She-Hulk #1 (2004)*

Alexandra Station commanded by Noah Baxter, seemingly destroyed in battle against Janus. *Fantastic Four #37 (2001)*

Asteroid M Early base of Magneto and Brotherhood of Evil Mutants, repeatedly rebuilt, finally destroyed by Fabian Cortez. *X-Men #4 (1964)*

Avalon Formerly Cable's station Graymalkin, co-opted by Acolytes, destroyed by Holocaust, remnants became Prosh and Providence island. *X-Force #8 (1992)*

Damocles Sword-shaped command base of Kang, brought from Earth-6311, destroyed by Avengers. *Avengers #41 (2001)*

Death Ray Satellite designed by Baron (Heinrich) Zemo imposter (Franz Gruber), destroyed by SHIELD. *Tales of Suspense #98 (1968)*

Death's Head Satellite Designed by Red Skull (Johann Shmidt) and Hate-Monger (Adolf Hitler clone) to broadcast hate-ray energy, destroyed by Captain America. *Captain America #226 (1978)*

Dr. Demonicus' Satellite Designed by Axon-Karr, removed from orbit by Shogun Warriors. *Shogun Warriors #7 (1979)*

Drydock Earth-691 space station commanded by Guardians of the Galaxy, briefly lay in orbit of Earth-616. *Marvel Presents #12 (1977)*

Fu Manchu's Space Station Designed to destroy the Moon, cast adrift in space. *Master of Kung Fu #49 (1977)*

Godseye Sentient SHIELD satellite designed to detonate nuclear weapons, destroyed by Hulk (Bruce Banner). *Incredible Hulk #89 (2006)*

Jerry Owens' Satellite Orbited Earth for 50 years with Owens aboard. *Uncanny Tales #48 (1956)*

Mandarin's Space Station Used to construct hate-ray, destroyed by Avengers. *Avengers Annual #1 (1967)*

Master Mold's Asteroid Base Mutant holding facilities, destroyed by Hulk (Bruce Banner). *Incredible Hulk Annual #7 (1978)*

Otomocorp Space Station Orbital base of Takashei Otomo, destroyed by Mys-Tech. *Gene Dogs #4 (1994)*

The Peak Space station headquarters of SWORD, destroyed by Skrulls. *Astonishing X-Men #13 (2006)*

Satellite of Death Used by Dr. Doom to destroy Earth's ozone layer, self-destructed by Dr. Doom. *Solarman #2 (1990)*

SHIELD Orbital Platform Earliest known use during Kree-Skrull War, briefly conquered by Steven Lang, destroyed by Deltite's followers. *Avengers #96 (1972)*

Silvermoon Designed by Harlan Silverbird to project anti-metal radiation from orbit, destroyed by Moon Knight. *Marc Spector: Moon Knight #51 (1993)*

Star Well Radiation-storing project by Roxxon Oil, commanded by Sunturion, destroyed by Roxxon. *Iron Man #142 (1981)*

Starcore One First Starcore Project research base, destroyed by Shi'ar wormhole. *Incredible Hulk #148 (1972)*

Starcore Station Incorporated temporal weapons designed by Tony Stark for Immortus, destroyed by War Machine (James Rhodes). *Force Works #20 (1996)*

Weapon Plus Space Station Facility where Weapon XV was designed, destroyed by Wolverine. *New X-Men #144 (2003)*

XERO Sentient satellite designed by Dr. Able Stack, destroyed by Machine Man. *X-51 #3 (1999)*

Art by John Romita Jr.